Role Playing
and
Identity

STUDIES IN PHENOMENOLOGY AND EXISTENTIAL PHILOSOPHY

General Editor
JAMES M. EDIE

Role Playing

AND

Identity

The Limits of Theatre as Metaphor

Bruce Wilshire

Indiana University Press
Bloomington and Indianapolis

for
William Barrett

First Midland Book Edition 1991

Library of Congress Cataloging in Publication Data

Wilshire, Bruce W.
  Role playing and identity.

  (Studies in phenomenology and existential philosophy)
  Includes index.
   1. Theater.   2. Role playing.   3. Identity (Psychol-
ogy)   4. Phenomenology.   I. Title.   II. Series.
PN2039.W54   1982   792'.01   81-47779
ISBN 0-253-35025-5   AACR2
ISBN 0-253-20599-9 (pbk.)

2 3 4 5 6 95 94 93 92 91

CONTENTS

ACKNOWLEDGMENTS

This book has formed itself over a lengthy period of time, and I am indebted to many persons; first, to actors with whom I have worked, colleagues of short but memorable duration: Manu Tupou, Frank Wittow, Jon Voight, Jacqueline Brookes, MacIntyre Dixon, Sandra McDonald, Douglass Watson, and others. A colleague of lengthy duration is Donna Wilshire, my Semiramis, Lavinia, Medea, Lucky.

I am indebted also to directors who have shared themselves and helped me to understand their creative ways of working, particularly Ira Cirker and Robert Wilson in New York, and Ludwik Flaszen and Adam Hanuszkiewicz in Poland.

A number of people read earlier versions of the manuscript and helped me find my way. I thank them: William Barrett, Edward Casey, John Fizer, Hugh Silverman. Conversations with Eugene Gendlin and Don Ihde were also very helpful. I alone, of course, am responsible for the shape the book finally took.

George Kanzler, librarian of the Alexander Library of Rutgers University, provided me with a private room in which to write, a prized haven. Study leaves granted by the university were also essential. The Research Council of Rutgers helped with injections of funds at crucial moments.

A visiting professorship at Texas A&M University was conducive to thinking and writing, and it was there that I finished the final version. I thank John McDermott and other officials of that institution.

No acknowledgment would be complete without mention of that group of philosophers assembled at New York University by Sidney Hook with whom I studied some years ago. Hook goaded and excited them into communication; it was impossible to bury the unfamiliar under a load of silence. Of the members of this department I am most indebted to William Barrett, *maestro amico*.

Finally, I thank my family—both immediate and extended—for their help and forbearance during the time I was engaged in writing. I owe a special debt to my wife, for we have worked so long together both in roles and "roles," both acting within the theatre and acting outside it, that the problem of theatre as metaphor would never have become so urgent for me without her, nor would my thought have developed in the way that it has.

Prologue

This is a book about art, particularly theatre art. But since art is a part of life, it is also about life. And since parts can be understood only in relation to wholes, and since attempts to understand life in its wholeness are philosophical, the book is philosophical. It is not intended primarily for the theatre artist as opposed to the psychologist, the sociologist, or the philosopher. It is intended for them all, and for all those who want to think about human beings. The book deals with concepts which all these persons share. We will begin with an example of theatre in order to reveal the nature of theatre, and to reveal that theatre reveals life—that it is life-like. At roughly the midpoint of the book we will reverse our emphasis to show that life is theatre-like—that concepts for life onstage and for life off are tied to each other. In the last section of the work we will show how this metaphorical connection of concepts, though powerful and irreducible, is yet limited in its ability to reveal human life.

Phenomenological methods will be employed to explore theatre as metaphor. They will help us see that theatre is an aesthetic detachment from daily living that reveals the ways we are involved in daily living—particularly our empathetic and imitative involvements. Theatre is the art of imitation that reveals imitation. The meaning of phenomenology, and of theatre as phenomenology, will emerge in due course.

It is an early spring evening in a semi-darkened warehouse in New York near the docks. The hour has passed at which Robert Whitman's theatre work *Light Touch* was to have begun. People are still buying tickets at the card table set up in the opened door at the corner of the building as the orange light of the nearly spent day falls through it. Some of those who walk across in front of the platform do not come up to join the audience, and the way they cross and lose themselves in the shadows beyond raises the possibility that they are performers. Is their saunter enacted or not?

Have they begun the performance? Is the large floor space in front of us the performing area? Or are the persons who walk by stagehands?

Awaiting the performance, we sat in the damp and gloom, uneasy over the continued delay and uncertainty. Finally lights illuminated the long wall a hundred feet in front of us, and a large roll of brown paper lying against the wall started to move and to shake at one end. This disturbance mounted and began to transmit itself slowly through the roll. At its height the paper stood about a third of the way up the wall. Then gradually, having transmitted itself to the end of the roll, the disturbance subsided and there was silence. There were persons within the roll, we surmised, but we saw no one. During the ensuing blackout we could hear the paper being pulled away.

Then a strange event of disclosure occurred—a disclosure of disclosure. In the darkness the main door of the warehouse in the middle of the wall before us slowly rolled up and opened. It went from floor to ceiling and was large enough for trucks to enter and exit. Gossamer curtains on each side of the opening billowed softly in a light wind. As if surrounded by a nimbus of silence, the sounds of the city could be heard—mostly soft and distant in this area—and cars appeared occasionally, framed by the door, as they passed on the street directly outside. Appeared, but appeared transfigured, as if a spell had been cast over them. Details of their shape and movement, ordinarily not noticed, leapt out, as if from a numinous aura. It was as if cars were being seen for the first time. Astonishing it was that persons could encase themselves in thousands of pounds of machinery and go rolling and lurching down a roadway. We wondered how any civility could survive it. Each rattle and sound of a car, and the flowing sound as it passed over pebbles and ruts, appeared through the nimbus of silence as if to name the part of the machinery from which it emanated. The driver's intent gaze on the road in front of him chipped out merely a fragment of the world in which he moved.

After a car had passed by in this side street the space in which we were living would relax and expand again to admit the sounds of the vast city—sounds delicate in the distance. Then again, as if we inhabited a breathing organism, events on the street would take prominence. Slowly and majestically matters unleafed through time; yet also sadly, as if all of us—rapt and silent inside the warehouse—were aware that the spell that had been cast was fragile. One felt grateful to be alive and conscious.

A police car then slowed down in the street and stopped. The warehouse door's being open at this time of night was apparently an irregularity that had caught the officers' attention. They stopped and the driver took a flashlight and shone it into the building and onto us. We began to laugh a little, and in embarrassment he withdrew the light. They drove away. Only the most brilliant actors could have enacted this with such verisimilitude and we were fairly sure that no actor was involved. The spell remained.

After some moments a truck appeared in the street outside. It stopped and began to back into the warehouse. The first approach failed. It jiggled and returned again slowly to the street. Each sound and movement the truck made filled up the space in which we lived. In the next approach it backed hesitantly into the warehouse and displaced the billowing curtains. It bore we knew not what, but we waited in hushed expectancy, as if its contents were the first specimens from an Earth as distant and mysterious as another planet.

The truck rolled slowly to a stop. After some minutes of silence its hold was opened by persons who appeared to be warehouse workers, and a few objects were exposed there by a spotlight: a cement block, an apple, a kitchen sink. These objects were carried one by one to the dock. The apple was an apple but could not be eaten by us. We were immobilized in our chairs at this "theatre work." The kitchen sink was a kitchen sink but it could not be used by anyone: the faucets were unconnected and its drainpipe terminated in the air. These things were useless. And yet they were meaningful in a much more vivid and complete way than they would be in ordinary use. Our very detachment from their everyday use threw their everyday connections and contexts of use into relief—connections and contexts vaster than we would ordinarily have suspected. Since these gave the things their meaning, their meaning was thrown into relief. Each thing stood within a nimbus, inviolable; it was a nimbus of relatedness, a context of intelligibility. We were not simply absorbed in the things— an absorption governed by that small fraction of their meaning relevant to our everday interaction with them. The things were perceived *as* meaningful. They became objects of art.

Just because it could not be eaten, the apple was perceived as something of loveliness and grace which had been grown upon the earth in the sunlight, and which could supply nourishment and delicious sensations when bitten and chewed. The sink, unconnected, was perceived as the sort of thing which connected us with a system of water supply and water disposal—as well as of life-sustaining and cleansing powers—a system which could easily be disrupted. The cement block, out of use, was seen to be useful not just to the person who owned it, but to anyone to build any abode to shelter any of us.

Integral to their enhanced meaningfulness, each thing stood in for all possible objects of that type or sort. Thus each thing was an incarnated universal, a physiognomic expression of a type; this without sacrificing its particularity as it sat there on the dock before us. It sat within its halo, inviolable.

Consider: what if the policemen had not believed that this was a theatre event, but had taken us to be trespassers, and had come in and had ordered us to disperse? And what if some of us, believing that they were only actors enacting policemen, had not dispersed? And they had directed the door to be lowered so that we could not escape, and had arrested us all?

Now some might still believe that these intruders were merely actors involved in ascertaining and testing the limits of people's belief in theatre— so testing the limits of theatre itself. And some of the believers might decide to cooperate in this presumed testing, to get in on the act, and to defy their orders. Let us say they were knocked unconscious for their efforts. The believers who remained might construe this as again more acting. The situation of these people would be exactly the same as the situation of those who remained conscious but who had ceased to believe this was a theatre event. Exactly the same, that is, in every respect that could be objectively identified, located, and measured. There would be nothing about the distance of persons to the policemen, nor their angle of vision, that—when generalized—would have distinguished those who took this to be theatre from those who did not.

In Whitman's strange theatre event we witness theatre experimenting on itself, discovering and underlining the conditions of its own possibility. Its value for a philosophy of the theatre is that through it a theatrical point of view can be separated out as a factor in any theatre event. *That is, actual things in plain view—not things dressed up or illuminated so as to appear to be what they are not—are nevertheless seen in an entirely "new light."* The difference, then, must come from a change in the interpretive attitude of the viewer, not from the things themselves. And this attitude is not localizable, nor is it weighable and measurable, as would be an object in the world. It is a state of mind, a way of freely interpreting the world. As Edmund Husserl would say, it is not in the world, as is an object, nor is it out of the world either. So it is not within-the-world. It is, rather, worldly.

The world viewable through Whitman's warehouse door is in point of fact the very same world that would be seen if one were doing a day's work within the warehouse. But the person at this theatre event is not absorbed in the narrow segment of the world relevant to one's immediate practical interests, as is the worker. One is not just a being in the world but becomes aware *that* one is a being in the world. One becomes aware of oneself as aware, interpreting, and free.

Theatrical point of view turns out to be continuous with artistic point of view: the detachment within involvement that is typical of any art. Whitman's production is an example of what makes theatre an art, and its writers, directors, and actors artists.

An absence in Whitman's production was so glaring that it became itself a presence: the actor, the paradigm of one who stands in for another (we ignore the problematical status of his "stagehands")—the actor, in whose co-presence we as audience participate in the re-creation of types and sorts of humanity. We stand in through the actor's standing in. Whitman's "theatre work," being a violation of the norm of theatre, shook us into awareness of this norm.

Experimental theatre remains theatre even while turning upon itself. It is not just an object but simultaneously a point of view on itself and the world; it is a view of the relationship between viewing and the viewed. If it could get out of itself it would cease to be itself. Nor can we observers regard it as just something going on in the warehouse or theatre, a strange event involving actors on the stage and audience in their chairs. For if we do not participate at some moments in its point of view we will not know what there is to investigate and to criticize.

In varying elements from the norm and in violating normal theatre, Whitman's experimental theatre revealed the conditions and structures of normal theatre more effectively than normal theatre itself ever could. But it could violate normal theatre only because of the tradition of the latter within which it moved—moved despite itself. We did not walk out impatiently when the door of the warehouse was opened and nothing came in—we did not think that the wrong button had been pushed and the artistic event had broken down—because we were primed by our sense of theatre art to expect that something special would be revealed through that opening, that frame. We were carried and led by a living history of artistic involvement, the very tradition of normal art that was being violated.

Above all, as I have noted, we were aware of the living actor, and of what in his normal ambience he does in our midst, just because he was not present here. As the particular sink stands in for all possible sinks, so the actor playing a character stands in for all persons of this sort, and we in the audience, identifying with him and his characterization, stand in through his standing in. We try out another life for size, we recognize— perhaps for the first time—how we are like the character or different from him. Our task will be to discover how such discovery is possible: how discovery of actual existence occurs just because of the fictionality of the proceedings.

In normal theatre we are confronted with manifest fictions: actors who are not princes, rubber knives that cannot cut, etc. The obviousness of this can lure us into the mistake of attributing the theatre event exclusively to the fictional things there onstage. Our encounter with experimental theatre reminds us that the "world" of the play requires the participation of the interpreting viewers and auditors—as well as the artists—and that these persons are located in a theatre standing in the actual world. The "world" of the play must be nested within the world in complex ways before the event of theatre can occur. "World" is progressively checked against world, and world against "world," so that reaches of the world-context that exceed our everyday ability to thematize them are pulled into the focus of the play's "world," and there become encompassable by the mind and the emotions. Our hypothesis is this: theatre is a mode of discovery that explores the threads of what is implicit and buried in the world, and pulls them into a compressed and acknowledgeable pattern before us in its "world." Theatre discovers meaning, and its peculiar detachment reveals our involvement.

Using actual examples of theatre as variations on the nature of theatre which reveal the meaning of it, and explaining how our procedure is phenomenological, I will argue in Part One of this book that theatre is life-like. Primarily it is so because, as the mimetic art *par excellence,* it reveals certain aspects of our mimetic reality as human beings. Offstage we imitate others deliberately and undeliberately, consciously and unconsciously, and are authorized by our models. The actors mimetically enact characters and relationships, and we in the audience experience these as ones that resemble and reveal either our own mimetically conditioned and imitative relationships offstage or those with which we are acquainted. Our guided detachment reveals our involvement. The actors pick up clues from the audience concerning our common mimetic life, and we pick up clues from the actors. A mutual mirroring is set into play. We utter our reality and our freedom through the evolving fiction.

In Part Two we will present a general theory of identity of self, unaided by any analysis of theatre *per se,* which discloses certain conditions of identity which are theatre-like: play, mimetic response, role, display, recognition of self through the other, etc. Thus I will argue that our conceptions of life onstage and our conceptions of life offstage are linked in an essentially metaphorical way. Neither "side" can supply an exhaustive set of literal terms adequate for itself which can then be applied metaphorically to the other "side." We balance perpetually in our conceptual system between notions of offstage and onstage. Each side feeds the other with digested material that was previously assimilated from it. We are caught in a circle of concepts that must be explicated.

Fallout from our analyses will include criticism of systematic attempts made by sociologists to extend theatrical concepts to offstage life in "role theory." At first glance this theory is beguiling. Since theatrical or theatre-like concepts such as *role* are already embedded in ordinary language for ordinary life, why not deliberately and scientifically extend a group of such concepts to offstage life?

Noticing people primping, for example, outside an apartment in which a party is being held and into which they are about to make their entrance, who can doubt the similarity to actors waiting in the wings to make their entrance? When the person enters the gathering, doesn't he fashion his face to elicit a desired response from those already in the room, and isn't this very much like an actor who conceals his other impulses and feelings behind a mask-like face? Don't we always feed off the presence of others, and desire, long for, and demand their attention? Each wants every other to confirm him in his living, breathing ideal of himself. This seems to be like an actor attempting to persuade the audience to believe the character he is playing.

The theatrical metaphor also seems capable of illuminating our less deliberate, more passive "performances" in offstage life. Often one's experiencing of oneself is so engulfed in his experiencing of others' experiencing that he has no effective sense of himself as a distinctive and self-responsible being. This allows us to raise the crucial question: to what extent—if at all—*is* he a distinctive and self-responsible being? He exists in a kind of spell cast by others, and in turn he may undeliberately cast a spell over those whom he expects to act in certain ways and who fall mimetically into the expected pattern. We trip each other into mimetic response.

For instance, to examine the typical conditions for calling someone charming is to find that he or she induces in one a narrowing of attention to a small range of preoccupations; the gulf of the past and the gulf of the future are masked out—likewise the gulf of space. In this fuzzy cocoon of hypnotic or quasi-hypnotic involvement with the other, the contour of one's identity blurs into his or hers. What happens in the theatre—the absorption of the actors in their own and in the others' assumed characters—seems to be a good model or metaphor for what is happening offstage. This suggestion is strengthened when we realize that the actor allows the archaic authorization of the audience around him to induce powerful mimetic tendencies within him as character, and to these he submits.

But we must make a distinction between the actor as artist and actor as character. As artist he controls the extent to which this submission as character occurs. A danger in using theatre as metaphor is that only the actor as character will be projected into our interpretation of the offstage world. The opposite danger is that the actor as artist will gain disproportionate emphasis. If the first occurs we will see in the offstage world only passivity, fascination, hypnotic-like engulfment, or—strange interdependency—instinctual cunning and calculation which is only inadequately acknowledgeable by the person himself. If, on the other hand, we disproportionately emphasize the actor as artist we will tend to see offstage only those situations in which we are consciously and coolly in control of a facade of behavior—a sedate cocktail party, for example. And we must make a third distinction: the actor as person. A philosophy of theatre must address the difficult question of whether the actor as person "speaks himself" in certain ways only as artist enacting a character. This requires a well-rounded and somewhat sophisticated analysis.

A survey of the systematic use of the role-playing metaphor by social scientists in the last five decades will reveal, I believe, that in general its use has been astonishingly crude. From Talcott Parsons to Erving Goffman, the more facile the skill for constructing a theatrical model and detecting initial similitudes in offstage life, the more confidently has the sociologist laid about with the instrument and chopped from sight fundamental questions. The most obvious feature of this failing is most evident in the work of Goffman. His theory of role playing onstage is not adequate. He believes that the actor merely hides his real self behind masks and costumes and lines that are not his own. This is the tendency of Goffman's earlier work, and when he takes it as the initial term from which to extrapolate to life offstage, then he must tend to conclude that all role playing and nearly all human behavior is defensive or phony. The tendency of his later work is to doubt that a real self exists, or at least to doubt that it is knowable. Since all "role playing" is like role playing onstage, and this is fictional, all "role playing" is a deficient mode of reality. Life must appear to be merely insubstantial and farcical, and because we cannot separate our lives from our view of our lives, our lives must tend to *be* hollow.

The role-playing metaphor is exceedingly slippery and dangerous because almost inevitably when we deliberately transfer the notion of role playing to offstage life we carry with us, smuggled in, the notion of the fictionality of the actor's portrayal. This tends to eat away from the inside our sense of the reality, seriousness, and appropriateness of our "role playing" offstage. We are divided against ourselves: on the one hand we dimly sense that we are responsible for our "role playing" offstage in a way that an actor is not for his onstage, and that it pertains to our actuality as persons in a way that it does not to his actuality as a person. But on the other hand, in the grip of the metaphor, we come dimly to believe that what we're doing offstage is an illicit version of what the actor is doing legitimately onstage, and so we attempt to flee our guilt and our responsibility for our unavoidable "role playing." This is a sort of schizophrenia that I think increasingly characterizes persons in our culture.

The role-playing metaphor as it has been appropriated by some sociologists breaks down and leaves us stranded. Intended to help us understand how we are mimetically involved with others offstage, it ends by undermining this very sociality. If any notion of a real self remains, it seems then to be a private and antisocial self hidden or semi-hidden behind the mere appearance of sociality. Instead of the occasionally tragic tension between our sociality and our particularity-and-privacy, we get a muddling of them, or one of them is slighted.

Our task will be to formulate an adequate theory of theatre and of role playing onstage that can account for the actor's "speaking himself" through a fiction. We can then take steps to determine in which respects offstage life is profoundly similar to onstage life, and in which it is profoundly different. To this task we now turn.

From what source things arise, to that they return of necessity when they are destroyed; for they suffer punishment and make reparation to one another for their injustice according to the order of time. . . .

—Anaximander

PART ONE

Theatre and the Reality
of Appearance

CHAPTER I

What Is Theatre?

How can a form of playing—a play in a theatre—be a serious matter? Perhaps no other form of human activity is more paradoxical on its face. We need to say that theatre is both playful and serious, and that while in one sense it is deceitful, in another it can be truthful. Can a certain class of truths be teased out for inspection only through cunning illusions? What are the various sorts of illusion? Plato has made us familiar with the idea that the actual particular can be revealed only through the ideal form of which it is an instance. What is fictional is compatible with its being an ideal, which reveals not only itself but the particular which is an instance of it. But also, notoriously—as Plato was aware—the fictionality of theatre is compatible with its being a self-deceiving escape from actuality. The appeal of the theatre is alternately darkly grand and suspiciously seductive. It slides before us like a film of oil iridescent on the ocean.

This art must appear paradoxical to us because of unquestioned ways of describing and categorizing it which raise misleading questions about it. For example: offstage we view reality itself, but how can we view anything but appearance, however beguiling and refreshing, when we view what is presented onstage? Offstage one is oneself, whereas onstage one feigns to be another self, and does so for persons seeking diversion in fantasy on a high and artificial level of society. How can we be anything but disengaged and diverted from our serious tasks while in the theatre?

Now, let us counter these questions with others. What if we could have no insight into reality unless it is mediated by appearance? What if theatre renders in a thematic and deliberate way what is already going on unde-liberately in the development of the self, hence extends and fulfills it—the incorporation mimetically into a conscious body of others' ways of being and of others' views of itself? What if a life is a human life because it is mediated by communal fantasy and belief about every life, and theatre and other arts articulate and consummate this mediation? What if what is dismissed as dramatic diversion can be a consummation of our being?

I will argue that theatre is, or can be, all this, and that therefore the familiar distinctions, traditionally parsed, that have hedged about its study must either collapse or be modified: appearance and reality; fantasy and reality; self and other; the useful and the diverting. All these distinctions must be reformulated from the ground up; some of them in the end will be barely recognizable.

The view I will develop is this: theatre is a consummation of the main line of human development—a development that is theatre-like at crucial junctures. Through the analysis of theatre's fictions we can see "writ large" the theatre-like conditions of the coherence and being of actual selves— large enough to see conditions which would otherwise be easily missed. In the order of time, participation in theatre in any strict and literal sense comes rather late in an individual's life, if it comes at all. But knowledge of the principles of theatre throws light on analogous conditions of being human that must be understood before anything else about a self can be. Thus theatre is historically posterior but ontologically or logically prior.

Surely one of the greatest obstacles to comprehending theatre is the many "obviously true" things that have been said about it—positions that conceal deep biases, vaguenesses, or ambiguities. For example, Hamlet's oft-quoted advice to the players—advice usually thought to encapsulate Shakespeare's own prescription for the theatre and to be self-evidently correct—actually bristles with problems:

> Suit the action to the word, the word to the action; with this special observance, that you o'erstep not the modesty of nature: for anything so overdone is from the purpose of playing, whose end, both at first and now, was and is, to hold, as 'twere, the mirror up to nature; to show virtue her own feature, scorn her own image, and the very age and body of the time his form and pressure.

The crucial ambiguity in the metaphor of holding the mirror up to nature is that it suggests that the use of the mirror may be necessary for nature to see itself (to arrange its cosmetics perhaps?), but that it may not be necessary for some observer of nature—however transcendent or ideal— to use it to see it. The latter can see nature directly, and might simply have told it about its features. Nature uses the mirror merely to make its face vividly evident to itself, but this only illustrates points that might in principle have been disclosed to it otherwise. Theatre just reproduces in gaudy and vivid form what is already grasped, or is already graspable, at least by someone somewhere. Thus theatre understood to be a mirror is superfluous.

But another, less obvious reading of this metaphor suggests itself, one much more nearly true of the reality of performance in the theatre, I believe, yet much more difficult, and maybe impossible, to interpret in exclusively literal terms: there *is* no transcendent or ideal observer—or at least this observer does not communicate at all with us—and we humans stand together, along with other things of nature, facing in one direction only and toward a void. We cannot turn to look directly at each other. Then, for us to put the mirror of theatre up to nature, and up to our common nature, may be the *only* way (or perhaps the only first way) to see certain features of our own looking faces and selves. Reality, then, would be graspable by us only in and through appearances, some of which would be irreducibly artistic and fictional ones.

Only on this second reading can we begin to explain the seriousness of the play, I believe; how it catches our consciences—and our consciousnesses—and reveals truths; at least how it does so when it is anything but mere entertainment.[1] Once we come down on this side of the pivotal ambiguity in the metaphor of theatre as mirror, we catch sight of a new vista of investigations, and we break out of the grasp of venerable misformulations of questions: for example, how can art be both creative and—on the other hand—reproductive or mimetic? Or, how could there possibly be a common genus for both representational and nonrepresentational art? But if the "mirror" of art is the only way, or one of the irreducibly fundamental ways, to see ourselves, and if seeing ourselves is fundamental to what we are as selves, then to come to see oneself is to effect change in oneself in the very act of seeing. To see what one actually is is to see this as only an instance of the possibility projected by the fiction—and it is to see the possibility as only one among many. Persons knowing persons is a special case of a general epistemological claim that cannot be overstressed: we grasp what actually is only after we have imagined what it might be. We see what a thing is only after we have imagined how there could be any possible thing of that sort.

To see ourselves must raise the magnetizing question of what more there is to be known, and to set out before us an array of possible ways of being. To perform the act of knowing is to be beyond it. Even to reproduce ourselves "realistically" would involve a creative act by way of a fiction, and on a different order from holding up a mirror in anything like the

---

1. Mere entertainment I take to be escapist. It is not concerned with recognition, but with distraction from recognition. Of course, if we can recognize how this distraction from recognition occurs, we will learn something about human beings. Still, I will not be centrally concerned with mere entertainment in this book.

literal sense. Hence already the rigid dichotomy dividing art that is reproductive or representational from art that is nonreproductive or nonrepresentational—"purely creative"—is loosened significantly.

Consider another example of an "obviously" true description of theatre that nevertheless conceals fundamental problems, Eric Bentley's attempt to condense theatre to its essence: A impersonates B for C.[2] This has an initial ring of truth, and it is not unenlightening. Reflecting, we realize that no written script is necessary for a theatre event, and that at least one actor is necessary; productions with no actors can generate a theatrical point of view but are borderline cases of theatre proper. There must be at least a one-member audience, for an audience—actual or possible—is ingredient in all art (we do not here question the status of the artist as his or her own audience). Moreover, there must be "impersonation" in some sense. As the sink, the block, or the apple cannot be viewed theatrically without becoming physiognomic universals, without standing in for all possible sinks, blocks, and apples, so the actor cannot stand onstage without standing in for a type of humanity. This characterization will occur even though there is no script and his character is given no name and he says nothing. We recognize him as a type in the family of man, and the fact that we abide in his presence and recognize him as such authorizes him as such; and since we stand in with the character only through his standing in, he authorizes us. There is a pact, an alliance.

But Bentley's word *impersonates* should put us on our guard. Not even the most skillful impersonation can be considered fine art. However telling, however haunting, mere impersonation is to enactment *qua* fine art as caricature is to portraiture *qua* fine art. As Aristotle pointed out, in rendering the particular fine art also discloses the universal, that which bonds us together in communality. And the particular enacted need not be an actual one. Fine art discloses those general characteristics and potentialities of human beings which we must be able to imagine if we are to imagine how any actual human being could be at all.

This is no mere quibble. There is a conceptual flaw here, a pre-critical nominalism, I believe, that prevents Bentley's many interesting and valuable ideas about character-type from coming systematically to fruition. Art gets at the general senses of things through "individuals" enacted by individuals. If this were not the case we could not explain the identifying attachment that the audience has to the play. They find what applies to themselves: the universal which resonates within each, so that the question of each life is put at issue. A skillful impersonator, on the other hand merely excites their curiosity or astonishes them for a moment, as a circus performer might do.

2. Eric Bentley, *The Life of the Drama* (New York: Atheneum, 1975), p. 150.

Of course, anyone who does anything anywhere becomes an example of how a person can behave. It is as if the impersonator were saying, "Here, go try this feat yourself." Merely by staying and watching him we authorize him in a minimal sense, and he authorizes us as potential mimics. In this sense we stand in through him.

But we emphatically do *not* stand in with the person he is impersonating. The power of the impersonation depends upon the realization that the performer has achieved a resemblance to someone not himself and not ourselves. The resemblance enthralls us because of our vivid awareness of what it is that individuates and sunders both us and the performer from the person impersonated. Our ability to identify with this person is blocked. We achieve only the shock of photographic resemblance, not the power of theatrical metaphor. We stand in merely with the performer's feat of standing in. The impersonator makes a spectacle of the person impersonated and we both are alienated from him. Impersonation is a form of mockery; enactment is a form of love.

Thus it is that "obviously true" characterizations of theatre leave fundamental questions unanswered and unasked, or suggest positions which turn out to be false. How are we to find our way? It is not sufficient to go to the theatre and simply open one's eyes. For just what does appear when one sits in the theatre or performs there? The nature of appearance is problematical. Appearances are meaningful only because they are interpreted. As Nietzsche pointed out, there is no immaculate perception. Typically, when one reports things "just the way they strike him," one of his tacit theories of what is happening has already interpreted the occasion in a limited way, and some unacknowledged egoistic or short-term interest has masked out portions of the meaning-giving context.

The first step toward reliable interpretation is a negative one: we must attempt to detect and uproot the nearly instinctual interpretations that bias and blinker us. Next we must give ourselves to the phenomenon, letting it unfold as it will, while at the same time remaining somewhat detached, our minds roaming, varying, comparing. This is not unlike the distinction maintained by the actor between himself as character and himself as artist. We stand in with him as character, but maintain our own sort of artistic distance as members of the audience.

But which example of theatre shall we choose? If we give ourselves to whatever happens to come along we will run out of time, perhaps without ever garnering a revealing variety of theatre, and we will forfeit our obligation to maintain some rational control over what we see. Robert Whitman's theatre event, the first example we chose, was a variation on theatre so radical that it used actual objects, and thus separated out for our inspection the usually hidden factor of theatrical point of view, or interpretive state of mind. This was a helpful beginning. What we now need is a variation that will separate out the factors we have just shown to be problematical: the question of mirroring of life by theatre, and whether this is a mode of discovering, and the question of the nature of our involvement with the character enacted. The two questions at a crucial point intersect: is our mode of involvement one of discovery concerning this involvement?

An example which revealingly varies its presentation along these themes is Bernard Pomerance's *The Elephant Man*. In contrast with Whitman's *Light Touch*, it is a conventional theatrical event, but not realistic in style. Although it depicts with some verisimilitude actual events and persons of nineteenth-century London, this is a "world" we see. Absence is called into presence through vividly evident artifice, fiction, and enactment. Unlike "realistic" theatre, no attempt is made to conceal the existence of theatrical point of view; it is just not glaringly and unsettlingly evident as it is in *Light touch*.

The title, *The Elephant Man*, refers to a monstrously misshapen man who was exhibited as a freak. On stage-left is a screen upon which are projected photographs of the historical person. Bony and fleshy protuberances disfigure in a ghastly way his large head and crippled body. Little or no expression is possible on his face. On stage-right stands a well-proportioned young actor who progressively contorts his limbs, countenance, and posture as the photographs are projected. The actor enacts the freak, and theatre displays the conditions of its communication and projection of a "world." It experiments on its own capacities as it experiments on the limits of our powers of involvement and identification. If we can identify revealingly with a monster, stand in for him through the actor's standing in for him, then we can identify with nearly anyone. Theatrical point of view and other conditions and conventions of theatrical production are kept constant while content projected is varied radically to reveal the limits of our power to identify with another human being.

Scene changes are made before our eyes as a cellist plays on stage-left, and we must imagine the time which has elapsed in the play's "world." In one early scene we see the misshapen man, John Merrick, displayed at the freak show. People pay to gawk at him simply because of the novelty of seeing a human being so *unlike* themselves, and with whom they have no involvement or identification—or so it would seem.

A London physician chances to see him, and, prompted mainly by scientific curiosity, pays the show's producer a fee and removes Merrick to his hospital. After failing to procure assistants who will relate to the monster as a fellow human being, the doctor seeks out the well-known actress, Mrs. Kendal, on the supposition that as an actor she can control or conceal the feelings of horror and revulsion that had prevented all the others from relating to him. He hopes that she will be able at least to seem to relate to Merrick as one human being to another.

Upon meeting Merrick, the actress is able to control her revulsion. He responds to her apparent acceptance of him and blooms as a person before our eyes. He expresses a kinship with her, noting that they both make spectacles of themselves for the entertainment of others. And yet the true self is just this very same body in its potentialities and in its actuality as it sits before her now: Merrick motions to his body with his one good hand. The actress motions in a hesitant way to her own body, as if to say, in a dawning consciousness, This too is just me right here. She begins to be pulled by the possibility of this strange kinship.

We find her standing in for him with her friends, presenting his case, introducing him to highly placed associates and acquaintances: artists, socialites, the wife of the Prince of Wales. They visit him and give him gifts. They accept him as a member of the family of man; they authorize him in the eyes of all. And strangely enough, they seem to be exalted by doing so, as if he were giving them something in return, authorizing them in some way too.

Most fundamentally, Mrs. Kendal—and perhaps each of the others as well—takes Merrick's place in the sense that she becomes able to see the world and herself through his eyes, and by way of his sensibilities. She is able to recognize his recognition of her because she recognizes him to be a human being. Her recognition of herself can be mediated through his recognition of her. And his recognition is one which is sensitive to aspects of herself that she has more or less successfully repressed. It is a recognition that is sensitive to the socially unacceptable and self-unacceptable in *her:* her moments—or more than moments—of not fitting in; the monstrous aspects of *her* life.

In a climactic scene she disrobes to the waist and asks him to turn and look at her. There is nothing disfigured about her body; indeed, in doing so she acts for the normal and the well-formed, welcoming Merrick into their company. But the hushed resistance within herself which she has overcome in so uncovering her body to him discloses to us that through him she accepts her own painful inhibitions and vulnerability, her own previously unacknowledged particularity and privacy. She is fully natural, fully herself, only with the monster. He authorizes her in *her* particularity and uniqueness.

Now we in the audience are made aware that we also feel a kinship to Merrick. We are reaching out also in a discovering empathy and identification. Assuredly, it is only actors before us, and the artist enacting Merrick is not actually misshapen but only enacts it in his posture and gait. But at this aesthetic distance from actuality our own potentialities for mimetic involvement and identification with Merrick begin to emerge in an acknowledgeable way. Usually, when confronting an actual monster, these capacities are realized for an instant and then are repressed, or they are eclipsed by other feelings such as fear.

Merrick tells Mrs. Kendal that before he met her he had no thoughts because he had no one to think them for. He finds himself because he finds himself in this other person. This grotesquely individuated man needs Mrs. Kendal to accept him as a human being, for this will include him in humanity; it will confirm his possession of those universal traits essential to his being fully *human*. He will be authorized.

But Mrs. Kendal—and we in the audience—need *him* as well; we find it releasing and discovering to display ourselves for him. Each of us is released to be more fully *a* human being, a single one. Through accepting him as human we gain access to his recognition and acceptance of each of us in our unique humanity. We objectify and accept elements in ourselves of which we had previously been only blindly ashamed or self-deceptively unaware. These he authorizes.

We stand in through the actors as they stand in for those who find themselves through each other's presence. So stretched and released by the art are we that at least for these moments we accept our kinship with monsters: we enlarge the domain of our being. The result of the experiment of theatre is discovery, and we come home to ourselves as we believe we are: beings of inexhaustible particularity as well as indefinitely extendable horizons of human concern and identification.

CHAPTER II

What Is Phenomenology?

What seems obvious often contains hidden elements and is misleading. Theatre is a prime example. Contrary to first appearances, to sit in a theatre is not just to eavesdrop on an artificial "world" and to be transported from actuality through inventions and charming fictional forms. Nor if theatre is informative does it merely illustrate what we already know. Despite what it obviously appears to be, theatre is a disciplined use of the fictionalizing imagination which can discover, I believe, aspects of actuality.

Phenomenology is the systematic attempt to unmask the obvious. In my use of examples of theatre I have already been employing some of its attitudes and techniques, but only now have I introduced the term explicitly. The delay enabled us to experience how complex and difficult to grasp some appearances are, and to be suspicious of an "obvious" dismissal of phenomenology, which might be stated thus: it is easy to know what appears to be the case, but hard to know what really is so, hence any discipline that concerns itself with appearances is unnecessary.

But I believe that phenomena or appearances are difficult to grasp, and that human reality cannot be understood independently of understanding them. Indeed, I will argue that human life is theatre-like, and that to understand the theatre-like we must understand the theatre. Theatre—from the Greek word *theatron*—means literally a place for seeing. We must devise a way of seeing this place for seeing.

Edmund Husserl was the first to use the word phenomenology to refer to a whole philosophy. He endeavored to formulate a method for revealing the meaning of things and events through revealing the structure of their modes of appearing. A method is required because ordinarily the press of our lives prompts us to be aware of things only in terms of that small fraction of their meaning which is relevant to our survival or short-term interest. To reveal fullness of meaning we must release things from this press and allow them to unfold their intricate and far-flung connections with other things in the meaning-giving context in which they are found. Thus, to free the thing in its *meaning* we must bracket out considerations of empirical *fact*—of what just happens to be the case in any particular situation in which we find ourselves.

To reveal the meaning of the actual we must relate it to many more actualities and possibilities than could be observed to relate to it in any actual situation. Phenomenology involves a detachment from the actuality in which the imagination so disciplines itself that it can return with the meaning of the actuality in hand. Phenomenology is a discipline of the imagination. For example, to determine what we mean when we call something a table we fictively vary in our imaginations the characteristics of any possible table until we reach those limits beyond which it cannot be varied and still remain a table. Can we vary it in our minds until it ceases to have a top? Can we vary its size or hardness indefinitely? No, because in either case it would no longer retain its function for human use. The limits of its variability determine the "shape" of the meaning of any possible table.

The phenomenological use of the imagination grasps the sense of what appears, and it does this through grasping those connections within the context of the thing's experienceability that supply the conditions of its appearance, but that are usually hidden from view because absent from the focus of our concern. For example, we walk down the aisle of a bus and see a leg protruding into the aisle. Normally, of course, we see the leg *as* the leg of a person, even though the person's body is not directly evident to our vision. But it is only when we imagine a situation in which what we mean—and what we expect to find—is disappointed—when we find *only* a leg as we walk to that seat on the aisle—that we are made focally aware of all that we did mean when we first saw it.

Phenomenology has been described as an exercise in seeing. We need the exercise because often we look but do not see. Our seeing is limited by prejudices so habitual that we have no awareness of them *as* prejudices. Phenomenology links the senses with the imagination in an effort to destroy constricting and distorting shells of prejudicial thought. To free the senses we must free the mind—and conversely. Even with things as banal and relatively simple as tables and human legs we may be somewhat surprised when we discover through imaginative variation the great range of what we mean by them; for example, when we see that a table must be of a certain minimal size to count as a table *tout court*, otherwise it is, say, a model table, a doll's house table.

But with a matter as complex and encrusted with prejudice as is theatre, our surprise can be great when we disclose what we mean by it. *Light Touch* and *Elephant Man* were cited as imaginative variations which theatre performs upon itself. We chose actual cases of artistic events which can be called theatre—strictly or loosely—in an effort to escape whatever prejudices lie so deep within the philosopher's "pure" imagination (spun out while he is alone within his room) that he or she cannot be aware of them as such; e.g., the prejudice that one can imagine all that theatre can be without ever going to the theatre. Whitman's *Light Touch* was a variation so extreme that we were uncertain that it was *theatre* art at all; it was as if we saw a structure with four legs but with no provision made for a top—is it a table? Whitman used real things in his production and persons who did not appear to be actors (not even those within the warehouse appeared to be such), thus he nearly expunged the lines that divide onstage from offstage activity. Yet several fundamental elements of theatre art were discovered through this procedure. First, though it was not clearly *theatre* art, it was *art* of some sort, and it was such an extreme denudation of specific artistic properties that we could see a general property of all art, a property which must apply therefore to theatre art: an attitude of detachment toward actual things sufficient to convert them into objects of art. They are seen as "meant to be seen and not used." Second, the very absence of actors underlined the point that actors are typically present; as things so seen become types of such things, so persons so seen become types of humanity.

It should be pointed out in addition, however, that Whitman's "stage-hands" did share with actors a characteristic that was thrown into relief through the problematic status of these persons: like actors, they behave consciously in the actual presence of the audience, and they follow some sort of prescribed routines—or some set of conventions of performance—however loose these might be. This prompts us to say that we have here a borderline case of *theatre* art. Whereas, if events occurred exclusively mechanically, on the one hand, or there was no prescription and no control, on the other—as was the case with the events seen in the street—we would be prompted to say that in both cases we were experiencing hybrid arts. Perhaps we would call the first "conceptual art," and the second an odd sort of "happening" or "found art." It should be clear, however, that boundary lines are somewhat blurred.

Once we sorted out through variations the fundamental theatrical element of aesthetic distance or artistic detachment, we were ready to appreciate an apparently paradoxical characteristic of theatre art. It is the art of *involvement*. When actors stand onstage and enact characters who must also be types of humanity, we not only identify these types as being of certain sorts—as we might identify creatures in the deep seas while looking through the window of a submarine—but in one way or another we identify *with* these types. By "identify with" or "stand in for" I mean tendencies to imitate that are either incipient or overt, ephemeral or more lasting, and the emotions of empathy that are integral to these tendencies. To laugh with those who laugh and to weep with those who weep I take to be a primitive impulse, though it can be counteracted by other impulses. Even when one is disgusted and revolted by an opponent, that opponent is one's *own* opponent, and the phenomenon of revulsion falls within the broad domain of that with which one identifies, the domain of the mimetic. If one were completely detached one would feel no revulsion. As art, theatre involves artistic detachment, but as theatre it is a detachment that reveals our involvements. Through the actors' deliberate identifications-with and standings in we discover our largely undeliberate identifications-with and standings in.

We chose the example of *The Elephant Man* for it was theatre producing a variation upon itself which revealed its own structure. In disclosing that we can identify even with a monster—and indeed sympathetically—it afforded us a glimpse of the full range of our powers of identification and standing in. Phenomenology explores meanings and maps them by discovering limiting cases through fictive variation.

Another variation upon this parameter of involvement, from a very different angle, is supplied by the theatre of Bertolt Brecht. His famous *Verfremdungseffekt*—estrangement effect—derives from an attempt to increase the element of aesthetic detachment until one's emotions of empathy can achieve no climax and release within the theatre; one retains them when one walks into the street, and they can become behaviorally effective there. But then, the effectiveness of his theatre requires that empathy and identification-with are not simply eliminated.[1] Hence, even when theatre

1. Although his own programmatic statement to the effect that his theatre is a complete reversal of the Aristotelian theatre of identification does much to obscure this basic point. Theatre that amounts to anything has always produced both involvement and detachment. But Brecht believes that only with his own theatre has the detachment necessary for critical reflection occurred. Notice how he speaks of his *Lehrstück*, learning play, and how he arrays himself against Aristotle:

Briefly, the aristotelian play is essentially static; its task is to show the world as it is. The learning-play is essentially dynamic; its task is to show the world as it changes (and also how it may be changed). It is a common truism among the producers and writers of the former type play that the audience, once it is in the theatre, is not a number of individuals but a collective individual, a mob, which must be and can be reached only through its emotions; that it has the mental immaturity and high emotional suggestibility of a mob. The latter theatre holds that the audience is a collection of individuals, capable of thinking and reasoning, of making judgment even in the theatre; it treats it as individuals of mental and emotional maturity, and believes it wishes to be so regarded. With the learning-play, then, the stage begins to be didactic. . . . the theatre becomes a place for philosophers. . . . (*Left Review*, London, 1936—translation by Willett)

The distinction he draws between a collection of individuals and a collective individual, a mob, should first be noted. It glosses over in a nominalistic way the deepest question, which

varies itself until no emotional release is possible within the theatre, identification-with and standing in remain.

Phenomenological methods, if employed sufficiently flexibly and imaginatively, can disclose essential characteristics of theatre art, that is, characteristics without which the event would not be theatre art. This set of characteristics might be called the "essence" of theatre. So I am denying that "theatre" is like the word "game" which—if Ludwig Wittgenstein is correct—refers to a range of activities which need share no characteristics as games. But it must also be insisted that these characteristics are very general and very few, and that the "essence" of theatre is not a Form pristine and discrete laid up in an eternal Heaven. Essential characteristics of theatre are created and discovered only within the immanence and cloudiness of the actual historical encounter of persons with each other and the world. Borderline cases and hybrid cases are indefinitely numerous, and the application of the concept of theatre can shift importantly over time, even though essential characteristics remain. Indeed, I propose to shift our attention shortly to the historical continuum of theatrical variations upon theatre.

The variations upon itself that theatre has produced in the examples we have cited were achieved through the variations in each of the elements of theatre. The historical cases we will cite in chapter 5 will specify more exactly the parameter of mimetic involvement, and will do so through implicit variations on the theme of standing in with a person in authority. In chapter 7, in the examples provided by the most imaginative contemporary theatre, the variations on this theme are so radical as to be almost explicitly phenomenological.

The academic-philosophical use of the imagination typically involves only the mental acts of an individual phenomenologist, while theatre involves the imaginative use of things and bodies by a community of persons. But isn't theatre merely an illustration or embodiment of what has already been imagined purely mentally in the privacy of some mind—particularly the playwright's mind—and isn't the theatrical production therefore derivative, a mere superfluity? The question suggests, of course, an affirmative answer, but we will argue that the true answer is negative.

---

is how the identity of individuals involves the identity of the group and the universal. The second defective distinction he draws is the one between the cognitive and the emotional. The whole point of great theatre is that the cognition it generates is of, through, and by the emotional involvement it produces. Finally, are we to think that the typical audience at a non-Brechtian performance of *Hamlet*, say, is merely a suggestible mob? Is it only with Brecht that the theatre becomes a place for philosophers? Brecht is really making a point that applies in one degree or another to all great theatre: it involves an involved detachment. His greater degree of detachment makes it more difficult for us to escape from life and to leave our pity and fear in the theatre. But he pays a price—his audiences may never become deeply involved in the first place.

Fictive variations, in one form or another, are essential to any phenomenology, I think. But the pivotal question concerns how they are to be performed. Husserl supposes that meaning is always objectifiable within the mind of the solitary philosopher, and in advance of communication between minds. Communication merely exteriorizes these meanings. A corollary of this idea is that "the meaning of 'I' is essentially realized in the immediate idea of one's own personality."[2] From these claims it is but a short step to the thesis that all articulation of meaning is essentially complete in soliloquy.

To accept these positions would be to beg the most important questions that this study raises. Theatre is concerned with illuminating through its fictive variations the actuality of mimetic relationships between persons. That is, bodies biologically human learn to become human persons by learning to do what persons around them are already doing. The learning body mimetically incorporates the model; it comes to represent the model and to be authorized by it; it stands in for the model and the model for it. But it needn't do this deliberately at all, for the selves are not neatly distinguished; they exist in a state of communal fusion, or semifusion. A person need be no more aware at forty years of age than he was at four months that he has responded mimetically and exists in mimetic fusion with others. A plausible theory which we will examine in due course is that only when the body can experience itself in the terms in which it experiences others can it experience itself to be, and can it be, a self or a person. But it needn't experience these terms *as* terms for others.

Now the hypothesis that I will develop and test is that actors standing in for characters in the theatre, engaging in deliberate and fictive mimetic enactments, can discover actual and nondeliberate mimetic enactments and standings in between persons offstage. The actor models modeling, enacts enactment, and reveals it. I think it plausible to hypothesize that since behavior and identity were laid down bodily, mimetically, and together, their recovery and recognition may very well be achieved only bodily, mimetically, and together—in the theatre, for example.

If this is the case, then the meaning of human relationships and identity is not discoverable by the isolated philosopher varying possibilities in his mind prior to all expression and communication. Nor is the meaning and identity of one's self essentially realized in "the immediate idea of one's own personality," for this will be a function of the meaning and identity of other selves and of the group of selves. For the philosopher to assume that he can on his own and immediately step to the Archimedean point from which the sense of all things is constituted and objectified, there to

2. Edmund Husserl, *Logical Investigations*, tr. J. N. Findlay (New York: Humanities Press, 1970), Vol. I, p. 316. See also pp. 321 and 327.

trace through fictive variations the structures of sense generated, is for him just to assume that he is *not* engulfed bodily and mimetically with others. In begging the questions of this study he begs the question of his own identity. Alone in his room he varies possibilities in his imagination, but within limits of variation some of which are hidden from him. He cannot imagine the limits of his ability to imagine. His aloneness as a *body* falsely persuades him of his absolute autonomy as a *self*, and eclipses his mimetic involvement with others so totally that this eclipsing eclipses itself.[3] We will regard theatre as a fictive variation on existence, conducted by a community of participants, in which each may surprise every other—as well as himself—with what emerges through their spontaneous interaction and involvement.

The limits of one's ability while isolated to imagine oneself are the limits of one's ability to objectify oneself in such a setting. To assume that all meanings are, in principle, objectifiable initially by the philosopher alone in his study is to obscure important questions about the limits of self-objectification. For example, imagining how one does things must be delineated in its scope by *how* one is imagining this how, but there is no guarantee that one will become critically aware of this primal how of imagining. There is a difficulty of self-reference here. Typically the philosopher imagines while alone in his study—he sinks into his armchair. But how about imagining while in action, say an actor discovering a character while in rehearsal with other actors? This is not just imagined involvement, but an involvement in the imagining that thoroughly structures the imagined. It is unreasonable simply to assume that this is unnecessary for discovery.

It is in rehearsal and performance that we can discover those tendencies of interaction between persons in each others' physical presence which can be discovered only when they are in fact in each others' physical presence. These are one's tendencies, e.g., of attraction, fusion, or repulsion, which must be experienced muscularly and viscerally to be known at all. They are too fleeting, too disturbing, or too habitual to be apprehended by the isolated phenomenologist imaginatively varying human behavior in his mind's eye. They may not occur to him at all in his isolation, for there are no others to provoke the tendencies and to "reflect" them back.

Husserl tended to think of imagination on the model of vision. Consciousness "looks at" essences or meanings (*Wesenserschauung*). Vision

3. Now perhaps a Husserlian phenomenologist will say that the philosopher must constitute all the levels of meaning in the proper hierarchy of founding and founded—*after* the deliverances of art are in. There is some point to this. But my method of ordering the levels of meanings will not be strictly Husserlian, even on this construal of his position.

is the distancing, discriminating, and objectifying sense *par excellence*. But in a rehearsal there is nothing seen as an object of an act of imagination. Imagining is a kinesthetic involvement with others, luring us all together, which is already determining the performance imagined. The characters and their relationships are discovered by the actors *ambulando*. If the bodily self is to become imaginatively aware of its own absorption in others, then its attempt to detach itself from itself in a calm and detached "visual" imagining is apt to freeze, distort, or mask from sight the very involvement one is attempting to imagine.[4]

At the level at which we wish to speak it is difficult to distinguish act of imagining from object imagined, and the fundamental Husserlian distinction between mental act and its object is thrown into question. The danger of speaking of mental acts is that we will then speak of *a* stream of them, and this predisposes us to a premature and unfounded theoretical commitment to individuation of self and to personal subjectivity. Even in Husserl's late *Experience and Judgment* where he speaks interestingly of an anonymous and pre-predicative self which does not thematize itself *as* its self, nor the other *as* other, still the assumption seems to be that it is an individual self, though anonymous. But this is just the question that we wish to raise. Is the anonymous self an individual self?

As we proceed, our orientation will move more nearly parallel to the phenomenological procedures of Maurice Merleau-Ponty and Martin Heidegger. I will be particularly concerned with the latter's idea that what in ordinary parlance we call an individual person or self is really but an instance of the group's identity, the "they-self." To be is to be "one" merely in the sense of being interchangeable with anyone else. It is to be neuter. One does "what one does," what anyone does.

I will not simply abandon the method of imaginative variations, but I will engage in them in special ways. The greatest danger consists in making them in a detached and impersonal way which obliterates the subject matter of the inquiry: the mimetic involvement between persons which is theatre itself, and much of life itself. One supposes that he is dealing with a problem analogous to those in a geometry of formal entities—or to ones in a domain closely related to this, say geometrically shaped material bodies. He supposes that the elements of these figures can be known immediately and exhaustively and in advance of sensory experience with actual figures: points, lines, angles, planes. He then varies an imagined figure from three sides to four sides, say, or from three intersecting lines on a

---

4. Although, as we shall see, somewhat detached observers—audience or director—are required to imagine through the actor, and to interact with him, if the artistic event is to be complete. And given the artistic fact, somewhat more detached participants, philosophers and critics, are required if the significance of the performance is to be systematically explored.

plane to lines that do not intersect, even though they are on the same plane, and he has discovered an invariant feature of all triangles: though there are more sorts than we might have first suspected, still none can be pushed to a point that permits this. Varying all the parameters, all the elements, he discloses the invariable essence of triangularity.

But the elements of theatre cannot be immediately and exhaustively known in advance of sensory involvement with theatre. Supposing that they can be produces a "constitution" of meaning all the more misleading because it seems to be complete. For example, one may suppose that the set of elements is exhausted by set, stage, audience, and actors of some sort. One then varies the element which is the actor to the point at which merely a wax mannequin remains stationary at center stage and the sets change mechanically around it. Fascinated by the reach of the drama, one has covered over the possibility of seeing that fundamental elements of theatre have been left out: particularly that mutually reflecting and dialectical relationship between live actor and audience which is the central element, if anything is: co-presence, awareness of awareness, participatory involvement. Theatre as a worldly mode of communal interpretation is lost. Remaining is but an especially complicated geometrical configuration within the world, from which one easily detaches oneself as reflector or observer, or so one thinks.

We do not set things straight by choosing examples of "material essences" which are distinct from formal ones. Husserl cites notches as an example: unlike triangles, they cannot be exhaustively specified as to their possible sorts and shapes. This is important. Yet as far as I know we do not become mimetically involved in any significant way with notches, and theatre does not deal in any way centrally with our relationship to them.

In the spirit of phenomenology William James once described philosophy as an approach to things in which we "pump free air" around them; that is, we detach ourselves from them and observe them in the many-sidedness of their relationships. In the case of the mannequin and the changing sets one has pumped so much free air around the topic of theatre that one has floated away from it. No doubt something is revealed, and it is perhaps the reach of drama: any disclosure through progressive tension (between things made sensuously present to us) of anything which has significance for us. But though this is drama—a conceptual drama or a drama of mechanical puppets—it is not theatre. Nor is this merely a technicality.

What deceives is that the mannequin is being viewed theatrically, but we cannot acknowledge this given the detached and ahistorical way in which the variations are being made. We must see puppets or mannequins as being like humans, and we must see the stage upon which they are placed as being like a stage upon which humans could perform. Its sense is parasitical upon the sense of theatre. But the variation in question has put itself in a position in which it cannot spell out its dependency. The use of the mannequin is an especially vivid tip-off: given our movement within cultural and theatrical tradition we must see the mannequin as a token of a human being, as standing in for a human being, and, indeed, for one who could in turn stand in for an indefinite number of others, i.e., we must see the mannequin as standing in for an actor and we must see all this as in-a-theatre if we would think that it is theatre at all. But the founding level of meaning which is theatre has been concealed from sight through the thinking that thinks the mannequin to be theatre. In short, to think that one can vary types of theatre with the detachment and facility with which one varies spatial figures—and can discover theatre thereby—is just to assume that one can imagine in advance all that theatre can teach one about one's involvements.

To avoid this error of formalistic pride we will examine a core of actual cases which no one through the decades and centuries—no one in his right mind—would dispute to be theatre. This might be construed as a dumb act of piety. It leaves open basic possibilities, one of which is that there is no Archimedean point beyond the world to which we can have access in order to survey and manipulate the world. It leaves open the possibility that theatre is worldly in an especially pervasive and encompassing sense: that it (among other cultural institutions) will determine how we look at things—for example, how we look at theatre itself.

Theatre cannot be articulated with the same dispatch as a spatial figure can be, for theatre is already an implicit phenomenological variation on the meaning of human being and doing, and it has sprung up between actual persons in the world. It is worldly, not just in the world as a spatial figure is. We can safely begin our imaginative variations upon it only after listening intently—lovingly, in a way—to the ones it has already made. We will call these given variations.

There is a new danger involved in avoiding the danger of floating away from the topic, however. It is to become so mired in actual cases that the full possibilities and meaning of theatre are obscured. Given our plan for the book, this would involve an obscuration not only of theatre but of existence itself. The one way open for us, as we balance between these dangers, is to stay in tune with our own involvement as we participate in an actual theatrical event, and at the same time to relate our experience to a variety of other such events, actual and possible. Only then can we discover the structures of theatre itself, rather than of some undisciplined creation of the philosophical imagination.

CHAPTER III

Theory of Enactment

Scanning the horizon of already realized variations, we note structures running through them all: in each case there are actors and persons comprising an audience for these actors, and they are in each other's immediate presence as bodily selves.[1] They are so for a given span of time. In the vast majority of cases the actors speak at one point or another, but important scenes may transpire with nothing said whatsoever, and in others in which they do speak the speaking may be peripheral to what the characters are doing. Although usually there are words written in advance for the actors to learn to speak, and stage directions for them to follow, a theatrical event can occur with neither of these being the case. We might hesitate to identify it as a theatrical event, however, if it were not repeatable in some recognizable form; art discloses types, and types invite repeated instantiation.[2] But the only conditions of its repeatability are that it be remembered by at least one of the participants, and that it be enactable again by someone. Thus it would seem to generate a "text" which is instantiable an indefinite number of times even if the "text" be no more than memories of participants, actors or audience.

Hence a theatre event has at least two temporal dimensions. First, it must be repeatable from one performance to the next. Second, each performance must occur for a given stretch of time. One could glimpse a piece of sculpture, a painting, or a work of architecture for a moment and one

1. There may be only one actor, and—perhaps—only one audience member. Yet a one-to-one relationship may limit the effectiveness of theatre.

2. It might be objected that the art object does not express types, but rather its particularity is manifested: its sheen, texture, qualities of shape and surface—its "aesthetic" qualities. But these are not contradictory claims. It is just because the art object's ordinary usefulness is put out of play that it can manifest *both* its sheer particularity and materiality *and* that transcendent, idealizing usefulness in which it stands in for all possible members of the class or type. We need only to concede that these two roles are seldom in the focus of consciousness simultaneously.

would be at least technically correct in saying that one had seen it; not so with theatre.[3] Actors and audience must remain together until something has transpired. In certain moments only a blank stage might be glimpsed, or in others a tableau quite unrevealing of the play itself. This is true for all works of art that require performance for their existence: there is no original which is signed by the originator and which can be glimpsed in an instant. An irruption in space-time must occur each time, and each time the event will run a somewhat different course.

However strange or remote be the "time" of the play's "world," it can be enacted only within the time in which actors and audience agree to be gathered together within the theatre's space, that is, only within the world's time. "Time" and time, and "world" and world, actors and audience, must intersect. This is the encounter which is theatre.

As long as the actor is not speaking in his own person—standing before the curtain, for example, apprising the audience of a role change—he or she need only to stand on the stage before the audience to enact a type of humanity. So strong is theatrical point of view. For instance, Samuel Beckett's *Act Without Words (#1)* features a single male actor, a knotted rope hanging down over the stage, and a bottle of water suspended on a string which is dropped toward the actor, only to be jerked out of his grasp repeatedly. No name or distinctive costume is given to the actor, nor does he say anything. Yet the actor is a proxy for each of us individuals in such a situation of desperation and tantalization. He says to us, in effect, "What if this should happen to you?" or "Go try this yourself." He stands in for each of us. He models a response to a difficult situation which, in one form or another, might befall any of us. Standing in for us in public, he authorizes our anxiety in such a situation, as well as our determination not to collapse in the face of the difficulty. But we also stand attentively in public in his presence. So, conversely, we authorize him to take our place, and we authorize his modeling of a response to the situation. Even if a performer should behave ridiculously as the character, and we should laugh at him, we all agree that this behavior should be counted ridiculous. His enactment authorizes our laughter, and our laughter authorizes his enactment.

Theatre is the paradigmatic mimetic art and it deals with the paradigmatically mimetic features of human life. The actor stands in for the character. But the character is a type of humanity with whom the audience member can identify, either directly as a stand-in for his own person, or indirectly as a stand-in for others whom the audience member recognizes, and with whom he can be empathetically involved. If the character is one who stands in for us, then we can also stand in for him, and indeed we do

3. I ignore here the many new hybrid art forms such as kinetic sculpture.

stand in for him through the actor's standing in for him. The basic facts energizing theatrical art are (1) that persons identify with others, even to the point of assuming permanently their modes of being and behavior (as in the family), and (2) that persons can bring this and related facts to thematic awareness through engaging in short-term artistic acts of identification and enactment.

In due course I will single out plays which are paradigmatically theatrical in that they reflect in their manifest content the structure of any theatrical event. That is, in them actors stand in for characters who stand in for other characters. The audience member stands in through the actor's standing in for characters who stand in an actor-like way, and if the audience member intuits a similarity to offstage existence then this existence must be seen to be theatre-like.

Now, these distinctions will all be necessary for our analyses of theatrical experience. But they are distinctions of reason only, and it will be disastrous if we think that they refer to moments or aspects of the experience that are actually separate in the experience. While involved in the performance we are not aware that we are standing in through the actor's standing in for the character's standing in. The whole point of theatre as art is to give release to our primal mimetic absorptions in types of doing and being; these absorptions are constitutive, I will argue, of our identity as persons, and they are usually quite unspeakable by us even when they are released. We articulate and express our awareness through a peculiar silence. We become aware of the unspeakably common, the fusion of human bodies through the group, the precisely nonverbal and nonanalytical supportive stratum of our lives.

As audience encounters actors, and world encounters "world," an inviolable rule typically regulates their intercourse. The anonymity and privacy of the audience member are protected as he sits in the theatre house. He is not expected to walk onto the stage and participate as an actor; indeed it is impossible for him to become a part of that "world's" scene, and if he walked onto the stage he would only disturb or destroy the scene. Nor, typically, is the actor allowed to walk into the theatre house and accost the audience members.

An aesthetic funneling and restricting—an aesthetic "distance"—regulates the intercourse of "world" and world. It is just because of this protection that the audience can uncover itself at its most vulnerable levels: its archaic mimetic fusions with others, and its odder and deeper sympathies, about which it has never learned to speak in words. And it is just because of its own protection that the cast of actors can reveal themselves as likewise vulnerable and mimetically involved.

Moreover, in this pact each can do for the other what the other cannot do for itself. That is, the audience participates in the "world" from the side of the world and in its relative passivity its mimetic involvements and engulfments in the world can be called forth through recognition of, and participation in, similar involvements in the play's "world." This release the audience expresses in manifold ways that supply clues to the actors, who then proceed to try further means to pull the far-flung structure of human involvement in the world into the concentrated and intelligible focus of the play's "world."

The actors, on the other hand, participate in the world from the side of the "world," and just because of the fictionality of their setting can initiate activity more daring, volatile, and free than the constraints and dangers of the world ordinarily allow. Even in those productions in which the artists strive for pure fantasy, not just any absence or nonexistence is pulled into the presence of the play's "world," but only that which can give us an experience of our power over possibility here and now in the theatre house; hence "world" and world augment and feed each other in this instance only when the internal coherence of the fantasized "world" most "obviously" sunders it from all relevance to the world. We beings—we actual beings—discover our power over possibility. Together the audience and the actors engage in incarnated imaginative variation on the meaning of human being and doing. Together they experiment on the nature and extent of mimetic involvement, identification, and sympathy—and on how these relate to the individual's identity.

Already incorporating others' mode of being, because one stood mimetically in their authoritative presence, one cannot simply step back and pinpoint and objectify this mode of being. Since it is one, one takes it with him as he steps back. The actor can discover this reality which lies between people only with and through the others; and the members of the audience can discover it only with and through the person who stands at the focus—but it is only the focus—of the experiment, the actor. The actor's challenge is to disclose the other incorporated in him as other, as character, but he can do so only in the presence of others for whom he is another who mimetically enacts their common life.

Usually unsuspected by the audience (during rehearsals the director and others in the rehearsal space are the audience), the actor is listening to the sounds they make. He hears the sounds that slip from them. He hears them in the encompassing margins of his consciousness. The actor's mimetic tendencies are such only relative to other persons, but the actor cannot see his own body and face when he is actively with and for others, and he must rely upon the audience to signal him when he is on to something telling and essential. Nor can he hear his voice as it really is—a voice mimetically with and for others—unless others let him know what they hear. Not realizing that they are being heard and followed, and thinking that it is only a fiction to which they are responding, they in the audience are not on their guard, and so reveal themselves deeply as beings who are mimetically with others. The goal of all involved is that hush of silence which discloses the habitually unspoken, or perhaps the unspeakable. It is that common life shared undeliberately and mimetically. One becomes aware of what one's body already is: something modeled on others mimetically. One also becomes aware of one's possibilities as an individual.

The shimmering fictional character is the locus through which the actor is given back to himself through the audience, and the members of the audience are given back to themselves through the actor. It is a play of mutual "mirroring." The audience supplies the communally constituted parts of the actor's body to the inspection of all. The actor is authorized by the audience, the audience by the actor. It is because the characters are fictional that we can push to limits and involvements which we would not ordinarily dare to approach. In rehearsal particularly, limits and involvements are sensed, flushed out, and approached because the art itself must prevent one from "going too far." Inhibitions and defenses can come down and greater disclosure can be achieved than in comparable situations in the offstage world. The theatrical situation is structured in such a way that all the parties, actors and audience, can let things escape them that add up dialectically to revelation concerning the limits and conditions of their common ways of being together in the world. Together they reconstruct the prototypical organism of human relationship.

If Paul Schilder is correct, as he seems to be, body and world are continually interchanged mimetically, and in the ordinary course of events quite unacknowledgeably. We will examine Schilder's views more thoroughly in Part Two. For now, we note only these key words of his:

> There is a community between my picture, my image in the mirror, and myself. But are not my fellow human beings outside myself also a picture of myself? . . .
> I sit about ten feet away from a mirror holding a pipe . . . in my hand and look into the mirror. I press my fingers tightly against the pipe and have a clear-cut feeling of pressure in my fingers. When I look intently at the picture of my hand in the mirror I now feel clearly that the sensation of pressure is not only in my fingers in my own hand, but also in the hand which is twenty feet distant in the mirror. . . .
> The experience of the sensation in the mirror is as immediate and original as the experience in the real hand. It is at least very probable that part of [one's own] experiences are given when [he] see[s] the bodies of others, especially when one considers how little the optic experience concerning one's own body-image differs from the experiences we have . . . of others.[4]

4. Paul Schilder, *The Image and Appearance of the Human Body* (New York: International Universities Press, 1950).

My fellow human beings are a picture of *myself*. Theatre, at its best, enables us to acknowledge this. Schilder's is a very valuable insight. Oddly enough, it is even more valuable when we purge it of the suggestion that one's optic image of oneself differs only a little from one's optic image of others. A crucial difference is that one has no primary experience of his own face. Item: I cut myself on the leg. Others rush over and I see them grimacing as they see the wound. Even if grimacing with pain should be natural for a young child who is blind, yet for me the face of the other as he sees the wound reinforces and molds my grimace through my sight of his face, and indeed his face fills out the body-image which is mine: *he* supplies a visually experienced face for *my* body-image. Notice that I do not say simply that he fills out my experience of my face, for in "the sphere" of relations—in the living context—my image of my body and my image of his body are not perfectly distinct. It is my body-image in the sense that it is experienced *by* my organism, but it is not my body-image if by that is meant that it is simply and directly *of* only my organism's face.

I am by-for-with-and-*in* others experientially. The ultimate problem is how to become aware of myself *as* by-for-with-and-in others *and* other from every other—I myself. I will suggest that the bodily and communal fictive variation that is theatre supplies me with the communally consti- tuted missing parts of my own experiencing body. Theatre is to be construed neither as a preeminently visual, nor auditory, nor literary phenomenon, but as a perceptually induced mimetic phenomenon of par- ticipation—an imagined experience of total activity.[5]

Consciousness is unwittingly self-limiting. We cannot be conscious of not being conscious of something. Deliberate choice, and the questioning of alternatives are possible only within limits and structures which are not questioned. Even if we should question the limits, the questioning itself must occur within limits that cannot at that moment be questioned. Each step of reflection must presuppose limits that it cannot question—ad in- finitum. Common ways of being together are at least initially unspeakable because all speech must presuppose them; but they are set resounding in the art. To push to the limits of a mimetic behavior is to release its "shape" in the silence—as if by a sonar of communal endeavor.

In theatre there is a sharing of secrets that the ordinary face-to-face encounter precludes just because such encounter is possible only by stay- ing within the limits that the encounter cannot question. Encompassed by the darkened audience, as if he were a child being cradled by his mother, the actor is guided by the pressure of their response. When it gives way to a hushed and perhaps reverent silence he knows that he is delineating

5. R. G. Collingwood, *The Principles of Art* (Oxford: Oxford University Press, 1975).

the mimetically shared life that is most basic and precious just because it is unquestioned. The profound hush at a great performance suggests something of an illicit disclosure of the private in public—except that theatre is an institution in which such disclosure is legitimated.

The actors as artists deliberately lay down various maskings, limits, and styles of life for themselves as characters, so that through their abandoned responses to each other as characters within these limits—and through their response to the audience—they can begin to tell which limits and maskings were *undeliberately* laid down by the characters, by these sorts of persons, in their mimetic involvements with and diremptions from each other. What "takes"? With what does the audience identify? Which of the actor's responses as character are most implicative and formative of a life? As artists the actors listen for what comes back to them as characters from each other and from the audience. In this experiment which humanity conducts upon itself, there is an element of trial and error. When the enactment is correct all involved rush into the characterizations as into the cavities of molds in a state of vacuum. We see as if for the first time.

The actors and the audience are co-creators of each character. Of course, they are speaking themselves, speaking types of their communal life, under the guise of the fictional other. They "sculpt" the character in Michaelangelo's sense: they release the character already formed in the grain of the block but entrapped by the excess stone. Yet, to release for exhibition mimetic tendencies already at work is to transcend them, for now one sees the actual as an instance of but one possibility. New possibilities and new questions concerning what each one is to be are put into play.

Before we can close this initial sketch of our theory of enactment, one more salient point must be covered. Theatre is a fine art. It is essential to every such art that the participants be aware that it is art. The audience has come to see not Prince Hamlet, but Prince Hamlet enacted; the Prince himself is long dead, if he ever existed. We see neither the character alone nor the actor alone, but this-actor-as-this-character.

Now, any theatre event is essentially durational, and the focus of our attention shifts and dilates from moment to moment. At times the focus includes the actor, and we are aware of him as artist, and of the technique he employs in enacting the role of the character; indeed there are moments in which our awareness of the character's "role" in his "world" is horizonal, not focal. But there are other moments in which our awareness of the actor as artist is so peripheral, and at the same time so secure and confident, that we can "let go" and identify profoundly with the character he or she is enacting. These are moments in which unprecedented extensions of our sympathy can occur, or in which regressions to archaic identifications and fusions with others can transpire. In extratheatrical situations such meltings and breachings of individuation typically involve mob actions, or a loss so complete of individual self in the dull wash of everyday conformity that not even the loss is noted. But in theatre the aesthetic distance that allowed the melting and breaching in one moment can trigger a critical response in the next that can, in principle, be awareness of the loss of individuation *as* such a loss.

Similarly, the catharsis of one's emotions of pity and fear when confronted with the tragic character's fall—as Aristotle describes it—is possible only because one has identified with a person who is nevertheless fictional. To confront an actual person in the grip of calamity may involve such a shocking identification that the witness is not in those moments perfectly clear: Is it *I* experiencing *him*? The emotions of pity and fear lose their shape in hysteria; or one represses the experience. Again, it is just the distance of the aesthetic point of view that allows access to one's own moments and movements of identification.

My use of the word *fictional* must be perfectly clear. The word is usually used in a more specific sense to distinguish works of art depicting beings or events that never actually occurred from works depicting things that did actually occur, e.g., "fictional and nonfictional literature." But I use the word in a generic sense to refer to all works of fine art in respect to their being embodied by beings which have a reality distinct from whatever actual things *or* inactual things are depicted by them. For example, regardless of whether or not there ever existed in world time a prince in Denmark who can be identified by the definite description of Prince Hamlet given in *Hamlet,* the actor before us has a distinct reality of his own. The enactment can occur only because there is in our sense, something *fictional* occurring. This is the idealization essential to all artistic communication. We express the sense of something through a different thing, something at hand: absence is called into presence.[6]

Before we present our first set of variations on the essential theme of mimetic involvements and authorization, we must further clarify how the

6. Thomas DeQuincey is excellent on this point: "If a man . . . should say that he would 'whistle Waterloo,' that is, by whistling connected with pantomime, would express the passion and the charges of Waterloo, it would be monstrous to refuse him his postulate on the pretence that 'people did not whistle at Waterloo.' Precisely so: neither are most people made of marble . . . it is the very worst objection in the world to say, that the strife of Waterloo did not reveal itself through whistling; undoubtedly it did not; but that is the very ground of the man's art. He will reproduce the fury and the movement as to the only point which concerns you, viz., the effect upon your own sympathies, through a language that seems without any relation to it: he will set before you what *was* Waterloo through that which was *not* at Waterloo. Whereas any direct factual imitation, resting upon painted figures drest up in regimentals, and worked by watchwork through the whole movements of the battle, would have been no art whatsoever in the sense of a Fine Art, but a base *mechanic* mimicry" (*The Antigone of Sophocles,* 1846. Excerpted at some length by Jacques Barzun in his *Pleasures of Music* [Chicago: The University Press, 1977], p. 23).

fictional idealizations of theatrical appearances can discover and communicate the reality of our lives when they need not depict or denote any actual particular beings. We will find that artistically structured appearance is involved in reality because it can *exemplify* sorts or types of human reality—which have indefinitely many instantiations in actual cases—without necessarily *denoting* any actual individual, so as to pick it out from others. What is this reality of appearance?

CHAPTER IV

Theory of Appearance

"Drama" and "theatre" are remnants from the Greek. "Drama" is a trans-
literation of the word meaning action or a thing done, while "theatre"
derives from *theatron,* which, as we said, means a place for seeing. Etymo-
logically, a theatrical production of a drama is a production of an action
so that it can be seen.

Such an exercise seems to accomplish nothing. Don't actions occur all
the time outside the theatre, and don't they appear just as clearly as the
nose on someone's face? Moreover, they are real actions. Aren't the ones
performed in a theatre merely pretended? But these words we use so
easily—"unreal," "real," "pretend," "see," "appear"—once filled the
Greeks with wonder (the words' Greek counterparts did), and they can
excite us to wonder as well if we pause a moment with them. In what sense
does the reality of a thing appear to us in the everyday world? What
appears to me, for instance, when I hear the whirring sound of a grouse
and say, "There is a grouse somewhere in the bushes"? Is it only the
sound, the "whirring motor," that appears to me? No, what is immediately evident is that I hear the *grouse,* not just the sound it makes. The
sound is an element of an absence given presence. Even if I should be
mistaken, and it turns out not to be a grouse at all, I still meant that it was
a grouse, not just a sound, and it is as indisputably evident to me now as
it was then that this is just what I meant. It is only because I know that
this is what I meant that I can later be proved wrong, if I am wrong.

But surely, it might be objected, if I am to be proved either right or
wrong, whatever it is in the bushes must appear directly—directly to sight,
most typically. Yet when we examine this "directly" we find that what
we mean to be there through the experience of sight is always more than
can be pinned down as actual contents of visual experience alone—the
barest visual images, "sense data." Nor can we say that what we mean to
be there is merely the sum of the bare sensory imagery of all the activated

sense modalities. Perception always involves interpretation—absence given presence. A corollary of this is that each occasion of presumptive sensory knowing of the world of nature, taken one by one, is conceivably deceptive. We could not say that they all are, for then the very concept of the deceptive would be without application and concrete meaning, since there would be nothing genuine and true with which it could be contrasted. So some occasions must be true, though in principle we cannot be absolutely certain which ones are. Hence the grouse itself, the very being or reality of the grouse itself, must be evident to us sometimes.

Even in the case of an alleged occasion of sensory knowing that is actually false—when something appears to be what it is not—*it* still must appear in *some* sense if it is to appear *as* what it is not. *That* it is must appear, though *what* it appears to be does not match what it actually is. But if what it actually is *never* appeared we could not know that it sometimes appears to be what it is not. So we must suppose that things can disclose themselves through appearing to be what they are—can disclose themselves truly sometimes. And we must suppose this truth to be not merely the truth of statements, because often no statements are made, nor do they need to be; and when they are made, we can begin to know what they mean and possibly to verify them only because that about which they are made can disclose itself in some measure of truth on its own. There must be this more fundamental sense of truth as disclosure.

It should not be thought, however, that this nonstatemental truth need be entirely extralinguistic. The name by itself—"grouse"—allows us to possess the thing in speech even if it is totally absent from the range of our sense organs. Plato thought that to have the *eidos*, the "look" of an object in speech, is better than to have a directly nameable instance of it, because when the object is present we have it given in only some of its ways of being presentable. But to summon it in its absence is to collect all its ways of being given.[1] This is profound, but it errs, I believe, in assuming that all power belongs to names and to disengaged reflection. Theatre is a perceptual and physiognomic mode of giving presence to absence and concealment. Here a sensuous presentation is also an elucidation of presentability—of essence. Here practical concern is disengaged and the thing as imaginable is freed. Why shouldn't such physiognomic means be essential for the disclosure of physiognomic elements of our existence?

Matters come to a head: both *that* and *what* something is must appear, but the appearance cannot be pinned down and limited to any statement just *qua* statement alone, nor to any set of actual—specific and peculiar—

---

1. Cf. Robert Sokolowski, "The Phenomenology of Naming," presented at the annual meeting of the American Philosophical Association, Boston, 1976, pp. 9–10. Professor Sokolowski has kindly supplied me with his manuscript.

disturbances within any set of sense organs. The sense of what things are must be common to all the sensory modalities (sight, hearing, smell, touch, etc.), but specific to none of them (these qualities of the thing are its "common sensibles," as Aristotle calls them). The activation of the sensory modality can be the occasion for experiencing this sense of the thing's being, but it alone does not constitute this sense, and the sense is not dependent upon any present encounter with any actual thing of the sort in question. It is integral to our sense of the context within which the thing normally functions. For example, a river is a river not just because it is composed of water, but because it is water of a certain minimal quantity (not precisely determined) which flows for a certain minimal distance (not precisely determined) between banks of earth, etc. The context appears at some time or other to someone, but it need not always be physically present if we would grasp the sense of *what* and *that* a river *is*.

An entrance to theatre opens up. We begin to see that our sense, or intuition, of what things are is not dependent in every case upon a present encounter with any actual thing of a certain sort in its actual context. It is dependent upon appearance, but the thing of which it is the truthful, everyday appearance need not be actual or physically present to produce the appearance in every instance; for example, not in the theatre. The appearance of a tree could be produced by papier-mâché and paint, the appearance of a murder by rubber knives and actors' movements.

Now, what if it were the case that theatre allowed us not only to see and to grasp an appearance of what something *is* when the actual thing is not present, but to see it *better*? Then theatre as that which allows us to see something done—as the etymology of the term suggests—would have been given an important and somewhat startling meaning. I am arguing that this is the case.

Aristotle pointed out in the *Poetics* that something cannot have artistic value if it is too large or too close to be taken in by the mind and seen all at once.[2] This insight can be generalized. Life itself is too large and strung-out to be taken in as a whole by the mind. It is just because we are assaulted by actual particulars in their ineluctable spatial, temporal, and conventional relationships to other actual particulars, that only a few can be present to us at once, and those most pressing given demands of survival or imperatives of ego. Hence others cannot be present, and usually we are absorbed in a meager portion of the whole so totally that we cannot be aware *that* we are thus absorbed. It is as if many musical instruments were being played at once and we were too close to some, while others were drowned out. The whole piece with its melodic line would elude us.

2. Aristotle, *Poetics*, 1450, b 38.

Our sense of what things are, including our sense of ourselves, is dependent upon the richness and depth of our store of "common sensibles," and upon our sense of the whole spatiotemporal and cultural context in which things are given their sense. Theatre with its fictions so organizes and compresses, or reduces, expands, or speeds up the presentation of events, that it can bring the whole—say a whole action within the world—before the mind; thus it allows it to be taken in as a whole. Most important, theatre fictively varies the key theme of mimetic involvement between persons until the theme is taken in *as* such, in its full dimensions, by the mind. It enables us to see thematically and acknowledgeably what previously has simply engulfed or blinkered us. It is not that in everyday life we cannot identify and classify things, but that we do so only within the straitened boundaries of immediate duress, custom, and opportunity.

The etymological exercise redeems itself and springs to new life. *Theatron*, the word for theatre, is related to *theōria*, spectacle, but this can also mean speculation and theory. Thus it is suggested that theatre, at its origins, was its own mode of speculating and theorizing about human nature and action. It is not identical with philosophy's mode of theorizing, for what it presents directly to histrionic perception—the conditions for the coherence of a life or lives—is argued for by philosophy. In ancient Greek civilization reality and appearance were linked essentially, and in certain ways they are still linked in ours. An occurrence was denoted by a word from which our "phenomenon" derives directly, and it meant literally "that which shows itself." Further, "phenomenon" is related to the Greek word for light (*phos*). An endeavor to get at the literal sense of *physis* (physical nature) renders it as "the appearing which stands there in itself."[3] The more nearly immediate perceptual sense of things is rendered by theatre, while analysis and synthesis of the concepts embedded therein are rendered by philosophy. Both are essential for revealing; they are interdependent.

With this we may have restored some of the wonder inherent in the basic terms of our discussion. If we have, it will be increased when we relate *theatron* and *theōria* to *theos*, the Greek word for god. As Karl Kerenyi has pointed out, in ancient Greek *theōria*, or its equivalent, meant "to look god in the face." Appearance is not mere appearance, or appearance set over against reality, but is the revelation of the ultimate powers and inexhaustible being of things. But how can god (*theos*) be looked in the face and at the same time be linked with theory (*theōria*)? It can only be because god was considered to be a living body, and that awareness of body was considered fundamentally revealing.

3. Martin Heidegger, *Introduction to Metaphysics*, trans. R. Mannheim (New Haven: Yale University Press, 1959), p. 159.

To make any sense of this crucial point we must try to pick apart the tight fabric of conceptualization that began to be woven around the time of Plato and which connects truth and theory exclusively to words and statements; we must try to look through it and behind it. For it is the bodies of the human actors before us that reveal through moving us to identifying involvement with them. Any other objects used to exemplify the power of appearing things are apt to mislead after a certain point— notches, grouse, whatever—since nonhuman things do not elicit from us the same sort of involvement. If we should grasp these other things only in words, our loss would not be as great as it would be if we somehow grasped humans only in words. As Husserl observed, the first other is another human being, and this establishes not merely an historical priority, but an existential one as well.

A modernizing and demythologizing attitude toward the florid and concrete life of the senses in folk religion developed in Greece during the fifth century B.C. Even Aeschylus and Sophocles meant to refine the traditional Olympian conceptions of the gods, and if we have no idea of the roots of this tradition which still informed the audience members' responses to the living actors before them, we will not understand the manner in which they were moved. And if we forget that the tragedians' texts were written primarily to be performed, not to be read, we will not understand the manner in which we can be moved.

Plato's ennobling of the abstract intellect is extreme, but in him we can see the attitudes of many others "writ large." For him imaging, which is the life of the senses, is the lowest level of mental functioning. Any fleeting image that occurs is merely particular, and worth nothing until it has been classified by the abstract intellect which itself is imageless. Plato is a source of the perennial idea of the "given": a prime matter belonging to the mind in its passive role that must be informed by the mind in its active role. This idea manifests itself in aesthetic theories as assumptions of art as "expression" of subjective states, and of art as the self's avoidance of actuality in disconnected idealization and diversions.

Any trace of this idea of the sensuous "given" will beg questions central to this study, for it assumes that persons are subjects already defined in opposition to other persons and to objects. This division destroys our ability to understand what is going on in the theatre. It prejudices our account of how we stand in through the actor's standing in. We must tend to ask, How can *I* possibly identify with *his image* of the *other*, the character? No more misleading formulation of the problem of theatre could be imagined.

The doctrine of the "given" connects one tacitly to these ideas: the self is immediately aware of itself as subject; the other is allegedly another subject whose body, as an object, is alone directly present to oneself; knowledge of the other's mind and intentions becomes the great problem. This prevents one from unbiased consideration of another possibility: that as a body-self one stands directly in the other's presence as a body-self—stands there with him in space—and that one's sense of his own self and mind is derived from his sense of the other's self and mind. Moreover, in theatre we better grasp ourselves because we better grasp the other as one of "our sort," and this disclosure of common being is pre-predicative, sensuous, undeliberate, and, at moments, anonymous—not the work of individuated selves at all.

It would be wrong, however, to think that Plato had no awareness of the Dionysian power of art to dig beneath the neatly demarcated existences which we like to picture to ourselves. It is precisely because he sensed this power, and sensed it to be dangerous, that he tried zealously to control it. He describes the poet—dramatic or lyric—as enthusiastic (literally, indwelt by a god), and he has Socrates say, "The poet is a light and winged and holy thing, and there is no invention in him until he has been inspired and is out of his senses, and the mind is no longer in him."[4] But he *is* "out of his mind" in some real way, and the poets "say many fine things but do not understand the meaning of them."[5] Thus Plato declares in *The Republic* that if any actor can act any part whatsoever—and act it well—he should be honored highly but conducted speedily out of the city. Such a talent is dangerous; it bespeaks a lack of settled character; it is a revelling in fusion and transformation which is an immoral influence on the fragile identity and autonomy of others. In the back of Plato's mind must have been the indelible memory of the citizens of the Athenian democracy, turned into a mob, who had condemned to death the individualistic Socrates, the "best and wisest of men."

Indeed, Plato's criticism of the arts must be understood as a function of a deep—if onesided—appreciation of their power. It is not just that the poets sometimes say what is untrue—about the gods, for example—but that they say things which should not be spoken at all. Plato seems to be recognizing that even when an immoral action within a play is presented *as* immoral—and the participants in the theatre authorize each other as disapproving of the action—still, the actor as character is such an immediately powerful model that he is communicating, "Go try this yourself." Plato's grasp of mimetic fusion was so good that he discerned its capacity to annihilate at times the distinctions that the intellect in its reflexive and analytical moments makes between *my* standing in for the *actor's* standing in for the *character's* action, as if there were to be an electrical short and

4. *Ion*, 534 b.
5. *Apology*, 22 a.

the fine circuitry with its insulated individual components were to be destroyed, melted.

But, on balance, Plato's work contributes to a tradition that still obstructs inquiry into theatre. True, Aristotle delivered key insights that linked sensuous experience of particular theatrical things and events with general sorts of things, with essences. Yet even he downgraded the "spectacle." It was not, I believe, until over two thousand years later, until Giovanni Battista Vico's *Scienza nuova* of 1725, that a conceptual shift sufficiently powerful to begin to break up the cemented prejudice against the theatrical event occurred.

Vico attempted to explode the idea of "the given" as unformed mental content in a particular subject or self. His method was to imaginatively reconstruct the experience of the ancient Greeks as they encountered Zeus the thunderer in the sky. Thus he attempted to dig behind the self-consciously scientific, demythologizing, and sophisticated thinkers and artists of fifth-century Greece and expose an archaic stratum of mimetic bodily involvement that persisted, both then and now, beneath the readily verbalizable surface. For though Sophocles' scripts, for example, may have been refined as scripts (particularly as we read them in the modern age), what they indicated was the mimetic involvement of audience in the immediately present bodily selves of actors who enacted figures of timeless myth. Indeed, if Vico—and later Nietzsche—are correct, the tragic hero always plays a version of the god Dionysus, that divine being who suffers and triumphs vicariously for the audience, and stands savingly in their place.

Vico labored to recapture the purer and relatively simpler experience of the earliest Greeks so that the idea of it could be used to decipher the more cluttered and self-obscured life of modern man. The prejudice blocking comprehension of this idea goes very deep. Indeed, given the structure of our language, which divides itself into first-person and other-person pronouns, and into acts and their objects, it is difficult even to imagine unprejudiciously what the ancient Greeks' experience was. Notice my own formulation above: "to imaginatively reconstruct the experience of the ancient Greeks as they encountered Zeus the thunderer in the sky." This supposes subjects-encountering who are set over against Zeus as object-encountered; and this begs the question.

For Vico there is no primordial "given." What is primordial is formed—formed by imagining and perceiving bodies imagining concretely in the "imaginative universal." In the single universal—in the name Zeus—is contained namer and named, both, and fear, fearfulness, and the feared, all three. "The as yet to be self-conscious subject and the as yet to be fully particularized object of thunder appear as a felt identity" in the awesome body of Zeus.[6] It is not merely that the bodies of the fearful recoil before the thunder. For these are bodies of body-selves, and as such these beings also *identify* with the grand body of Zeus, the god and ultimate protector. In this primordial experiencing of fusion the *god's* body informs the humans' experiencing of *their* bodies. After Vico, Sartre, for instance, can rearrange our descriptive schemata: instead of saying, for example, "I fear the gorilla," or, "Fear is present in me as a subjective attribute of a substance," we can say, "The fear gorillas me." It is difficult to overestimate the importance of this conceptual turn.

Vico uses his analysis of rudimentary experience as the first step in a cosmogony, an account of the evolution of the experience of the world in which the true and the made, *verum* and *factum*, are convertible. The naming of the experiential whole as Zeus cannot be achieved without some distinction beginning to be formed between the whole and the locus of the thunder, the sky. Zeus is the sky. The thunder is the generalized action of the body of Zeus. "In the separation of earth and sky the world can occur." That is, in falling out as elements they can appear as elements of a whole, of a world.

6. Donald P. Verene, "Categories and the Imagination," in *Categories: A Colloquium*, issued by the Department of Philosophy, Pennsylvania State University, 1978, p. 198.

CHAPTER V

Variations on the Theatrical Theme of Standing In and Authorization

It is over twenty-five hundred years since the plays of Aeschylus and Sophocles sounded within the theatres and reverberated with the responses of the poets' contemporaries. Some of the scripts remain, as do some of the theatre structures, and scholarship can help us piece together what some of the conventions of production were.[1] If we would try to imagine intelligently what the theatre event was, it is perhaps to the theatre structure we should go first, for this is where the theatre event occurred.

Hewn in the hollow of a hillside, in rising concentric tiers of stone seats which could accommodate over ten thousand spectators, this auditorium of greater than semicircular plan opens out onto the sky and the seasons. The sky above and the bowl of the amphitheatre below comprise a world before us in miniature, a "world" upon which the world at large can—at this climax of cultural achievement—be mapped. The theatre converses with the world about immensity.[2]

At its heart beneath us is the bare circular area, the orchestra, and behind it the open stage, upon which actors, singers, speakers, and dancers performed. Two small stones scratched together at the center of the orchestra can be heard in the most distant seats. To speak from this point is to be placed within an immense megaphone that broadcasts one's voice to sur-

1. For example, see T.B.L. Webster, *Greek Theatre Production* (London: Methuen & Co., 1956). And note references made by Webster to works by Sir Arthur Pickard-Cambridge.
2. Cf. Gaston Bachelard, *The Poetics of Space* (Boston: Beacon Press, 1969), p. 69.

rounding spectators, and returns it vibrant with their response. Actors in the Greek tragedies—masked—spoke and acted as characters in the memorial or immemorial past of their people. Group, individual, space, time, heaven, earth, culture—each element was framed as an element so that it could fall out as an element and be apprehended as an element of the whole. This theatre was a place for seeing.

One wonders why the twin modes of thematizing the world, philosophy and theatre, arose together in Greece in the sixth and fifth centuries B.C. Perhaps the physiognomy of the land was a factor. The clarity of the dry air makes the spheroid of the sky above compellingly evident; the irregular land sets itself off from the blue water upon which it seems to float; the fire of the sun burns brightly in the sky. Earth, air, fire, and water: these were the basic elements, according to some of the pre-Socratic Greek thinkers, of the world itself. But people had seen sky and earth for as long as there had been people, and we must utilize as well something like Vico's explanation of the archaic experience of Zeus, and of him as lord of the sky, before we can have an idea of why people saw the sky *as* sky, the earth *as* earth, and both as elements of the world apprehended *as* world. This experience must antedate by far the sixth and fifth centuries. We will suppose, however, that the audience's experience of the actor before them reactivated at crucial moments some such primal experience of a navel of the world, a center around which the world could turn, where world could be experienced as world because compressed and articulated through the "world" generated by the actors.[3]

The Greek theatre's openness onto sky and countryside lodged it comfortably in the world, and put it on an equal footing with the city and with Nature. Plays were performed in broad daylight; there was no doubt that real persons performed there on the stage and that real persons in the real world were in the audience. To turn to one's fellows in their seats or to glance above the bowl of the theatre at the olive trees on the hills was to see an indubitably real world that was indubitably meaningful. To turn again to participate in the play's "world" was to see not only meaningful things and persons, but to see them—given the reality of theatrical point of view—*as* meaningful. It was only the peculiar detachment of the theatrical point of view, and the explicitness of the meaningfulness of things within the play's "world," that distinguished these things from those of the world. Certainly there was a difference between them, but it was not

---

3. It should be noted that the sacred city of Delphi, the home of the oracle of Apollo, considered itself to be the center of the world. The notion of a "navel" of the world arises in this context. Also relevant is the *omphalos*, a large phallic-shaped stone, elaborately inscribed, which seems to have figured in Dionysian festivities in the theatre of that city. Notice the idea of the body of the god as the generative source of the world, and recall Vico.

the difference between symbols, on the one hand, and things which can be symbolized, on the other—"mere fictions" as opposed to facts. Talk of symbols almost inevitably brings with it modern subjectivism and individualism and prejudices our understanding of theatre.

The actor before them enacting his character was an imaginative universal in Vico's sense. He stood at the intersection of "world" and world. Participating with the audience seated on their stone bleachers, he pulled in connections from the world and exhibited them in such a perspicuous, unified, and condensed way that discoveries of meaningfulness were possible. He stood in for the audience, and they for him, in a mutually mirroring, augmenting, and beneficial way. There could never be a question of how it was possible for signs or symbols to refer to the real world, for the "world" of the play could exist only in perpetually shifting and restabilizing interdependencies with the world.

The world at large was meaningful because for those who could experience it one thing in it led to another. Things existed in a context. The "world" was meaningful because it was an articulation and focusing of this context. In general, one thing leads to another, and one thing is associated with another, in our experience. Thus the world is protometaphorical. The "world" that nests within it, even as it strives to encompass it meaningfully, is consummately metaphorical. Things exist within the "world" only *as* meaningful, *as like* actual particulars.

World and "world" play into each other's hands, or there is no play at all. We cannot perceive the world in its own terms and then check to see if the terms of the "world" reflect it accurately, for our sense of what the world is has already been determined in part by the play's "world." Nor, of course, can we decipher the "world" of the play in terms that belong only to it, for its sense is an explication and development of the sense of the world. Only a technical exercise in theatrical nomenclature—a history of theatrical conventions, say—can try to confine itself to terms relating literally and solely to the theatre "itself."

Stated analytically, the actor in the world stands in for the character in the "world," and thereby stands in also for us—we who are likewise in the world. Speaking experientially, however, we must say that the body of the actor speaks directly to us and for us. It is revealing that the supreme valuational terms are spatial—the heavens above and hell below—and that terms for our emotions and moods are spatial and at the same time temporal, bodily, and rhythmic: effervescent, lofty, exalted, high, or depressed, down, dejected, halting. Each has its directly perceivable physiognomic pattern, rhythm, and stance in and through the body. A person moves about upright, with feet on the earth and head pointed to the heavens. This fact determines the meaning things can have for us, and of the meaning we can have for ourselves as beings-in-the-world.[4]

Husserl observed that the first other is another human being, as we saw. Human physiognomy is more insistent and primordial than are the shapes of tables and chairs, trees, and boulders. The actor uses his body for the disclosure of meaning *as* meaning; he differs from the life actor whose meanings are usually lost in the things meant by them, or if they become apparent as such they are seldom organized to achieve a systematic impact of appreciation and apprehension; if they do they become art of some sort. In the very projection of meaning, the actor, and we in the audience, must become aware of the conditions and limits of the projection and of how the meaning projected applies to—and is made possible by—all of us. Of course, the body not only moves but sounds, speaks, sings, and what Baudelaire said of the poetic phrase applies also to communication by the actor's body in space and time. Indeed, Baudelaire grounds the meaning of the poetic line in the meaning of moving bodies in space:

> [T]he poetic phrase can imitate (and in this, it is like the art of music and the science of mathematics) a horizontal line, an ascending or descending vertical line; . . . it can rise straight up to heaven without losing its breath, or go perpendicularly to hell with the velocity of any weight. . . .[5]

Not only can we see physiognomic patterns as meaningful, we must do so. For example, an oval or circular shape with three dots placed like an inverted triangle at the center must appear to be a human face; cloth wrapped conically around the handle of a knife held blade upright must appear to be a female human. Sometimes acting students are directed to wear neutral masks—masks with an allegedly expressionless expression— the intended function of which is to direct the audience's attention to the rest of the actor's body, and thus to direct the actor's attention to his whole body via his absorption in the audience's attention. But, in the first place, we do not see the mask as completely expressionless, and as we expect the person to be feeling in some new way we see the expression change slightly. In one case in which the student, still wearing the mask, was harshly criticized by the instructor we seemed to see right through the mask the abashed and humiliated face of the student. Of course we might have been wrong about what was underneath the mask; if the mask had become transparent at that instant we might have seen an expression

4. See Erwin Straus, "The Upright Posture," in *Phenomenological Psychology* (New York: Basic Books, 1966).

5. Charles Baudelaire, draft of a preface to *Flowers of Evil* (New York: New Directions Books, 1955), p. xiii.

of impassiveness. But we do see—in an important sense— this expression of abashment and torment now, and we fear that if the mask were to become transparent we would see something even worse. Perception is not just an ocular phenomenon which we control at will. It springs up irresistibly from our whole selves as beings-in-the-world.[6]

Nietzsche's description of Greek theatre as music made visible is helpful. It is a spatiotemporal whole of meaningfulness which evokes spatiotemporal wholes of meaningfulness. The rhythmic and temporal aspect of the theatre event is best brought out through a description of it as music. For example, of some music it is true to say that it is expressive of nervousness. It must be so, given the bodily reality of those who perform and listen to it. The melodic lines are short, stabbing, agitated, and tear away from each other in dissonance. This is just what a person typically does when nervous. It is not just his body that moves thus. *He* is nervous; he jumps up, paces, stops short, darts about, etc. We do not apprehend the artistic event as a symbol which applies to an actual fact symbolized. We directly and necessarily apprehend the meaning in the artistic event as it directly and necessarily articulates our actual lives (though it need not express a present and actual nervous state in ourselves, but only what it would be like if we or anyone were to be nervous, and this is the ideal and timeless aspect of art).

The theatre event is very complex, and perhaps other, simpler examples of the rhythmic structure of sound will factor out for us the rhythmic aspect of the bodily life of theatre: bells before mass—their steady rhythm is a summons, an insistence; bells of celebration, a jubilation in which no moment is ever twice the same—life at its consummation of joy; bells for a funeral, the dirge—each stroke sounds at about eight-second intervals, it sounds alone, and it means that the continuity of a life is broken and that nothing more can be expected of it. These artistic or quasi-artistic events are so tied up with the life of the group that all who are members of it must perceive their meaning. Actors communicate through the rhythms of their bodily life, and it is a communication frequently in tension with what is being enunciated verbally. We live through the dramatic progression with the enacted characters: struggle, release, jubilation, death; or, purpose, passion, perception; or, fusion, diremption, reconciliation, etc. Plot is that movement of soul and articulation of energy with which we can identify, a meaningful unit of duration.

Now, of the myriad theatrical events that have occurred, which will we pick as given variations? We have already determined that if an event is to be theatrical an actor must stand in for a character, for a type of humanity,

6. This was observed in the studio of the mime Jacques Lecoq in Paris. It is the exercise employing the *masque neutre*.

and through this standing in the audience member stands in for this character, this type (or identifies with him in some way, e.g., "that is someone who falls within my ken, someone whom I recognize"). Involvement and identification are the essence of theatre.

All right then, which plays involve us the most? Attempting to select the plays that continue to grip us despite changing times and circumstances, we survey the history of theatre. Undoubtedly we would pick a Greek tragedy, but which one? Probably some play by Aeschylus or Sophocles. The least arbitrary choice would seem to be *Oedipus Rex* by Sophocles. It has prompted continual comment over the millennia, from Aristotle to Freud; Lane Cooper has described it as infallibly plotted.[7] Then we would feel constrained to pick some play from the Christian age. Since *Hamlet* appears to be the paradigmatic play of all times it would have to be the representative in this category. Probably we would like to round out the picture with a contemporary drama. This is the most difficult choice. At such a short distance it is easy to mistake infatuation for love, as it were. There would seem to be the least disagreement about *Waiting for Godot.* Given the perspective of a quarter century and more, this is as certain to be a classic as is anything else.

Assembling these before us, we note among them a startling similarity. The content of each is a variation on the theme of standing in. The actors stand in for characters who stand in. Oedipus stands in illicitly for his father the king, and with destructive effect. Hamlet stands in licitly for his father the king, and yet with destructive effect also. The two tramps in *Waiting for Godot* seem not to have been able to stand in for the authority at all, and there is a destructive effect here too, a strange insubstantiality in their lives.

Inevitably this is suggested to us: theatre, the art of involvement and standing in, involves us most intensely and enduringly when it deals explicitly with problems of standing in and involvement. The "form" of theatre as art dictates the "content" in these cases and with great success. This suggests that something fundamental is being taught about theatre just because something fundamental about ourselves is being taught simultaneously. It suggests that we stand in most profoundly with problems of standing in, that this problem interests us so much because it is the problem *par excellence* of our own identity as selves. For example, it has been asserted that "of all the plays written by Shakespeare, *Hamlet* has enjoyed the greatest popularity."[8] But just why this should be the case is not clear

---

7. In all references to *Oedipus Rex* we will use Lane Cooper's translation in *Fifteen Greek Plays* (New York: Oxford University Press, 1943). This reference is on p. xv.

8. Louis B. Wright, *Hamlet*, The Folger Library (New York: Washington Square Press, 1958), p. vii. All references to Hamlet are to this edition.

at first sight. A. C. Bradley has maintained that both for sheer beauty of poetic expression and for darkness of tragic color and effect, other of Shakespeare's plays surpass *Hamlet*.[9] I agree, and think therefore that its universal appeal wants explanation. I believe that this study can begin to supply it.

I will adopt the hypothesis that standing in and authorization is the essential theatrical theme, the content in which the form of theatre art most directly and obviously consummates itself, and that in learning something about the conditions of its enactability we must learn something about the conditions of our own identity as selves. Through two sets of three given variations I will develop and test the hypothesis that great theatre is revealingly life-like. Our analysis of the conditions of enactability in these paradigmatic theatre events will supply clues concerning conditions of identity of self which will later be confirmed when we examine human life independently and discover it to be theatre-like. We will conclude that the identification in life with persons in authority, the rupturing with them, and the confirmation of all this by others, are articulated and developed by the essential structures of theatre: standing in or role-taking, dramatic rupture between persons in mimetic involvement, and the attestation of all this by the audience. We will conclude that onstage and offstage life are essentially bound together in a metaphorical manner.

As long as we see the characters in these plays as perfectly individuated entities we will be unable to see how their identity involves a mimetic engulfedness in each other which is like a morass in which they struggle to individuate themselves. One must be authorized and empowered by one's own mimetic source. But how can one be and at the same time establish oneself as an individual being with his own interests? This is the problem that lies at the bottom of all these plays and gives them their perennial attraction. We sense that it is our problem as well and that the characters are set before us to solve it vicariously. It is the domain that Anaximander marked off long ago with the dark saying that stands as epigraph to this volume: What reparation must we pay to the other as the cost of our becoming an individual being along with him in the world? What reparation must he pay to us as the cost of fathering us? The question concerns the price of individual identity itself.

Once we feel the force of the theme of mimetic involvement and authorization we easily see how the contemporary *Waiting for Godot* exhibits kinship with the two older theatre events. Each plays out before us variations on the essential theatrical theme. In this given variation empowering and authorizing standing in with the authority has been pushed to

9. A. C. Bradley, *Shakespearean Tragedy* (Greenwich, Conn.: Fawcett Publications [a Premier Book]). Originally published in 1904.

its limits and has broken down. Standing in has become merely wretched waiting-for. Yet even here the characters cannot escape the power of the authority and while trying to divert themselves with flaccid entertainments and bootless digressions, still they wait, hoping against hope that the empowering one will appear—and do what?—assign to them some authorized role? In all likelihood, yes, they need to act for him and in his place. They need to stand in for him, represent him, etc. And they need him to stand in for them. Since they have not yet been authorized through this standing in they cannot get on to the more obviously dramatic problem of individuating themselves, sundering themselves, and paying the reparation for individual identity. The prior mimetic involvement and authorization essential for any human identity at all—whether individual or communal—has not jelled. Through the wraith-like insubstantiality of the characters we engage dramatically with a peculiarly relevant problem of our own existence. This we find strongly dramatic.

If *Oedipus Rex* is the sharp positive print, and *Hamlet* a slightly blurred image, then *Waiting for Godot* is the negative of the same picture.

A note of caution before we turn to our first example: I am not maintaining that these plays are the only possible examples, but only that no other examples could be any less arbitrary. These are paradigmatic; and certainly those that are not paradigmatic do not thereby cease to be examples altogether. One confirmation of plays' paradigmatic status is that once we have them in hand we can see how other plays can be used as examples of the essence of theatre, whereas if we had started with these others we could not do this so easily. As an instance, take Aeschylus's *Agamemnon*. The somewhat less focal structure of standing in and authorization—and the problems involved—now comes into sharp relief: Clytemnestra stands in for her daughter Iphigenia in revenge against her husband Agamemnon, who identified more with his warriors and their cause than with the girl, his own flesh and blood. Electra and Orestes then stand in for their father against their mother to avenge his murder, etc. Notice as well how other plays illustrate the essential pattern. In *Antigone*, Oedipus's daughter takes the place of her dead brother and of the gods against Creon who fills the "role" of secular authority at that time in the city ("by the power vested in me"); and of course each of these characters is represented by an actor who stands in for them on the stage. In Arthur Miller's contemporary *Death of a Salesman*, the son is discomfited when he finds that his father is no longer a model he can emulate and mimetically reenact, and the father is demoralized when he discovers that the "role" of businessman is ineffective in the crises of life. Again, of course, each of these "roles" is enacted in the role of the actor; roles clarify and develop "roles." We could go on.

1. The "World" of *Oedipus Rex* and the World of Its Theatre

The idea I will develop is that the theatre event in the stone megaphone on the side of the hill enabled the assembled persons to see what they were too inured to see, or too afraid to see, or too close to see, or too far to see, or too ashamed to see otherwise. It compressed and summarized in the "world" of the play the wide context of sense which is the world itself; it was the absent given presence, articulation, and precision through theatrical proxy. The "world" stood in for the world.

In attempting to determine just how theatre discloses the nature of human action, we may presuppose that it is an individual's action that is in question. This would be anachronistic. Aristotle rightly spoke of the dramatist as a poet of plots who arranges events in such a way that the *play's* action is rendered mimetically. Thus the action of *Oedipus Rex* is to discover and to eradicate the source of the pestilence in the city of Thebes. This sense of action is aptly applicable to dramatic tragedy, and I agree with Francis Fergusson's construal of it, "Thus by 'action' I do not mean the events of the story but the focus or aim of psychic life from which the events, in that situation, result."[10]

But the psychic life in question is not merely that of any individual, not even the hero. Also explored is the psychic life of a people. The chorus of fifteen, weaving and chanting as one body before the spectators, was an effective image of that strange, other individuality which is corporate. By "image" we do *not* mean a mental entity in a mind, but things or persons viewed theatrically—that is, perceived *as having* meaning. The word "image" means that which is intuited directly "before all predication," as Aristotle noted. As someone may perceive something circular, and act commensurately with his perception, but be incapable of defining "circle"—or even perhaps of saying that it is a circle that he perceives—so the body of the chorus was directly perceived. Individuals composing it (Theban elders in *Oedipus Rex*) defined and ever redefined the frame within which the principal individual characters pursued their intersecting paths. The chorus prayed, recounted, ruminated, meditated, questioned, and totted up the balance after each encounter between the principals. A part of the scene—particularly in the person of its leader—it nevertheless also stood outside it.

A different dialectic of presence and absence applied to the chorus. Unlike the other actors—both the principals and those in crowd scenes—once they of the chorus have made their early entrance, they never leave

10. Fergusson, *The Idea of a Theatre* (Princeton, N.J.: Princeton University Press, 1968), p. 36.

the stage or orchestra. Through their praying and recollecting they periodically and majestically summon what is absent into the presence of intelligibility and concern, but they themselves are always present. This suggests, of course, the abiding, interpreting, structuring, and all-pervasive life of the people—the corporate identity—and doubtless the chorus mediated between the scene and the spectators. It suggested to the community ways of construing the action. The legend of Thebes was a living one for them, and the assembled Athenians would empathize and identify with their Greek half-brothers of times and places past, the Theban elders in chorus. And as they did so they seem to have experienced the enactment of their common memories—their living past as legend and daydream. We can imagine the audience melded through identification with the chorus and comprising a single corporate organism stretching through time and summing itself in a kind of timeless now. The chanting of the chorus would mold their breathing, and as they sat there they could know: This before us is what we Greeks have been through together, and this is what we will continue to commemorate for as long as we endure.

Perhaps an arboreal metaphor would be helpful as well. Through each branching of the elders' identifying—through their attunement with earlier Greek movements and events, say, cataclysmic or redemptive encounters with the gods—the current audience's identifying could run apace. Until the body of their life in time had again—and newly and novelly—been recreated as a great tree of life. To recreate the discovery and purging of the ancient pestilence at Thebes was to purge and purify their own current lives vicariously.

One does listen and look in the theatre, but it is misleading to say that the audience has a direct visual and auditory experience of the actors before them, whereas the characters enacted by them are merely suggested to them. This is to be beguiled by a physiological analysis of the body present in the present moment, and is to miss the realities of lived time and of mimetic involvement of persons one with another. It is simplistic and misleading to say that the actors as symbolizers are real while the characters as symbols are unreal. The weaving, chanting, dancing chorus rendered in their rhythms a life through time that was common to all. Even an individual actor renders a type, a range of possible individuals. We must so gear our presentation that ultimately we can test Nietzsche's observation that drama is a species of enchantment—the enchantment of entering into another's body—and this can occur whether we think of it as the actor's body or as the character's. When the actor's body is seen from the theatrical point of view it gives presence to the character's body.[11]

11. Friedrich Nietzsche, *The Birth of Tragedy* (New York: Doubleday & Co. [Anchor Books], 1956), p. 56.

The musical, rhythmic, and physiognomic chorus—music made visible—along with the individual actors could activate legends: memories which are also fantasies of possibilities; abiding images of numinous powers and supernatural beings; curses and blessings. The most ingrained tendency of the modern mind is to experience the world according to a model that allows no room for serious consideration of legend, communal memory, fantasy, and mythical time—"timeless" time. It is an ideational "world" built up around us by our cultural works—particularly by technology and by the demands for accountability made by the nation state. This nonthematic and normally unacknowledgeable "world" through which our modern intercourse with the world is mediated can be illustrated roughly thus: to exist is to be a discrete entity, bounded within its surfaces, which exists in one moment after another in time. Each moment is disconnected from every other, and only what is present and actual, moment by moment, is real. To be real is to be like a stone in the bed of a river. The waters of time wash over it, as do debris and other stones that click against it and wear it away. Reality involves relationships, but only the relationships of clicking or grinding contiguity and particularity, and ones limited to the moment. This is an unwitting and misleading worldly model—an interpretation of the world—which construes itself as something which is merely *in* the world. It must construe us to be like separate stones which are worn away by time because it cannot appreciate the significance of its own—or of any other—act of interpretation: the summoning of absent moments into presence that this act presupposes.

It would be best if the "world" of *Oedipus Rex* could be presented in such a way that it shattered this "world" of the ingrained model. We would then have a chance to remodel our notion of the world itself in a much less biased way. We would perhaps see that the "substance" of human life is worldly and communal, and, in the appropriate senses, timeless, mythical, and fantastic. We would see how human "substance" is measured by the degree of presence of absent time and absent others within each of its instants. Past and present are given presence simultaneously in the self. This is a level of experience which is more fundamental than the shaky analytical consciousness of dating and denoting. Memory and anticipation are immemorial and abiding. To be most intensely is to be most expansively in participatory presence, and art is the clue to this. We engage artistically in myths in order to come to grips with the myths we live unthematically every day. To be is to exist in the presence of the absent.

As Bachelard puts it,

> In the theatre of the past which is constituted by memory, the stage setting
> maintains the characters in their dominant roles. At times we think we know

ourselves in time, when all we know is a sequence of fixations in the spaces of the being's stability—a being who does not want to melt away, and who, even in the past, when he sets out in search of things past, wants time to "suspend" its flight. In its countless alveoli space contains compressed time. This is what space is for.[12]

The principal characters of *Oedipus Rex* are creatures of *polis* and world as mapped into the Athenian institution of the theatre. They exist at no particular time and act under time-dissolving curses and blessings theatrically rendered. In participating mimetically in the conditions of these characters' identity, the audience participates in the conditions of its own identity, and in a way that it begins to gain some sense of them. These conditions are potentialities and limits of existence so universal and enduring that without them we would fail to recognize a human being at all; they are definitive of persons, if anything is. This we find when we begin to read our own existence in the light of them. Great variability in their manifestation and intensity from culture to culture and age to age does not undermine them, but just the reverse, it undergirds their generality. To violate such a limit or condition does not render it inoperative, but rather leaves one cursed, and if a curse is no longer intensely felt, this seems to mean only that one no longer intensely *is*.

Oedipus stands in for every man and lives out his curse for him. The rite, or near rite, which the Greeks lived through repeatedly from generation to generation, and through theatrical and extratheatrical rendering, was this: The king and queen of Thebes, Laius and Jocasta, are cursed with the prophecy that their son will kill his father and marry his mother. To avoid this they pierce the infant's feet and abandon him in the wilderness to die. Out of pity, a shepherd saves him, and gives him to a person who carries him to a childless king and queen in Corinth, a sufficient distance from Thebes to avoid, one would think, the prophesied entanglements. Later, a drinker at a banquet in Corinth taunts Oedipus, now a young man, that he is not really the son of the Corinthian king and queen. To test their protestations that he is, Oedipus goes to Apollo's oracle at Delphi.

> At last I rose—my father knew not, nor
> My mother—and went forth to Pytho's floor
> To ask. And God in that for which I came
> Rejected me, but round me, like a flame,
> His voice flashed other answers, things of woe,
> Terror, and desolation, I must know
> My mother's body and beget thereon

12. Bachelard, *The Poetics of Space,* p. 8.

A race no mortal eye durst look upon,
And spill in murder mine own father's blood.

Dazed, he flees from Delphi in the opposite direction from Corinth to avoid the prophecy, and encounters a party of men—one of them King Laius—who crowd him from the path. Not recognizing them, Oedipus strikes at them fatally in anger, and thereby fulfills the prophecy of killing his father. He performs the act which both he and his father had striven so zealously to avoid, and the act occurs because of what they had done to avoid it. Reaching Thebes he wins the crown through courage and intelligence, thereby winning the vacant throne, thereby winning the queen, his mother, for his wife, and thereby fulfilling the prophecy. So that he will no longer be tricked by his sight which had been limited to the present and actual merely, he blinds himself, and in mortification and disgrace goes into exile:

If one should dream that such a world began
In some slow devil's heart, that hated man,
Who should deny him?

The chorus struggles with the question of how the natural order of things—potent and right—could be so subverted, and speaks to the blinded Oedipus,

'Tis Time, Time, desireless, hath shown thee what thou art
. . . .
O great King, our master,
How oped the one haven to the slayer and the slain?
And the furrows of thy father, did they turn not nor shriek,
Did they bear so long silent thy casting of the grain?

Apparently, the only answer that might have been supplied to them within the context of the play is that there had been a curse on Oedipus's family. To what extent can we—at a distance of 2,500 years—make anything more of this?

While the brief account I just gave of *Oedipus Rex* is an accurate narrative, it is misleading just because it is a narrative. Absent is the unfolding dialectic of presence and absence within the experience of the characters as rendered by the play for the audience. A god's-eye point of view was feigned in which everything pertaining to Oedipus could in principle be present at any moment. The play actually opens on the last day of Oedipus's reign as king, and it proceeds inexorably as that unfolding dialectic of presence and absence which was possible for him on that day, in that city, in that world. As he inquires into the antecedents of King Laius's death—into the murder which is reputed to be the cause of the pestilence—he inadvertently delves into his own antecedents. His past and his present actions become revealed together, both for him and for those about him, and within the growing area of comprehension they are at last felt by all to constitute one life.

A single character in the play possesses a god's-eye point of view, the blind prophet Tiresias—although even he suffers from the truth he possesses, which is more than would happen to a god. The corollary of his inability to see present and actual particulars is his ability to summon what is absent, and absent in every sense: temporally, experientially, spatially. This is a variant of Plato's insight that the wise man is one who learns to die in the sense that he dies to the present and actual for the sake of the larger vision of the look of the *eidos* or Idea. But the image of the blind prophet is also a theatrical one *par excellence*. Through him one can see the limitations of ocular seeing.

Pitted against him, demanding that he speak what Tiresias knows will doom him, is a man of peculiarly sharp sight, known for his ability to pick up signs in men's faces and voices, and to pick out cunningly the thread which will unravel a riddle—Oedipus. The hidden—and in that sense absent—dimensions of his own self can come home to him only with the progressive collapse of these calculative and analytical purposes of his which occupy the consuming focus of his behavior. Beneath all his plans and devices is a tide of fusion and mimetic involvement that is undeflectable. It is a preestablished and opaque synthesis against which his analyses break apart. As Oedipus comes to realize this constituent of his identity he is transformed. Standing in for us, we realize through him conditions of our common human identity, but at a distance from the shock—as in echo—and our rationalistic and analytical purposes are chastened but not destroyed by the impact.

The action—or identity—of the play is simultaneously the rendering of Oedipus's identity, and this occurs in the tragic rhythm of which Kenneth Burke has spoken, and which we can term purpose, passion, perception. Oedipus's purposes collide with what can only seem to him at the time to be fortuitous and opaque collocations of events; he then suffers (*passio*) the collapse of these purposes; and in so suffering achieves a new kind of insight. His very identity, he now sees in his blindness, involves prerational and undeliberate fusion. His eyes could see none of this, so rooted were they in the individual beings cut out so clearly, it seemed, from the background of the present and actual scene. To blind himself is to destroy the tyranny of the present and actual, and to be able to give presence to the immemorial realities of fusion. He longs to be like Tiresias.

It might be objected that the new insight is on an analytically comprehensible level; insight into short temper and cruelty as a defect of character,
the tragic flaw: his impatience with Tiresias and his threatened violence
against him, his abuse of the old shepherd toward the end of the play, etc.
No doubt this is a point, but if it is not placed within its context it is fatally
misleading. For one should notice similarities between father and son,
even though they had spent such a short time together. The father was
willing, under the pressure of the curse, to sacrifice his son in a very cruel
manner, and it was the impatience and violence of both that precipitated
the disaster on the road leading Oedipus from Delphi and his father toward
it. Note how the cunning ferocity of the father matches that of the son:

Wife, I will tell thee true. As one in daze
I walked, till, at the crossing of three ways,
A herald, like thy tale, and o'er his head
A man behind strong horses charioted
Met me. And both would turn me from the path,
He and a thrall in front. And I in wrath
Smote him that pushed me—'twas a groom who led
The horses. Not a word the master said,
But watched, and as I passed him on the road
Down on my head his iron-branched goad
Stabbed. But, by heaven, he rued it! In a flash
I swung my staff and saw the old man crash
Back from his car in blood. . . .

Oedipus, though he be a mature man and a separable and independently
maintainable organism, and so long absent from his father that he cannot
recognize him, still seems clearly to be identified with his father, and to
inhabit his body mimetically. They share the same temperament and the
same curse. And his disaster is not complete until he takes his father's
place sexually with his mother. What was meant to be kept separate and
protected by shame and reverence has collapsed under the pressures of
fusion; this is the curse. Only Tiresias can see the fatal commingling, and
the price he paid for this insight—legend had it—was a commingling in
his own body, hermaphroditism. Legend speaks of the breasts of Tiresias.
So we are left with our question, what exactly are we to make of the curse?
   Knowledge of the defective characters of two individuals, father and
son, does not in itself enable us to understand the dynamism of the play,
nor does the addition of chance and ill-fortune round out the picture.
There is a necessity in the drama, a necessity of mimetic involvement and
engulfment, and a necessity for violent rebellion against it, but it is not a
necessity which simply eliminates freedom. We cannot be perfectly sure,

for example, that Oedipus could not have restrained himself at the crossing of the three ways; that he simply did not have the capacity to restrain himself in the face of each intense provocation. The very distinction that poses freedom and necessity as opposites seems strangely brittle and inadequate, and we feel the need for conceptual reconstruction of human reality. The agent freely initiates actions whose ramifications and consequences are not fully knowable or controllable by him. His *freedom* involves him *necessarily* in the workings of a world external to his particular consciousness. He is a hazardous task for himself which he *must* take up *freely.* As Max Scheler has written,

> Tragic necessity is not the necessity of the course of nature, a necessity which lies beneath freedom and the power of the will. . . . Rather is tragic necessity of such a kind that it lies *above* freedom: it is to be found only in the conclusion of free acts or of "free causes" in the total sphere of causality, in which may be found even "unfree causes," that is, those which are the results of prior causes. . . .
>
> The tragic . . . contains this paradox that when we behold the destruction of value it seems completely "necessary" and at the same time unpredictable. . . .
>
> A specifically tragic phenomenon is to be seen in the interruption—even in the midst of external victories—of a course of life directed towards certain values as goals. Tragic necessity is to be seen above all in the essence and essential relations of inevitability and inescapability of things founded in society. . . . The tragic consists . . . in the fact that the guiltiness cannot be localized.[13]

The tragic would be as impossible in a completely satanic world as it would be in one that is divine. We are left with the tragic world of human society in which freedom mixes inextricably with engulfment. In need of reconstruction are the notions of human identity and human action themselves.

Let us return to the unfolding action of the play. Still pursuing his analytical vision, Oedipus picks up the thread in the report about a herdsman, reputed to be the same as "the thrall on the road," and said to have somehow escaped the killing there. Finding, on his return to Thebes, Oedipus on the throne, this man had asked of the queen to be sent to the mountains. Oedipus now summons him:

OEDIPUS. One shred of hope I still have, and therefore
 Will wait the herdsman's coming. 'Tis no more.
JOCASTA. He shall come. But what further dost thou seek?
OEDIPUS. This, if we mark him close and find him speak
 As thou hast, then I am lifted from my dread.

13. Max Scheler, "On the Tragic," *Cross Currents* 4 (1954):185–87.

JOCASTA. What mean'st thou? Was there someting that I said . . . ?
OEDIPUS. Thou said'st he spoke of robbers, a great band,
   That slaughtered Laius' men. If still he stand
   To the same tale, the guilt comes not my way.
   One cannot be a band.

"One cannot be a band." Even at this advanced point in his agony, Oedipus cannot question this principle; it is axiomatic. And indeed it conflicts with all principles of mathematics, grammar, and of logic to say that one man can be a band of men. Yet the play is suggesting that the principle of individuation for human persons is problematical. To say, "I am my family," or "Jones is his own father" is to predicate a plural predicate of a singular subject, or to use a predication of relation as if it were one of identity. It is patent nonsense mathematically, grammatically, and logically. But the play prompts us to question the limits and validity of these studies. Freud's notions are relevant: that in the "work of the unconscious" we "know not not"—and hence cannot make the distinctions essential to all analysis. The ultimate question is whether this inability to distinguish himself from others within his own experience undermines his identity as an individual being.

Let us touch on a matter bordering on the central perplexity. Through its system of artistic appearances and masking, the theatre shows us the necessity of masking in the actual world. This is a necessity on the tragic level itself, neither clearly a matter of freedom simply understood (e.g., a deliberate act), nor of necessity so understood (e.g., transmission of power in a chain of gears). Shame and reverence before the privacy and inwardness of the other are fundamental, it is suggested, in order to counterbalance powerful tendencies of identification and engulfment, themselves also fundamental. This suggests that a dimension of identity is fragile; that there is a "screen" in the self and if this does not stop the other's gaze or physical approach at a certain point, the self will be damaged: as if it were to be punctured, and the breath of spirit were to escape.

It is the violation of this essential masking that the masking in this theatre reveals, so it is suggested. At the heart of love is distance, reverence, shame in the face of the other's precarious sanctity and individuality, not shame as disgrace but shame as reverence. Psychology must frequent the precincts of the religious if it would contact its subject matter. As Kurt Riezler noted, "One of the only two sentences from Aristotle's *Erotikos* that have been preserved runs: 'Lovers look into each other's eyes, not at other parts of their bodies. For in the eyes *Aidos* [shame] dwells.' Sex without love avoids the eyes."[14]

14. Quoted in Carl D. Schneider, *Shame, Exposure and Privacy* (Boston: Beacon Press, 1977), p. 56.

In that reconstruction of his life which is Oedipus's tragic fulfillment, and which we and the actors live through vicariously, it is the revelation of this violation in the order that is central. His identity demanded that he find his own source or roots:

Tis mine own birth. How can I, when I held
Such clues as these, refrain from knowing all?

But when he finds these roots they are twisted and contaminated.

Behold the brother-father of his own
Children, the seed, the sower and the sown.

It is that for which the chorus stands—the ritual order of the world—that has been violated. Above all, it is that order—protected properly by shame—which divides him from his own beloved source that has been violated, and wherein the defilement most consists. Why must he spring from his source *and* leave it if he would escape defilement? Is the thrust toward the newly autonomous and the transcendent of the human essence?

Stranger. Fear lest thou take
Defilement from the two that gave thee birth?
Oedipus. 'Tis that, old man, 'tis that doth fill the earth
With terror.

And what is the logic of reparation which can guide Oedipus once he has found, in the company of witnesses, his violated source?

Nietzsche, in the *Birth of Tragedy,* advanced the promising thesis that Athenian tragedy of the fifth century is a dynamic equilibrium or syncretism of Apollonian and Dionysian influences in the culture. Apollo—the air god of equability, light, vision, individuation, clarity and distinctness, analytical and sequential reason. Dionysus—the earth god of revelry, ecstasy, darkness, "timeless" time, choral sound and rhythmic movement, sudden insight, global intuition, and communal fusion. The full drama—the something done which is comprehended in the theatre—has at its heart the storm front that builds around the focal, deliberate, analytically conscious purposes of the principal individuals as these interact with factors of fusion, irruption, and loss of individuation which are not predictable and not neatly analyzable by the analytical intellect.

The undercurrent of Dionysian fusion, thematized in the chorus but left unthematized in the principals, seeps up into the deliberate projects of these "individuals" and collapses them as if they were castles of sand on the shore. What is being realized in *Oedipus Rex* for all to see is that the conditions which seem so clearly to individuate persons and to establish their autonomy are egregiously limited in their ability to do so. Even as king, Oedipus is attached to and identified with his parents in overwhelming ways that none of them can prevent or even understand. Moreover, they are entangled with "forces" they call ancestors, gods, fates, and curses, which lie beyond their ability to further comprehend.

The drama suggests that the dialectic of absence and presence is related to that of concealment and exposure, and that these revolve around the question of how the person is individuated from the group while yet remaining a part of it. Oedipus's problem is that he is so engulfed in his present and actual environment, and in the consuming focus of his analytical intellect, that he loses touch with his own source. To be properly in touch requires a degree of disengagement from his present and actual body. Clothing, and the screenings and restraints that go with it, enable one to be a present and actual body and at the same time to transcend it. The clothes evoke the historical group and its traditionally sanctioned limits on individual behavior; they define and at the same time conceal a particular body. To disrobe before his mother, and to take his father's place sexually with her, means that he has forfeited his ability to be in proper touch with her as his historical source. His clothes kept him at the proper distance. The event of his conception and birth—his initial involvement with his mother's sexuality—is an absence in time that can be given proper presence only as an absence. Thus Oedipus is in improper touch with his mother and has violated his source; and in violating her he has violated the conditions of his own identity.

The power that binds these persons mimetically and communally is so great that unless it is curbed and channeled the individuality of all is violated. To become an individual Oedipus must leave his source and at the same time respect it as his source. To relate to his mother as if he were her husband is to violate her, himself, and the order of time. He must become a new source in time.

How does this relate to the time of the theatre event in which it is enacted? What are we doing in the theatre? We witness through enactment a man who has violated his source and has violated time. Silent and safely ensconced, and confronted with a presence that is at the same time an absence—an actor who enacts someone not himself—we can discover through the character frightened desires that all of us may have for illicit and destructive union. The actor stands in for us and we for him. We shudder communally over what would so badly disturb any individual alone that he probably could not confront it. At the same time we express our collective disapproval of Oedipus's act. The theatre event is a Dionysian revelation of a defilement of source—through artistic participation in that defilement—which is simultaneously an understanding and transcendence of that defilement. It is a new source in time.

To reveal through physiognomic patterns what things mean to us, so that this meaning and its conditions can be apprehended as such, is the truth of art. In the case of theatre it is primarily what we mean to ourselves that is revealed, and this is that we are temporal and self-constructing beings who are irreducibly individual and irreducibly communal. The plays we examine suggest that to realize for the group in the theatre house the status and the role of the individual in the group is a primary way in which to realize (quite literally, make humanly real) both the individual and the group.

Within the proxy world of the theatre, present and absent and person and group are woven together in a living whole. Within the safety and compression of the art, we can assemble a vast array of particulars—ordinarily spread out beyond our comprehension in space and time—on an equal footing and perspicuously before us. Notice I say "us"—we subject our artistic-experimental views of the concealed, the intimate, the absent, the particular, the group to the confirmation or disconfirmation of the audience. These elements can enter into communication and into dialectical exchange. The concealed can be revealed here as the concealed, the absent as absent, and can be given presence as such. Much the same can be said of the related art of Greek religious architecture: the god or goddess is revealed behind the columns within the shadows of the temple, revealed *as* concealed, to the congregation standing in the sun before the temple. Narrative or argumentative verbal language limps lamely after these perceptual encounters with existence artistically structured.

There is a danger that we will not let theatre art speak for itself; that we will plot in advance what effects we want from it, and so subvert it to being merely a means for conveying insights achieved antecedently to theatrical creativity. Nietzsche maintained, correctly I believe, that such a subversion occurred with Euripedes. As he observed the work of his elders, Aeschylus and Sophocles,

> Euripedes perceived in every line, in every trait, something quite incommensurable: a certain deceptive clarity and, together with it, a mysterious depth, an infinite background. The clearest figure trailed after it a comet's tail which seemed to point to something uncertain, something that could not be wholly elucidated. A similar twilight seemed to invest the very structure of drama, especially the function of the chorus.[15]

Congruously with Socrates' and Plato's equation of goodness with intellectual knowledge, Nietzsche goes on, Euripedes equated the dramatically beautiful and valuable with what can be fully explicated analytically prior to the theatrical event. Indeed, Euripedes constructs his dramas not from

15. Nietzsche, *The Birth of Tragedy*, pp. 74–75.

the stage but from his seat in the theatre as spectator—"the thinker Euripedes, not the poet." Drama merely illustrates what he already knows.
Hence mysteries appear to be mere superstitions, and ill-fortune and suf-
ferings the conniving work of petty and jealous gods. Nor does the hero
learn from his suffering; he merely endures it. The knotted plot, the apparent dead end, is resolved by a "cynical method" of a *deus ex machina:*
for instance, the goddess Athena, fully revealed, descending from the top
of the stage house.

Great tragedy, says Nietzsche, arises not from a dominantly visual and
precogitable theoretical source, but from the spirit of music, dance, and
poetic speech as it springs to life on the stage and in the orchestra itself.
In fact, only from a core of musical dissonance can it all spring and be held
together, and only this dissonance can express the joy, the release, and the
pain. The individual's return to his source via the theatrical event is a
revelation and not a defilement. The pain of his individual identity is felt
along with the joy of its dissolution in archaic participation, and yet he
reclaims himself as an individual through the artistic event.

We must endeavor to reflect "from the body," as we find ourselves
springing into action artistically on the stage, and as we find ourselves
identifying empathetically with the performers. We must endeavor to reflect while in action. Aristotle noted that the tragedy arose from the improvisation of the dancing and chanting chorus, and the separating-out of
a few individual protagonists in the tragedies we know—first one, then
two and three—seems to recapitulate the conditions of individuation: individuals are shaken out of the group through their action, and play out
their destinies within the magnetic field of its action.[16]

To conclude this variation: we have proposed to give an account of three
plays that revolve around the topic of standing in and authorization, and

16. Gerald F. Else in his scholarly *The Origin and Early Form of Greek Tragedy* (New
York: W. W. Norton, 1972) disputes Aristotle's contention that tragedy arose from the
improvisations of the dithyrambic chorus in worship of Dionysus. He claims to find "no
evidence of Dionysiac ecstasy in the plays" (pp. 30–31). The problem is that Else is employing
a tacit definition of Dionysiac ecstasy that is far too narrow to be helpful. He traces tragedy
to Solon. But Else himself writes of Solon: "The Athenians, having failed to capture or
recapture Salamis . . . had forbidden anyone to propose a resumption of the war. Solon, we
are told . . . feigned madness, then burst into the market place with a cap—a traveler's cap,
it appears—on his head, and recited an elegiac poem of his own composition, calling for a
crusade to win back the island. The stratagem was successful . . ." (p. 40). Solon feigns
madness, impersonates another, and risks his individual well-being. This is a very ecstatic,
even Dionysian thing to do. Else refers to Nietzsche's *Birth of Tragedy* as a "great book"
(p. 10), but we are given no idea from what Else writes of why this should be true. The
professor is trapped in the literalism of modern realism. Regardless of whether historical
antecedents of Greek tragedy in Dionysian worship can be traced (other than through Aristotle), important Dionysian elements certainly appear in the plays. And there is the indisputable fact of the Dionysian setting in which the plays were produced. Else's is a brilliant
defense of an impossible position.

that present three possible forms for it to take. We have completed our account of the first. Oedipus stands in illicitly for the authority. If to stand in for an authority licitly is to be authorized, to stand in illicitly is to be condemned and defiled. In the theatre event the community stands in licitly for Oedipus's illicit standing in and thereby transcends the defilement in the very act of participating in it vicariously. The community of individuals authorizes itself as a community and as individuals.

Hamlet, the next play, exhibits a son who stands in licitly for his father, but only after crucial delay and only with the most disturbing consequences. *Waiting for Godot,* the third, exhibits persons who fail to stand in effectively at all with the authority, and who are as frail and insubstantial as wraiths.

Now, there are plays in which people stand in licitly and effectively, and are authorized and apparently enhanced. Why not discuss these? The answer is a simple one: they are not towering classics; they do not grip us and involve us in the deep, fascinating, and perennial way that the ones we discuss, and others like them, do. And the reason for this can only be that the difficulties in the human involvements in the "world" of the plays speak to us of difficulties in these sorts of involvements in the world of our daily lives. These are the plays that most compellingly draw us in, and challenge, frighten, intrigue, exalt us. We must conclude, at least tentatively, that these plays most interest us because they most directly pertain to what interests us most: our own identity as selves and the problematical structure of that identity.

What the variations will suggest is a deep ambivalence, turbulence, and instability between individual and authority, between individual and group, *and* within each component. They will suggest that if the individual is to be human he must be caught in a mimetic involvement with the authority that amounts to enchantment. He must undeliberately and unwittingly take the authority's view of him as his own view of himself. He fuses with him. Yet to be human he must also be an individual human. But if his enchanted mimetic involvement has made him one—one experientially—with the king of Thebes, for example, then how can he be individual without displacing or killing the king, for there can be but one king? But if he does this he must defile his own source.

The plays document various responses to this tragic reality; and as all of them *qua* theatre must involve us participants mimetically in reciprocal authorization, the plays will seek to authorize each of us in his or her tribulations of becoming an individual self. The plays appear as artistic enchantments designed to decode and to deliver us from the enchantments of everyday life. They are accessories to the struggle of individual bodies struggling to become individual selves.

Might they not enchant us and engulf us anew? Let us see what form they take.

2. The "World" of *Hamlet* and the World of Its Theatre

Hamlet emerges deep in the Christian era, two millennia after *Oedipus Rex*. Their similarities are the more significant just because of their great differences. Using the theatre as pivot between art and world, we can begin to plot the shifts in the metaphoric reach of that relationship. Gone, first of all, is that openness onto sky and countryside that lodges the Greek theatre so comfortably in the world, and that puts it on an equal footing with city-state and nature. So directly and automatically is the world mapped into the Greek theatre that a question of the metaphorical status of the relationship can hardly arise. Hence, of course, the question of which element in the relationship is primary cannot arise either. Merely in making this metaphorical relationship explicit, Shakespeare's theatre effects a shift in it, and in so doing alters its participants' sense of their relationship to the world. This, I will suggest, alters the participants' identities as selves.

Shakespeare's Globe Theatre is enclosed. Atop its high octagonal walls a canvas canopy cuts it off almost completely from the sky. Upon this canvas are *depicted* heavenly bodies, the "fretted fire" of sun and stars. Direct sight of the outer world is prevented; it is symbolized within. Nothing better sizes up the change in the situation. Theatre continues to orient man within the world, but now a new distance for commentary and questioning has been interposed between him and the world. The world continues to be given presence, its appearances rendered, but at a distance which takes much larger risks concerning the intelligibility to be achieved. The very distance makes greater the possible payoff in terms of sweep and depth of intelligibility, but the risk of failing to grasp what is touched by this reach is much greater. Skepticism concerning the meaningfulness of the world at large is already planted in Shakespeare's day, and his *Hamlet* prophetically projects its possibilities.

Francis Fergusson, commenting on the work of George Kernodle, has written,

> The Elizabethan stage itself, that central mirror of the life of its times, was a symbolic representation of this traditional cosmos: it was thus taken both as the physical and as the metaphysical "scene" of man's life. Mr. Kernodle has shown this in detail in his illuminating study, *From Art to Theatre*. He traces the genealogy of the symbolic facade of the Elizabethan stage house back

through street pageantry to painting and to the architecture of tombs and altars; and thence to the arcade screen of the Greek tragic theatre itself. . . . "[T]hat facade was itself a symbol of castle, throne, triumphal arch, altar, tomb"—in short, an all-purpose, eminently practicable setting, implying the constant elements in the Elizabethan world picture, yet flexible enough to serve the shifting make-believe of the actors. . . . The symbolic character of this stage seems to imply a conception of the theatre akin to that of ritual. . . . And the ceremonies which Shakespeare and Hamlet's Danes engaged in . . . were taken as celebrating and securing the welfare of the whole, of the monarchy, and of the "lives of many" that depended on it.[17]

And yet in *Hamlet* it is as though every one of these ceremonial elements had been elaborated by a process of critical analysis. Fergusson continues,

Even the ritual process itself is, in *Hamlet,* directly dramatized: i.e., presented in a tragic, ironic light. There are no rituals in *Oedipus:* Oedipus is a ritual. But Hamlet has an extremely modern and skeptical, a Pirandellesque, theatricality as well; Shakespeare plays with the basis of his own make-believe.[18]

The theatre event can occur only at the intersection of "world" and world. When we speak of ceremonial rite we are speaking of an event in the world which exhibits an affinity to theatre. We might be tempted to speak here of an intertwining of world and "world" rather than an intersection. The rite embodies a "text" that is "enactable" an indefinite number of times—although not necessarily by the same participants—and there is a protective framing for the display of the rite which is analogous to the aesthetic distance essential to a theatrical production.

Greek religious rite exhibits more specific affinities to tragic theatre. It would seem to be essential to all religious discourse and practice that an authoritative person or event be commemorated in the rite, and commemorated at times and places established once and for all through reference to this original authority. Its authoritativeness includes its power over world time. The tragedies of Aeschylus and Sophocles occurred regularly within the world time of the culture: at the yearly festival honoring Dionysus, and in the precinct of Athens—as designated by Pisistratus—bearing that name. They occurred at a holy place and on a holy day, and this distinguishes them from nearly all the theatre of the modern world. And probably it was felt that the actors were vehicles possessed by the god, or by the mythic heroes, at least for that time and at that place.

Moreover, a fairly good case can be made that the content of tragedy overlaps with the content of religious ritual. Recall Oedipus: seeking to

17. Fergusson, *The Idea of a Theatre,* pp. 116–19.
18. Ibid.

relate properly to his constituting source, he relates improperly to it. Rectification can occur only after he renounces his own improperly gained and grounded position in the culture and mutilates his body. It is contended that this is a counterpart of the religious rite of sacrifice, the mutilation of the body of the hero (*sparagmos*).[19] In the rite proper an animal stands in for the hero. Consumed by the god's followers, the animal's body imparts to them the god's strength and the atoning virtue of his payment for wrong. Theatre, we can suppose, is an analogical extension of this, however dim: the audience "consumes" with their eyes and their emotions the body of the actor, who stands in for a god or a god-like figure. They participate vicariously through the actor.

An economy of substitution and atonement emerges at the heart of human identity, and it appears in both rite and theatre. This will seem absurd only if we assume that the conditions of the identity of the body—understood as a physical object only—are simply isomorphic with the conditions of identity of the self whose body it is. One body is separate from another, and so it follows that one self is separate from another. Nothing more is required to invalidate this assumption than to show how the names of persons differ from the names for nonhuman physical things. Identifying names can be given to the latter without any entailment for our specification of the identity of the thing, but from the name we give to a person something does follow for his identity. The name is not merely a sign related contingently to the person—so that we can easily imagine it to be changed and the person to remain the same—but rather is integral to that presence of the person to the world and to himself which is integral to who he is. He *becomes* that named being. Thus, for example, the ancients thought that to gain control of a supernatural person's name was to gain control over him, and still today to forget a person's name is to forget something of his very being, even though "we know perfectly well who we mean"; that is, we can point him out as an object, or can follow his movements symbolically in a conversation through the use of a marker for him, such as a definite description. Still, if we cannot recall his name we are uneasy and believe that something is missing. That there is an element of sympathetic magic here is clear. A name is in some way an equivalent of the person: it carries his presence far and wide through the world of persons. To forget his name is to diminish and humiliate both him and ourselves.

Given these points we can begin to grasp why the relation of individual to group is ambivalent, unstable, and volatile. Put schematically: if to

19. Gilbert Murray, "Excursus on the Ritual Forms Preserved in Greek Tragedy" in Jane Ellen Harrison, *Themis: A Study of the Social Origins of Greek Religion* (New York: Meridian Books, 1962), pp. 341–63.

become at all, a person must be named and otherwise designated by the culture, and if exemplar individuals must be lifted up as stand-ins for the culture, then individuals, to become themselves, must identify with these exemplars by taking *their* attitudes toward *themselves*, e.g., by taking as their own the names given by them. In a kind of magical or alchemical equivalence, the other becomes identical with oneself. But only in certain respects, one might object. But the reply to this is that the person is in no position to analytically distinguish these respects as respects, and his very identity cannot be sundered from his experience of it. This leaves a question for our section on identity. For now, we simply gather clues from the plays. And *Oedipus Rex* suggests that for the individual to go his separate way and increasingly take responsibility for his life—a move typically enforced by this same authority—the initial magical bond must be loosened and the authority's presence "within" one diminished or displaced. As dominating presence he must be killed.

But this is a defilement of one's source. One is caught in a tragic bind: no matter what he does he is guilty. This defilement can be purged only if one—or a substitute for one—dies to atone for one's crime. This economy of substitution and atonement, which appears in both religious rite and theatre, is the procedure used to render the tragic bind endurable, and to dampen the explosive instability of the individual's identity.

To be sure, this economy appears in a somewhat attenuated form in the Greek theatre. The artistic event stands with one foot in the religious tradition and one foot slightly outside it. The step of removal suggests a distance in which mimetic enchantment between persons offstage can begin to be reflectively framed. Also, prizes were given to the best artists. It is unlikely that a prize would be given to a person with strictly sacerdotal functions; it would be blasphemous.[20] Beneath all the gravity and ecstasy was an element of skillful play and experimentation.

It is clear, however, that *Hamlet* stands at a much greater remove from rite than does *Oedipus Rex*. First and foremost, its production is not governed by the commemoration of an event; it is not bound into world time in any periodic way. It can occur whenever material circumstances allow and whenever fancy strikes. The reason for this is not, of course, that the Christian era leaves nothing to commemorate, or that the economy of substitution and atonement is radically different in this era. It is difficult not to be struck by similarities between Greek mystery religions and Christianity. God incarnates himself in Christ and as the "second Adam" makes reparation for the sin of the first. He dies for us, in our place, and

20. It has been suggested to me that these should be construed as gifts. But do we give gifts to persons because they are the best, the most skillful? But perhaps the *Greeks* did something like this, and we have lost the relevant conception and the relevant word.

so reconciles us to our source. For, as one man created the example of rebellion and sinned for all, so one man stands in for all and makes reparation for all. This sacrifice of the body of Christ is commemorated in the ceremony of the bread and wine in communion. Likewise there is the rite of baptism: it both symbolizes and furthers the redemptive fusion of all believers with Christ. As Paul the Apostle writes,

> Know ye not, that so many of us as were baptized into Jesus Christ were baptized into his death?
> Therefore we are buried with him by baptism into death: that like as Christ was raised up from the dead by the glory of the Father, even so we also should walk in newness of life.
> For if we have been planted together in the likeness of his death, we shall be also in the likeness of his resurrection:
> Knowing this, that our old man is crucified with him, that the body of sin might be destroyed, that henceforth we should not serve sin.
> For he that is dead is freed from sin.
> Now if we be dead with Christ, we believe that we shall also live with him:
> Knowing that Christ being raised from the dead dieth no more; death hath no more dominion over him. (Rom. 6:3–9)

"For if we have been planted together in the likeness of his death, we shall be also in the likeness of his resurrection." Rites and rituals are behavioral metaphors, belief acted and lived. No account of human identity can pretend to adequacy that has not attempted to explain the power of such mimetic involvement to integrate, direct, and galvanize a life. The rite of baptism could stabilize the self as both individual and cultural, and at a level of its deepest energies: not that of conscious dating and planning merely, but that of the immemorial and the abiding also.

Still, though *Hamlet* occurs in the Christian era, it occurs at a great distance from its source; moreover, Christianity itself has introduced a conception of time as linear, not cyclical.[21] *Hamlet* must be construed as an acidic commentary on the decay of rites, and as an attempt to authorize us on a different basis. *Hamlet* is about "maimed rites"—marriages that are false, funerals that are truncated, entertainments that are stratagems. Fergusson makes passing reference to Hamlet as the royal scapegoat, thus to his role in the greatest rite of all, that of redemption.[22] Perhaps, but we must first decide what can be meant by redemption in this context. There

21. That is, time is construed as bringing genuine novelties. The direction of time, however, was thought to be guided by the return of Christ in worldly triumph. Thus the mass, the communion, was to be celebrated until "He comes again." With the weakening of the bonds of this rite must come a weakening of the directional control of time and change.
22. Fergusson, *The Idea of a Theatre*, p. 132.

is something also to be said for Jean S. Calhoun's observation that *Hamlet* presents us with a "dark vision of sacrificial possibilities."[23]

As we shall see, Prince Hamlet is deeply ambivalent toward his father, King Hamlet. He is both magnetized by him and wayward with respect to him. The relationship seems to be another instance of the perennial fusion-rebellion complex which we have noted. There is a peculiar vacillation here, however, which seems to speak of an attenuation of mimetic bonds in general—as if the world at large had begun to lose its power to hold and to enchant. Hamlet's relationship to his father cannot be understood by itself. It is a function of Hamlet's being-in-the-world. This is now diffuse and questioning, and all of his relationships are of a piece with it. He alternately embraces and doubts his father's authority. One cannot imagine Oedipus doubting his father's authority. When he discovers he has aggressed against him he immediately takes steps to make reparation.

Shakespeare seems to see prophetically that without rites offstage for mediating the fusion-rebellion complex there will be trouble for us. It might be objected, of course, that there never has been a foolproof rite to deal with this problem. Still, it is clear that a whole network of rites tended to ameliorate it: e.g., the "performance" of marriage authorized by heaven militated against incestuous relationships, and the anchorage in the transtemporal domain condemned hasty remarriage. The yearly anniversary commemorates the event, and the participants stood in and "played a role" that bound moments of time in a coherent whole. Children participated periodically in ceremonies of respect for parents, etc. Time was transcended within time. At the very least we can say that the rites often delayed or deflected destructive energies of fusion and aggression.

Being patently theatre-like, rites can be examined perspicuously both in their parallels to, and contrasts with, theatre. Standing in through *Hamlet*'s "world" maps the attenuation of ritualistic standing in in the world. But more than this, Shakespeare presents his theatrical standing in as if it might substitute for this decaying standing in. *Hamlet* as a play stands in for this lack of standing in. The actor who enacts Hamlet the character enacts one who feigns madness, for example; he enacts an actor; he enacts one who invents a "world." When we in the audience stand in through the actor we are authorizing him in this enactment of an actor, in this radical invention of a "world," and the actor authorizes us to do so. All of us participants seek to authorize ourselves in this invention of a "world" with its "roles" in order to fill the void in the world left by the crumbling of rites. We can begin to imagine the character Hamlet as a redeemer of a new sort: as a sacrifice to the void, he stands in for all of us.

23. Jean S. Calhoun, "Hamlet and the Circumference of Action," *Renaissance News* 15 (1962):297.

Oedipus Rex would never have commented on its own possibility in this way. Its make-believe is ensconced in the solid matrix of the Greek city-state, its religion, its customs, and its history. *Hamlet*'s propensity to comment on the conditions of its own possibility as an artistic event— and of how it might substitute for decaying rites—betrays an anxious concern with the conditions of our own possibility as selves. The conditions of enacting a self onstage throw disturbing and suggestive light on the conditions of being a self offstage.

At the beginning of the play we find Hamlet isolated. His father has recently been killed; his mother has too soon remarried, or thus Hamlet believes; and she has married Claudius, the man who now occupies the throne that should have been Hamlet's own. On the night on which we meet him he is called to the battlements of the castle by his lieutenants and friends, and there encounters a supernatural presence which is the ghost of his father. He is overcome with terror and awe:

> What may this mean
> That thou, dead corpse, again in complete steel,
> Revisits thus the glimpses of the moon,
> Making night hideous, and we fools of nature
> So horridly to shake our disposition
> With thoughts beyond the reaches of our souls?
> . . . .
> Hold, hold, my heart!
> And you my sinews, grow not instant old,
> But bear me stiffly up.

The ghost tells him that the present king, his own brother and Hamlet's uncle—"that incestuous, that adulterate beast"—"won to his shameful lust the will of my most seeming virtuous queen," and killed the man whose ghost now speaks. After commanding Hamlet to avenge his murder, the ghost's last words to him are "Remember me," and Hamlet protests nearly hysterically that he will wipe away all else from the table of his memory,

> And thy commandment all alone shall live
> Within the book and volume of my brain,
> Unmixed with baser matter. Yes, by heaven!

Yet he does not remember, at least not consistently, and the ghost must reappear weeks or months later to "revive his almost blunted purpose." We learn to doubt the potency of the oath made in heaven's name.

I agree with A. C. Bradley that Hamlet's thoughtfulness, his concern with angles and projected consequences, only exacerbates his inaction, and is not the central root of it.[24] I agree that the root is a melancholy unto death. I go further and wish to understand in a quite literal sense Hamlet's wish "Oh, that this too too solid flesh would melt, thaw, resolve itself into a dew." To be sure, there are his perfectly manifest problems, which are formidable: Claudius is king and he controls the army. But these problems are in principle attackable through calculation and analysis: e.g., might a loyalty to Prince Hamlet amongst the commanders—and a residual loyalty to King Hamlet—be exploited? This possibility is never entertained by Hamlet because he is grappling with even greater problems, ones that elude his calculation and analysis. He can no longer stand in legitimately for his dead father, and the chief reason for this is that he has lost involvement in rites, so lost involvement in the time-transcending and time-binding reality of heaven and the supernatural. He wonders whether he might not have seen a "goblin damned." Having lost his deep mimetic involvement with his father, he has lost the power to be authorized and empowered as a self, and the conditions of his identity are so disturbed that he longs to expunge them altogether, to cease to be.

There was a presence, but did it give presence to the divinely supernatural—that which reveals the past reliably? The clicking of linear time leaves the past behind and wears away Prince Hamlet's involvement with his father the king. The vast reach of the play's dialectic of presence and absence trembles with interrogation and doubt. This is a crucial difference from *Oedipus*. The chorus there had chanted,

> Nothingness, nothingness,
> Ye Children of Man, and less
>   I count you waking or dreaming!
> And none among mortals, none,
> Seeking to live, hath won
> More than to seem, and to cease
>   Again from his seeming.

Persons must have their being in appearances—hence they are "nothing" and appearances are always potentially misleading and ensnaring ones, at least taken one by one. But there never was any doubt in Sophocles' productions that gods exist, say, Apollo or Zeus, who can properly read appearances, and that there are oracles who deliver the purport of their reading at any moment in which it is desired. When Oedipus is convinced that he has been cursed, all the ambivalent feelings toward his father that

24. Bradley, *Shakespearean Tragedy*.

he may harbor are swept away and he acts absolutely decisively.[25] His crime is regicide and incest, and definite forms of expiation and reparation fit this crime. He has fouled the transmission of energies of individuals bound mimetically and enchantedly with others, and the full force of this numinous power must be turned upon the violator. The familial violation is a social and also a cosmic one. The rings of his spheres of reality in the world, inner to outer, cohere and reinforce one another even as they crush him.

As Jean S. Calhoun has pointed out in her masterful "Hamlet and the Circumference of Action," Shakespeare generates his action and forms his characterizations within a display of included and including "worlds": the castle, Denmark, other countries, the earth, the cosmos, or the heavens. Different characters are defined by the scope of their concern, and so take their place within the action of the play. The women are defined by the activities of their men, the soldiers by their immediate orders and environs. King Claudius's concern ranges out only as far as the secular affairs of men and states, with but a sporadic and unfulfilled sense of the heavens. But Hamlet ranges out through them all. He is the "complete reflector," as Calhoun puts it.

However, we must point out that he fails to achieve a single coherent image in all that he reflects. Let us pause over these pregnant metaphors of "image" and "reflector." First, though Hamlet is crucially involved in the action, he still distances himself more than Oedipus did; this is suggested by "reflector." That is, he did not kill the king, nor did he commit incest with his mother; his uncle did those things. At this point the metaphor of the reflector is peculiarly helpful. The problem for Hamlet is compound: not only can he not achieve a coherent image, but the very attempt to maintain the detached stance necessary for the image throws him out of touch with the forces with which he must be engaged if he would understand himself. In Nietzsche's terms, there are Dionysian forces at work that elude the Apollonian intellect, the stance of equability, vision, detachment. Note well: it is not merely that his detachment prevents him from accomplishing the avenging act, but that it prevents him from knowing what it involves. It involves a fusion with his father as mediated by supernatural forces. Hamlet is bereft of a set of rites which guarantee the presence of the supernatural. He suffers from a wound of absence. No mere image of himself as avenger and as stand-in for his father will suffice as long as he remains detached. He must put his body on the line, take his father's place bodily, and risk death for his father's sake if he would know what it is that is involved. His shaky belief in the supernatural is not just an intellectual problem in theology, but affects adversely

25. Indeed, ambivalent feelings, which loom so large in the modern world, are so easily overruled in the Greek world that they are of questionable significance.

his very ability to act and to be. Hamlet is present to himself as a task, as a to-be, and he is so daunted, befuddled, and dismayed by it that he balances between it and yearning for dissolution and suicide. He fails to stand in for his dead father in a way that authorizes and empowers him to accomplish his task.

Of course, Hamlet does not simply cease to believe. He is caught in the middle. At the time, his encounter with the ghost was an actuality that palsied him. But one moment in his life does not hang together organically and coherently with the next. The chorus, the historical life of a people circulating around the principals, is gone; that which fuses present and past, individual and group, mundane and supernatural, is gone. Lacking historical coherence and power, Hamlet cannot properly play his social role as avenger. But because the presence of the ghost still haunts him somewhat, he cannot play other social roles open to him as a chief figure in Claudius's court either. The heavenly sphere of reality becomes disengaged from the social, and Hamlet is torn and disorganized between them: "What should such fellows as I do crawling between earth and heaven?" Zeus the thunderer and the protector no longer sounds in the sky.

It is not so much that the Freudian explanation of Hamlet is mistaken as that it is misleading because it is incomplete. Of course, it is a supernatural father whose place Hamlet has trouble taking. What would repel him from doing this? Immediately we suspect an archaic fear of fusion. If he takes his father's place he will either be dead, or he will take his place sexually with his mother, or both. The Freudian reading also suggests, interestingly enough, that on the subconscious level of his experience Hamlet will identify himself with Claudius as well—as displacer of his father—and that this is also a reason that he cannot kill him.[26] The repression of a desire for fusion occurs on a level of his experience that he dare not acknowledge, and concerning which he constantly deceives himself.

But it is not just sexual disorientation that afflicts Hamlet, it is world disorientation, and particularly the disruption of world time. Hamlet is troubled unto death, and the springs of his action fail him because the world as he experiences it is falling apart and his own identity is disturbed. This is the answer to the question he raises late in the play:

Why do I yet live to ask myself why has not this been done,
When I have the will, the means and the power to do it?

The question is whether he does have the power—whether he can pull himself together to do it. The antecedent moments of his life do not consistently feed, inform, and detonate their successors.

26. See Ernest Jones, *Hamlet and Oedipus* (New York: Norton, 1976).

If it is the essence of the dramatic to identify with someone as he struggles with a problem, then Shakespeare's creation of *Hamlet* is a dramatic event in western civilization. For as Shakespeare identifies with Hamlet and his struggles, so we identify with Shakespeare and his struggles with Hamlet's struggles. New crises of action and belief in the world map themselves onto crises of action and belief within the "world" of *Hamlet.* And at this point a very dramatic thing happens. The theatre, and the model "world" that it generates, is asked to carry a greater burden than theatre had ever been asked to carry before. The "world" of a Greek play is at least equally balanced by the culturally mediated world in which it is staged. There is easy give and take between them, and the "world" of the theatre is at home in the world. But with *Hamlet* the playwright and his players ask questions of the world that the culture at large cannot answer, and in response to the echoing in the void the theatre turns in upon itself. Instead of attempting merely to mirror the world within its "world," this "world" also reflects itself within itself as a " 'world.' " Actors play actors, a stage is set up on the stage. This process of self-reflection could go on indefinitely, with quotation marks added perpetually within quotation marks. One might think that if theatre does this it can dredge up from its own creative sources a notion of all possible worlds. Then, what is invariant between them can be extrapolated to the world at large. At least we can say that since the world does not supply adequate independent means for checking on the theatre to see whether its productions are life-like, we will project from the theatre into the world and we will find perhaps that it is theatre-like. Thus the high drama of this drama, its dangerous and prophetic "Pirandellesque" quality of which Fergusson speaks.

The moment in which this happens is brilliantly staged by Shakespeare, and we seem to feel his excitement as he feels Hamlet's. A group of traveling players arrives, and for the first and almost the only time in the play, Hamlet is happy, in fact nearly ecstatic. That which weds language to the rhythms of nature—the murmur of the wind, the fall of waves, the pulse of time in insect life—or to the stately forms of traditional cultural life—poetic diction in iambic pentameter—this has broken down into a rushing prose that treads eagerly on its own heels. He greets the players familiarly as the old friends (and associates?) they are, and says, "We'll e'en to't like French falconers, fly at anything we see. We'll have a speech straight." He asks for a particular speech from the first player, and going beyond what is needed to cue the actor, gives him thirteen lines. We already know that the first stratagem he thought of following his interview with the ghost was "to put an antic disposition on"—to act the part of a fool or madman—presumably to throw the kings' men off the scent of his work of revenge. The actor who plays the part of Hamlet plays the part of one who has already adopted the techniques of theatre as a way of life. There is no life in the raw "out there" waiting to be cooked by theatre. Theatre "reflects" what has already been influenced by it.

Hamlet no sooner hears that the players are on their way than he says, "He who plays the king will be welcome." He has already hatched his second and more direct stratagem: he will have the players enact a play in the king's presence similar to the account given to him by the ghost of how he was murdered by his brother. If Claudius has a guilty conscience, this will cause him to "blench" and to reveal it. All this is to test the ghost to see if it be "honest." In the absence of rites which guarantee the presence of the supernatural, theatre is a way of discovering what remains of truth.

Life is so concentrated in the theatrical image that in this form it cannot be overlooked. It forces a recognition from the parties involved and it can discover things. Left at this point, however, these words could apply to the Greek theatre as well. In *Hamlet* we begin to see a shift in the balance between theatre and world. Life comes to be thought of as more radically theatre-like than it was experienced to be before. In the metaphorical relation between theatre and world, theatre threatens to emerge as *proton analogon*. Hamlet's problem is that he cannot act and be, because he cannot stand in for his father. We cannot help but think that he is drawn to the theatre because it is the art of standing in, and because it can teach him to be, he breathlessly hopes, through teaching him to stand in, to play his "part." To act offstage would become the direct analogue of to act onstage as would an actor.

We see, cropping out here, a distinctively modernist attitude. One cannot suppose that there is an objective order, divinely instituted, in which one's place, value, techniques, and duties can be read off. Recall that Hamlet's "paragon of animals" speech, his disquisition on man's high place in an ordered cosmos, ends with, "And yet what is he to me, this thing of dust?" Let us suppose, rather, that we proceed from something man-made that we know well—say, a play—and project it testingly into the world to see if anything out there is like it; as if a blind man were to cast out ropes, and were to grope along them to see what they had outlined or what they had ensnared. Life, then, may be theatre-like, and the closest truth about oneself may be that one is actor-like.[27]

And yet we must forget neither Hamlet's, nor perhaps even Shakespeare's, profound ambivalence toward the theatre, nor the desperateness of Hamlet's situation. It is not that theatre is so bright but that the world

27. Recall Vico's idea of the convertibility of the true and the made.

is so dark. Because Hamlet cannot experience spheres of reality as nesting, cumulative, and coherent, the springs of his action lack coherence. He seldom can act effectively from reason, nor yet can he fall neatly into place and act out a social "role." But it is part of the tragedy that the techniques of theatre which Hamlet seizes are inadequate to save him. This is revealed not only by the manifest content of the play, but by the form it takes as a theatrical event.

Hamlet's mother asks him why his father's death "seems so particular" to him, since, as he admits, death is common. Hamlet replies,

> Seems, madam? Nay, it is. I know not "seems."
> Tis not alone my inky cloak, good mother,
> Nor customary suits of solemn black,
> Nor windy suspiration of forced breath,
> No, nor the fruitful river in the eye,
> Nor the dejected havior of the visage,
> Together with all forms, moods, shapes of grief,
> That can denote me truly. These indeed seem,
> For they are actions that a man might play;
> But I have that within which passeth show—
> These but the trappings and suits of woe.

While granting that men customarily do act in ways similar to a player's acting, still he maintains that he has that within which "passeth show."

An illuminating view of life is being achieved from the activity and viewpoint of theatre, but it is also an illumination which indicates its own limits. A player is in fact uttering all these lines of Hamlet's and showing himself on stage even as he says that he has that within which passeth show. But this is not self-stultifying, for he is playing in such a way as to suggest the limits of the play. The actors are showing by means of theatre the theatre-like show of life, and without this we could have no idea of that which "passeth" it. The actor playing Hamlet shows this in the sense that he shows what cannot be directly shown. Great theatre sounds its own limits and in this sense transcends them because it can fetch the unspeakable into presence.

Whereas the play within the play has only the play as its limits, the play itself borders on—and so intimates the shape of—that which transcends it, life itself. As the player's play within *Hamlet* is to the other events depicted in the play, so presumably the latter is to the world. As *Hamlet* is grander and vaguer and messier than the player's play, so the world is grander and vaguer and messier than *Hamlet*. Exactly what it is we may not know, but it is along that line of extrapolation, in that direction. There is no attempt to carry the theatrical metaphor wholesale into life and to stamp it upon it. Nor is there an attempt to spin out formalistically and from theatrical sources alone the invariant components of all possible worlds, hence of this actual one's also. The theatrical metaphor generated is essential, but piecemeal and tentative, for it gropes toward a world that is intimated by it, but that cannot be exhausted by it.

This, again, can be made evident in Hamlet's response to the first player's passionate enactment of Aeneas's tale to Dido (the part whose first thirteen lines had been delivered originally by Hamlet himself):

> O, what a rogue and peasant slave am I!
> Is it not monstrous that this player here,
> But in a fiction, in a dream of passion,
> Could force his soul so to his own conceit
> That, from her working, all his visage wanned,
> Tears in his eyes, distraction in's aspect,
> A broken voice, and his whole function suiting
> With forms to his conceit? And all for nothing!
> For Hecuba!
> What's Hecuba to him, or he to Hecuba
> That he should weep for her? What would he do,
> Had he the motive and the cue for passion
> That I have? He would drown the stage with tears. . . .

The actor playing Hamlet enacts a passionate response to a passionate enactment of a player. Extrapolated down the line we gain a new experience of how persons in life work themselves up, theatrically, through their own "conceits," imaginings, beliefs. But at the same time Hamlet's enactment in response to the actor's enactment projects the greater complexity, density, and extensity of acting offstage. For the conceit concerning working oneself up through a conceit suggests the limits of conceit in life. That is, it is one thing to work oneself into a passion over an idea in which one can absolutely believe for a few minutes while onstage, or even for a few minutes off. It is another thing to be possessed by an idea that drives and steers one through the choppy seas of life day after day until its end has been accomplished.

It is just this steadiness that Hamlet finds he does not possess, and it is just this lack that the modern audience can detect in itself when it finds itself through Hamlet's finding of himself. We are fascinated with Hamlet's dilemma, for it is a way of discerning and coming to grips with our own. We see that many of us, like him, oscillate between lassitude and fanatical flareups of attachment. Our lives are not both steady and passionate. Too often, our acts, like his, spring irruptively from a dread of being locked into roles that lack all supramundane and extra-analytical sanction or excitement. As in Hamlet's mistaken killing of the concealed Polonius, an action emerges as a desperate reaction to passivity and doubt.

On the other hand, when Hamlet's actions are reasonable they often lack conviction and power. Like many of ourselves, we see, his thought and belief tend to disengage themselves from his action. Though he believes that "there's a divinity that shapes our ends, rough hew them as we will," this amounts more to a vague fatalism than to a doctrinal matrix for behavior which holds magnetizing and stabilizing councils of perfection or of prudence. So he consents grandly, casually, to Claudius's invitation to duel Laertes, not stooping to investigate the poisoned foils, and participates in that denouement as debacle, that tangle of accidents which accomplishes the action of extirpating what is rotten in the state of Denmark at the cost of destroying Denmark itself: killing himself along with the rest of the royal family and opening the state to occupation by a foreign power.

At this point the revelation of the limits of theatre through the form of theatre merges with the disclosure of its limits through the manifest content of the play. For the debacle occurs even though the play within the play does cause the king to "blench," does uncover his guilt. The ancient problem of standing in for the father takes on new dimensions.

Hamlet asks us what we can make of ourselves in an age in which rites disintegrate. We must take this in a quite literal sense: what we can make of ourselves. If rites interconnect individual and group, past and future, and society and nature in the world-time of the ceremony, then when the rites lose their power the individual will be forced to try to create his life in a more radical sense than ever before. Must he try to invent a self for himself? Instead of living within the power of recurrent rhythms and cultural patterns which have been made one's own through the rites, possibility will stand before one like an abyss. Either that or one will confine oneself to limited "roles" and endure through the inertia of boredom.

If one is not merely in the world, but is worldly; if he has no identity in himself, as does a nugget sewn into a pocket, but his identity is a function of the identity of the world as it is experienceable and appropriatable by him through time, then if the identity of that world disintegrates so will he. Either that or—again as we said—he will withdraw, schizoid-like, into a domain that is small but apparently safe, boring but enduring. Thus *Hamlet* is prophetic and speaks to us about ourselves. As Heidegger has put it, man has no nature but only a history, and possibility is prior to actuality. But we do have a history in which we are formed mimetically, and if we are sustained as adults it is through mimetic attachments, however subtle. Where are they to be found? Rather, where are minimally rational attachments to be found? The twentieth century is a grim and rapidly changing record of saluting masses, crowds with little red books in their hands, and consumers gorging themselves on the latest fad. And all of this is attended by the exclusion or the slaughter of those who cannot be absorbed in the identity of the group. Dionysus will have his due, and fusions there must be, but where are the fusions that will not destroy our fragile and problematical integrity as individuals? Can it be that we can trust only the mimetic involvements with our fictional characters? Modern art takes on a curiously self-involved and desperate quality.

A production of *Hamlet* brings us together, but after it has done so it presents us with the possibility of things flying apart: the individual flying apart from society, or being engulfed by it; society flying apart from nature; thought flying apart from belief and perception to the detriment of coherent and cumulative action; ultimately, the beads of continuity in an individual's experiencing threaten to fall apart and to roll away on their own. How can we make the world our own—our own as experienceable by us—and feel its generative power as our own? In the Greek theatre and mystery religions explicitly, and in Christianity tacitly, rites and the rite-like weave ourselves and the rhythms and seasons of nature into a single continuous fabric of power and significance. But as Sartre once remarked to Merleau-Ponty, "Nature is in tatters." And as Edna St. Vincent Millay has written,

> It is not enough that yearly, down this hill,
> April
> Comes like an idiot, babbling and strewing flowers.

Hamlet comments upon itself. It is a play that is about playing and make-believe in situations in which rites disintegrate. The largest questions it poses for us are these: can its play, in which we participate mimetically, authorize and empower us afresh in the very process of playing out the disintegration of that which has authorized and empowered us previously, our play-like rites offstage? Could such artistic exercises so permeate our lives in world-time that they become something very like rites themselves? *Hamlet* is a play that documents the inadequacy of playing for Hamlet. We are left with the question of its adequacy for ourselves. We ask in the end whether our "role playing" offstage can establish us as authentic individuals in a thoroughly secularized world.

3. The "World" of *Waiting for Godot* and the World of Its Theatre

The initial stage directions for this play read:

A country road. A tree. Evening.[28]

The scrawny little tree—sculpted for the original production in 1953 by Giacometti—is near center stage, and as the play is usually mounted, the

---

28. All references to *Waiting for Godot* are to the Grove Press edition (New York, 1954).

two tramps, Vladimir and Estragon, lurk at the periphery of the perform- ing area. The stage picture, intuited unmistakably, is of a world that is empty at the center—or that is centerless. Perhaps in some dim way the tramps remind us of the Greek chorus. To some degree they stand in for us, the audience. They comment on the scene, inquire about some absent but awaited authority—Godot—but they are inadequate to manifest the nature of this absent Godot, or to present a coherent picture of any level of their reality. Nor can they achieve any conventional resolution of their action, which is simply to await him. Hamlet's wound of absence has become a near amputation. They are perpetually looking into the distance, but it is a distance that forever recedes in front of them. Anything that might lure or guide them through this space is absent. Nothing they do sets up a reverberation within it. The tramps stand in the position of the circulating, surrounding chorus—the aura of the stage—that position from which an interpretation of the world might be expected—but no such interpretation is forthcoming.

To recall Aristotle's distinction, Beckett as dramatist is a poet of plots, of actions, not of verbal arrangements as ends in themselves. We are gripped by the tramps' waiting. Why should we be? No doubt for the same reasons we were gripped by Oedipus's relation to the king and to the gods, and by Hamlet's relation to the king and to the spirits. Oedipus's habit of decisive action—modeled so closely yet unwittingly on his father—is gone. What was a festering, sprouting germ in Hamlet—his inability to stand in decisively for the slain king, his father, and to be authorized and empowered by him—has come to a vast, static maturity in the waiting tramps.

The point seems to be that the authority whose view of them, and certification of them, the tramps must incorporate and make their own if they are to be vitally alive is absent in such a way that his felt presence in the world cannot sustain them, at least not beyond merely waiting for him. He is felt merely as a serious—a gaping—absence. Since he has not been introjected, he cannot be defied. And since he has not been defied, there can be no meaningful expiation, for no meaningful sin has been committed. Nothing is to be done except to wait.

The upshot of all this is an emotional emptiness, an anaesthesia, in which their own selves are not compellingly present to themselves; their lives are flat and pointless (beyond the waiting). They are wraiths of dust. They do have their friendship, which is important to them, but it is a flame flick- ering in the void, and they frequently lose emotional contact with each other. Trivial rites, very much like burlesque routines, take on great im- portance as surrogate structures of significance and continuity, and as time killers (since time as pulverizer has become practically unendurable); for example, taking off one's hat, looking into it, knocking on its crown, replacing it on one's head (a picture, a stage metaphor, for looking for one's mind or brains?). Taking a step beyond *Hamlet*'s maimed but conventional rites, these odd rites comment mordantly on the nearly total absence of any conventional ones.

The smallest victories take on immense, if ephemeral, significance: securing a carrot when a carrot, not a turnip, is wanted, regardless if it is a wizened specimen; an erection—or the felt possibility of one—being a rare and priceless joy, etc. The magnetizing magic of identification—or whatever we are to call it—which makes action possible and exciting has gone. A curse hangs over nobody in particular; a vague and diffuse curse hangs over their world.

Hamlet's inability to consistently remember—or to be sure he has recognized—his father has spread to nearly every object and person in the tramps' world. They are not sure they see the same person twice:

VLADIMIR: And you are Pozzo?
POZZO: Certainly I am Pozzo.
V: The same as yesterday?
P: Yesterday?
V: We met yesterday. [*Silence.*] Do you not remember?
P: I don't remember having met anyone yesterday. But tomorrow I won't remember having met anyone today. So don't count on me to enlighten you.

Pozzo, a slave driver they encounter on the road—alive and obstreperous in the first act, blind and frenzied in the second—may even be Godot:

ESTRAGON: Are you sure it wasn't him?
VLADIMIR: Who?
E: Godot.
V: But who?
E: Pozzo.
V: Not at all! [*Less sure.*] Not at all! [*Still less sure.*] Not at all!

These dislocations and incongruities are comical when properly enacted on the stage, but the deepest problems of identity of self are suggested when they are extrapolated to the limit. As emotional atrophy and withdrawal reach the point at which things and persons in the environment are not re-identifiable as the same, then the identity of the self as subject-for-that-object is endangered. The re-identifiability of my experiences as mine, which is essential to my sense of myself as the same through all these experiences—which is essential to my identity—is itself dependent upon my sense of objects as being the same. That is, if it is not known that an experience is an anticipation of seeing X, the very same X that will be perceived when it arrives, and remembered later, then how can there be any assurance that it was really a sequence of experiences belonging to the same stream of experiences? And if not this, how can there be a single enduring subject to whom anything appeared, and by whom it was experienced? If we do not presuppose a single experiencing self, we cannot suppose that the same thing has been differently experienced by it. And if we do not suppose that the very same thing is differently experienced, then we cannot suppose that it is experienced by a single self; there is mutual entailment here.

A dialectic of presence and absence requires the continuity and identity of a self which can repeatedly manifest the presence of self-identical things, even if these things be physically absent or nonexistent. Indeed, a provisional sketch of human reality as self might be: at a point in time a being is a self if it can manifest absence *as* absence: knowingly manifest it as its *own* manifestation of *it*, the very same thing that can be experienced and manifested by it differently at different times. This we examine systematically in Part Two of this work.

If things are not *recognizable* and *rememberable* all this is impossible. But of course the problem goes beyond mere cognition, particularly if cognition is understood on the model of vision. The tramps' identity problems involve not merely disruption in the entailment relationships, and contrast relationships, linking knowing subject and its objects. They have no *identification with* a center of energy and authority in the world that they can manifest as energy and authority when out of its local environment. Vladimir does not wish to hear Estragon's dreams. Perhaps they suggest to him too painfully a lost community of mind or spirit in which absence is given structured presence habitually. Perhaps they suggest too pointedly each man's aloneness as a center of subjectivity.

Pozzo the slave driver is a creature hemmed in by his poses and fronts, and sickened by the helplessness and degeneracy of his servant Lucky's dependency upon him. The tramps ask Pozzo why Lucky does not put down his load as he stands there:

> POZZO: . . . Why he doesn't make himself comfortable? Let's try and get this clear. Has he not the right to? Certainly he has. It follows that he doesn't want to. There's reasoning for you. And why doesn't he want to? [*Pause*] Gentlemen, the reason is this.
>
> VLADIMIR: [*to Estragon*] Make a note of this.
>
> POZZO: He wants to impress me, so that I'll keep him. . . . The truth is you can't drive such creatures away. The best thing would be to kill them. [*Lucky weeps.*]

The misplaced fusion and dependency—an ancient theme.

When his hat is on his head, Lucky "thinks" upon demand. This at first seems no more than a hysterical or schizoid word-salad, yet a theme recurs, which was made vividly evident in Jack Macgowran's enactment of Lucky in New York in 1972:

> . . . that man in Essy that man in short that man in brief in spite of the strides of alimentation and defecation wastes and pines wastes and pines and concurrently simultaneously what is more for reasons unknown in spite of the strides of physical culture the practice of sports such as tennis football running cycling swimming flying floating riding gliding conating camogie skating tennis of all kinds dying flying sports of all sorts autumn summer winter winter tennis of all kinds hockey of all sorts penicillin . . . for reasons unknown but time will tell fades away. . . .

As with Hamlet's "Oh, that this too too solid flesh would melt . . ." the problem is ontological, the undermining of individual human reality (which undermining may also be desired). The tramps' reality is so scanty and ineffectual already that they can take no action, not even to hang themselves. The best we can say is that in enduring at all they achieve a strange inverted sort of ecstasy.

> VLADIMIR: We always find something to give us the impression that we exist.
> ESTRAGON: We're magicians.

The last three lines of the play encapsulate its essence. The tramps cannot remember why they are standing there waiting.

> VLADIMIR: Well? Shall we go?
> ESTRAGON: Yes, let's go.

The last line in the play is a stage direction:

> [*They do not move.*]

4. Summary of the Variations and the Nature of a Text

Beckett is using the theatre, and the verbal language it involves, in such a way as to draw the limits of verbal language itself. He is saying that silence lies within language, close to its heart. The very contrast between the tramps' verbal speech and the rest of their behavior speaks of the limitation of that speech. They cannot put into words the depths of their dependency upon Godot, but there it is before us plain as day. It is not that the play is not about dependency between human beings. It is about how this dependency becomes pathetically greater when their dependency upon an ultimate authority is unresolved.

Seated in the audience we become aware of our own silence, of our dependency upon the production, and of our questioning which the production occasions. An absence is being given presence: the absence of authority and authorization, which amounts to an absence of being, and it is more nearly total than it was in *Hamlet*. Through the process of giving the absence presence an attempt is being made to heal this wound of absence. The standing in and involvement, which is the production itself in this theatre house, has pitted itself against the manifest content of the play being produced: failure of involvement and standing in, a withering detachment.

We become aware of the disturbing possibility that the failure of mimetic attachment present in the focus of the play's "world" will not be overcome by the mimetic attachment and authorization reciprocated by audience and performers in the encompassing theatre house and world. The drama occurs in the theatre house between stage and audience. To what extent can we be authorized in articulating together through the actors our lack of authorization? We do not participate in this performance periodically at a hallowed time and place in such a way as to deeply habituate the observance in cyclical and sacred time; nor is a whole community assembled, but rather a fragment of one. The experience of authorization probably cannot become cumulative and strong, and we vaguely suspect this. We wonder if the total experience of the production can be sealed off from the manifest content of the play, or if this content will soak through, as blood would through a bandage. The content is a pervading questioning of the meaningfulness of human existence and mimetic involvement in time, and the unsettling worry is that it will seep into the foundations of community participation and mimetic commitment necessary for the production itself to occur.

The key to all great theatre is the silence of the audience. It discloses that each person has cut the continuity of everyday talk and everyday concern, those activities in which one can always find more to occupy oneself if one wishes to lose oneself in them.[29] The random life of the senses has been cut as well. The silence reveals that each person has reserved this time for discovery, rediscovery, and contemplation of that which each in his own person would find it difficult or impossible to speak. Mimetic fusion and disruption too profound to be speakable is

29. Concerning the nature of silence in general see Bernard P. Dauenhauer's *Silence: The Phenomenon and Its Ontological Significance* (Bloomington: Indiana University Press, 1980).

entrusted to the proxy life lived through the characters on the stage. The audience at *Oedipus Rex* and the actors lived the timeless and unspeakable suspense of the disruption of mimetic attachment to authority. Commenting on their enchanted involvement with authority, we believe we can say what the troubled question was that moved them at the outer margins of their consciousness: how is one to be mimetically authorized by an authority in whom one is engulfed, and yet at the same time be a self-responsible individual with his own interests?

At crucial instances the silence in the theatre house is total. It is those moments in which the characters themselves are silenced by what they cannot speak. The backbone of *Oedipus Rex* is those moments which add up to disclosure, but which Oedipus jams from the focus of his consciousness until he is overwhelmed by them: moments of his dialogue with Tiresias in which he glimpses that it may be he himself who has produced the intractable and mysterious pestilence in Thebes, and this is a possibility which he cannot fully acknowledge. We in the audience live through his struggle, knowing what it is he cannot speak, but instructed to participate in his silence. At the close of the theatre event each of us can say, "There but by the grace of the gods go I." We are delivered into speech.

There are a few such moments in *Hamlet*. But the locus of silence has shifted somewhat. Whereas in *Oedipus* the moments of silence within the play are counterbalanced by a sense of the awesomeness and mysteriousness of the world at large—a world of unspeakable amplitude which contains us all—in *Hamlet* it is as if the outer silence were so great and unmanageable that a din of bustle and words must be set up within the play to keep it off, to keep it at bay. Toward the end of the play the silence flows in for a moment when the gravedigger gives Hamlet the skull of Yorick, the man of "infinite jest" who had tended Hamlet as a child, who carried him about on his back. At that instant the actor playing Hamlet will be overcome and cannot speak. Thus conveyed is that absence which is the absence of death, that to which we can never fully give presence. Through this inchoate presence the innocence of Hamlet's relationship with Yorick opens out onto a time of innocence with Hamlet's father. Yorick is a proxy father that Hamlet can love absolutely, before all competition, rebellion, and confusion can begin. But words, now quiet words, beat the silence back again, and it is not until Hamlet's last statement as he dies,

the rest is silence

that the vast unspeakability of things is acknowledged, and the world flows in around him and all else in that "world" as if the Red Sea, instead of remaining parted, had flowed in and closed over Moses. Horatio's encomium,

> Now cracks a noble heart. Good night, sweet prince,
> And flights of angels sing thee to thy rest!

rises above the ruin as if the Elizabethan world were calling to its aid the last of its resources, the ghost of a Christian civilization, so that it could hover above it at the end.

With *Waiting for Godot,* silence itself is the theme. It runs through and between the words, and they float within it only to draw attention to its limitlessness. A corresponding openness of questioning is set astir within the audience. The question of the meaningfulness of the world is put at issue in this play's "world," and hence the question of the meaningfulness of our selves, for we are the worldly beings who must try to make sense of the world. We believe instinctively that one's being is a matter of one's presence, and this is a function of the presence of the world one communicates, and of one's place within the world.

The reality of the play includes the audience and the theatre building. As we have pointed out, the Greek theatre, open onto the sky and countryside, was lodged comfortably in the city-state, the seasons and nature. The gathered community on its high terrace seats contemplated its history and its possibilities. However disturbing might be the questioning it generated, still this questioning occurred within a more or less ordered and traditional sense of the universe. This aspect of the production is more emphatically evident in the Romans' modification of the Greek theatre. The central fact of the Roman edifice is the back wall of the stage which looms up before the audience. In its center, above the stage, is the niche for the statue of the emperor, two or three times life size, that looks out levelly at the audience, his breastplate on.[30] The Greek theatre had participated more in the air, and in the sense of possibility. Here, one feels the subjection imposed by the massive walls. They are made of sandstone and are yards thick. Today, so out of use and old, the theatre's rounded shoulders bear bushes and weeds and the nests of birds. The structure shows mainly its materiality and the stability, determination, and might of those who heaped it up. Their other traits have almost vanished from our immediate perceptual comprehension, but we know that each spectacle, however frivolous, bizarre, or terrifying, was experienced as engulfed in this marginally apprehended concretization of Roman stability and power. The edifice contained and modulated every interpretation sug-

---

30. I am thinking particularly of the theatre in Orange, southern France.

gested by what occurred on its stage. In articulating the continuity and power of the state, it functioned like a silent, encompassing chorus.

In our treatment of *Hamlet* we have emphasized the questioning, the skepticism, that breaks out within the play. But we would be remiss if we did not emphasize now that the theatre building silently reinforced traditional elements of the play. Impacted within the theatre house were unquestioned social, historical, and cosmic articulations. For example, differentiation among social classes was embedded in the seating arrangements of the theatre, which were hierarchical: a place to stand before the stage for the plebeians ("the stinkers in the pit"), places on the stage margins for the gentry, the surrounding tiers next to the walls for the nobility, and a special box for royalty. It was the latter who were divinely ordained to fill their position and to oversee—in principle—the production. This dimly analogizes the place for the priest of Dionysus in the Greek theatre. Whatever questioning of the sacred occurs within the play was silently modulated and contained by the encompassing theatre house and its place for representatives of the divine.

Contemporary theatre belongs in no particular edifice or institutional setting. It is as if the cultural and institutional disruption characteristic of the present age had shaken the drama of our period and winnowed it down to a questioning of all fundamentals, as if all clichés and conventions of interpretation had been destroyed, and we were left with the task of interpreting from the ground up, which means the reinterpretation of interpretation; as if we must put together again earth, air, sky, time, the seasons, place, people. What are the elements necessary for any rendering of human identity and agency? This is the question confronting both contemporary drama and philosophy. With the destruction of traditional interpretation in its contemporary "realistic" incarnation—the cliché of the living room or drawing room—we are left with the stark realities of space, time, and the interrogation of those irreducible human capacities presupposed by any factual account of persons. From Beckett to Whitman, Wilson, and Grotowski, one is struck by the starkness of the vision, and, in a sense, its primitiveness. It is as if this theatre were trying to create a community without which neither theatre nor community could survive. In one way or another, it seeks to sever its dependency upon conventional theatre buildings, managed so as to cater to conventional theatre audiences. Beckett has been produced mainly in off-Broadway-like settings around the world; Whitman produces in a warehouse, Grotowski in nearly any large, high-ceilinged room, and Robert Wilson has produced out of doors.

It is difficult to overestimate the importance of this shift. *Waiting for Godot*, with its paper moon that slides up the back wall and its scrawny tree (disenchanted nature—Pan is either asleep or dead), could be produced perfectly well in a garage. This theatre would reassess its own capacities for mediating and articulating the world: nature, culture, time, and all. Consider also Whitman's warehouse that opened onto the street. This building, rented for a few weeks, lacked the structure of traditional theatres with their unquestioned social, historical, and cosmic articulations. A world was given presence in traditional theatres anterior to the mounting of any particular play within them; and thus was embodied institutionally and architecturally the presupposition that the world could be understood to a decisive extent independently of any play mounted within them.

Of course, these buildings were the product of another art, that of architecture, and this raises for us the question whether the world can be understood independently of the arts in general. Still, the theatre house was not questioned by the audience; they came to take it as much for granted as they did the ground upon which it stood. Hence the idea that it embodied and conditioned only one viewpoint among other possible ones did not come up in any easily acknowledgeable way. It lent to the audience the sense that the world was simply given, or simply instantiated, through the edifice of the theatre itself. So the conclusion tended to be drawn that within this edifice, so within this world, the artistic event of the play occurred. The play was wrapped in cotton wool, its explosive charge hidden and even defused. For the audience was guided and constricted in its interpretation of the world without realizing it. The building mediated noiselessly between the "world" of the play and the world that contained the theatre, and buffered the impact of the possibility that this art is not just another event within the world, but a decisive work of human freedom and interpretation of the world.

The contemporary theatre which we have begun to study appears to be an attempt to interrogate itself—and human life—from scratch, as if the world and our existence could be reconstructed element by element before our eyes. When Whitman opened his warehouse door onto the street he revivified the presence of the world through his art. The city and then the world ballooned out before the opening. But it was an ephemeral, fragile, and incomplete vision. In its acute self-consciousness, it disclosed disclosure, but offered a vision of that which yearns after fuller vision. It is no accident that the roots of the word "holy" interweave with those for "whole" and "heal." During certain charged moments a nimbus of completeness hovers about the contemporary theatre. It discloses a wound of absence. The disclosure is an effort to achieve coherence through giving presence to this absence itself.

The "worlds" of contemporary plays form themselves within the contemporary world. It is predominantly a world of technology and instant communications. We can give more things presence than we can possibly care about. Our communications networks fill announcers' mouths with data; they speak of the deaths of passengers in a plane crash in Ecuador in the same tone of voice they use to report the stock market closings or the weather forecast. Each day uses up its "news" and leaves fading wrappers and bones: remnants of what was plucked from various times and places and thrown together in whatever place the experiencing person now occupies. Let us say it is the street: peeling broadsides for massage parlors, quotations from scripture, images of last year's fashionable faces, faces of those who stand before one now, oil from Arabia filming the wet street, the cacophony of sounds and sights from television sets and transistor radios—a heap of the incoherent, untimely, and inappropriate. In the midst of this world we endeavor to create "worlds" in which absence is given presence coherently and concernfully.

But we may well object at this point that there is more to theatre than the moments of performance. There is the script, which is written in advance, is there not? And the script transcends any momentary intersection of "world" and world, and, indeed, can link such intersections cumulatively in a tradition of performance—can it not? The answer is that while there is always a text, there is not always a script, as we shall see with Robert Wilson and Jerzy Grotowski.

Nevertheless, it is typical to have a script, and one was written for each of the three plays we have examined. We must now investigate this feature of the plays. Scripts involve configurations of matter—markings—which are conserved through space and time. Obviously this feature enables scripts to transcend individual performances in theatres; but there is a danger that this one feature of productions will be taken to be exhaustive of their being. Scripts are scripts only because their material markings are meaningful as signs to those who can read and write. Even with regard to those few scripts which are written primarily to be read rather than performed—in the more obvious sense of that term—still, the writer and the reader as they write and read must imaginatively stand in for the characters. What is true for the novelist is even more obviously true for the playwright. Gustave Flaubert has written,

it is a delicious thing to write, to be no longer yourself but to move in an entire universe of your own creating. Today, for instance, as man and woman, both lover and mistress, I rode in a forest on an autumn afternoon under the yellow leaves, and I was also the horses, the leaves, the wind, the words my people uttered, even the red sun that made them almost close their love-drowned eyes.[31]

31. *The Letters of Gustave Flaubert*, ed. Francis Steegmuller (Cambridge, Mass.: Harvard University Press, 1980).

We must say of the playwright that he is the master actor who acts out all the characters in his imagination while he writes, and he does so for an imagined audience of readers and performers.

Why, then, do we need a performance in a theatre at all? The first thing to be said is that playwrights imagine their dramas as thus performable, and indeed imagine them performable within an already-standing tradition and institution of performance. Even a revolutionary piece presupposes that against which it is revolting. The playwright *must* imagine his play as performable by a group in which each participant contributes syncretistically along with all the others, both ones present and actual and those given presence through artifact and memory. The connection between the writer and the theatrical tradition as institution is often very close indeed, and this is no accident. Shakespeare, Ibsen, Molière and Strindberg had their own theatres. Aeschylus, Sophocles, and Euripides wrote for a public institution in their own city. All functioned as a part of a theatrical tradition of performance. Even when the connection to a standing institution is not so close, the writing of a script cannot be an act of creation out of nothing and into nothing. It may not be imagined as being actually performed, but it must be imagined as being performable by a group of historical beings.

We can now be more specific about the connection between script and performance. Like all humans, the writer exists in an absolute here and now, in the physical presence of an environment of particular things. It is not correct to say that the meaning of the situation is confined by the mere immediacy of these things themselves. Things experienced must summon absence into presence. The meaning of these things is articulated, for example, by all the writings that have been read by the writer—or which characterize his culture generally—and that now inform his response to present things. The play that he writes is a new act of giving presence to absence, a new distancing by the writer from out of his here and now and its present complement of meaning, and from out of whatever dialogical situations involving a plurality of actual individuals typically structure his daily life. His here and now is transcended, and the semantic autonomy of the script that he writes opens it to an indefinite range of potential readers and actor-artists in an indefinite range of situations and in an indeterminate time.[32] A whole new "world" is sketched in outline so that the world can be re-described and freshly illuminated from a new instant in its history, a new moment of its funding. Alone in his study, the writer simply imagines selves-for-others, and imagines an audience for them.

When production begins—if it does begin—the script is regrounded in

32. Cf. Paul Ricoeur, *Interpretation Theory: Discourse and the Surplus of Meaning* (Fort Worth: Texas Christian University Press, 1976), pp. 35ff.

the dialogical situation of actual others in each others' actual presence. The pure imagination of the writer is checked out, corrected, extended, and transformed by the perceptual imaginations of all those involved in the production, and of course in their own new here and now. Does the script play? If so, how does it best play, given the actual selves involved in this production? It will be art, and not mere fancy, if the perennial concerns of persons are summed up afresh and lead to new modes of questioning by those assembled.[33] The script is regrounded in dialogical situation as amplified and articulated in the new distancing—both perceptual and metaphorical-symbolical—supplied by actors and audience. We can call this dialectic an accordian movement—indefinitely extendable in time—of instances of distancing, of giving presence to absence. Out of the production may emerge new writing, and it may be writing done by the author himself—rewriting done during the rehearsal, transformation, and embodiment of the script.[34]

Typically the writer writes alone in his study, and there are limits to his ability to imagine what actually happens when body-selves are thrown into each other's physical presence, for example, that which glimmers and flickers in their eyes for an instant and will not be caught, to adapt William James's phrase: the instant of fear, vulnerability, hatred, fascination, longing, contempt. But it can be caught by the actor—trained as he is in such receptivity—and he allows it to spread through his behavior and to manifest itself in surprising ways. What the actors contribute to the total act of creation of theatre, where a script is involved, is often—though not always just this by any means—the more irrational aspects of persons' relationships, those that can be caught only on the wing, when conscious bodies are cast into each others' actual physical presence. At some stage, if a production of theatre is to be complete (I am not speaking of that maverick form "reader's theatre"), the world must throw itself out immediately into a "world" of bodies if it would reflect itself.[35] It is the

33. See T. R. Martland, "Art?" *American Philosophical Quarterly* 15, no. 3 (July 1978).

34. In the case of the printing of the first folio of Shakespeare's plays in 1623—seven years after his death—so incomplete were the scripts that, for example, actors were canvassed to contribute their "sides" (pages with just their character's lines and the immediate cue lines from other characters). This occurred in some cases even when stage managers' copies existed, so mangled and interlineated were they by changes introduced by one or sundry in the course of multiple productions. In certain cases actors were asked to reenact scenes from memory. The plays of Shakespeare could not be taken off the shelf of a study or a library. He did not consider them to be part of his strictly literary life at all. This is a difficult point for some persons to comprehend.

35. No doubt there have been writers who would have liked (at certain moments at least) to dispense with actors, e.g., Beckett: "Not for me these Grotowskis and Methods. The best possible play is one in which there are no actors, only text. I'm trying to find a way to write one" [D. Bair, *Samuel Beckett* (New York: Harcourt Brace Jovanovich, 1978), p. 513]. Thus when Beckett has directed his own plays he has insisted that the actors follow his own enacted

director's function as multivocal audience for the cast of actors to coordinate and augment the imagination of all the artists involved.

Of course, we should not forget that the writer also is a body-self, that he writes with his hands and arms, and has a kinesthetic imagination. Arthur Kopit has related how he composed his *Wings*, a play about persons who have suffered strokes. "He listened to countless tapes of stroke victims in therapy, and then typed and retyped their conversations in an effort to achieve 'a kind of muscle memory of their language patterns.' "[36] Nor should we forget that important writers have been principal performers in their own productions—Aeschylus and Molière come immediately to mind. Their imagination as writers is also their imagination as accomplished actors. Likewise to be recalled is that writers not infrequently write for particular actors of known abilities and propensities. We know that Shakespeare wrote *Hamlet* for Richard Burbage, the son of his business associate James Burbage, and we will never know how much of Hamlet's character had already been suggested to him by this person.

Nevertheless, we are entitled to generalize cautiously, I believe, and to speak of the more nearly abstract imagination of the writer. Although the writer's words typically constitute all that is said in the performance, they constitute merely an outline—and in places very sketchy—of what is to be done. The writer leaves room for silences, and for the unpredictable contributions of other artists as co-creators of the performance. In great plays the words outline situations, contact assumptions, and generate consequences in performance which exceed the power of the words alone to express. Plays that should remain on the page unperformed are those in which there is more in the words as lyrical poetry than as dramatic poetry—as structure for enactment.[37] The great script is the great seed which excites its own moving ground of mood and of propensity to act in its performance—and in each viable production somewhat differently.

---

readings, gestures, and stances. On the basis of the production of *Waiting for Godot* in New York in spring, 1978, based on his own earlier production in Germany, I would say that he has failed as a director, and done his play a disservice. An interesting parallel can be found in Harold Clurman's *On Directing* (New York: Collier Books, 1972), pp. 36–37; in *Golden Boy* Clurman directed Fuselli, a gangster, as a sort of Renaissance prince. The author, Clifford Odets, was at first appalled; but by all standards the characterization, by Elia Kazan, was a great success. Clurman concludes that in this case Odets' intuition as a writer was greater than his visual stage sense. That is, he left room in his writing for a possible realization of great aesthetic value, but which he himself could not perceive to be valuable when it occurred before his eyes. He later thanked the other artists.

36. Another point is made in this interview which is of general interest to us: "neurologists who have seen it are anxious to use it as a teaching device because it does what textbooks don't do; it forces you to empathize with the victim." *New York Times*, June 25, 1978.

37. Perhaps the plays of W. B. Yeats are a case in point. But it is difficult to tell for certain, because of the paucity of talented actors and directors in this *genre* of theatre.

We have not yet commented on the word *text*. This is because it is fatally vague, despite the fact that it is much loved by philosophers and critics. It easily moves into a position of synonymy with "pre-written script," or with the meaning of such a script, and this is but another lapse into a formalistic and ahistorical approach to theatre as art. It is an instance of intellectuals' most basic prejudice, one which conceals itself from itself: namely, that "meaning" must mean, fundamentally, writable meaning (*litera*, literature, and particularly what is literal in literature). It is very difficult to become aware of this prejudice when one's awareness is me- diated and dominated by the practice that one values most highly: writing.

But once we clearly distinguish *text* from pre-written script, so that we can then explicitly relate them, the word *text* has an important role to play. We must distinguish between a dramatic performance of a play and the play itself, or what we can call the text itself. We are clearly in the domain of theatre art—and not merely of something theatrically viewed— only when the play is replicatable. *Text* should merely mean what is re- plicatable in the work of art, and it should not prejudice us against cases in which nothing is written in advance, or in which something is written as a transcript of what evolved through improvisations in rehearsal or performance. Because as *litera* it is supposed to capture the dialectic of presence and absence which is believed to be the play itself, the pre-written script assumes a quasi-Platonic status as the basic element of the art. Shorn of this association with pre-written script, the notion of text is a valuable one.

Rightly understood, a text is the evolving precipitate of encounters of persons with each other in time, the precipitate of a tradition, and texts themselves will evolve, however slowly perhaps. They will develop as they inform and excite new ages in new ways of typical response and under- standing. Though we can seek again through historical research what we might call Shakespeare's own text—the text as it was in the Elizabethan age and in his own theatre—and though we might achieve a much different reading from ones which are now current, still the text must always be the text-for-us-at-this-point-in-history.

We will now develop the notion of encounter as a form of communal experimentation in which models and metaphors for life are tried out. The problem is to excavate conditions and structures of identity and conduct which have been laid down by body-selves unconsciously, undeliberately, and in greater or lesser degrees of mimetic engulfment with others down through the generations. These conditions and structures have been laid down by us bodily, mimetically and together, and I will suggest that they can be exposed by us in the theatre because they are exposed there bodily, mimetically and together. We assume that in this area we have insight only because of our ability to construct and reconstruct; the true and the made are convertible, as Vico would say.

We conduct incarnated thought-experiments on the conditions of identity of self, and our analysis of theatre pushes the experiments to revealing extremities. Presuppositions of existence—particularly those pertaining to the connection between mimetic standing in and identity—are exposed for investigation which would have gone unquestioned or been simplistically understood. To stage a drama is to intervene in the circuit of life and to build a model of it which disturbs life even as we find it conforming to the model. To try to attain an utterly detached view of ourselves is to try to remove ourselves from ourselves; it is to try to play God. The guiding hypothesis of the book from this point through the remainder of Part One is that when we project a "world" of persons as staged and fictional, hence as other, we achieve sufficient distance to give what is habitually so close to us, and so much our own, a revealing presence and intelligibility— presence as presence. We excavate ourselves. We cannot ascertain the limits of this approach until we have pushed it as far as it will go.

Two hundred years ago Kant wrote,

> When Galileo let balls of a particular weight, which he had determined himself, roll down an inclined plane, or Torricelli made the air carry a weight, which he had previously determined to be equal to that of a definite volume of water; or when, in later times, Stahl changed metal into lime, and lime again into metal, by withdrawing and restoring something, a new light flashed on all students of nature. They comprehended that reason has insight into that only which she herself produces on her own plan, and that she must move forward with the principles of her judgments, according to fixed law, and compel nature to answer her questions, but not let herself be led by nature, as it were in leading strings. . . .[38]

Now, I find this very valuable, but our approach must be understood as carrying a wing that involves it much more intimately in existence than did Kant's. His *Critique of Pure Reason* had committed him to the distinction between phenomenal and noumenal selves, and to the view that only science gives us reliable knowledge of objects. Hence despite the brilliance and ingenuity in his later philosophy of art, he had radically limited the domain in which he could work. For him, art is the unpredictable synthesis of imagination and understanding (without the aid of concepts of objects) which gives us some sense of the ultimate fitness and purposiveness of things in the world, but nothing definite, and nothing

38. Immanuel Kant, Introduction to *Critique of Pure Reason*, 2nd ed., trans. Max Muller, in *Kant: Selections*, ed. T. M. Greene (New York: C. Scribner's Sons, 1957), p. 12.

that can be pinned down scientifically. I believe we should allow the possibility that art can tell us more about who we are.

But in the spirit both of Kant and of Vico we can formulate this hypothesis: as science is the theory of technology in the broadest sense—or what we must suppose about objects if we would understand how our techniques for inquiring into them could possibly grasp them—so theatre, philosophically understood, is the theory of acting and identity—or what we must suppose about persons if we would understand how it is possible for them to be convincingly projected and enacted on the stage. In sum: to recreate the world in a "world" of theatrical imagination makes us aware of conditions of the world's being and meaningfulness that had before lain in the obscurity of the "taken for granted."

CHAPTER VI

Theatre as Metaphor and Play as Disclosure

What sort of reality has Shakespeare's character Hamlet? One can point him out right there on the stage, and the question seems perfectly simple. But the danger is that a putative reference will be achieved at too great cost—a cost one does not perceive. One may think that he has achieved this reference, but it will have been sought in such a way as to mask out the context which makes the act of reference possible, and which gives the referent itself the significance without which it cannot *be* itself.

The ontological question about Hamlet is easily misleading. It presupposes that whatever reality Hamlet has, it must be that of a demonstrable particular thing. Addressing it as such we find, however, only a particular actor speaking words someone else has written and apparently pretending to be someone he is not. Hence we are tempted to conclude that only the actor is real, and that the enacted character is unreal, for we cannot suppose that there is more than one real being on the stage, and given a choice between the actor and the character, we must surely pick the actor.

William James spoke of the psychologist's fallacy as the substitution of what the observing psychologist takes to be the causal source in the "external world" of a thought for what the thought itself thinks about the world, just as it thinks it in its full context of sense. It is the fruit of an obsession for locating the referent, and it is part of a strongly felt need to secure the foundations of natural science against the threat of solipsism. This threat hangs in the air of modern philosophy. The thinker who commits the psychologist's fallacy will sacrifice everything to establish the existence of particulars in the "external world"—however impoverished the sense that remains to them—which are "rigidly designated" as referents by proper locutions of reference.

An instance of this fallacy is to suppose that all one directly perceives when one hears a grouse in the bushes is the "whirring of its motor." Here we suppose that all that Hamlet could be is what could be touched there by us. But we saw that the observer in the audience could not in principle touch Hamlet, but could only touch the actor playing him, for if he rushed onto the stage he would destroy the production of the play, and Hamlet as an element of the production. If we avoid the unwarranted inference that the character is therefore nothing, and if we reflect that another actor while enacting his character could—if the play calls for it—touch Hamlet, then we see that the character has its reality only within the "world" of the play.

But there can be a play only within a theatre, and a theatre only within the world; and so we must see the character within these nesting spheres if we would see him at all. The "world" he is in, and the world that contains the theatre in which this "world" is enacted, are condensed in our perceptions of the character as we sit in the theatre. We see neither Richard Burton alone nor Hamlet alone, but Burton-as-Hamlet. Thus we do not place Hamlet directly in our world when we see him enacted, yet we are returned to our world as it is mediated to us by Hamlet's "world," and it is a world newly illuminated and newly experienceable by us.

So we see that the character cannot be without his full context, which includes the actor within the world enacting the character within his "world." Now, I do not believe that we can experience any being as being what it is unless we experience it in its world, because it cannot *be* unless it is thus experienceable in its world.[1] So the character cannot be unless he is placed within his "world" and this cannot be unless it is included in the world. But, since the theory I will develop is that world and "world" are related essentially metaphorically, world cannot be meaningful unless it is related to the "world" of the theatre. Thus, for *us* to be it is necessary to understand ourselves in part in terms of the "world" of the theatre— and of other cultural and artistic works.

It would follow, then, that the character Hamlet is real just insofar as we constitute ourselves by experiencing ourselves and speaking about ourselves through him—both as stage actors and as audience, or life actors; that is, when we experience ourselves and speak about ourselves through the proxy of Hamlet. The character's reality is a function of our own reality as playing, experimenting, self-knowing beings. So it is futile to try to locate the character Hamlet in a quasi-Platonic domain which hovers there in the light of the stage in front of us for a few hours— as if in epiphany—a merely diverting spectacle. Hamlet is not an art ob-

1. I am here simply assuming the validity of this Kantian and post-Kantian point.

ject at all, but is ourselves speaking to ourselves about our essential possibilities.

Aristotle defined metaphor as the application of a thing's name to something else which resembles that thing in certain ways. This definition has drawbacks: it presupposes that all metaphors are names, that in every case the name refers in a literal sense to something else, and that the literal sense is a clear and obvious matter. For us, however, characters enacted onstage are not verbal but physiognomic metaphors; we *see* and *feel* them to be like ourselves. And it is not true that there is always an adequate literal way to refer to the persons or things in the offstage world which are referred to metaphorically by the characters onstage. The whole point of art is to put us in touch with things that are too far or too close for us to see in our ordinary offstage life. We said that Hamlet is not an art object at all, but is ourselves speaking to ourselves about our essential possibilities. For both Hamlet and ourselves our possibilities do not exist for us in our isolation, but in our relationships to others, particularly to those who are our source.

Thus it is blinding to dismiss ghosts as either fanciful or dead metaphors. Because it may be only when literal meanings of the word "father" have been *destroyed*—or an habitual encasement of appearances shattered—and the perception of the father drawn into conjunction metaphorically with the fantastic idea of ghost, that one can *first see* what has pulled him or repulsed him in the face of his actual father. Even a dead father's presence can haunt one. In crucial instances the actual can be represented revealingly only when it is re-presented through the fictional. All reference is through sense and connotation, and it is just the destruction by artistic fiction of habitual lineaments of connotation that clears our gaze and redirects it so that hitherto concealed aspects and relations of the referent first click into view. The real is conducted to us through the irreal, or through the surreal, or through the supernatural.

It is said that Shakespeare himself played the ghost. This but adds emphasis to what we can already discern: the deepest motive power of the play is the relationship between Hamlet and his father, and if the "small" part of the father's ghost is not played with convincing force the play cannot generate momentum. To play the ghost today is to be faced with a greater artistic problem than that which confronted Shakespeare. How does one play the part with any integrity in an age that finds it almost impossible to entertain in any way the presence of the supernatural? The actors playing the parts depend upon one another. If the actor playing the ghost simply tries to terrify the actor playing Hamlet through some "supernatural quality," we will get camp and bathos. But if the mimetic bond linking fathers and sons is really tapped by them in the presence of witnesses, this is enough to make the flesh crawl; numinous power is released in the twentieth century. The actor playing the ghost stands open to the son's fear and love of him. He finds himself as the feared, loved one who is Hamlet's father—he finds himself as the ghost. A weird presence is released in the room.

Later, when Hamlet doubts whether this supernatural presence was his father's ghost, still he is mimetically involved and fused with his father, albeit invertedly. We intuit this directly, before all predication, because Hamlet stands in proxy for ourselves. As the father's life has already been cut away from the son's, so the son experiences his own life as cut away from himself. In effect, he experiences himself as having already died. He droops. Hamlet's mother tells him,

> Do not forever with thy veiled lids
> Seek for thy noble father in the dust.

Most of us do not believe that ghosts are actual beings. Hence to see a ghost enacted is to witness something which is obviously metaphorical. It must be pointed out immediately, however, that *all* enactment is physiognomic metaphor, obvious or not. For example, Burton is not an actual prince named Hamlet, and we are aware of this in the theatre; otherwise we would not be aware of the enactment, of the fact that it is an artistic event. Burton enacts Hamlet through displaying behaviors and bearings which are merely similar to his. He is like the character (in certain respects) who proves to be like ourselves (again, in certain respects).

Oddly enough, through experiencing the differences intrinsic to the metaphors we best see the linking resemblances, because the differences break the hardened shells of association within which the resemblances habitually slide by unnoticed in the everyday world. Resemblances become thematic through being seen to hold despite the differences. The fact that the actor is not the character and the character is not ourselves allows this recognition of kinship to occur. The detachment of theatre, its aesthetic distance, reveals our involvement. If resemblances between persons disclosed by art prove inescapable in life, then essential characteristics of human beings are revealed.

It must follow that enactment as metaphor is at the same time fictive variation. For example, the relatively invariable meaning of being a dispossessed son—as is Hamlet—is revealed through variations in enactments by actors who need not themselves be dispossessed sons. It is not necessary to enact a "far-out" character such as a ghost to achieve a physiognomic metaphor which is a fictive variation. All enactment breaks out of the constrictions of the literal and the actual and adumbrates far-flung but fundamental segments of the meaning of the literal and the actual. The meaning-giving context is revived.

It must follow as well that enactment is a playing which is serious; it belongs to the playfulness of experimentation. We try out physiognomic models and metaphors until we produce those into which our own natures fit; we discover our measure. In the three plays that comprise the second set of variations on the theme of standing in and authorization we witness experimentation of such a vivid, free, and imaginative sort as to be almost explicitly phenomenological: the plays of Ionesco, Wilson, and Grotowski. We will prepare for this section by deepening our theory of enactment already sketched; through developing the connection between the encounter of audience and actors which constitutes the physiognomic metaphor of enactment; and by relating this to fictive variation, playing, and incarnated thought experiments.

Paul Claudel has given these illuminating lines to a character in his *L'échange* who is an actor sensing his audience:

> I glance at them, and the hall is nothing but living flesh which they inhabit.
> . . .
> They listen to me and think what I say; they look at me and I enter into their soul as into a vacant building.[2]

The dominant experience is that of felt possession. One possesses the other and returns to himself through him. There is a process, a rhythm, a doing with which the audience member identifies—an ongoing internally developmental quality quite distinct from any experiencing of something "out there" as an "objective state of affairs." In the moment of creation, and in that of appreciation, there is no actuality or possibility "seen" as an object of a mental act; it is possibility luring us within us. Henri Gouhier adds, speaking for a member of the audience,

> The actor does not see me, but he sees this hall in which I figure. The actor does not think of me, but he thinks of that being without a face which derives from my face a bit of its substance. I am not anyone in particular for him; I am, however, not nothing: we live one through the other.[3]

The intimate relationship between actor and auditor is not a face-to-face encounter, but a presence in a "mask" indwelling a presence "without a face." It is an anonymous indwelling and proxy standing in, but nevertheless intimate, for this very anonymity allows the sharing of secrets that a face-to-face encounter would discourage or make impossible. The actor onstage creates a "space of complicity."[4]

2. Quoted in Henri Gouhier, *L'essence du Theatre*, Nouvelle edition (Paris: Aubier-Montaigne, 1968), p. 26. Translation is mine.
3. Ibid.
4. Ibid., p. 20.

Gouhier points out that it is just because the everyday self is permanently installed at what it feels to be "the center" of the world experienced by it that it is oblivious to its most characteristic and habitual modes of action. These are really mimetic. One is already an other for others who has been formed by others, so he cannot be that center which is in itself and for itself as he feels himself to be (I expound now freely on Gouhier). One exists on a periphery of mimetic fusion with others which remains unilluminated for him for two reasons, first, because this periphery is so constant and contrastless that it remains unnoticed—only when we observe another culture are its lines of mimetic fusion clearly evident—and, second, because the distinctiveness of the person's bodily position and bodily point of view convinces one of one's distinctiveness as a self. True, one's body tends to vanish in the objects of its concern, but it is just because one *must* presuppose it to be distinctive even when one has no focal consciousness of it that its mimetic parroting of others so completely eludes one's attention.

At the theatre I cease to vanish from myself through a delusive "center." I am "supernumerary," "at the periphery," hence free to follow another's action as a character "with all my soul." The actor stands in for me. At the periphery I sense myself as "that sort there." When most intense, we sense the limits and contours of the self with a quasi-religious awe; we sense our secret, mimetic self fleshed out in the guise of the other. Concomitantly, we feel our everyday sense of individual identity to be threatened. In the face of mimetic attraction and fusion, our previously unwitting assumptions about individual identity are now ignited *as* assumptions merely.

To be sure, theatre is usually dramatic, i.e., desiring, acting persons—characters—encounter obstacles to their desires and actions. It is these obstacles that test and expose the characters' mettle, expose the "roles" they are playing, and who they are. But equally truly, this dramatic element falls within the reality of the mimetic—the domain within which we identify. The obstacle is the character's *own* obstacle. Opponents belong to each other, and, as Nietzsche said, we become dependent upon our opponents. Or, to use the formulation of Heraclitus, things which oppose each other fit each other. Moreover, we in the audience identify with these confrontations: these are *our* conflicts—or ones which might be ours. We resonate in mimetic attunement.

To understand more fully how theatre is an experimental procedure for uncovering mimetic fusion we must better understand the being without a face, the corporate identity which is the audience. The director during rehearsal and the audience during performance participate in the creation of the "world" from the side of the world. They do not enact characters, they are dressed in street clothes, and they conform to conventions for behavior in public places. They bring from the world their mimetic fusions, modes of being with others which are tacit and normally unthematizable by the participants.[5] It is as if persons were playing games, but with the odd characteristic that they cannot articulate the rules of the game. Each culture and subculture is distinguished, for example, by tacit rules of approach to others in space—say, rules of approach to parents. What is too close for comfortable and effective communication in one culture is just right for another. A movement must mean something regardless of whether the person moving can define it. It is a "silent language," and we are inducted into it unwittingly, and perform according to its dictates unacknowledgeably.[6]

The audience comprises a passive community bound up in its fusions. It is faceless in the sense that the individuality of each person no longer casts such a glare that the mimetic and communal periphery need remain hidden. This is the case for the director and his assistants much of the time and for the audience at the performance all of the time. There is a significant element of truth when Claudel's actor says he enters into the soul of the audience as into a vacant building, but we must not take the word vacant literally, for the mimetic life of the community is there waiting to be called into presence on the stage. Now how is this presence evoked?

At the focus of the experiment—but it is only the focus—stand the actors. As artists and persons they also stand in the world and participate in the world's fusions, but as artists who play characters they participate in the "world" and its relationships. All play involves limitation. When a child or an animal bites in play, for example, it is not that it does not bite, but that it places limits on the bite that it makes.[7] When an actor plays a character he not only limits himself in the obvious ways (for example, when the "world" of the play calls for the character to hit another character the actor playing him stops short of actually hurting the other actor), but also in the more fundamental sense that he attempts to determine the limits that apply to the character as character, not just to the actor who plays him. The two limitings are related, of course. To limit himself as actor creates a sanctuary in which we dare to explore the outer limits of behavior as character. The actor as artist attempts to determine

5. Michael Polanyi, *The Tacit Dimension* (New York: Doubleday Anchor Books, 1967).

6. Edward Hall, *The Silent Language* (Garden City, New York: Doubleday & Co., 1959). The discerning reader will see that phenomenology as I practice it allows cross-fertilization with structuralism, e.g., with the work of Claude Lévi-Strauss. Another book would be required to spell out this connection, however.

7. Cf. Gregory Bateson, "A Theory of Play and Fantasy," *Psychiatric Research Reports*, no. 2 (1955), pp. 39–51.

just what it is that he as character cannot at each moment know, and dares not at each moment do.

Here the director and the audience must make a contribution to the search for the character's limits. For though the actor while playing always exists in a dual capacity, as artist and as character, he is necessarily so involved in the character that his abilities as artist to objectify him are limited. We in the audience are able to experience simultaneously both what the characters want and do and know *and* their total situation in their "world" which lies beyond the limits of their comprehension, so immersed in that "world" are they. They act within limits; working with the actors we seek to become aware of the limits within which they act. We are looking for limits that have been laid down undeliberately by the characters. Both in rehearsal and in performance the director, and others in the audience, assist the actor as he attempts to feel his way to occluded limits and mimetic involvements that cannot be within his consciousness as character. Only when they lie tentatively within the margins of his consciousness as artist can he abandon himself as character within them and allow an unpredictable surge of life to emerge through them. Neither we in the audience nor the actors are able to predict this surge of life in all its aspects, for it emerges from connections and a context which is precisely other than the agent (the character) can thematize; and the actor as artist has begun to put his fingers only on the boundaries of the character's life, not the uninsulated contents which fire off in the character's ignorance.

But once the surge of life occurs between the characters, we in the audience will either confirm or disconfirm it. For after all, it is just our common life, the mimetic organism of the community, that the actors attempt to pull out of us and into the focus of the experiment so that it can be recognized by us all at an aesthetic distance. When the enactment of our common mimetic being is correct, we rush into it as would inchoate material into a chamber under vacuum. A deep silence signals the recognition of that silent language which persons who are bodies learn mimetically from one another. Together with the actors we alienate ourselves as characters so that we can return to ourselves as persons.[8] Hamlet is ourselves speaking to ourselves about our essential possibilities.

Joseph Chaikin, actor and director, has said some perceptive things about the elusive and crucial matter of the presence of the actor:

> This "presence" on the stage is a quality given to some and absent from others. All of the history of the theatre refers to actors who possess this "presence."

8. Of related interest, see Albert Hofstadter's valuable essays in *Agony and Epitaph* (New York: G. Braziller, 1970).

It's a quality that makes you feel as though you're standing right next to the actor, no matter where you're sitting in the theatre. At the Berliner Ensemble Ekkehard Schall possesses such a quality. Some other actors with very different approaches than Schall who possess it are Ryszard Cieslak, Kim Stanley, Ruth White, and Gloria Foster. There may be nothing of this quality offstage or in any other circumstance in the life of such an actor. It's a kind of deep libidinal surrender which the performer reserves for his anonymous audience.[9]

In the experiment of theatre, the great actor can allow himself to be possessed erotically. He lives vicariously and others live vicariously through him. The actor lends his body and soul to use by the community: its exploration of actual and possible types of personal and interpersonal existence.

To articulate fusion and engulfment, the actor allows an artistically controlled engulfment with the audience to occur. As they feed off his characterization, he feeds off their passivity, their fusing, *and* their objectivity in regard to the character before them. His artistry consists in maintaining a precarious balance between abandonment to archaic fusion authorized by the audience, and artistic control of what enactment is allowed. He permits himself to be possessed erotically by his "anonymous" audience, but only within an artistic setting in which what escapes him and what escapes them can add up dialectically to revelation concerning the organic life of their interpersonal being. The deepest involuntary impulses and currents of fusion yield themselves up *as* such only through the most delicate probings of the art. There is an element of artifice in the art. The actor is "a presence in a mask indwelling a presence without a face." The "mask" is the character, the work of the art; it seeks to become the face of the corporate body. The slightest movement of the head, for example, evoked in a passing moment of rehearsal, is seized by the artist because it is that speck of material around which a whole scene, possibly the whole characterization, begins to crystalize. The artist touches things in such a way that the next moment he can keep his hands off them. Let us vary the metaphor. Creating a work of art is like exploring an organism while living inside it. We touch various organs and then await a response; we go on from there.

"The I is an other," said the poet Rimbaud, and here is a key if anything is. It is not merely others who present themselves to me and make their presence felt by me, but for me to be, my own presence must be felt by me. And it is a presence which is already modeled mimetically on others, although in the natural course of events one will tend not to realize this

9. Joseph Chaikin, *The Presence of the Actor* (New York: Atheneum, 1972), p. 20.

(assuming, contrary to fact, that art is not a part of the natural course of events). I do not experience my identity within a space-less, self-illuminating point which is the center of my world and which is myself, although I may uncritically think I do. When I actually encounter myself there is a shock of de-centeredness. I come upon myself as one who is already underway, already "out there," already speaking a public language, and already shaped by attitudes and practices common to my fellows. I find myself, not always happily, "playing a part." The theatre has long ago embedded itself deep in everyday life in the form of this metaphor which has burnt out and lost its fire and life; but there it lies, impacted like a meteor, both at and under the surface of life.

We seek to revive the question of the powers of theatrical metaphors by seeking first to revive the question of the powers of theatre itself as metaphor. We are experimenting with the idea of theatre as experimentation: an experimental construction of physiognomic models or metaphors which either command our recognition or do not. We have completely avoided "theories of expression." For far too long such theories have been forced upon the actor and the theatre like procrustean beds which fit the facts by mutilating them first. It is to the actor's work that we must go if we would understand that knife edge of delicacy, that strange reciprocity of abandonment and control, upon which pivots the metaphorical relation of "world" and world. Through this approach we are trying to understand how the "world" of the theatre event is set back into the world that contains the theatre as an institution, and in all that "world's" inventiveness and ideality institutes the preservation for our comprehension of what would ordinarily fly by in the world uncomprehended.[10] "World" mediates, in part, our commerce with world, and we must leave open the possibility that we compose our art in response to our deepest need to compose ourselves. We leave open the possibility that art and self are com-posed.

It is next to impossible for any theory of expression to be adequate, because the concept of expression distorts or begs every fundamental question. Expression connotes ex-pression: that something already exists inside the self and gets pushed or pressed outside. But this naive dialectic implies that the self in turn is inside the world—*innerweitlich*—like a marble in a barrel or a stone in a stream. Expression is supposed to be an event in which the inside is pressed outside that inside. And this implies that we can know the world independently of knowing what will come out of the inside as artistic expression. From this point onward the inquiry is hopelessly poisoned, and the study of art must be relegated to being one

---

10. Cf. Martin Heidegger, "The Origin of the Work of Art," in *Philosophies of Art and Beauty*, ed. Hofstadter and Kuhns (New York: Random House, 1964).

of the frills of philosophy which can be dissected analytically into component strands to let dry in the breeze.

Even theories of expression which have something to teach us assume that we can know the world independently of grasping its nature as artistically expressed; they do not grasp the epistemological parity of "world" and world and the *essentially* metaphorical relationship which links them in our experience; hence what these theories have to teach us is sharply limited in value. Take for example the idea that a musical line which falls in a certain way is expressive of dejection because it is similar to the falling line of ordinary speech that typically expresses dejection.[11]

But "ordinary speech" is really extraordinary; it is not a response to dejection in the way that the jerk of the knee is a response to the tapping of a hammer on the knee. Vico and Shelley have asserted what seems to be true: that ordinary speech arose from—and still retains the marks of—cries and expressions which are metaphorical in the sense that they mean, because they are intimately similar to, and indeed enmeshed in and integral to, a whole gamut of behavior typical of a situation. Thus ordinary speech (though not necessarily every bit of it) is art-like, and it is in addition influenced by the art of the culture—fine, applied, and ritual. Hence ordinary speech which is advanced as an explanation of the expressive power of music can supply no foundation, but presupposes the domain of expressivity which it would explain. It is just as worldly as is music. There is no more reason to explain ordinary language by music than music by ordinary language.

The same critical reasoning applies when we try to use human physiognomy as the *proton analogon*, the base line for explanation which is supposedly independent of all artistic and artistic-like concerns. It seems to be an elemental truth that our perceptual life is anthropomorphic. For example, we cannot see a bassett hound's face without seeing it as if it were a human face, and one that is expressive of dejection. There is an important element of truth here but it is limited. Humans do not have their emotional states in the same way that a substance has properties. No matter how "absorbed" one is in his emotional states, and in their typical bodily "expressions," he still takes an attitude toward them, so cannot be literally absorbed in them, identical with them. As Heidegger will say, and as Grotowski will exemplify, each emotion and mood has its mode of understanding and interpretation. One allows himself to be "ab-

11. Note the distinction between "expression," which connotes an actual state of dejection manifested in ordinary speech, and my use here of "expressive of" which need not connote this. It is essential to the ideality and presencing power of art that the emotion of which art is the expression need not in fact be present in the artist at the time of the art's composition. I am indebted to a talk given by Professor Peter Kivy at Rutgers, February 13, 1978, in which he outlined a theory of expression.

sorbed"; one allows the world, and himself in it, to be given presence in this way. It is not the case that the world is solid fact and that the "world" is mere fantasy. We must leave open the possibility that the world in which our bodies move is theatre-like.

For human reality, the apparently basic distinction which divides the natural from the conventional and the cultural seems to be simplistic, if not sophistical. A person is not in space in the way that a marble is in a barrel or a match is in a box; the way the person is in space is a cultural, interpretive, interpersonal—and in part—an artistic and artistic-like matter. So we cannot simply check the artistic rendering of X onstage against X offstage to see how the likeness of the former to the latter renders it expressive of it. *The "world" in which* X *appears onstage is a world phenomenon, and this "world" aims to be a key to the nature of the world.*

Theatre's fictive variations are incarnated thought experiments. Factual considerations are bracketed out in such a way that the *sorts* of human *involvements* can be revealed. The main problem for any thought experiment is to be able to imagine what would *really* happen—not to come up with just any fantastic construction. The aim of theatre is to put us in touch with the essence of what really happens in human relationships. What is varied only by the individual in a detached manner in his own mind in Husserl's fictive variation is enacted bodily in the theatre for all of us. In theatre it is not just a bracketing in of the act, as we bracket out factual considerations, but a bracketing in of the act *in act*. As philosophers we vary in our imaginations the manner in which one person can strike another, for example. When we believe that the variations can proceed no farther along the various parameters of striking, then we must believe that these limits of variation demarcate the essence of striking. The theatre, on the other hand, bodies forth quite literally our imagining of one character's striking another. Of course, the striking is not actual in the full sense of that term. The swing of the actor stops short of its target, so it is fictive in a somewhat different sense from Husserl's fictive variation.

No doubt, even though fictions are employed in both cases, theatre's attempt to reveal involvement in the world through involvement in the "world" must disturb the world more than does the philosopher's thought experiment conducted from his armchair, alone in his room. This raises serious problems concerning the truth of theatre as art which we must confront. And yet the difference should not be exaggerated, for the audience certainly imagines—one should say perceptually imagines—that one *character* has been hit by the other. A similar effect is achieved in the armchair, but without the surprises of physiognomic disclosure, and one might say that the act of sitting in the armchair is a way of pulling one's punches.

Ultimately we must ask: So theatre's play must limit itself to be play and to be revealing; now what does this limitation conceal? But we must not ask this question before it is clear what theatre appears to reveal, for appearances are not easily grasped. Nor must we ask it in a way that simply assumes that theatre is not an essential metaphor and that we can grasp ourselves in the world perfectly well without any reference either to it or to its conceptual relatives in ordinary talk and experience.

We sit in the theatre. The play occurs in that illuminated stage setting before us. What do we experience? Most vividly, it is space, contracted into the stage or into the set, which bursts forth in meaningfulness. While classical geometry is the attempt to abstract completely from the human qualities of spatial being, theatre is just the attempt to "locate" these by contracting around them. Able to see the characters in space, and to participate mimetically and identifyingly in their seeing of things in their space, we in the audience can also detect the nature and limits of their seeing and doing in space. We can see what they—and we—are ordinarily too absorbed to see outside the theatre, namely that being-in-space is a function of absorbed concern in things and people in space and a function of all the assumptions and prejudices that govern this concern. We are, then, creatures of distances, even when it is only a matter of gaining a distance on our absorptions. A desert dweller has written of the discovery of "something intimate—though impossible to name—in the remote."[12] This does not altogether defy explanation: the more profound the distance made one's own, the more profound the de-distancing, and this is to be most intimately oneself. One is a function of one's powers of giving presence to the world. Theatre contracts around these powers in the form of the "powers" of "selves" onstage so as to be able to reveal the conditions of the powers whenever and wherever they may be.

The roles great actors play can break us free from our "roles" offstage so that we can see aspects and limits of these "roles" that we had not previously seen. The momentary transformation may become a long-term one. Take an actress playing Ophelia to an actor's playing her father, Polonius. Granted, it is a fiction in certain fundamental ways; for example, the young woman enacting the older man's daughter is not necessarily his daughter offstage. We see this possibility as a part of seeing her enact the daughter onstage. In contingent fact she is not his daughter, but how about in essence? Note the way I use "in essence": to refer to one's potentialities as a particular (say, sexed) member of the species human. Now, while the woman has no potentiality to be *this* man's daughter, she does have the potentiality to more deeply realize through acting with him what the potentialities of being *a* daughter are; thus devolves upon her the potentiality

12. Edward Abbey, *Desert Solitaire: A Season in the Wilderness* (New York: Ballantine Books, 1968), p. 45.

of altering what she *is* as a daughter. As Aristotle, Hegel, and others have
seen, the mission of art parallels for a certain distance that of philosophy:
to grasp the universal in the particular. Within the frame of the theatre,
where there can be no enactment without typification and generalization,
the particular human, either actor or member of the audience, stands open
to a revealing restructuring of his humanity, a restructuring to which he
allows free experimental play for the moment.

I wish to suggest that when theatre's restraints free it from some of the
restraints of everyday life, it can do something to shake free the essential
woman-as-daughter, as perhaps both she and we want her and dream her
to be and possibly—now!—could be. I suggest that theatre shakes us free
from mere contingency, from triviality as well as from accident, for example, the fact that the actress's actual father may have died when she was
an infant. Perhaps the seeds of the woman's potentialities as person and
daughter—unthematizable as they have hitherto been—may bloom only
as something to which all can relate, as an archetype of a human relational
reality, and may first be shaken loose for growth only in an enacted fiction;
in that setting where we need not be afraid and defensive or at a loss for
appropriate behaviors. The suggestion is that the real self of the actress is
mediated to some extent by the fiction she enacts; it is not merely her
professional reputation that is affected by the fiction. Likewise the selves
in the audience are mediated by the fiction she enacts. We can confront
afresh the issue of what it means for us to be sons and daughters.

The deepest prejudices are ontological ones—commitments to the nature of the real. The largely unquestioned prejudice today is that reality
is only what is observable from a third-person point of view, that is,
thoroughly objectifiable and measurable entities or events. This must prejudice us against our own reality, for we are the beings that idealize and
fantasize and that exist in others' fantasies and idealizations concerning
us. Theatre is an attempt to fantasize in a way that breaks the encrusted
grip of fantasies and exposes them. We would be restored to our freedom.

André Breton's delineation of surrealism has a general significance for
art:

> Everything tends to make us believe that there exists a certain point of the
> mind at which life and death, the real and the imagined, past and future, the
> communicable and the incommunicable, high and low, cease to be perceived
> as contradictions. Now, search as one may one will never find any other
> motivating force in the activities of the Surrealists than the hope of finding
> and fixing this point.[13]

13. André Breton, *Manifestoes of Surrealism* (Ann Arbor: University of Michigan Press,
1972), pp. 123–24.

This crucial insight should be augmented by Francis H. Bradley's "On Floating Ideas and the Imaginary": no idea of fantasy or imagination "floats free" as an element of unreal content in a particular mind; no such idea is simply negated and excluded by reality.

> Can we speak of the Universe as being merely real or as being merely imaginary? Is it not on the other hand plain that such a distinction falls within the Universe?
>   There is not on one side a single "real" world of fact and on the other side a single world that I call "imaginary." On the contrary a man has . . . an indefinite plurality of worlds.[14]

A person has a domain of imagination that is linked to empirical existence—and forms a structure of his reality—even when in the full light of consciousness it is actively excluded from empirical fact.

> The star that I desire does not wander outcast and naked in the void. My heart is drawn to it because it inhabits that heaven which is felt at once to be its own and mine.
>   In the end and taken absolutely . . . there can be no mere idea. Reality is always before us, and every idea in some sense qualifies the real. So far as excluded it is excluded only from some limited region, and beyond that region has its world. To float, in the absolute sense, is impossible. Flotation means attachment to another soil. . . .[15]

Theatre is play which is in earnest. Insofar as its very existence depends upon keeping it insulated from the appearance of empirical fact, it is play. But insofar as it occurs within the actual world, and requires actual agents, and illuminates and redefines empirical fact in its very exclusion from it, it is earnest. It is both and neither. Theatre is its own category.

Bradley maintained that play need not always involve make-believe but that it always involves limitation, which frees it from the constraints of empirical fact. To use our example, a play bite is a bite, but one that limits itself in order to articulate itself; in order to articulate a context or a "world" for itself. An ordinary bite stuns or terrifies, and in one way or another limits or destroys the full context of its intelligibility. In their correspondence, Bernard Bosanquet objected that play always involves make-believe.

> [P]lay which is to refresh or distract the mind, must possess the make-believe that it is earnest. While you feel play or amusement to be mere play or amusement, i.e., not to matter, they do not . . . take you out of your self, that is,

14. Francis H. Bradley, "On Floating Ideas and the Imaginary," in *Essays on Truth and Reality* (Oxford: The Clarendon Press, 1914), pp. 44–45.
15. Ibid., pp. 35–36.

do not effectively amuse or recreate. . . . In short, to be well amused . . . you must think you are taking the thing seriously, though you must not really take it seriously.[16]

This is a point, but the key phrases "make-believe that it is earnest" and "think you are taking the thing seriously, though you must not really take it seriously" require analysis. One suspects there is paradox because the proper level of analysis has not been achieved.

The germ for resolution suggests itself in Bosanquet's next paragraph: "I suppose the sense that some pursuit which interests us very much at the moment has little value ultimately, is found all through life, and constitutes no sharp division between play and earnest." I would reconstruct this as follows. Make-believe is always involved in the theatre, but only to the extent that the artist makes-believe for himself as character that the only time that matters is the time in which the character exists in his "world." Even if the character is depicted as anticipating his own imminent death, for example, it is just now—in that "world's" time—that he is doing it. Unknown to him, factors may be at work within that "world" which will prevent that death from occurring. The actor as artist brackets out from his consciousness as character the full span of world-time that as artist he knows pertains to everything, and which contains the total time of the play's "world."

So his activity as character is serious within the limits of time that he, as artist, has allotted to that character for his activity. This bracketing is a suspension of belief, as character, in what, as artist, he believes to be fully, factually the case. As artist he is playing in a certain way; as character he is serious in a certain way. All this can happen because as character the actor is not directly in the world as a separate individual (it is always the character-enacted-by-this-actor). Thus it is very tempting to say that, as Hamlet, Burton really does ask the other actor, as Horatio, what strange thing he has seen on the battlements. Just because as artist he knows what the other actor is going to reply is no reason, we are tempted to believe, to say that as character he does not really ask the other character. For if he did not really ask, the bracketing which can bring out the limits, conditions, and sense of one's really asking about such things would not do so, for there would be nothing there worth bracketing and revealing. We are further tempted to say "really ask" because actors spend many long and arduous hours learning to "really ask" and "really listen," etc.

But we must restrain ourselves, because the actor asks *as* the character. True, the actor does not cease to be a person, and as a person who is an

16. J. H. Muirhead, ed., *Bernard Bosanquet and His Friends* (London: George Allen & Unwin, 1953), pp. 173–175. I am indebted to Arther Smullyan for this reference.

artist he utilizes his own psychical acts and his own emotions—particularly during rehearsals—to give shape to the character. Through techniques such as emotion memory and sense memory the actor is trained to get in touch with his own emotions as a person. But these acts and emotions of his are always framed, in the margins of the actor's consciousness, by the communal act of imagination which is the artistic performance. These acts and emotions are "bracketed," cut off from a commitment to a factual state of affairs; they are idealized. If we simply say that the actor really asks we obliterate the distinction between artist and character, between world and "world," and between that unique mode of worldly activity which is artistic activity and other modes. We obliterate our own laboriously laid foundation.

There is some reason, however, to refer to artistic asking as super-real, surreal, as well as ideal. For in matters close to the heart and strange, it may be only within this artistic stance that we can be deeply serious. Without the bracketing out of fact we are too vulnerable or horrified to reveal ourselves at all; or we do not know, clearly enough to tell even ourselves, what there is to reveal. Offstage, we typically move just close enough to our presupposed limits and suppressions to sense, out of the corner of the eye, "move no further." In art we lay them bare, we believe, just because we are "only playing."

Theatre uses actual things and persons for its fictions and intervenes in the world in order to impose its frames upon it. To underscore this I will speak of it as a *de facto* phenomenological bracketing—through fictive variation—or as an aesthetic interruption. Martin Heidegger writes of absorption in—and in a real sense, obliteration by—everyday objects of our concern in their utilitarian connections:

> In this familiarity Dasein can lose itself in what it encounters within-the-world and be fascinated with it. . . . How can the worldly character of what is within-the-world be lit up? The presence-at-hand of entities is thrust to the fore by the possible breaks in the referential totality in which circumspection operates. . . .[17]

Theatre is aesthetic interruption of the referential totality. The artist interrupts absorption and displays it as such.

In *Being and Time* Heidegger attempted to reopen the question of reality, or being, and he assumed that the first step was to interrogate the nature of the being who asks the question of being—indeed, the being who throws its own being into question. He wished to develop a "hermeneutics of facticity," a way of interpreting human life which avoids all

17. Martin Heidegger, *Being and Time* (Oxford: Blackwell, 1962), p. 107.

assumptions concerning the nature of consciousness and the attendant assumption of subjects over against a world of objects. He believed he had discovered at least four conditions of life, basic potentialities of being human, which were not reducible to each other or to anything else—the ontologicals, the *existentialia*. They function as do categories. To deny that they aply to persons would be not so much false as absurd, for they are definitive of persons: language, being with others, projection of possibility, and mood.

As a part of our effort to test the idea that an enactment is convincing only because through its fictions it condenses conditions of human being and behavior offstage into perceivable patterns, I will show how the four contemporary plays we examine reveal these same categorial conditions and potentialities. We have already seen that *Waiting for Godot* is a language in which the limits of verbal language are revealed. As given presence by the play in its theatre, language is a background structure more fundamental than any clockable span of verbalization, or even such a span of silence. It is this "giving presence" itself; it is an accumulating background that makes it possible for us to pick out stretches of meaningful silence. Not just any stretch of silence is meaningful, is language. So we must say (and we will henceforth capitalize this use of the word): as to Language— the ontological or categorial characteristic concerning human potentiality—either it is verbal language, which is one factual realization of the potentiality, or it is nonverbal, the other factual realization of the potentiality. We project a world in Language, whether it takes sounding or silent forms. This ontological characteristic must be presupposed by all factual or empirical inquiries, so it cannot be established by them. Indeed, so fundamental and unshakable is this ontological characteristic that we can understand the possibility of the language-less and the meaningless (assuming the actuality of any such pure state) only on the foundation of Language: it is a privative form of Language, its absence.

Now, by itself this parallel to Heidegger cannot establish that theatre reveals conditions of human being, for we have not established that Heidegger's account of these conditions is correct. And it is not until Part Two that we confirm Heidegger when we develop a theory of the conditions of human identity which is independent both of his account and of any reference to theatre *per se*. But bringing in Heidegger here helps to focus our phenomenological investigations of the plays and prompts us to look for things that we would not otherwise have imagined to be relevant.

We will offer three more variations on the essential theatrical theme of standing in and authorization, with the analysis now augmented by the Heideggerian strand. We examine contemporary plays which speak directly to us of our contemporary world, and which display vividly the conditions of their possibility as plays. They offer us a particularly good chance to see whether the conditions of the imaginative projection of "persons" or characters overlap with the conditions of our possibility as persons. They offer us a "mirror" in which we may be able to make discoveries about ourselves. The final variation will be followed by a preliminary discussion of the question of theatrical art and truth.

In sum, theatre is physiognomic metaphor. Being this it is also aesthetic interruption, incarnated thought experiments, *de facto* phenomenological bracketing and fictive variations—the phrases are interchangeable. In the play we next examine, Ionesco constructs a situation of extreme, absurdly extreme, isolation in which the presence of others is not only not eliminated, but intensified. The infrastructure of the play is a set of fictive variations in which the inescapability of the presence of others is revealed. As a whole, the play is but one variation on the theme of standing in and authorization. Into these "mirrors" we now look.

CHAPTER VII

Second Set of Variations on the Theatrical Theme of Standing In and Authorization

1. Eugene Ionesco and the Potentiality of Being-with-Others in "Roles"—Fallenness

To understand theatre it is necessary to understand the mating of playing and disclosure. One of the factors that entitles one to say that a certain current of contemporary theatre returns to the sources of the art, is the reappearance in it of the crude vitality of play. We think of the satyr-chorus gamboling in worship of Dionysus, and of how this formed a root of Attic tragedy. The burlesque-like routines of the characters in *Waiting for Godot* have been mentioned. This theatre's content includes a commentary upon its own possibility; it is theatre which theatricalizes the essence of theatre, and tragedy, comedy, and burlesque all have their turns. Surrealism is also an important element in Beckett, and even more centrally in the work of the "absurdist" Ionesco, and in that of Robert Wilson. We have already noted André Breton's delineation of surrealism as the domain of twilight and fusion which Nietzsche described under the rubric of the Dionysian. The role of play in communicating this in productions which are in some measure surrealistic must be explicated.

Some have seen the fantastical events of Ionesco's plays as merely a heightening and underlining of the absurdity in everyday life. No doubt the plays can be greatly appreciated on this level. But when they are, they are registered in only a portion of their spectrum: that of mere farce, or cruel farce. Ionesco accurately depicts his great opus *The Chairs* as tragic

111

farce, and it is—to vary the metaphor from visual to aural—the full undertones of the tragic that this aforementioned level of appreciation fails to hear. Beneath the chirping and carping foreground figures of farce is the somber base note of tragedy. This is what is difficult to understand by means of the methods typical either of contemporary literary criticism or of linguistic philosophy.

I believe that we can begin to understand it only when we concede the possibility—improbable as it seems *prima facie* given Ionesco's absurdist techniques—that he has uncovered some of the conditions of the experienceability of the world and of the identity of self through his absurdity and playfulness. This is what arrests us and fills us with the tragic hush. By such conditions I mean those limits of action and experience laid out in advance—"chosen" in a pre-deliberate and tragic manner—that impart intelligibility to a life in the world. These are the sources that the merely factually informed mind could never predict through induction or ordinary calculation, because they are tacitly presupposed by all that the empirical intellect knows and does.

To reduce something to absurdity is to carry it to the point at which the conditions of its recognizability emerge from the shadow of presupposition in which they are usually hidden. Through the obstacles to its recognition that the artists have placed in our path, we are forced to make the conditions of its recognizability focally present to consciousness. Differently put, the grotesque exaggerations of Ionesco's theatre are integral to an experiment of fictive variation which aims to reveal the normal conditions and limits of life through violating them one after the other, until something like a complete picture of the human situation emerges. These are the conditions of any self being for itself as self; of any selves being for each other as selves; of any selves being at all. This is theatre as phenomenology: it pushes the concept of human selfhood to the points where it breaks down; these points outline the concept.

The Chairs[1] strips things down to fundamentals. The characters are a ninety-five-year-old man and his ninety-four-year-old wife. They've reached the point—who could doubt it—of wanting to sum up their lives; at least the man has. They live in a large, bare, circular, windowed room of what is perhaps a lighthouse. The curtain opens on this room—empty, the windows open, lit with a dim blue light, as if the atmosphere of the whole world were circulating through it. For a minute or two no characters appear. Such thematization of space and time through denudation is typical of much contemporary theatre, and suggests a denudation of cultural forms; artists seem to be registering that shock in which they have found

1. All references to the play are to the English translations by Donald Allen in *Four Plays by Ionesco* (New York: Grove Press, 1958).

nearly all conventional theatrical forms and settings wanting, and in which they have been sent scurrying into the ground-conditions of any human life. At least the continuum of space-time remains and persons in it! Ionesco raises the question whether a life can be summed up and unified when it is no longer possible to view it through cultural forms which place one at the standpoint of the gods, under the aspect of eternity. In *The Chairs* the old persons attempt to render their lives coherent through memorializing them: they attempt to retrieve their lives and to project them toward an ideal in one single unifying movement. *The Chairs* is Ionesco's memorial to this attempted memorialization. He seeks a new cultural and artistic form in which the disintegration of culture can be thematized as such—contained as such, so reattached and rewoven in some way.

The old man hobbles onto the stage and goes to a window where he looks out with a small telescope. His wife enters and bids him come back before he falls out the window or catches a cold. The old man sits on his wife's lap and laments his misspent life. She consoles and mothers him while they recall with delight things they apparently did as children together. She is mother, wife, sister to him—lines of relationship are almost as tangled as they are in *Oedipus*, if we can but see them. Hope seizes him at certain junctures, and he declares that he has prepared his "message" for the world, his statement of his "mission." He has planned a party for old friends, we learn, at which the emperor will appear. An orator has also been invited who will be the old man's surrogate, and who will read his message to the group.

The perennial themes which we have been tracing in this book jump again into focus: the need to be authorized by a great authority, and the need for some person whose virtues will be imputed to one, and who will stand in for one and mediate between one and the authority. Tiresias leads Oedipus back to his affronted sources. Prince Hamlet must stand in for dead King Hamlet and mediate between him and the divine demands for justice. Scripture states that there is one mediator between God and man, the man Christ Jesus, etc.

We hear the distant sound of what may be a bell—is it the bell of the lighthouse or of a rolling buoy?—and the old man hastens with both glee and apprehension to open the door for the first guest. He lets in "the Lady," warmly greets this old friend, introduces her to his wife, Semiramis, and shows her graciously to a chair. But no lady is visible. One by one these "invisible guests," as Ionesco calls them, fill the room. The old man and old woman, back to back, flirt with old beaus and girls, all invisible. Complex conversations develop. More and more guests ring and appear at the door. Shouting and racket mount; the old couple hobble about lugging chairs and trying to seat the phantoms. Pandemonium ensues as they cannot find enough chairs quickly enough to seat this milling unruly throng. Staged properly, it is a Dionysian frenzy. Finally, in a hysterical climax, the old man welcomes the emperor to the group, and, while standing on a chair so that he can see him, weeps and pleads with him to be patient until the orator arrives and reads his message.

The orator does arrive. He is an actual, physically present person. As the old couple shudder in silence, he takes his place, ornately dressed, in the corner. The old man resumes:

> OLD MAN: . . . I count on you, great master and Orator . . . as for me and my faithful helpmeet, after our long years of labor in behalf of the progress of humanity during which we have fought the good fight, nothing remains for us but to withdraw . . . immediately, in order to make the supreme sacrifice which no one demands of us but which we carry out even so. . . .
>
> OLD WOMAN [*sobbing*]: Yes, yes, let's die in full glory . . . let's die in order to become a legend. . . . At least they'll name a street after us. . . .
>
> OLD MAN [*to Old Woman*]: O my faithful helpmeet! . . . you who have believed in me unfailingly, during a whole century, who have never left me, never . . . alas, today, at this supreme moment, the crowd piteously separates us. . . .

Above all I had hoped
that together we might lie
with all our bones together
within the selfsame skin
within the same sepulchre
and that the same worms
might share our old flesh
that we might rot together. . . .

> OLD WOMAN: . . . Rot together. . . .
> OLD MAN: Alas! . . . Alas! . . .
> OLD WOMAN: Alas! . . . Alas! . . .
> OLD MAN: . . . Our corpses will fall far from each other, and we will rot in an aquatic solitude. . . . Don't pity us over much.

In an ecstasy of joy the old man and woman leap from the windows simultaneously in twin immolation and suicide.

The orator strides to the head of the room, takes a pregnant pause, and then emits the awful gutteral sounds of a deaf-mute. He accompanies these with fragments of symbols marked on a blackboard. The play peters out with these sounds and signs, and the stage fades slowly into darkness and silence.

We have laughed at the old couple but we have felt uneasy for doing so.

Their antics are ludicrous and at the same time very sad. It is as if Ionesco had invited us to witness the demolition of a building, vacant and old, and we had found that the electric wires were still alive, sparking and fuming in the rubble. We laugh at the old couple and at the same time love them and pity them. On the outer margins of our consciousness we recognize a kinship to them. In these strange moments of sharing we see that what matters to them also matters to us: we must make our presence felt to others if we would fully be our own selves; we must live in the presence of others whether they are physically present or not; we must be authorized by a presence we consider authoritative; we yearn for union with others and at the same time long to be individuals. Through the invisible guests in the gaping void of space we were put in touch with something child-like and archaic that felt very familiar to us. We were secret sharers at these proceedings.

We participated with the actors in a kind of rite. Each of us was authorized by the others to give up for a moment in exhaustion and to acknowledge the child-like longing for magical union. If before formal rehearsals commence the actor begins to work alone on the character of the old man it will nevertheless be in the company of his own invisible guests. The character may begin to be formed in a manner such as this: one moment in exhaustion his jaw goes slack, his tongue becomes thick and heavy, and the strangest puling, slurring, child-like sounds come out of his mouth. This is the character: a naive child with a message for the world of others, struggling to get it out through a worn-out body. The character, in outline, will crystallize instantly around this unpremeditated sagging and slackening of the jaw and thickening of the tongue, as if a particle of dust had chanced to fall within a supersaturated solution, and the crystalline lattice-work structure had emerged instantly throughout the container.

Heidegger concluded that we cannot be without being with others. To be we must have already fallen into "roles," into what others expect us to be and to do. Ionesco's play tends to confirm this. At the end of their lives and isolated, the old couple cannot escape the presence of others who move in upon them, and who do so irrespective of logic and the chronological sequence in which they were first met. The others have a timeless reality for them, and they are not bound by space. We are on the level of mythical time, but it is not ordered by established rites. The Presence of others must be presupposed by any contingent state of human affairs. If others are present then they have Presence; if they are absent they can still have Presence; and if we can somehow speak of absence of presence then it is a privation of Presence of which we speak. Presence in this basic sense is inescapable; it is a categorial condition of human life.

Integrally related to this is the condition of authorization. We are authorized by others whom we consider authoritative. The old man's message is never given, and his intercessor with the authority, his stand-in, is a deaf-mute: Ionesco seems clearly to be making a mockery of the idea of authorization. And yet when we consider the idea at the categorial level we see he is concerned with it. As to Authorization, not authorized—apparently.

It might be argued, however, that Ionesco is intending to dislodge authorization on the categorial level. This may be true, but if it is then we do not think that he is successful. At most we can say that he modifies the form that authorization takes. His production authorizes all involved to give presence to the absence of *authenticating* authorization.[2] Insofar as new authorization occurs between actors and audience a new power will appear. But quite surely it will be a power of lower magnitude, and it sets us to questioning our own identity. "I am in, for, and by others mimetically. Now how can I also be other from every other—I myself?" It is a very troubling question, for if our humanity is a function of fusion, then we may wonder if sufficient fusion remains even to ask the question of individuation in a behaviorally effective way. Are we coming apart as did Hamlet for so long, or simply losing our substance, as happened to the tramps?

The Chairs is an experiment with our lives, a model organization of human possibilities, which cannot help but disturb and redirect that on which it experiments. Its "world" is set up within the world. To deploy actors to stand in for beings like the old couple is no merely farcical matter. Ionesco sets up a model—however negatively, ironically, or indirectly— for human beings; he does not merely reflect what is already there. Or at least we can say that he creates a setting within which questioning must occur. We are brought home to ourselves as interrogative lines of development within a particular horizon of possibilities. However disturbing these possibilities are, there hovers about the play, strangely, a sense of wholeness. The encompassing absence is itself a presence.

I take it to be manifestly clear that traditional sources of authority have decayed. Into this vacuum rush untold varieties of surrogates, some of them menacing, others too weak, still others simply untried. Theatre is experienced as an attempt to experiment with human identity and to try out new possibilities of involvement before we are frozen mimetically into "roles" offstage too deeply ever to break out of their fractionalizing of our being. We begin to believe that the ultimate subject matter and responsibility of theatre and of all art is freedom and autonomy.

2. The topic of authentic individuation is treated in the second part of this book.

2. Robert Wilson and the Potentiality of Projection of Possibility—Understanding

A young contemporary of Robert Whitman who likewise bases his work mainly in New York, Robert Wilson is an important and original talent. He harks back to the roots of theatre, and the new life he finds in his work stems from the life he finds in the roots. Like the improvisations of the dithyrambic chorus which formed, said Aristotle, the source of Attic tragedy, Wilson does not work from scripts but develops his productions out of improvisations in which he himself participates. Certain traditional themes such as standing in and fusion are retrieved, but they are thrown into a horizon of possibility which encourages their radical reevaluation. He shows some of the things that can happen when we are allowed to improvise in a bright new setting on "the dark and hidden springs of our conduct." His method is, so to speak, free association by living, presencing bodies.

I hope to accomplish a dual purpose in the analysis of his work: to deal more systematically than before with some of contemporary theatre's methods for exposing presupposed conditions of human identity; and to orient my analysis around Heidegger's notion of the ontological potentiality of projection of possibility (or understanding) in such a way that this both guides our investigation, to some extent, and is tested and criticized by the investigation. There is no presumptive incompatibility here, because if we were to be working on the proper level in our philosophical analysis of theatre, then this give and take between philosophy and theatre is just what we would expect to find taking place. The presupposition of understanding or projection emerges quite naturally from the total matrix of presupposed human potentialities which begins to emerge when we break the plays down into what makes them work dramatically.

How can absurdist or surrealist theatre be a serious matter? The example we wish to use is Wilson's *A Letter for Queen Victoria*. We suggest that it is the very playfulness of this theatre that accounts for its seriousness— that this playfulness is a *de facto* bracketing and experimentation that contributes to a phenomenological understanding of human action and self.

A Letter for Queen Victoria is the first Wilson production to have been staged in a Broadway proscenium theatre, and the incongruity of it in this show-business setting further emphasizes the absurdist character of the work. As we enter, we see two dancers already spinning on the two sides of the apron of the stage, spinning as they will do for the next three hours of the production. They will vary their speeds empathetically or contrastingly to what is happening between and behind them on the stage, but later one will have to strain to bring them to the focus of consciousness. It as if their cycling continuity were the condition, the living but forgotten temporal frame, without which the bizarre events between them would fall apart.

And the events are indeed bizarre, a churning flux: shots and people falling, falling and standing up again; repetitions of words and parts of words printed on large flats; arias of screams in what is billed as an "opera"; an autistic boy wandering about and speaking (in a way) to others, then carried above them on a harness through the air; great silences amidst great spaces where only the scratch of a match or the rustle of clothing can be heard; an Oriental figure speaking at us through a large Venetian blind that opens and shuts at random, etc.

Item: an entr'acte in *A Letter for Queen Victoria:* Robert Wilson himself stands in front of the proscenium curtain, which is painted with repetitions of words. He looks across the stage at his fellow performer, the autistic boy, Chris Knowles. Chris is facing us and keeps smiling at something in his mind's eye. We are aware that Chris is aware of Robert. Robert keeps looking. Then he stalks directly across to Chris, bends and shouts into his ear, "You son of a BI [*pause*] TCH!" Without looking up, as if he were a cherub being assaulted, Chris says softly, "Please go away." Robert does, but only to return to his original position, and to repeat the whole thing several times, as if it had not happened before: the shambling onslaught through space, the slowed-down words, the same little reply.

Now, the bare fact that something is done onstage constitutes already a disengagement of our practical concern from it, and is a *de facto* bracketing and fictive variation of it. We do not simply see a man walk across and speak menacingly to a boy. Our horizon of concern expands to include a greater awareness of the conditions that make this sort of act possible for any of us, as well as a greater awareness of its ramifications and consequences.

But in addition to these general considerations, there are methods of fictive variation specific to Wilson's theatre:

1. *Repetition.*—If action is not employed merely to get on to something else, but is repeated, it is framed; it stands out; and we finally see portions of its ordinary context and its significance hitherto passed over. That is, we have varied offstage action, which occurs only with effect (and so is not exactly repeatable), beyond this normal state of affairs. Onstage it occurs without effect and is repeated without effect. Hence the nature of *normal* action comes into thematic focus: in this case its *effect.* The normal is revealed through being violated. It emerges distinctly because it is related to contrasting behaviors which highlight its meaning, and we cease to be absorbed in it as an exclusive possibility of existence.

2. *Action slowed down.*—Again, its utilitarian function is disturbed or blocked, and only then do we stop to grasp this function. We have varied offstage action, which is normally utilitarian, beyond the point of its being normal and utilitarian. Hence the nature of normality finally comes into thematic focus: in this case its effectual rhythm. We see that it is effectual only on condition of having a routine rhythm that crowds out other possibilities of existence. We see the normal only by violating it in the art. And, in seeing it, we cease to be absorbed in it as an exclusive possibility of existence. In so defining the normal we both understand it and break out of its grip. We can, if we wish, be freshly and appreciatively normal. We shall shortly note a third method of fictive variation specific to Wilson's theatre.

Vulnerability—whether our own or others'—is seldom seen in its full context, because in threatening situations offstage we must narrow our attention, focus on those instrumentalities which may quickly achieve our survival, and tightly control or suppress our emotions—or be shocked into unconsciousness or delirium by them. Here in the theatre we are detached enough to see that as infants we have lain for years at the mercy of others in space; we walk even now in constant vulnerability, which is usually felt only peripherally and unacknowledgeably. We see that we will fall one day in this space, fall and die.

That one is embodied as *a* human being means that one occupies a unique space-time point, hence is open to every hazard that chances to impinge on that point, and is absolutely individuated. This despite one's coordinate sociality: that one become a *human* being only by learning to do automatically the sorts of things that others do. Within this context questions emerge vividly, e.g., convention—in dress, speech, manners— just how does it allow us to participate in the identity of the group, protect us moment by moment, and make an individual identity possible for each of us? Just how—as Wittgenstein put it—is convention the "rock bottom?" Wilson's production displayed vividly the human predicament evident in all the plays to be examined: we both need others and are threatened by them, and we are threatened because of our need. That is, we need others to be concerned about us and to approve us, and we are threatened because they can fail to do so (perhaps because they do not appreciate the conventions governing our behavior). Others can haunt us even when they are not present, or when they do not exist.

Notice another scene. Two female characters appear on the deep stage: a short white actress in profile with a flowing, white cape hanging from her shoulders and stretched behind her on a rope. A tall black actress in a flowing black cape stands atop a pedestal. Words pass between them without syntax and with no obvious or sequential sense. We see that this being together in space is the condition even for their noncommunication.

They cannot escape each other. Finally, accompanied by a protracted groaning and tearing sound, the black actress raises her arms, slowly disgorges herself from her black cape and appears slim and willowy in white. The white actress tears away slowly from her cape and appears in black. They keep up the monotonous nonsensical exchange in the strange gravitational field that binds them together. They approach each other from across the stage, and it appears that they will meet or collide, but at the last minute do not touch as they pass, and do not look at each other. This is repeated in a constant slowed-down motion that approaches suspended animation.

There was evident here a third method of fictive variation specific to Wilson's theatre, a third method of bracketing action in action:

3. *Action aborted, unconsummated.*—When the action of meeting and encounter is unconsummated and our expectations are disappointed, we finally see, through contrast, what *consummation* always amounted to, and what some of its conditions are. And these are the ones usually most hidden from us. That is, Wilson has taken an action, which offstage is normally consummated, or at least has a chance to be, and repeatedly left it unconsummated. Hence the nature of action as normal and consummatable finally comes into thematic focus. The potentialities of human intercourse can be realized only if the situatedness and vulnerability of body-selves are respected, and only if the continuous nonverbal context necessary for verbal exchange is maintained from moment to moment. Suggested principles of relevance, without which the texture of human being-together would be impossible, include: meeting, distance, deference, encounter, and joint absorption in a common subject of concern. And, again, since our daily absorption in conventional consummations is exploded within the larger one of grasping their intelligibility, we are brought home to our freedom.

The sense of the unsaid—or perhaps unsayable—which hovers over the production was typified in one instance by the white girl's finding a smudge on the black girl's dress. She interposed a magnifier between the smudge and the black girl's wide-opened eyes. Simultaneously the smudge was projected large on the rear wall. Then the white girl turns her head toward us and opens her mouth in a long silent scream. I can never recall a scream's being so clearly connected to its conditions, e.g., its relation to the unspeakable.

Wilson's scenes add cumulatively to one another. Item: A vast white and pink space with ladies and gentlemen at small, posh tables. We soon notice that something is not quite right: one gentleman is lacking shoes, another has no shirt, etc. Shots ring out and people fall down dead, but only to get up again and resume their conversations as if nothing had happened. Repetition of this until the pink and white space seems on the verge of floating away.

In addition to repetition and the other methods of fictive variation, the fantastic nature of the scene frames and thematizes the conditions and limits of the experienceability of *this* world. We can imagine people getting up after being shot dead, but it is out of *this* world. Here we can rattle off into a corner and, beyond anyone's sight, hearing, or help, drop once and for all in death. This world is where we are mortally vulnerable. It is the condition of all my possibilities, including the possibility which ends all my possibilities, death. But it is also the condition of my being able to imagine and enact what could only be enacted within it: the fantastic. It is only within the world that we can try to frame and thematize it with our art and our absurdity, and only here that we can either meet or miss any of our fellows. Here in the theatre we are together. Here at least for this brief while we can help each other somewhat, help each other see. The graveness of the situation comes home to us.

Members of Wilson's audience enjoy a peculiar sort of involved detachment. In ordinary contemporary theatre, one's awareness of fellow members of the audience, and of the actors as persons, is seldom focal. In Wilson's theatre it often is. Usually, both in the theatre and out, we are rushed—rushed to see a point, rushed to get something done. In Wilson's theatre there is time to reflect upon our condition. There is respite from that rushing superficiality of ordinary life in which our experiences and our actions simply fly by, and leave no more trace on us than what is necessary for our practical pursuits or for our survival, or perhaps for retention of a sentimental feature of our lives. But here: the mind's wandering, the mulling-over one's fellow spectators, produced a curious self-criticism, a detachment which was a retrieval of self.

Wilson's theatre had become metatheatre. The bizarre stretchings of theatrical conventions had "put out of action" and hence revealed that basic coaction integral to theatre itself: the relationship of audience to actors. Paradoxically, with the relationship suspended, we were drawn closer both to our fellow spectators and to the actors: closer in a feeling of common humanity, and closer in awareness of similarities of on and offstage life.[3] Yes, there was the theatre critic Walter Kerr sitting in his accustomed aisle seat, but looking a bit strange on this occasion, and it brought us up short.

We looked up to the stage to see an enclosed cavity of space. There had

3. I am indebted to Professor Edward S. Casey for thematizing this insight (and for his other remarks) in his comment on a paper that dealt with these topics and was read at the Convention of the American Society for Aesthetics, Toronto, October 27–29, 1976. The paper was coauthored by Donna Wilshire.

been an abrupt but noiseless scene change while our minds had "wandered" and the dancers cycled—we assumed they had—on the stage aprons. In a vast, symmetrical bare room, dark except for extraatmospheric light pouring coldly through a large opening to the side and rear—an opening as onto outer space—stand four goggled and suited aviator-like figures, motionless, their arms casual on each others' shoulders, up against and facing the back wall. Then darkness. The light reappears. Their arms have moved somewhat, and one of them is slowly drumming the wall with his fingers. You see, there is life here—of a sort. Now in the silence one of them is evidently lighting a cigarette. With a match, a torch? A dim light glows and flickers before him and on the wall. Smoke appears between him and the wall. (So this is what smoking is? A little light and fire to call our own in the midst of this immensity?) Darkness. They reappear now before the large open window; they lean out, speak monotonously and nonsequentially, and then find something out there at which they point. What is it? We have no idea, but we can tell that it makes little difference. It might be a very important astronomical event, but these men have seen it before. They are no longer moved, if they were ever moved at all. It has no relevance to their problems as men, aside from prompting them to turn from the window and absorb themselves in a world small enough to feel at home inside their room. How incomparably mundane are these aviators—the space out there being sundered from the space in which they move together. What would change them? Perhaps novelty for a moment, or worship for a moment, but nothing for long.

The customary slow motion, the repetition, the sense of a practical purpose disappointed, and our own involved detachment etched out a condition of existence: an abode is more than a shelter from indefinitely numerous threats (the aviators are perfectly equipped to venture out into space), and more than a convenient place to meet, or avoid, one another. It is a purposeful masking out of the larger world, a necessary partialization of experience that we must undertake together. The abode protects us from the incalculable weight and darkness of all that we turn away from. It is a little space within space, a place where a fire can be built to replace the sun. As enacted, no motivation for ever leaving the abode presented itself, hence the abode's obscuring and masking function (usually itself masked and sunk in the background of consciousness and eclipsed by the abode's apparently more important functions) emerged focally. One might say that it emerged blindingly. It was almost more than one dared take in. As if one saw the face of a blackened but intensely luminous sun. It was experienced as the boundlessness of the experienceable world.

The play ended fittingly with a long scene dominated by a Japanese figure sitting behind large Venetian blinds which opened and closed at random; he spoke sentences that never came to the point. Other characters on the periphery of this figure attached themselves, child-like, to others and emitted puling, repetitious, mimicking sounds; it was mimetic behavior with an autistic aspect. The play we have seen has been an original projection of possibilities which has transcended the normal in the very act of defining it. The sudden emergence of the ancient theme of mimetic repetition and fusion with authority might be compared to throwing from a moving vehicle a weighty anchor with hooked and tentacled extremities. The vehicle lurches to a stop as the wind and debris which it had kicked up keep moving ahead. A problematical future opens before us. The dissonant juxtaposition of blind repetition and creative possibility laid hold of one as does the last line of a Rilke poem which one would never predict to occur, but which, when it does, strikes one as being inevitable:

You must change your life.

Our theatrical probe reveals, I believe, a condition of existence which our section on identity must elaborate: without the capacity for one's repetition of action to be given presence to oneself and to one's fellows *as one's* repetition, we cannot suppose that the beings in question are human. But this presupposes that a past and a future be projectable in a unitary manner from present moments. This capacity must be presupposed by any actual attributions to persons either of autistic-like noncreative and fixated repetition, or of creative and ever-new appropriations of the past— appropriations in the light of a present that is fresh and new because it buds out of a future that is being projected newly and novelly. So we can say, following our formula: as to Repetition and Projection, merely repetitive; or, as to Repetition and Projection, not merely repetitive but creative.

We believed that Wilson's "nonsense" revealed the conditions of making sense. We recalled Piaget's theory that the primal accomplishment is the child's repetition of its own spontaneous motions and sounds. The autistic child does not get beyond this point; he does not open out onto others and onto the newness of time. If the child imitates others, it is automatic; the child never does so freely and responsibly as a person. Something awesome was occurring on stage, and we felt that Wilson was poking close to those conditions for making sense of which no ordinary sense can be made. An epiphany of humanity was occurring there, if you will. This was the suggestion: that in witnessing the conditions necessary for persons' making sense of the world we were witnessing the conditions necessary for persons' existence; that what a person *is* is a function of his or her making sense of things—of that process of world involvement and involvement with others which is identical with itself over time.

We had not before seen so clearly the porousness and precariousness of an absolutely individuated human existence which nevertheless verges simultaneously on the communal and universal. Nor had we ever seen so clearly the danger that lies in confusing individuation (understood from a third-person viewpoint merely) and identity. Because different persons have different bodies, they must stand at different points in space-time; so merely assigning them different numbers will individuate them decisively. But tracing the conditions of an individual's *identity* as a *person* finds that person bound up with others and the world in bonds of communality, responsibility, and freedom. The autistically tinged mimetic behavior of Wilson's characters indicated that the dialectic of particular and universal, in which individuation of self evolves out of engulfment, had broken down; thus that dialectic was revealed. That is, the characters were merely fragments of the group, not individual centers of freedom and responsibility who nevertheless must exhibit common traits; they were not individual beings who could count as paradigm examples of individual persons. The openness of the question of identity dawned on us.

The use of the autistic boy, Chris, was central to achieving this result. Without the contrast between ourselves and someone abnormal, does not our vaunted normality lose its shape and begin fading into the void? Must not we, who must make sense in order to be, also make sense to some degree of our making sense, and how can we do this without an art-form that returns to us the strange ones, with their strange ways of making sense, as an ineluctable foil to us? Contrast presupposes kinship.

3. Jerzy Grotowski and the Potentiality of Attunement to the World—Mood

The categorial condition which Heidegger locates in all attunements and moods is *Befindlichkeit*. Difficult to translate, it can perhaps be said to mean that one always finds oneself, one is always present to oneself, however obscurely or inarticulately. This manifests itself as mood. What we ordinarily think to be our "center" is really a hum of mood in which we are lost in a mimetic periphery which we cannot acknowledge. The individual abides with himself in apparently aimless involvement which reveals itself only in moods. And as Heidegger has pointed out, we seem never to be without moods, for even in that dull satiation with self which we might call a flat or moodless state, still that is a mode of finding oneself in the world, of being present to oneself; it is the mood of blankness and satiation.

The self cannot escape itself. Because it is a being-in-the-world it cannot be and escape the world. Thus the self must be attuned to the world in one way or another. Even to be alienated, disgruntled, stagnated, or rebellious is to be so in reference to the world. It is to be attuned in the inclusive sense of the term, and it is to be engulfed in the mood that is one's being so attuned, and which speaks this attunement. Or, one can be attuned in the more common and narrower sense of the term: at home in discovering and working out one's ownmost potentialities as a being who can project possibilities. Thus attunement in the broader sense of *Befindlichkeit* is inescapable; it is a categorial matter: as to Attunement, attuned—or unattuned.

The capacity to recreate or reproduce mood is fundamental to theatre; it must be presupposed if persons are to be convincingly enactable on the stage. Yet it is just what a visual model of cognition and reproduction cannot adequately grasp, because mood cannot be singled out in advance as an object in the foreground or in the distance, with the means for grasping it being calculable. Only bad art or amusement art assumes it can be. It is too close and encompassing, too already present in and through the body, to be discriminated and seen. Mood resists being bracketed in and revealed by conventional phenomenological reflection, for some consciousness must always hover outside the bracket unreflected, and nothing conceals itself in the shadowy margins of consciousness more successfully than the pervasiveness of habitual mood. For example, we may be chatting amiably enough, but a background mood of stagnation and despair circulates through every word we say. Or, we may be lamenting an occurrence, but a mood of elation buoys us on every side: "It did not happen to *me!*"

We can get at mood only indirectly and we may have to wait until it is artistically reproduced before we can recognize it. Often it is reproduced only after a series of trials and errors and of successive approximations (e.g., putting on a recording of "mood music" is just what great art will not do). The approximations involve what we can deliberately intend as artists: verbal speech, intentional projection of time and possibility, calculated modes of approach to others. But none of these fall into place as enactment of character until a certain combination of them evokes spontaneously a mode of being attuned to the world from which all of them *and* others can then spring in a coordinated and organic way. Artistic creativity exists on the balancing point between activity and passivity.

Often it is just meaningful silence, silence as language, and a hush and closing down of broadcastable plans, that signals the potency of appropriate attunement. Things begin escaping the actor in such a pattern that actions emerge from it as from their matrix. These are the gestures, postures, sounds, joys, moods of the character enacted. Actors influenced by Constantin Stanislavsky call this the "sub-text": that which the script suggests to the actor or the perceptive reader, but which it can directly say only at the cost of being superficial. It is the character's "world," and the audience's world answers to it. The works of Anton Chekhov and Eugene O'Neill are classic examples of plays that will not be born until their subtext is tapped. The verbal language on the page must limit and situate itself as verbal language relative to what cannot be directly spoken by it. To achieve the requisite attunement the actor can only block in voluntarily what the character is known to know and say, stand open as artist and as character to what is happening around him, and then this attunement—once discovered—just happens, as it were, automatically. The actor lets it happen—lets it carry all else on its moving ground.

Following Heidegger, we have suggested that the thrust of the plays we have examined can be grasped in terms of four fundamental sorts of human potentiality. These are language, being with others, repetition and projection, and involuntary presence to oneself through one's world—attunement or mood. For Heidegger the four categorial potentialities must be present if a being is to be human. Examining convincing enactments of selves on stage we find that these potentialities are present as essential conditions. Our recognition of our selves through the enactment and projection of "selves" on stage leads us to believe that theatre is essentially involved in life, is life-like.

We can now state more clearly the relationship between theatrical experience and philosophical reflection. The gravest occupational hazard for the philosopher is to become so absorbed in the high abstractions which are the objects of his thought that he loses intellectual touch with his own identity as a particular human being. Of course, he remains himself nevertheless, and his particular needs, yearnings, attunements, and deficiencies are projected surreptitiously into his thought; he simply loses awareness and control of what is happening. This is most vividly evident in the thought experiments philosophers carry out and in the examples they cite. With distressing frequency we find what appears to be highly disciplined thought which contains, nevertheless, an imagination out of control: irrelevancy and dislocation are produced, which usually go undetected, because to move out of touch with one's own existence entails not being aware that one has done so.

The philosopher caught in this malaise imagines merely abstractly, either as if he were speculating about an attenuated physical reality, a science fiction world, or as if he were engaged in formal inquiries into mathematical or logical possibility only. He fails to imagine the coordinated range of what is really possible for human beings. Roger Wertheimer comments sagely,

> When I present myself with . . . science fiction fantasies, I am inclined to respond as I do to a question posed by Hilary Putnam: If we build robots with a psychology isomorphic with ours and a physical structure comparable to ours, should we award them civil rights? In contrast to Putnam, who thinks we can now give a more disinterested and hence objective answer to the question, I would say that our present answer, whatever it is, is so disinterested as to count for nothing. It seems to me that such questions about the robot . . . can't be answered in advance . . . Odd as it may sound I want to know exactly what the robot looks like and what it's like to live with it. I want to know in fact how we—how I—look at it, respond to it, feel toward it.[4]

Wertheimer is saying, I think, that we are too engulfed in our reality and too unthematically involved in things to be able to imagine abstractly in advance just what a situation will be. In our armchairs we conjure up oversimplified scenarios in which our own feelings, moods, and involvements are left out; hence we understand neither ourselves nor that about which we speak. Are robots like ourselves? But we no longer understand ourselves.

Yet Wertheimer fails to point out that all too often when situations are actually realized we cannot even then understand what has happened to us, just because we are engulfed in the factuality and have lost all perspective on it. Or that we do realize, in part, what has befallen us, but that there is no reversing a disastrous sequence of events. What is needed are thought experiments in which imagination becomes concrete, affective, perceptually engaging, and communal; which is to say that what is needed is art, particularly theatre, understood phenomenologically.

As the last example of theatre, I will cite—especially in connection with mood—the work of Jerzy Grotowski. Like the approach taken by Robert Wilson, his work springs from improvisations by actors and only afterwards, if at all, does there appear a script, which is merely a transcript of what occurred. Wilson improvises as an actor with his actors, only occasionally stepping back to see the total effect. Grotowski builds his theatre around "the revelation of the actor": improvisations and exercises which train the actor's body, not to illustrate a "movement of his soul," but to *be* such a movement; either this or to be originary disclosures of

4. "Understanding the Abortion Argument," in James Rachels, *Moral Problems* (New York: Harper & Row, 1975), p. 87.

his "inner impulses."[5] Both artists concur, at least tacitly, with Nietzsche's observation that Euripedes failed to think from the stage—failed to become an actor in his own imagination as writer—but rather calculated in his writing as if he were merely a thinker in the audience looking on at a spectacle.

Building on the work of Breton and Antonin Artaud, as does Wilson, Grotowski invites the actor to a confrontation with his own impulses, some of them "mythical," which waver on "the borderline between dream and reality."[6] To do this he must break "the life mask": those clichés of fashionable self-interpretation—newly minted conversational argot, idle talk, and distracting curiosity—which keep him closed off from the range of his potential presence to himself through his body. Similarly to what happens in Wilson's work, only when the sacrosanctity of his life mask is violated can it be revealed for what it is. Likewise, only when patterns of mythical participation, fusion, and sacrifice are violated can we touch their buried nerve, and have them spring to new awareness and new life within us.[7]

When the actor does this he abandons his pretense to be an attractive individual, for he stands in for others who experience themselves through him, and in this act of his sacrifice the community confesses its confusion and its alienation from its own deepest potentialities (insofar as one can be alienated from these):

> For when in the theatre we dispose of the tricks of make-up and costume, stuffed bellies and false noses, and when we propose to the actor that he should transform himself before the spectator's eyes using only his inner impulses, his body, when we state that the magic of the theatre consists in this transformation *as it comes to birth*, we once more raise the question: did Artaud ever suggest any other kind of magic?
>
> Artaud intuitively saw myth as the dynamic centre of the theatre performance. Only Nietzsche was ahead of him in this domain. He also knew that transgression of the myth renewed its essential values and "became an element of menace which reestablished the derided norms" (L. Flaszen). He did not however take account of the fact that, in our age, when all languages intermingle, the community of the theatre cannot possibly *identify* itself with myth, because there is no single faith. Only a *confrontation* is possible.
>
> I am speaking of the surpassing of limits, of a confrontation, of a process of self-knowledge and, in a certain sense, of a therapy.

5. Jerzy Grotowski, *Towards a Poor Theatre* (New York: Simon & Schuster, 1968 [A Clarion Book]), p. 310. I do not explicate the complex manner in which fragments of literary texts are interwoven in the production. This is the work of Grotowski's "literary adviser," Ludwik Flaszen.

6. Ibid., pp. 35, 63. For an introduction to Artaud's work, see his *The Theatre and Its Double* (New York: Grove Press, 1958).

7. Grotowski, p. 121.

A confrontation is a "trying out," a testing of whatever is a traditional value.

An honest renewal can only be found in this double game of values, this attachment and rejection, this revolt and submissiveness.[8]

It is particularly the Christ myth of sacrifice and vicarious atonement that concerned Grotowski in his last plays. The actor sacrifices himself when, even as an unbeliever, he submits to previously buried or inchoate sacrificial and mimetic impulses within himself. He submits to them in order to grasp them, to determine their limits and to surpass them. Only when we catch up with our past can we truly get beyond it: "If he does not exhibit his body, but annihilates it, burns it, frees it from every resistance to any psychic impulse, then he does not sell his body but sacrifices it. He repeats the atonement; he is close to holiness."[9] The actor stands in vicariously and sacrificially for the audience in this confrontation with, and in some sense transcendence of, the myth of sacrifice itself. The annihilation and burning of the body is clearly Nietzschean in its overtones, and recalls the Greek Dionysian tradition as well as that of the Christian. As enacted, it is a remarkable gathering of the civilization. Of course, it also suggests a civilization in upheaval: one which must violate its myths in order to regain contact with them. To what extent this upheaval is the disturbance which is violent growth—rather than being merely a flailing in the gulf dividing two ages—remains a question. It may, however, be the most potent and solidifying question we can pose for ourselves, given our circumstances.

Grotowski's penultimate play, *The Constant Prince*, is such a radical alteration of the Calderon play of that title that the original is not recognizable.[10] Developed out of improvisations, it has the effect of violating the earlier text of the romantic tale. The ransom is paid for the kidnapped prince, but instead of leaving his captors and returning to his homeland, the prince chooses to exercise his freedom by dying for his captors. The principal actor is Ryzard Cieslak, and the play centers around the trance which he induces in himself, and in which he is called to empty himself sacrificially of his individuality. Rising like a phoenix from his bed of torture, the Constant Prince says,

What am I? What am I more than a man?
Who am I to retaliate against a crush of men?
Is it that I am a child?
But, I am no longer a child,

8. Ibid., pp. 119, 121, 131, 122. (I have arranged the quotations.)
9. Ibid., p. 34.
10. Actually, it is billed as "after an adaptation by J. Slovacki of the piece by Calderon."

I am only a slave
ready to live as these other slaves,
to live here and to enrich my master.
And who then pays so dearly
for a slave?—But he is the one
who pays with his body and with his head,
because he has lost his liberty,
because, I tell you, he has died for the other men.
Thus I have been dead for a long time.[11]

The space of complicity in this play is a ring of benches above a sunken acting area, as if the house were the theatre of an operating room in which students could observe a forbidden act—the Prince's torture and immolation. That the audience stands at a halfway point, both within the scene as "passive participants" and outside it, suggests the Greek chorus; but no playwright or director has mapped their responses against a "world," and they must discover, in the world if they can, their own commentary on the scene. The relation of "world" and world is only posed for them as a question with which they are to deal.

Grotowski's theatre—*qua* theatre—came to fixate itself, and perhaps to expire, in a single work, *Apocalypsis cum Figuris* (original version 1969, greatly modified version 1973; it is the latter I will discuss). Grotowski sees the play as so fundamentally transitional as to lead the company, eventually, out of theatre itself. Its continuity with the preceding *Constant Prince* is significant: as in that play there is a Christ figure, "The Innocent," and he is also played by Cieslak. But the discontinuities are significant as well: in the new play the Christ figure is never allowed to consummate the sacrificial act; there is a moment of collapse of The Innocent, but it is marked by his bitter self-recrimination; and if there is a sacrificial emptying of his individuality, it seems incapable of atoning for our deficiencies and authorizing us. If authorization is now up to us, are we capable of doing it? We come to grips with ourselves as interrogative lines of becoming.

In *Apocalypsis* the audience sits on the floor very close to the actors and surrounding them, but no touching occurs and no eye contact is made. This is a more egalitarian setting, and the psychological distance between actors and audience is in some measure decreased. With all of us positioned on the floor together, the production begins. Rousing himself from apparent somnolence, the actor enacting John the disciple rises, chanting, and describes with his finger a cross on the floor. The actress enacting Mary Magdalen rises also, and while he spreads a cloth she approaches with a loaf of bread. It is clear that they mean to celebrate the communion

11. Translation of the French transcript of the original Polish by B.W.: *Les Voies de la Creation Theatrale*, I, ed. Jean Jacquot (Paris: Editions du Centre National de la Recherche Scientifique, 1970), p. 81.

meal. Then with great dexterity the actor simulates masturbation, as if it were a kind of milking of his mimed generative organ. They consume the enacted emission from out of the cupped palm of his hand. The communion meal is celebrated with bread and sperm. This is followed by violent competition for the remaining bread.

The scene is shocking and powerful, much more so than something explicitly pornographic would be, for we have participated in a forbidden commingling of creative impulses at the core of the self, a commingling of sexual love and Christian charity. Released in improvisation, the actor's impulse to celebrate Christian sacrifice is also mixed with his impulse to exercise his sexual power of insemination and subjugation. Each domain of activity is violated by the other, and from each springs new, if tortured, life. We in the audience are left with the distinct conviction that this is the sort of behavior that might happen if we contemporary scientific or agnostic individuals would confront our own "mythical roots." As polymorphic or dissonant as the resulting chord might be, there would yet be a kind of resonant attunement. In the play, as we witness it, the schizoid hollowness which Grotowski attributes to modern civilization—the separation of thought from belief and feeling—is replaced by their violent and ringing contact within the self.

I speak of contact within the self, but this is a somewhat misleading spatial metaphor. The separation, Grotowski maintains, is between the head and the rest of the body. Expressivity, thus conscious sense of self, comes ever more and more to be located in the face alone, and the head—packed with its thoughts—suppresses, restricts, or manipulates the rest of the body. Apollo, or some maimed version in which only his head remains vital, subjugates Dionysus. But with this goes a mangling or suppression of our pervading attunement with the world, a ripping apart of the controlling matrix of mood: that encompassing webbing which cannot be directly managed and manipulated, but which must be allowed to flow and fall together on its own.

The Grotowskian actor has, as it were, spread his face through the rest of his body, and his body through his face. For example, in his exercises he speaks gesturally through his feet, or allows the sounds of his voice to resonate in, and emanate from, his back, chest, or stomach. To attune himself to his own resonance in the world he emits sounds while crawling on his hands and knees, and responds in a supple way to the sounds heard. Or he turns his hand into a "face" which looks into the "face" of his chest and "converses" with it. One can but think of Rilke's "Archaic Torso of Apollo":

We knew not his amazing head,
in which the eye-fruits ripened. But

his torso still glows like a candelabrum,
in which his countenance, now more centered,

is held and shines. Or the bend of his breast
could not blind you, and by gentle turning
of the loins could not a smile rise
at that center, which bore issue.

Or the stone would stand disfigured and short
below the shoulder's transparent fall
and would not glitter so like a panther's coat;

and not burst from all its limits
forth like a star: for there is no place,
which does not see you. You must change your life.[12]

Apollo's torso is a "more centered countenance." It is not merely that this repeats or mirrors the countenance which we could imagine as the face; it may dialogue with it, dispute it, or overrule it, but there is some kind of attunement, even if polyphonic. There is co-realization instead of suppression or detachment. The actor, tapping his "inner impulses," transforms himself for the audience so that his body becomes this second countenance. The power of the theatre is this transformation as it comes to birth. Here Nietzsche's notion of enchantment is cashed: it is to stand mimetically in that other's body who has recaptured integration and attunement, and this is to be brought home to oneself through the other. Grotowski's metaphoric claim that the actor's body is burned connotes not only the sacrificial and vicarious aspects of the act, but also that his body no longer offers resistance to the transmission of his impulses.[13]

Taken out of the context of the production, many of the episodes of *Apocalypsis cum Figuris* would seem to be merely sacrilegious. But the mood of the production is religious in a fundamental sense that has been adumbrated by William James:

Religion, whatever it is, is a man's total reaction upon life. . . . Total reactions are different from casual reactions, and total attitudes are different from usual or professional attitudes. To get at them you must go behind the foreground of existence and reach down to that curious sense of the whole residual cosmos

12. Rainer M. Rilke, *Sämtliche Werke*, vol. 1 (Insel Verlag, 1955), p. 557. Translation by Orus C. Barker, Jr., whom I thank for permission to quote.
13. Grotowski, p. 238. Cf. Artaud: "The actor should be like a martyr signalling from the flames."

as an everlasting presence, intimate or alien, terrible or amusing, lovable or odious, which in some degree everyone possesses.[14]

James specifies religious experience still further: it is the sense of the primal and enveloping reality to which the individual feels impelled to respond solemnly and gravely, and neither with a curse nor a jest. One experiences a submission which is solemn but glad. Grotowski's production is play which is nevertheless solemn. It is a challenge which he has set for himself and for his actors, a self-imposed contest of openness, a sacrifice which is ecstatic. Its purpose is a giving of self which is disclosive of it.

Cieslak's character, The Innocent, is a creature of mood, and he is modeled directly on Nietzsche's speculative depiction of the leader of the satyr chorus in primitive Greek tragedy: the "union of god and goat," "the wise and enthusiastic satyr who is at the same time the simpleton. . . ."[15] Yet he is also a Christ figure. He is ecstatically giving and open, and he enters so completely into the enthusiasm of the others that the rhythm of their meetings and celebrations excites him to superinduce his own faster rhythm. His syncopated gallop is like a young colt's. The resulting cacophony disturbs the others. They need and admire his empathy and spontaneity but they cannot reciprocate fully. His spontaneity gives rise to the chirp of a lark, theirs to the howl of wolves and the grunts of pigs. They feel wretched by comparison to him, learn to hate him, and finally drive him away. Neither is accepted and authorized by the other.

Adapting the scene from Dostoevsky's *Brothers Karamazov* in which the Grand Inquisitor lectures Jesus, Simon Peter—keys and all—denounces the Innocent, who collapses on the floor in an agony of self-deprecation. Only the two remain on the stage. Peter blows out the candles around his prostrate body, and says, "Go and come no more." Peter leaves. Darkness and silence. There is no curtain call.

This is theatre that borders on rite. But at most it is a broken rite. The Greek word for the grace of God is *charisma*, that from which we derive our faded and impoverished word of the same spelling. The Innocent has charm and a certain kind of charisma and power, but he lacks *charisma:* others do not abandon themselves to him and he does not stand in for them so as to authorize and empower them. They do not consume his flesh and drink his blood and participate in his power. They merely cast him out. Thrown into the periphery through the centrifugal force of the fiction, the member of the audience senses, as in a dream, a likeness into

14. W. James, *Varieties of Religious Experience;* from the early section, "Circumscription of the Topic."
15. Friedrich Nietzsche, *The Birth of Tragedy* (New York: Doubleday & Co. [Anchor Books], 1956), pp. 8, 57.

which he fits. He senses possible ways for him to be: mimetic impulses of
his own toward fusion, and tendencies to seek empowering authorization.
But probably he will experience these tendencies and impulses to be broken and aborted, just as are the characters' in the play. He is left with a
question which lives, at least during the moments of the performance, in
his body: what new possibilities of mimetic involvement, and of authorization and legitimation, remain viable within the debris of traditional
culture?

Throughout the six plays we have examined we have been following
variations which they make upon the fusion-rebellion complex as it pertains to individuals and their authorizing groups and group leaders. In
Oedipus Rex and *Hamlet* tragic difficulties attend the individuation of the
protagonists. *Waiting for Godot* is an ironic solution of the fusion-rebellion problem: the failure to achieve fusion in the first place prevents the
sins of sundering from occurring. But then the problem emerges as an
insubstantiality of the characters' reality as selves; individuation that
amounts to anything can occur only within a prior identity produced by
human fusion with authority. *The Chairs* is another variation on the essential theme of fusion and individuation which reveals insubstantiality of
self: the self is mad and fantastic because its relation to authority—both
its submission to it and its statement of its particular message—is mad and
fantastic. Wilson's *A Letter for Queen Victoria* presents extremely individualistic projections of possibilities, projections which grasp the normal
in the act of exploding its inevitability, and yet the play ends with a disclosure of infantile, and perhaps intractable, mimetic involvements. Grotowski's *Apocalypsis cum Figuris* presents a failure of fusion with the
authority, the Christ figure (and a concomitant failure in his authority);
but fusion there is: the "disciples" are an animal-like mob who are ruled
by a Simon Peter become bully and bureaucrat.

We have participated in variations on what seems to us to be the defin-
itory problem of our identity as selves. Fusion and individuation—to some
minimal degree at least—with all the attendant problems there must be;
and if we fail to achieve fusion with one authority then either there is
insubstantiality, or a fusion with another authority, perhaps the unsavory
mob of the "disciples." The words of St. Paul to his scattered churches
create for us perhaps a nostalgia: "You are one in the body of Christ."

Somewhat similarly, Grotowski's theatre event confirms a community.
But now it is a strange and troubling confirmation. It does not occur with
regular periodicity in the world-time of a people; hence they cannot memorialize themselves in a monument built of time. It confirms a fragment
of the community in the very dissonance and changeableness of its members' impulses, in its fractionalization, and in the disturbance of the ques-

tion with which it is left. Though the pace of the community be brisk and the voices animated, there is a background mood: "Something is wrong." Behind the animation is depression. Mimetic bonds, which are basic because they authorize through vicarious participation, have atrophied or been disturbed. Many feel insubstantial, worthless, unauthorized, rudderless, and lonely, despite the presence of others. The plays we have examined throw explanatory light on the condition aptly denoted by David Riesman in his title *The Lonely Crowd.*

Given unavoidable human dependency and interdependency it would seem that some form of authorization will always be needed. If so, can the secular group, closeted in its contemporaneity, authorize itself? Or, can each individual authorize his or her own self? These questions presuppose that the self has sufficient vitality to appropriate itself as one of its own disturbed and seeking kind. But does it? Can the self return to itself systematically and ritualistically as a questioning of its own being?

CHAPTER VIII

Theatre and the Question of the Truth of Art

It may seem obvious that in watching *The Elephant Man*, for example, we are relating only to an enacted monster—and one enacted by a well-formed actor—and so we are discovering only our ability to relate to enacted monsters, not to actual ones. Or it may seem obvious that in watching a fist fight on stage we are relating only to an enacted fight, only to one in which the fist does not actually make contact with the jaw, so we are discovering only our ability to relate to enacted fights, not to actual ones: theatre pulls its punches, and so must relinquish any claim to being true in any significant way about existence beyond the theatre.

But if we were very hungry and we were told, "There are apples in the cupboard," would we object that we were being given only the words and not the apples? Or would we object that we were discovering only our ability to relate to the words, and to understand them, and not to understand that to which they refer? We could object reasonably only if being given the words about the apples prevented us somehow from understanding the apples, or prevented us from achieving contact with them. But this is not typically the case. It is just the words that put us in touch with the things, or are a necessary condition for this to occur.

It is a fundamental misunderstanding of the ideality of all communication to think that the ideal which reveals the actual cannot reveal it truly because it is ideal and not actual. If it reveals the actual at all, it can do so only because it *is* ideal. It gives presence to what it itself is not. There are genuine problems involved in conceiving how art can be true, but they are found on more subtle levels of analysis than are frequented by these objections.

The identity and truth of the work of art cannot be sundered from our

136

own identity and truth as selves. In speaking for us it is not something isolated from us which is set over against us. Just how it pertains to our identity is a nice problem that requires the full length of this book. But we can say here that the work pertains to our identity because it mediates us and reveals us as essentially natural and essentially idealizing and conventional; as essentially bodily, private, and particular and essentially social; and because it sums up, funds, and gives presence to more absence than our everyday acts ever could. Thus, since the self—as we shall see—is an activity of cumulatively giving presence to absence, art pertains to our identity as selves. We need art or at least the art-like to be ourselves.

In the contemporary age one of art's major functions—and particularly theatre art's—is to sum up and give presence to our questioning about our involvements and our sources of authorization. It is a funding involvement in our involvements that is integral to our identity, no matter how troubled our identity might be. Indeed, contemporary art has reached the point, one might say, of desperate creativity and desperate involvement, as if it would compensate for the loss of traditional involvements.

The "world" of the art work occurs, it is real, only at the intersection of "world" and world. There is no art object in itself. In the art event the artists and participants cannot help but reveal themselves as they are—as artists and persons. The only question is whether they will reveal themselves profoundly or less than profoundly. One way in which a less than profound disclosure can occur is that what they reveal themselves as being while engaged in the art event is only the way they are during the event. One way in which a profound disclosure occurs is that what they are during the event knits itself up with other times of their lives so that these various times become linked together in a context and are rendered intelligible.

Although theatre is predominantly physiognomical communication, it is nevertheless ideal. Actual persons and things are used in the production but their factual reality is bracketed out so that what they are as types and essences can be revealed. Of course, words and statements are typically part of the production. But any move to consign these to non-assertoric uses of language manifests a naive dualism that misses the threads of ideality which connect life within and life outside the theatre. An actor neither asserts nor does he not assert. As character he asserts within the bracket. Just as a play bite is a bite, but one which limits itself and thereby signals itself to be a bite, so the character's assertion is one which signals itself to be an assertion and in so doing reveals some of the conditions of its own meaningfulness. Given our everyday absorption offstage in states of affairs asserted, rather than in the act of asserting and in the conditions of meaningfulness of the assertion, the self-framing assertion onstage can better reveal these conditions. Thus we take up the artistic stance when we do not *simply* assert.

We can now see how it is possible for theatre to be true of actual life while being itself a fiction. It can be true if it can exemplify the essences, sorts, types, universals which make actual persons and things what they are. We are particularly concerned with sorts of involvements. Hence a simple assertion outside the theatre is true if and only if it refers accurately to a set of actual particulars via the sorts of things which the particulars exemplify. On the other hand, an assertion made by a character in a play is true if and only if it refers accurately to any particulars—any *possible* particulars—of this *sort*. Of course, I am not saying that all assertions, simple or bracketed, are about particulars, or that truth is manifested only by verbal language.

Our book now makes an important transition. Up to this point we have pursued a phenomenology of the theatre. We have pointed out how the setting of the theatre with the interactions it allows prompts us to moments which we can only believe to be moments of recognition of our common extratheatrical mimetic life. We generated the hypothesis that conditions of convincing enactment of persons onstage include the recognition of universal features without which persons could not be recognized at any time or place (the features of any possible person). This seemed to be confirmed as we sat in the theatre. We enriched this hypothesis by adopting provisionally Heidegger's four existential conditions of being human; it was just these that we saw exemplified in the four contemporary plays we discussed; we could not imagine these conditions removed and imagine the enactments to be convincing. If our hypothesis is true, then in understanding the features which make characters convincingly enacted onstage, we will be grasping the features in terms of which we recognize actual persons offstage.

But is the hypothesis true, and are the convictions that we hold in the theatre correct? We have shown how they might be true, but are they actually so? Moreover, even if we should grasp the features in terms of which we recognize actual persons offstage, do these features constitute what these persons really *are*? We have not yet proved that theatre discloses what we must suppose about persons if we would understand how it is possible for them to be convincingly enacted in the theatre. A new stage of inquiry is demanded.

We will be in a much better position to answer these basic questions if an independent account of the conditions of identity of self offstage tends to confirm the convictions we hold in the theatre. If these conditions of identity turn out to be *theatre-like* then theatre as metaphor will have an excellent chance to grasp them. Of course, if theatrical metaphor in all its versions and ramifications turns out to be essential, then a strictly independent account of the conditions of identity of self will be impossible. All that we can hope to accomplish is an account that makes no reference to theatre *per se,* in which nevertheless theatre-like terms show up inevitably and naturally. Such an account we will attempt to give; we will also dispense with Heidegger's formulation of the conditions of identity. Adopting a transcendental deduction of these conditions of identity of self at any time or place, an account which is broadly phenomenological but which does not employ much of the technical terminology, we will expose conditions of identity that are very close to what Heidegger formulates in most respects, and which are theatre-like as well. Theatrical metaphor will turn out to be essential—although not all-powerful.

Let us be unmistakably clear about what we have in mind: if the theatrical metaphor is essential, then instead of just sliding inexorably and naturally from an analysis of the conditions of theatrical "individual" (the character) and "world" into an analysis of the conditions of individual and world, we should also slide inexorably and naturally from this other "side" back into theatre. I think that this does happen. We will endeavor to show, through a general theory of the conditions of identity of the self, that a theory which is exclusively mentalistic and which relies solely on memory is inadequate, and that a key condition is that there be a body which is able to "express" itself, to deploy and display itself in a theatre-like way in space and time. That this body-self is inescapably theatre-like will, of course, be evidence for the essentiality of theatrical metaphor in all its forms, because to understand the theatre-like presupposes an understanding of the theatre.

We will deduce conditions of identity which are spatial, temporal, interpersonal, mimetic, bodily, dialogical. The space and time we have in mind are not just those of geometry and chronometry. They are the space and time which we directly live: a domain in which objects and persons of our concern and care are de-distanced and given presence through the bodily stances of these attitudes themselves. This is a domain of paths and routes, as if it were an organism of mimetic relatedness—with sinews and shapes and varying degrees of density—within which we live. We will lead up to the distinctive emergence of theatre-like behavior as a condition of identity.

In sum: we have already shown how theatre is life-like in appearance, even when it is not in the naturalistic style. Now we will change the direction of our inquiry and show that life is theatre-like, within certain broad limits. The ultimate point will be to show that we are confined to a single circle of concepts, and that we must move either clockwise from theatre to life, or counterclockwise from life to theatre. If this point is made, we will have to conclude that metaphorically loaded appearance is co-extensive with reality—at least for as long as we can grasp appearance.

PART TWO

Reality and the Self

CHAPTER IX

Space, Time,
and Identity of Self

It is vexing to realize that the term *identity* has no single sense. When coupled with the term *self*, as in *identity* of *self*, each of the terms exacerbates the difficulties in the other. *Identity* can pertain to atemporal entities like numbers, to temporal ones like persons, to atemporal and temporal groups of entities, and possibly to the universe itself as that which is identical with itself and with nothing else. Pertaining to a temporal being that is a person it means, presumably, that the being is identical with itself through time and change. The first danger here is that a sense of identity appropriate to a static entity such as a number will be tacitly assumed to apply to a person also, and that this will set up an artificial and highly distracting problem: how could *this* identity possibly be maintained through time?

At the other end of the continuum of initial misunderstandings is a sense of identity which includes the sense of time and change, but it is properly applicable to identity of personality, not to identity of person or self.[1] In cases in which there has been disruption of identity of personality it does not follow that there has been disruption of identity of person. We commonly say of another who has undergone a conversion, or a crisis, or simply the passing of a great many years: "He's not himself, you wouldn't know him." But if we speak literally we contradict ourselves: He—meaning that person there whom we have always known—is not himself? To know that there has been a great personality change in him, we must assume, rather, that there has been a change in *him*. We must assume that that man himself has undergone the change, and so we must assume his identity through time.

1. For the purposes of this section, I will use "person" and "self" as synonyms.

143

Let us push the case of personality change to the limit. Assume we have an instance of precipitous and violent insanity with no periods of remission. It is not clear what sense this human being has of his own distinctiveness through time. Still, we observers would have to say that he is the same self, otherwise we could not say that it is *he* who has gone mad. Moreover, we would probably bridle at saying that this was merely a necessity of speech. If we could exhume the criteria at work in our judgment, they would probably include: (1) That human body there is the same body; it has followed the course of a single history in space-time which is just the life of this person, John Robinson. (2) That body there may perhaps be restored to its accustomed character of action and self (an argument from potentiality, somewhat akin to saying that a bicycle in pieces is still the same one, because it can be put together and function as before). (3) That being is the same person because we, his family and friends, continue to be responsible for caring for him. If we are responsible for caring for that body because we are responsible for caring for John Robinson, then that body is John Robinson.[2] Identity here would be implied by the moral responsibility of others.

Even if the man should die we are not utterly and immediately sure that the self or person has ceased to be. This uncertainty is reflected in our language. We say either that John Robinson's corpse is in the casket or that John Robinson is. We are even now providing for his funeral, so how could we have ceased to be responsible for *him?* At the wake we are somehow with him, even though he, somehow, is not with us. That body has memorialized itself there in space as John Robinson, and we stand within its presence, but we do not think that John Robinson can stand within our presence. It would simplify things a great deal if we could eliminate the body altogether from the criteria of identity of person or self, for then its strange status relative to others could be eliminated also.

John Locke sought to give univocity and clarity to the term *person* by narrowing its sense, and by making its application depend upon the satisfaction of a single criterion imposable only by the being himself, and only in mentalistic, "inner" terms:

> . . . This being premised, to find wherein personal identity consists, we must consider what *person* stands for;—which, I think, is a thinking intelligent being, that has reason and reflection, and can consider itself as itself, the same thinking being, in different times and places; which it does only by that consciousness which is inseparable from thinking, and, as it seems to me, essential to it: it being impossible for any one to perceive without *perceiving*

2. As we will discuss below, a person does not own his body in the ordinary sense of "own." In that sense we can take care of a person's house, say, without taking care of him.

that he does perceive. . . . For, since consciousness always accompanies think-ing, and it is that which makes every one to be what he calls self, and thereby distinguishes himself from all other thinking beings, in this alone consists personal identity, i.e., the sameness of a rational being: and as far as this consciousness can be extended backwards to any past action or thought, so far reaches the identity of that person; it is the same self now it was then; and it is by the same self with this present one that now reflects on it, that that action was done. . . .[3]

I agree that any adequate view of the person or self must include its capacity, whether nascent or matured, to take itself as self and as the same. But I wish to deny that this condition can be satisfied in the mentalistic manner of Locke's account. It is wrong to assert that it is "impossible for anyone to perceive without perceiving that he does perceive." Presumably infants perceive before they have sense of self, and even adults perceive much of the time without any thematic sense—any "perceiving that"—it is they who perceive. Indeed, often there is perception without there being any thematic sense *that* there is perception going on. Locke seems to be misled by the structure of our language about perception to assume that the state of mind which is essential for such language to be used about perception is essential for perception itself to occur. Since perceiver, lan-guage-user, person is posited by our language about perception, he infers mistakenly that it is also posited by perception itself.

This position ignores the evidence that perceiving is characteristically lost in the presence of the perceived. Though perceiving is not without its own presence, even in pre-reflective life, it is one which is typically eclipsed by that of the perceived, and it need carry no thematic or ac-knowledgeable sense of itself, or of itself as a self's perceiving. How a conscious body is to achieve thematic self-reflexiveness is the very difficult problem of how it is to be returned to itself as itself from its objects, and I believe it can be shown eventually that theatre or theatre-like activity plays a role here.

Thinking that the person can establish himself from within himself alone—indeed from within the luminous atom of his own mind alone—Locke thinks that the person might be transferable from one body to another:

For should the soul of a prince, carrying with it the consciousness of the prince's past life, enter and inform the body of a cobbler, as soon as deserted by his own soul, every one sees he would be the same *person* with the prince, accountable only for the prince's actions: but who would say it was the same

3. John Locke, *An Essay Concerning Human Understanding*, ed. P. H. Nidditch (Ox-ford: Clarendon Press, 1975) Book II, Ch. 27.

man? The body too goes to the making the man, and would, I guess, to everybody determine the man in this case, wherein the soul, with all its princely thoughts about it, would not make another man: but he would be the same cobbler to every one besides himself.[4]

It would be the same *man*, the cobbler, but a different *person* would inhabit that man, the prince. I will dispute the bifurcation Locke makes between criteria of identity of man, as a natural form of life, and criteria of identity of person. I will argue that criteria of identity of person involve reference to body, and that criteria which in principle can be imposed only by the being himself in reference to his own mental states may be necessary, but they are insufficient to establish that person's identity.

First, the sequence of mental states has a continuity which presupposes *prima facie* a distinct sensory point of view in space, a sensing body; perspectives of things experienced unfold sequentially and coherently only for it, and only in accordance with its motivations to move. If this is claimed to be merely a contingent matter of the person just happening to be in some body or other, and the sequence of perspectives just happening to unfold coherently, then it would follow that the person could in principle jump instantaneously, constantly, and at random from body to body and from place to place. But this he cannot do, since for him to be in a situation he must find it minimally intelligible, and this must be compatible with his being in the situation in which his current body is, and for a certain stretch of time; he must be able to know what he's jumping *from*. The sense of being anywhere is at least the sense of an abiding sensed, a changing sensing, and an abiding senser. So the person must abide for some moments in a body, hence cannot do what in principle he should be able to do if his relationship with bodies were purely contingent and nonessential: he cannot jump constantly and at random from body to body.

This constraint applies within the first-person point of view. But the same sort of constraint applies also to the ascertainment of identity from the third-person point of view. To assume that the string of words, "I am John Robinson," being emitted from the mouth of a body is a sentence uttered by a single person, I must assume that a single person occupies that body throughout the string. Otherwise, one person might have said "I am" in this body, and then said "John Smith" from another body two miles away. While someone else, who had traded places, has said "John Robinson" in this body. So no single person has said "I am John Robinson"; we have a mere string of words and no intelligible sentence. And this is not merely a necessity of speech, for we must suppose that intelli-

4. Ibid.

gible sentences are possible, and we must suppose whatever makes them possible, if we are to suppose that any investigation is possible.[5]

Notice what we are doing. We are excavating what we must assume about the identity of beings if we are to assume that they are identifiable as the beings we take them to be. What makes our experience of a person— either ourself or another—possible? This is a transcendental investigation, and it falls within the tradition stretching from Kant through Heidegger and others. For Heidegger we cannot identify a person in isolation of the world of space, time, and others in which he finds himself and lives; all the ontological and irreducible potentialities are ones of a being-in-the-world. To demonstrate the breadth and depth of this general approach I will now proceed independently of Heidegger. I will follow the thought of others, and generate my own as well. First I utilize that of the contemporary English philosopher P. F. Strawson. Not only is it valuable in itself, but gaining a sense of its limitations is valuable additionally.

As Strawson has noted trenchantly of any transcendental argument, we do not assume that there exist in the mind concepts of possible sorts of things which pose the problem of how these concepts get applied to actual things "out there" in the world. For if they did not already apply in some way to these particulars we could not think of the latter at all. It is only because we have assumed a solution to the "problem" of their application that the genuine problem arises. This is *how* do they apply—what makes their application possible—given that they do apply.[6] So we have a concept of a person. What does its application presuppose? Instead of speaking in theatrical terms of a person's presence, as we did in the first part of this book, we are now attempting to articulate conceptually the conditions of the person's identifiability in the prosaic offstage world. We leave open the possibility that we will rejoin the initial approach. This would happen if conditions of identifiability of self were to involve conditions of identity of self which were theatre-like.

Given the conceptual scheme within which we find ourselves, how is it employed to identify the things that do get identified through it? Whatever the identity of a person turns out to be, it must at least include those of its features without which we would not be able to identify it. The identification of anything presupposes a single, common, continuously extendable framework within which it can be identified both for the identifier and for others. It can be identified as a single thing only because it can be picked out from others, and it can be picked out only because it

5. I have adapted some points made by Sydney Shoemaker in his *Self-Knowledge and Self-Identity* (Ithaca: Cornell University Press, 1963).

6. P. F. Strawson, *Individuals: An Essay in Descriptive Metaphysics* (New York: Anchor Books, 1963), p. 30.

occupies a position in time and space which is unique relative to other things; but it is a unique position only within a common framework. The idea that a thing can exist as the very same in indefinitely numerous and simultaneous editions of itself destroys the very idea of its identifiability.

Strawson argues that a person is a basic particular within this framework of basic particulars, and so some of the attributes of material particulars must apply to persons; thus he argues directly against Locke. His argument hinges on the idea that the identifiability of persons involves the use of person-predicates: whatever can be ascribed to persons *qua* persons: "is afraid," "is bald," "is looking at the sky," "is writing a letter," etc. Given the nature of language and predication, predicates are general and so must be ascribable to more than one person, so to more than oneself. To ascribe them to others means that one must be able to identify other subjects of experience. But one cannot do this if he can identify them *only* as subjects of their own private experience, for this would not be directly accessible to him. So in order to ascribe mental states to myself I must be able to ascribe to myself predicates ascribable to others, and these involve ascription on the basis of certain publicly accessible corporeal characteristics of others. First-person ascription of predicates presupposes knowledge of third-person ascription of these same predicates. Of course, many of these predicates are ascribable by me to myself without the need for observation of the sort that I must make of others; but that does not change the main point for Strawson.

The mentalist supposes what his official picture of the world cannot justify him in supposing: that there is an isolated and disembodied consciousness which can identify itself and its contents as its own. The skepticism concerning other minds and other persons that is naturally involved in this position makes it impossible for him to acknowledge a condition of his initial self-identification: that the private and personal consciousness presupposes some contrasting sense, which is that of the other's being and consciousness. He is tempted to say that he just *has* an individual consciousness, as a person just *has* an individual head. But one doesn't *just have* an individual head; one learns to identify it in terms necessarily applicable to others' heads as well; likewise with one's consciousness.

To use the person-predicates that we do use in identifying persons, one must be both a self-ascriber and an other-ascriber, and must see every other as both too. It must follow, then, that one's depression, say, is the very same depression that is felt by oneself and observed by others—if it is observed at all on the occasion in question. Thus mental states are intrinsically "expressive." But that word is misleading, because it suggests that something already existing is simply pressed outside. So on Strawson's view one's depression is already as equally "outside" as it is "inside," and though one can try to conceal it—for what can be observed can also be faked or concealed—it is this concealment that requires added explanation, not its "expression."

That persons have material bodies is a necessary truth in Strawson's view. We cannot identify them without identifying material bodies, and what we must always use to identify we must regard as pertaining to the person's identity. Moreover, I must experience myself as a body identifiable by others, so my identity must include how I experience others' identifying and experiencing my body. Since in the normal course of events there is similarity of response to human bodies by human bodies, I must experience myself to be, and I must be, essentially similar to others. This begins to clear the way for a theory of mimetic behavior.

I believe that Strawson is in outline correct—at least as far as he goes. It is his way of arguing the point that for the person to be aware of himself he must be aware of himself as one of "our kind." That my sense of myself is in any way dependent on my sense of another is a rewarding switch from Locke. It becomes even more enlightening when one goes beyond Strawson and the limitations of an approach which gravitates so closely around the conditions of the verbal identification of things. When we broaden the scope of the inquiry phenomenologically to include the full gamut of ways in which we stand open to others, then inquiry is freed to explore the implications of one's dominantly nonobservational sense of oneself as person being dependent to some considerable degree upon one's observational knowledge of others. It points toward a theory which can link enactment in the arts with one's sense of self and with the identity of that self. For what can be observed in oneself by others, and in others by oneself, is not only what can be concealed or faked on occasion—which puts it all very negatively—but is what can be enacted as well.

After concluding that a person is an individual to whom both mentalistic and physicalistic predicates must apply—and that the concept of a person is a primitive one within the conceptual scheme we do use—Strawson writes, "[W]e may still want to ask what it is in the natural facts that makes it intelligible that we should have this concept. . . . I do not pretend to be able to satisfy this demand at all fully." But he mentions some things "which might count as beginnings or fragments of an answer."

> First, I think a beginning can be made by moving a certain class of P-predicates [predicates for persons] to a central position in the picture. They are predicates, roughly, which involve doing something, which clearly imply intention or a state of mind or at least consciousness in general, and which indicate a

characteristic pattern, or range of patterns of bodily movement, while not indicating at all precisely any very definite sensation or experience. I mean such things as "going for a walk," "coiling a rope," "playing ball," "writing a letter." Such predicates have the interesting characteristic of many P-predicates, that one does not, in general, ascribe them to oneself on the strength of observation, whereas one does ascribe them to others on the strength of observation.[7]

As a tentative explanation of why we have the person-concepts and predicates which we do have, he cites certain characteristic patterns of bodily movement that imply state of mind or intention; patterns which we incorporate in our own sense of ourselves, but nonobservationally. These are actions, things done—and things done as displayable. Strawson writes, "it is important that we should understand such movements [of others] for they bear on and condition our own."[8] Just how they do, he does not say. I think it is plausible to believe that one's observational knowledge of others is built into oneself nonobservationally and furtively, and through play-like "enactment" offstage and enactment onstage. We discover the others built into ourselves mimetically. Strawson admits that the body may be a "necessary part" of the explanation of self-ascription, but he does not explain how it is so.[9] These are crucial matters. We must leave open the possibility that theatre as a *de facto* phenomenological investigation is what can move key "P-predicates" and actions to a "central position in the picture," and by varying them give us some idea of "what it is in the natural facts that makes it intelligible that we should have this concept." We may be able to see how concepts are generated in our experience at large, not merely how they must apply to things, given that they are already embedded in our verbal language.

7. Ibid., p. 108.
8. Ibid., p. 109.
9. Ibid., p. 94.

CHAPTER X

Self as Body-Self

The typical empiricist's fixation on the role of memory in identity betrays his tacit belief that consciousness is a chamber-like thing in which mental events occur. Since the events are all actual, the self can contain only what has actually happened, and this is all past or passing. Certainly, some mental states are anticipations, but these are only passing or past events.

No doubt the latent or matured capacity to give presence to what is past is an essential condition for a being to be a person. Locke pointed out that consciousness feels its contents to be its own, and this is "extended" to contents which are of events long past. We come up with something important: to now remember something experienced in the past is to remember it experienced by someone, and to truly remember this must mean not only that that something did happen, but that the being by whom it was experienced is identical with the being who now remembers it—I myself. Who else could remember the living-through of the experiencing? Even though the past experiencing and the something experienced are remembered somewhat differently each time, the self *is* just this identity of process, this ever growing and changing remembering of past experiencings.

But giving the past presence is only one facet of that transcendence of the present and actual by which we transcend time in time, and are constituted as one experiencer of a world experienced. And it is misleading to try to construe this transcendence after the model of events occurring within a chamber-like consciousness. First, little sense can be made of the necessary distinction to be drawn between act of experiencing and what this is *of*—what is experienced by the act. Second, it is not just past experiences that are "owned," but possible, future ones in anticipation and imagination. How one sets himself, either habitually or irruptively, to face the future cannot be properly construed as just a passing event within a consciousness.

Perhaps the most misleading feature of the metaphor of self as chamber-like consciousness is that it generates the idea that the identity of the self is a dyadic relationship in which the presently occurring events within the chamber somehow reflect events which occurred in it in the past. This tendency is abetted by the tradition of formal thought for which identity is that of a formal entity which coincides statically and eternally with itself, $A = A$. But the identity of the self is dialectical, at least triadic, and it is other-directed and future-directed. Charles Peirce, for example, contended that the self is a coherent sequence of signs which must be interpretable by self and others (there must be signs, interpretations of signs, and interpreters). This becomes a fascinating and difficult triad because the self's interpretations of itself as a sequence of signs must in large part be in terms of others' interpretations of this same sequence. We will develop our own idea of identity as dialectical.

It can be argued that it took philosophy over two thousand years, until Hegel, to reach this insight: a human being can become itself, its self, only when it makes its own what others have made of it. Ultimately, it must make individually its own what others, who are of its own sort, have made of it. The individual self is individuated within what is ours. Each experiencing body can become its own, can become a significantly individuated human self, only because it can become an other for itself which is other from every other, even as it makes its own what others make of it.

To establish this view, I employ a mode of transcendental deduction: the progressive exposure of the conceptual conditions of the identifiability of a self, with these conditions explained just insofar as they explain within the unifying context of reflective experience. Unavoidable conditions of identification will be conditions of identity. I include Strawson's approach within a larger whole. This, in brief, is the sequence of the argument: It is a conscious, or potentially conscious, body which must be identified as a self, and it is so under the following conditions: when it can experience objects or persons which are in fact other than itself—but with whom it is mimetically involved—and then can reproduce them *as* other in their absence. This includes its ability to deliberately reproduce its undeliberate mimetic involvement and identification *with others' identification and objectification of it,* and in their absence. The body must be able, to some extent, to appropriate *as* its own *its* mimetic reproduction of *them.* Art and art-like activity—and most specifically theatre and theatre-like activity—will be shown to be a condition of the body's realizing this; a condition of its being *its* self. To be a self is to be for oneself as one's own through an articulation of what one is for others.

Ultimately I will argue that theatrical art and theatre-like play are sensuous consummations of the activity of owning purely ideal essences or sorts—not merely those which were in fact, or which could be in fact, instantiated in human relations. The development of self requires the ability to give presence to the purely ideal.

Now, it would be pointless and counterproductive to ignore the indebtedness of all these approaches—Heidegger's, Strawson's, my own—to Kant. But it is equally incumbent upon me to point out just where I diverge from Kant. It is the element of mentalism in Kant—the residue of Locke and Hume—that I reject. Yet I am greatly indebted to his argument that the sense of self is dependent upon the sense of something which is not the self. A self can become itself only if it can gain a sense of itself as its own through time, and it can gain this only through a construction of itself as the experiencing correlate of, and contrast to, the objects known through its experience: e.g., now expectation of manipulating X, now perception of X and of manipulating it, now memory of having manipulated X, etc. One moment does not replace another, but they hang together in experienced time, and not just because the object is apprehended as the same in each of its presentations—when it is presented as not actually present, for example, or even if it is presented as not actually being any longer—but because it can be presented as the same object only when it is presented as the same *for* a being that remains actual through all its diverse activities and moments. This being is just what one means by one's self.

Moreover, the self is not merely the passively registered constant correlate of a sequence of mental events within an atom. As Kant put it, the intersubjective transcendental imagination spans time through creating schemas or images of things—things as possible. This is the root of Heidegger's conception of the understanding as a projecting of possibilities. Because possibility can be envisaged, the relevant past can be retrieved and a living present can be experienced in which a single being chooses, decides, and acts.

Moreover, as Kant noted, objectivity requires intersubjectivity. For an object to be presented as fully itself it must be presented as apprehendable by others. And, I add, if the person is to apprehend himself as a real constituent of the world—and this apprehension is essential to what he is as a self—then he must also apprehend himself as intersubjectively apprehendable. Of course, this means that he must experience himself to be a body.

But this last inference is made too simply and directly for Kant himself to follow it. A number of factors prevented this. His notion of experience as *Erfahrung* involves a conception of representations or appearances in which experienc*ing* and phenomenal attributes of objects experienc*ed* are never clearly distinguished. Because the notion of experiencing is never properly developed, there can be no effective investigation of how a sense of the experiencer's own body might be essential to his sense of his own experiencing and his own self. To secure belief in physical objects against skepticism seemed sufficient task to Kant, and for him the human body turns out to be just another object of scientific knowledge.

No doubt, thematic and scientific knowledge—the conditions of which Kant sought—is actually achieved at a certain level of maturity of self (or at least capacity for it at times when it is appropriate). By thematic knowledge I mean knowledge in the form of explicit verbal judgments, or else perceptions which are, in principle, verbalizable. But Kant was too willing to suppose that this is the only level of knowledge and of the self worthy of having its conditions "deduced"; consequently some of the conditions of knowledge and self were slighted. It is here, we will find, that an analysis of art and the art-like should enter the "deduction," for it can penetrate into the more immediate and personal moments of what Kant calls "the immediate consciousness of the existence of other things outside me."[1] We need to expose first some of the conditions for nonthematic knowledge to become thematic, and for the self to be itself. To do this we must understand the self as essentially and peculiarly body.

I will analyze the body not just as object of scientific knowledge, but as a condition of identity of the knower himself. Kant's idea of the fugue-like construct which is experiencing-self and experienced objects will be retained, but with the body essential to the self and to its experiencing. I will then tie this analysis of body as self into the "expressivity" of it via others and back to itself, and articulate the point that objective reality for human beings—which includes the objective reality of the self—must be intersubjectively experienceable. However, I will also leave room for what is directly experienceable only by the self.

I see something now, I remember it later; any theory of mind must be able to distinguish different acts of experiencing from the single thing that is experienced by them. Experiencing and experienced must each be presentable as varying without the other being so presented; otherwise neither could be known. Now, if we develop the manner in which one's body is typically and pervasively present in one's experience—present without being presented—and if we extrapolate on one of Kant's own distinctions, I believe that we will be able to see how the experience of the body is indispensable to the person's own conscious and pre-reflective experiencing, and hence is indispensable both to his sense of self and to his self.

For example, in perception it is only because the body is perceptually engaged with the perceivable world that the world is perceived at all, yet

1. Immanuel Kant, "The Refutation of Idealism," *Critique of Pure Reason,* 2nd ed., trans. N. K. Smith (New York: St. Martin's Press, 1958).

it is only because the body gives way to this world beyond it (it is not focally perceived itself) that perception of the world can occur. The body must "step aside" to allow the rest of the world to appear to and through it. As Merleau-Ponty, William James, and others have seen, we do not first recognize things and then manipulate them, but, on the level of recognition which is discovery, manipulate and then recognize. It follows that the body is not first known and then set in motion in the world in order to understand the world in terms of the already understood responses and skills of the body, but that the world is understandable only within the context of already occurring, nonthematic, concernful manipulation and perception of the world, which world includes, as one *eventual* object of study, the manipulative and perceptive body. That is, we experience our bodies only through the-world-perceived-and-manipulated-by-our-bodies. The primary perceptual meaning of things is global and interinvolving.

Thus the body refers beyond itself in a very odd and complex sense: I experience my body primordially only when I look right through it, and experience it through the responses of others and other things to it. And if I focalize the body in secondary experience—say, look at it—I respond to it in terms first set by the responses of other things and persons to my body; not by my body "in itself"; e.g., that image in the mirror, though distinctive to be sure —"brown eyes, long nose, scar on the left cheek—me"—is not built up on its own basis alone, but is an image involved in, and precipitated by global *interpersonal* meaning and general nonthematic senses. The body is such that to look at it is to look back at it from the world; it must be reflected, in a literal and trivial sense (in a mirror), and in a nonliteral and important sense. It might be compared to a transparent instrument viewable only through the mirror of the world it has already manipulated and modified; except the body is not strictly speaking an instrument, nor is the world strictly speaking a mirror.

The key distinction in Kant upon which I mean to extrapolate is that between synthetic and analytic apperception. The analytic, dissecting unity of the prosaic perceptual as well as judgmental consciousness presupposes synthetic unity, e.g., it is only because I can think John and Jim together that I can think that John is not Jim. Things to which we refer must be *along with* each other in the field of consciousness if they are to be discerned *to be* different from each other, or *to be* factually absent from each other. I will develop the idea that the body present in awareness, but marginally and not as an object of scientific knowledge, is *along with* focal referents in the field in just such a way that it functions to be *of* these referents without necessarily being experienced as *being* with them, i.e., being in their physical presence, or being simultaneously with them in the world. Thus the body in experience will be integral to the self's experiencing.

Involved in the meaning of something taken to be there in space is the idea of something which at that instant presents itself to us on only one of its sides; it presents itself perspectively. Involved in this is the concept of a line of sight, and with this the concept of a perceiving being so set and stanced in space that it sees only along this line. Cognition and expression cannot be conceived to be sundered in the self as it actually exists. I cannot visually perceive something, for example, without facing it with open eyes, thus without expressing that I am perceiving it. When remembering I cannot help but disengage (to some extent) my sense modalities from the events of the passing scene, thus I cannot help but appear "evacuated," and to express and to experience my remembering. Nor is my entertainment of non-present but past events indistinguishable expressively from my entertainment of non-present but possibly present ones. In the latter case I am on my toes—my senses alert, roving, scanning. Even if no bodies existed, it would be essential to my sense of my experiencing—as I must understand it—that I sensed and felt, however vaguely or unveridically, a body appropriately deploying and positioning itself.

The point is that the body must be experienced *along with* everything else in each case, but it need not be experienced as *being* together with everything else. This is compatible with the lived distinction between experiential activities which are mine, and the things upon which these activities are directed. Each is experienced as varying in its own appropriate ways without necessarily occasioning a change in the other; for example, while still perceiving a snowball, I see it melt; while passing from perception to memory of a rock, I still take it to be enduring.

Or take this case: my present memory that last year I perceived the constellation Orion would be sketched in terms of this analysis thusly. Within the current field of consciousness this body is sensed to be identical with the body which was visually *along-with* those celestial bodies which themselves were presented as *being* Orion. My bodily self is given as looking at Orion last year.

I am preparing the way, I believe, for an adequate theory of mimetic behavior. Since, contrary to the usual procedure, the self is not being pegged in advance as a subject over against objects, but as involved essentially in a body which is involved pre-reflectively and non-thematically in others and in other things, we are already on our way to a theory of the conditions of mimetic behavior both offstage and on which does not stack the cards against itself from the beginning. We should then be able to relate mimetic response to identity of self without begging the question of identity.

Just because the body is ubiquitously but peripherally *along with* everything else in the field of experienced objects, it can be absorbed experientially in these objects. But then what happens to the painfully won distinction between act of experiencing and object experienced? No doubt this distinction is essential to any account of the structure of experience. And, indeed, it is only because we have made the distinction that we can then go on to say that at crucial times in the pre-reflective life as it is actually lived this distinction becomes blurred, and is only partially or inadequately made. This occurs in mystical or oceanic involvement with others and with Nature. For example, the power of van Gogh's painting of turbulent cypresses thrashing in the wind derives from the painter's ability to capture his mimetic fusion with them—to capture the fact of their turbulence being perceived in and through the turbulence of his body-self, and of each turbulence reinforcing and commingling with the other. The turbulence of the experiencing compounds the turbulence of the experienced, and conversely. As we will note, actors train themselves to slide into this "hot spot" of mimetic interfusion and involvement.

This blurring of the body-self's act of experiencing and the object experienced has a vitally important corollary: since the distinction is essential not only for distinguishing self and other, but also for distinguishing a present act of remembering from a past event remembered, the blurring of individual identity will go hand in hand with a blurring of time and change. Perception blurs with memory and the present blurs with the past. Thus engulfment in others is characterized by a peculiarly timeless quality. When this engulfment is habitual and impedes individuation of identity, it will have a death-like quality which radically obstructs its recognition and alteration.

The absorption of the experiencing body in the experienced object can proceed to the point where the *along-with* slips nonthematically into a magical or quasi-magical merging with the other, that being which officially (in Apollonian terms) one is not. The *along-with* slips into *being with* or *being in*. Thus, for example—to take a case which is not negative— the transports and ecstacies of love in which lived time slips away, unregretted, or seems to stand still. The body experienced primordially is not thematic, hence cannot be thematically apprehended as *not* being the same as the other. From a third-person point of view, the separate bodies are sufficient to individuate. But individual *identity* involves also the person's own sense of himself as body, and this is what is merged with the other. In Kant's terms, analytic apperception becomes swamped with the synthetic. We are involved, then, in a transcendental deduction of Nietzsche's idea of the Dionysian strand in existence; it is a rational reconstruction of it—employing "rational" now in the most flexible and, it is hoped, most creative sense.

It might be objected, however, that the body is not really indispensable in the self's experiencing, but is merely another experienced object, albeit unique in some ways. The body as experienced may become absorbed in other objects, but since it is quite distinct from the self, the self does not. A variant on this theme is that the body is owned by the self as is any possession. And like all possessions it is possible in principle (though perhaps not in fact) both that this body be owned by some other self, and that there be some means of specifying the owner independently of his owning of this possession.

On the contrary, I think that the body in experience, the living and lived body, is an element constitutive of the self. Even if (*per impossible*, I believe) there should be some way of conceiving of the self as existing independently of its body, yet if we do conceive of it having a body we must conceive of it having it essentially. That is, unlike any other of its actual possessions (e.g., its house), there is no way of conceiving of the self independently of conceiving of its body, if we once conceive of its having a body at all. We can conceive of a person without conceiving of his house, but if we try to conceive of him without his body we can no longer do so. This is rather odd, to be sure. My body is mine *and* me: it is primordially mine; and it is so just insofar as it is not thematized, not identified *as* mine. It does not presuppose the independent identifiability of the self which owns it, because it is not a simple object owned. As body-subject it is an element constitutive of the self, the subject.

I believe that it is impossible to specify the self independently of the body. Even persons' reports of having left the body—e.g., of "looking down on it lying there in bed"—presuppose a position in space from which it is viewed, and a perspectival view which implies the presence of sense organs, and presumably *some* body, at that point. Granted that they experience themselves with an "astral body," or whatever, but their notion of this is parasitical on their normal experience of their normal body, which now lies down there. That this departure from their normal body actually occurs, as they think it does, is exceedingly less likely than that while in their normal bodies they dream or hallucinate that they are in their astral bodies. But even if we say that this does occur, these persons must still have at least one body that is essentially their own for the time they are "in" it.[2] And since it would seem that their experience of the

2. And it would seem that it would have to be in some ways like the old body: e.g., capable of spatiotemporal continuity within a situation. If the proprioceptive experience were utterly different it is difficult to see how this could be integrated with memories and expectations in such a way that the person experiences this body as primordially his, so experiences *himself* in a situation, as he must if he's to know that he's jumping from situation to situation. Philosophers who conjecture about transplanting brains from site to site sometimes forget (1) that this is a crucial portion of body, and (2) that the immensely complex coordination of experience involved in even "simple" perception, which is usually supplied by the regular body, will have to be supplied from some other source. If we should grant the

body down there would be an experience of their *own ordinary* body, it would also seem that their identity as selves would involve a remembering of both bodies, and in the appropriate sequence of one-body and two-body experiences.

It is much easier to *say* that the transmigration of self from body to body occurs than it is to imagine what would have to be the case for it to *really* happen. Talk of out-of-body experiences (or of transfer of brains from body to body) generally overlooks how deeply intertwined our conceptual system is with the commonly alleged *fact* of persons (and brains) belonging to particular bodies. However intriguing such speculations might be, I will not further indulge in them. Those unconvinced by my argument can think that it applies to them only when they are in their mundane bodies, and to this they will probably accord some significance at least.

To the objection that there are no bodies of any sort in space, I reply, adapting from Kant, that one can take the idea of the self seriously only if one takes the contrasting notion of bodies in space other than one's self seriously. Strawson's version: I must apply to myself predicates that are applicable by me to others, and since I apply the predicates to others only because they have bodies to which they are applicable, I must also have a body. The self *is* a body, although it is very peculiar in being capable of experience in the way it is.

I will now argue more systematically that the lived-body is the locus through time of multitudinous acts of experiencing by this real self—by I-myself. Also that the body lives itself in a "transitional synthesis," or continuity (rather than as an objectifying or "identifying synthesis").[3] Only out of this arises any sense of self. Hence the body as owned is also the owner of itself; so its being owned cannot beg the question of the identity of another being as owner.

Provocative ideas along this line are found in William James's seminal *Principles of Psychology*. Consonant with the manifest dualistic program of that book, the identity of the self is first sketched in a mentalistic and somewhat Lockeian way. Identity is constituted by "remembering and appropriating thought incessantly renewed": I am I because thinking finds continuity, resemblance, and "warmth" in experiences and in experienced objects identified *as* mine (although the warmest and most constant is the body called mine). Identity is very much a matter of identification—an annotated history of subjective data.

---

possibility in principle that an actual body could supply this—some diaphanous body, say— it becomes more improbable than was perhaps initially expected that such an event would ever actually occur.

3. Maurice Merleau-Ponty, *The Phenomenology of Perception*, translated by Colin Smith (London: Routledge & Kegan Paul, 1962), pp. 423, 429, 440.

But James presses the question. What is thought itself? Isn't it that which appropriates as its own the appropriated? The present pulse of consciousness, however, being "the darkest in the whole series," knows nothing of itself.[4] And moments of reflection which follow reveal not it, but the most intimately felt, though marginally apprehended,[5] part of its present field of awareness, the body, as that to which the objects of experience—things perceived, remembered, or planned—are tied, *and by which they are appropriated.* Thought itself is revealed as empty, as nothing to which anything could be tied, and knowing seems but a relationship knit upon the field of experience which peculiarly involves the living and experiencing body as the so-called *subjective* term, the "I," the agent. The suggestion is left that I *am* this body which is not focalized—but which is at any time focalizable, as distinct from other bodies—and around which the perspectival panorama of the world always turns. I am the experiencing-experienced body.[6]

This is a very disturbing thought in a dualistic book which must sort everything into subjective and objective bins; if the body does not go into the latter, what would? Yet in the *Principles* itself James takes some steps toward understanding the body as subject. He suggests how it can be both mine and me, i.e., mine without begging the question of the identity of the self which owns it.[7] He does not drop the idea of thinking, but what emerges is the notion of the thinking (and feeling) body which *is* the self: The appropriating thought has a "sense of bodily existence," "the bodily life which it momentarily feels." But being the darkest in the whole series it does not identify itself; hence it does not identify itself as a part of "my" series of experiences, as a part of that which constitutes "me." Neither does it identify the momentary bodily life *as* its own. Furthermore, this moment is a member of a sequence of moments in none of which need thought identify itself or the bodily life *as* its own. Finally, the self must be assumed to endure even in the extreme case of amnesia, in which, presumably, nothing in the nonimmediate past can be remembered and

4. William James, *The Principles of Psychology*, Vols. I & II (New York: Henry Holt & Co., 1890) (hereafter abbreviated by a volume number and page), I, 341.

5. James writes, "We name our thoughts simply, each after its thing. . . . What each really knows is clearly the thing it is named for, with dimly perhaps a thousand other things. It ought to be named after all of them, but it never is. Some of them are always things to be known more clearly a moment hence. Our own bodily position, attitude, condition, is one of the things of which *some* awareness, however inattentive, invariably accompanies the knowledge of whatever else we know" (I, 241).

6. The objective (accusative) case—"lived-body," "experienced-body"—may mislead: It tends to beg in the negative the question whether we can live or experience our bodies-as-subjects. We might also have written, "body experienced experiencing," or "body lived living."

7. James, *Principles*, I, 341.

identified thematically as mine. The apparently paradoxical but very interesting conclusion emerges that the body which is primordially mine, the lived historical body, is an element constitutive of me precisely when it is not identified by me *as* me and *as* mine.

Let us flesh out the intentional nature of the body as nonthematic historical subject; let us analyze memory phenomenologically. A. J. Ayer has acutely observed in his commentary on James that we need not beg the question of the self's identity in offering as a part of the explanation of this identity its appropriation of the body as its own, if we can show

> that the claim to ownership of a past experience can be made in such a way as not to involve the concept of self-identity. This would be achieved by construing the making of the claim as the production of certain signs which would sooner or later be interpreted by experiences which could be described without any reference to their owner. The signs in question would have to exhibit the use of the first person, or something which did duty for it. . . .[8]

But Ayer's notion of signs is cryptic and undeveloped because he does not explore the expressivity and intentionality of the body. Moreover, any notion of body as sign is dangerous because it suggests that the referent meant by it can have an existence independently of the body (e.g., the sign "cafeteria" and the referent meant, the cafeteria, can exist independently of one another). We will prefer to speak usually of the meaningfulness of the body as self, and the meaning which it has cannot be divorced from the referent meant by it, at least when it refers to itself in the past, because this pertains to its own being.[9] So we will appropriate Ayer's insight in this manner: an appropriating thought which involves a sense of present bodily existence could appropriate a body as past and as its own, and would "do duty for the first person," just by meaning or "signifying" this historical body. And the body as thus meaningful would be both mine and me precisely when not meaning itself *as* this meaning, i.e., when not reflexive and not thematic. Thus the very vagueness and marginality of the body's ubiquitous presence—its inattentiveness to itself—is its virtue.[10] It is the background against which and around which and before which a life can be played out. It is essential to identity, I argue. And when we understand that its various postures and rhythms are nonthematic, in con-

---

8. A. J. Ayer, *The Origins of Pragmatism* (London: Macmillan, 1968), p. 297.

9. Nor can we regard the body as an iconic sign, for such a sign is numerically distinct from the thing which it resembles, and to which it refers. And I do not regard it as an indexical sign, for then it would be the necessary effect of itself as past and as referent, and this undermines freedom. The notion would have to be heavily qualified.

10. As well as being the source of complexities of mimetic involvement and of potentialities for self-deception which bear on identity and with which we must grapple in due course.

sciousness only marginally, we begin to grasp that pervasive emotionality and attunement to the world which we call our moods.

To hear the doorbell and to sit up and turn the head toward the door behind which a welcome guest is expected to be standing is to experience the body on the way to the door, and in some way meaning this action. Differently put, it is expressive of the action. To unfocus the eyes in reverie is to experience the body as disengaged from the present and actual situation, and thus meaning a reverie. Indeed, James construes reality itself as that which can stand over against our bodies in a practical relationship of doing and concern (or which is spatiotemporally continuous with that which can); thus the body in such practical stances "signifies" the real.[11]

What if a critic objects that the identification of the body as one's own presupposes rather than explains self-identity? He says, "I know it is my body because I make its arms move, I feel and see its mouth move in the mirror, etc. Obviously the use here of 'I' and 'my' begs the question of identity."

Now, it is true that I can identify my image in the mirror as mine—or pre-reflectively, as me—but this is possible only because I have a primary sense of my body as mine. How else could I know that that is an *image* in the mirror and that it is of *me?* Identification of the body in the mirror is secondary. And on the level of primordial experience I am *not* aware that "I am making my arms move"; they just move in the presence of things apprehended as needing to be moved—a chair blocking the door, for example—and my awareness of the arms moving is part of my awareness of myself. Allusion to the setting in which the concept of my body is learned is of value in indicating the conditions of application of the concept, hence its meaning, and it is clear that the concept is not learned by looking in a mirror but rather in the response of things to us and in the "mirror" of other peoples' eyes, which is a very different matter. Whenever the body is identified in the same sense that things or objects are identified, then it is not mine primordially. The critic's objection is superficial; it deals only with the focalized and secondarily experienced body. All of the experienced-experiencing body—the body I am—cannot be in the focus at once.

This primordial body is displaced from the focus of consciousness in a way which figures, I argue, as an element in the founding level of what we mean by my life, my past, or myself. Let us take memory. Remembering something involves a present bodily sense of perceptual disengagement experienced marginally, which is strictly correlative to a world unfocused

11. James, *Principles*, II, 290.

in its perceptual aspect. Thus the body leaves room for, "points to," and is merely along-with a content other than perceptual, i.e., a content which can therefore be given as not present and capable of being remembered. For this "pointed-to" content to be itself a perception (of anything but one's body), instead of a memory (one can remember rememberings), the body must figure in this content also marginally, but as perceptually engaged. If what is remembered is a dream-like fancy or anticipation, the body must figure marginally in the remembered content, but as perceptually disengaged, and as "pointing to" and leaving room for whatever is presented as "not yet." On this analysis the very meaning of lived time and personal existence is established in the "specious present" as founding level and germ of sense. The future—the "not yet"—as well as the "just past" is present in a phenomenal sense: a single pulse of consciousness combines them both, and the stance of the lived body is the key in the directionality of time; the stance is at the same time a tense.

But even if I should remember a remembering, I will ultimately be landed in the reliving or recollecting of the perceptual situations of interpersonal encounter in which the very meaning of my bodily stances and tenses is learned in conjunction with my seeing of other's seeing of them; and my seeing of other's seeing of anything, *and* my seeing of their anticipating, contemplating, and remembering. I come to learn about all this by experiencing others as historical bodies-along-with-me-in-the-world. Thus the expressivity of my body even for me is a function or precipitate of general, interpersonal senses and global meanings. I do not experience this body in isolation of my experience of others' experience of it.

To recapitulate the argument for the noncircularity of the appropriation of the body: A memory claim such as remembering that one has seen Orion involves a perceptually displaced and disengaged body which is meaningful in the sense that it leaves room for, "signifies," and is interpreted by experiences of the perceptually engaged body which "make no reference to their owner" in that they were *then* a "now" which need have involved no thematized awareness of this self or the body. Nor need there be any identification of the body now as mine; it is absurd to think, for example, that before I can remember taking a walk one night last year and seeing Orion I must identify this body as the same one I remember having then. The present moment is the darkest in the whole series, and every moment is or was a present moment. This "production of signs" would *be* agency, or at the very least would "do duty for the first person," as Ayer says. As James put it, "The 'I' is primarily a noun of position."[12]

12. William James, *Essays in Radical Empiricism* (New York: Longmans, Green & Co., 1940), p. 170.

We would prefer to say that it is primarily an historical body, the meaning of which is a nonthematic personal construction within and upon the interpersonal.

We involve the body in the dichotomizing and synthesizing functions which Kant locates in transcendental subjectivity exclusively. Intentionality or referentiality of mind to world must involve the motility of conscious body as "signifier." What things in the world are, their possibilities, is a function of bodily possibilities, of what I can do with them.[13] The body is "the common texture of which objects are woven," as Merleau-Ponty put it. And yet it also must be able—to some extent—to distinguish itself as a distinct element in the fugal structure of self and world. Art, particularly theatre, will be seen as the inevitable consummatory attempt to articulate and thematize the self-structure or self-dynamism *as* prethematic, engulfed, and immediate.

13. Merleau-Ponty, *Phenomenology of Perception*, pp. 137, 148.

CHAPTER XI

Body-Self and Others: Cognition, Expression, Mimetic Response, and Transformation

One cannot conceive the person's cognition and expression to be really separable from one another, nor from his identity. The person cannot visually perceive something, for example, without facing it with open eyes, thus without "signifying" and expressing that he is perceiving it. Of course, he can attempt to prevent expression, but it is this which requires added explanation, not the expression. When remembering, he cannot help but disengage (to some extent) his sense modalities from the events of the passing scene, thus he cannot help but appear "evacuated," and to express his remembering.

The habitual body is the middle term between presence and absence. What I am is a matter of what I, as this body-subject, can make of my situation now, which is a matter of how I approach it, set myself within it, and anticipate within it now, which must be related to how I have habitually done so then (either as reaction against it or as continuation of it). No matter what novelties break forth through me, as I face the future in the present, I must also express my past. Any change in activity or any change in the self that is meaningful presupposes an irreducible minimum of continuity and identity over time; otherwise there would be no change in *me*, in I-myself. The self is not the continuous identity of a substance which is a subject, but is a temporal unity of caring, and is the "phenomenon that in saying 'I' expresses itself as-to-be-in-the-world."[1]

I cannot grasp myself without grasping myself as expressive to and for

1. Martin Heidegger, *Being and Time* (Oxford: Blackwell, 1962), p. 107.

others, and without grasping my expression in terms of their expressive response to it. I am a function of my recognition of myself, but this is a function of my recognition of others' recognition of me—as Hegel put it tersely in *The Phenomenology of Mind*. But then this involves a mimetic response to others, which is a point of central importance in this study. Actions of mine recognizable through others' recognition of them are actions which are generally recognizable (are of the sort others would do), hence some must be mimetic of others' actions. Nor do I mime these others only face to face. I must mime what others do and say about things if I am to learn about things, and so I must mime others continually. Most crucially, however, absorbed as I am in my objects, I must undeliberately mime others' attitude toward myself, and so I must become a social object *in my own eyes* (an idea developed by G. H. Mead[2]).

This is an explosively significant point, but there is a danger which resides just in that fact. We may be so eager to track down its implications and repercussions that we give it an initial formulation which begs crucial questions of identity of self; the formulation would catapult us immediately beyond itself and we would never give it the critical attention that it needs. The danger with beginning on the Hegelian level is that we will assume that the recognition is between consciousnesses—rather than between bodies that are occasionally conscious. To conceive of *a* consciousness almost inevitably involves the tacit attribution to it of self-identity and self-consciousness anterior to its mimetic involvement with others, and this vitiates the account of this involvement and begs the question of its significance for identity of self. There is a variant of the danger in Strawson: that we must apply to ourselves predicates which are applicable to others is an important point, but in concentrating so exclusively on fully thematic verbal language about others and self his theory runs the risk of tacitly presupposing a high degree of self-consciousness as condition of the use of any language, hence a state of individual identity anterior to involvement with others; this is unjustified. It is an echo of the disability of Locke's approach to perception through our language about perception.

2. "The self arises in conduct, when the individual becomes a social object in experience to himself. This takes place when the individual assumes the attitude or uses the gesture which another individual would use and responds to it himself, or tends to so respond. . . . It arises in the life of the infant through what is unfortunately called imitation, and finds its expression in the normal play life of young children. In the process the child gradually becomes a social being in his own experience, and he acts toward himself in a manner analogous to that in which he acts toward others. Especially he talks to himself as he talks to others and in keeping up this conversation in the inner forum constitutes the field which is called the mind. Then those objects and experiences which belong to his own body, those images which belong to his own past, become part of this self." G. H. Mead, "A Behavioristic Account of the Significant Symbol," *Journal of Philosophy* XIX (1922). There are some basic points of agreement between Mead's "behavioristic" and my phenomenological approaches.

We must be phenomenologically astute and hew close to the situation of bodies open to other bodies in the instant of sensuous encounter. We must develop what Hegel, Strawson, even Heidegger—each in his particular way—leave dangling: the role of bodies in self-consciousness, self-attribution, and identity. For example, the young child Johnny takes toward himself the attitude of a parent, he "enacts" "Johnny is a bad boy!" and while saying this strikes himself (which extreme behavior is sometimes seen), but without in any deliberate way thinking, Now I'll enact my parent toward myself. Even though we have said that he does not take over their attitude toward himself deliberately, we run the risk of falling into an anachronistic notion of mimicry in which we do, despite our intentions, read into this undeliberate *mimesis* by the child the structure of deliberate mimicry as adults would engage in it. What many parents have long suspected now seems to be confirmed: that infants only two weeks old learn rapidly to imitate adults' facial expressions of various sorts, and presumably these can be the germs of attitudes toward the world.[3] But it is highly doubtful that these infants possess either a deliberate will or a sense of individual self. Merely as conscious bodies they take the roles and expressivity of others in the group, and a nascent self appears because the body begins to react to itself as such a being. It is even plausible to suppose that the body's response to this mimetically induced other "in" itself is itself mimetically conditioned by others, and that there is an open-ended spiraling and compounding of identifications with others' attitudes toward one. One is caught up in a contagion of engulfment with the others in which one stands in for others, and conversely.

The drawback in any mentalistic approach to interpersonal involvement, for example the Hegelian approach, is that it will not properly appreciate that one's recognition of oneself as mediated by one's recognition of others' recognition of oneself is not necessarily a thematic recognition *that* one recognizes himself in terms of others' recognition of him. Thus will be concealed the fruitful and difficult problem of just how the conscious and mobile body is to make experientially its own those of its attitudes toward itself which are in fact mimetically and pre-reflectively modeled on those of others toward itself. But with this drops away the true problematic of the structure of the self. Dropping into obscurity as well is the problematic that gives initial seriousness to art: how is nonthematic and pre-reflective involvement with others and other things to be rendered as what it actually is—rendered *as* nonthematic and pre-reflective involvement?

We suppose that the conscious body must nonthematically and non-

3. Andrew Meltzoff and M. Keith Moore, "Imitation of Facial and Manual Gestures by Human Neonates," *Science* 198(4312) (October 1977).

deliberately take the attitude of others, which includes the attitudes of others toward itself. This is very unlike deliberate imitation and mimicry. This is very unlike deliberate positing of oneself by oneself. A common way of behaving, a "role" *available* in the immediate social setting, is adopted, but it makes little sense to say "I adopt it" or "he adopts it" because the self is just now in process of formation. The evolving self has an element of the impersonal gaze: the body neither addresses itself nor the other through the "role"; it is just a doing and a speaking which is also a learning and a listening for all involved; it is a communal activity.

Before the child identifies his body as his own, or uses the pronoun "I," he knows his "call." To know his call—"Johnny"—is to take what other people take him to be doing and being in the world, and this is a taking or intending which is not a reflective taking of this taking, and not, by stronger reason, a taking of his taking *as* a function of other's taking of him. His name names for him his world. His body is experienced "along with" all of this. It is tacit, and subject to manifold mimetic involvements (and distortions) which we shall discuss. Because of this ubiquitous "along with" status, it is not his as is a typical possession. Only under threat of injury does the body become possessive of itself in something like the ordinary sense. At other times it is peculiarly beyond itself; it stands open to the other, and to his needs, desires, and cognitions concerning it. If one must be a social being in his own eyes, and if he is thrown in with others so that he cannot avoid them, then this presupposes that others' attitudes toward him have already been incorporated in his behavior before he can be a self. The body gains presence to itself in terms of what it is for others—but nonthematically.

Merleau-Ponty has employed an artistic metaphor which is justified as long as it is not applied prematurely. Undeliberately, and not necessarily acknowledgeably, we respond to things mimetically: we "sing" them. We reproduce their rhythm and magnitude through rhythm and magnitude of body and voice—we speak with and for them. With a quiet thing we grow quiet in order to hear it, and with a noisy thing we shout over it to make ourselves heard. With a small thing we kneel down, contract the body, squint and narrow the focus of the eyes; we unwittingly mime it and speak for it as small in the very act of perceiving it to be small. Our response to humans is likewise directly participatory and mimetic. It is the *parents'* smile or frown in which the child is absorbed when he sees them look at him. It is *their* holding and feeling of him that he feels when he is in their arms. Whether rigid and distrusting or molding and trusting, this structures him as trusting or distrusting of himself. Yet, he need have no clear or acknowledgeable awareness of the distinctness of selves; no thematic awareness that it is *their* feeling of *him*. It is just because of this that the mimetic response is so pervasive and complete. I was inducted into a mode of being-in-the-world that is both mine and others'. This body becomes myself by taking over, say, my mother's stance toward myself as her son, or if I rebel it is not just against her, but against that of her "in" myself, that I rebel. And, not surprisingly, my rebellion against her may be modeled on her patterns of rebelling, whatever they might be. Thus Paul Schilder has argued that the child's body-image (his lived sense of his own body) and a parent's body-image are made of "similar material." We examine this more fully in the next chapter.

Even when there is confrontation, and the being cringes before the other's aggression, it is plausible to suppose that he covertly mimes the other's attitude toward him even as he overtly cringes from him. How else can we explain, for example, the interdependence of sadism and masochism and their facile interchangeability? It is plausible to suppose that the person mimetically takes over the other's attitude toward himself without realizing it; without realizing that it is *he* who is taking over the *other's* attitude toward himself. As he responds cringingly to aggression, for example, he mimes unwittingly both victor and vanquished and does so simultaneously "within" himself: as himself toward himself. Having already incorporated mimetically the roles and expressivity of others in the group, he relates to himself as such a being *and* does so in the manner that others would.

For a being to be a self it must be its self, its own unique being. Insofar as the body appropriates its actions, movements, and experiences *as* its own, it is an individual self. But how is this possible? At first sight, Schilder seems to be right when he says that although the child's and the parent's body-images are made of "similar material," still the child's body-image is *his*. But I believe that we will find it more accurate to say that the body-image belongs to that body. It does not follow necessarily that the body has the capacity at every moment to acknowledge itself and its body-image *as* its own. So it is not yet a full-fledged individual self.

But then, how is it possible for the body to acknowledge itself as its own? That one is mimetically involved so intimately with the other would seem to eclipse to some degree his sense of being other than the other. That the body is unitary, separable, and self-moving is a fundamental fact and is no doubt necessary for the possibility of individual identity of self. But great problems remain. For example, even though a shout does emanate from a particular body and not from the others, it is the sort that others would give, and if it is in reference to something of common concern in the environment, it may verge on being apprehended as "ours" and not clearly and distinctly "my own." Of course, there is behavior attributed by others to one alone, e.g., "It was Johnny who smelled the fire and cried out!" But the prevalence of mass movements of all sorts throughout history, and of semihypnotic mob behavior, suggests that identity of individual self is unstable through time and is a matter of degree only. It seems to be an ideal which we can approach only asymptotically from an initial condition of engulfment in others. The motor power of approach is the particular body's hunger to be more completely its own.

While I have been alluding to the responses of children, it must be emphasized very strongly that I am not pursuing that branch of empirical research called genetic psychology. I am interested in the interconnection of the concepts of expression, mimetic response, and identity, and on the most general level. I have alluded to mimetic response in children because a phenomenon at the inception of its development is often most clearly revealed because it is free of secondary accretions. If one were conducting empirical research and one inferred directly from isolated facts about children's behavior to purported facts about adult behavior, then these conclusions would not necessarily be true, and one would be guilty of committing the genetic fallacy. Children outgrow certain things.

But I am not involved in empirical research, but rather in a phenomenological and transcendental version of conceptual analysis. I am inquiring how identity of self is conceivable in the light of a large set of concepts: that of body, others, mimetic response, cognition, expression, and meaningfulness. If investigation of the phenomenon of mimetic response in children releases a concept which contributes to a more encompassing and mutually illuminating set of concepts for *all* human behavior then it has justified itself. The investigation must pan out on the most general level of conceptual analysis. I think it does. For example, it is only with this way of seeing mimetic response that we can get to the bottom of self-deception and regression in adults, and it is only when we have done this that we can get to the bottom of the role of art and the art-like in the articulation of identity. By "get to the bottom" I mean that it renders the concepts coherent, mutually reinforcing, and illuminating. We hope to show how mimetic engulfment pertains especially to mood, and how it and the other ontological potentialities—filled out through a conception of the body articulated through the theatrical metaphor—ground the possibility of identity of self.

Let us consolidate our position. Cognition presupposes expression which presupposes mimetic response. The other person is with me and through me from the beginning of me. And since the identity of a self involves how it makes itself its own, e.g., how the person dreams (in every sense) his possibilities, and since the self is mimetic, then the person is a function as well of how he dreams other persons' dreams of his possibilities. Does he do so as engulfed or as his own? Neither cognition, nor expression, nor mimetic response is possible without a particular body with a particular history. It is an expressive body, and it is expressive by way of others' expressivity, but this never submerges absolutely the significance of its particularity. Each of its acts must occur at a unique point in space-time. This true even of that act in which engulfment is maintained and noncreative repetition is allowed to continue. Any projection and repetition of an event involves at least minimal novelty. To be able to remember something is to be able to apprehend it as apprehended before, and this involves a sense of the current apprehension as never before having been.

The particularity of the body is inexhaustible in its potentialities; a positive effort must be made to limit it (an effort that is often made). Any event can be apprehended as reproducible by me in more manners and connections than are presently imaginable by me. My future opens out before me in more ways than can be bounded by me, and this may cause anxiety. The body thinks, cares, and imagines. Any system of thinking within which the body-self operates contains the potentiality to jump outside of the system and to objectify it within an encompassing system . . . and so on indefinitely. Psychical identity is achieved as a function of the transformation of biological identity. To be is to be an identity of a process of transformations of a particular body that never wholly escapes its history and its socially structured habits. To be most vitally I must live in the new, but I live in it authentically (*eigentlich*—as my own) only when I live in it so as to catch up to my past through it. This may be an attitude of repudiation—anything but forgetfulness or engulfment. To anticipate later arguments in this book: I live in the new authentically when I project my past afresh, and in such a way that I simultaneously memorialize my. possibilities for achieving change, individuality, and novelty. This is a complex corollary of the principle that we can grasp the actual only when we project in imagination possible ways for it to be.

Here, we will find, lies the root of the tension between self as particular and self as intersubjective and universal, between itself as unique potentialities in time and itself as general ones, which is at the source of its fully realized creativity in art. The need for confirmation by others of one's uniqueness lies at the basis of self as creative reproduction—in the domain of the art-like as well as the strictly artistic. The impulsion to make the personal public is a self-impulsion. Since I am a social being for myself, to become myself I must make ever more and more of my experienceable world experienceable by others. This can happen only through what can be experienced of me by other body-subjects: my bodily activities and my structuring of materials. It would seem that even the uniquenesses of my sensory life—whatever they might be—can slip into dissociation and forgetfulness unless the attempt is made to make them fully my own through appropriating others' responses to them.

The self's identity involves a fusion—and at times confusion—of its more nearly direct experience of itself (e.g., awareness of its bodily sensations) and its view of others' view of itself; art and art-like activity is the unavoidable attempt to articulate and structure this fusion and to dispel self-deception. Since this articulation is open-ended in its possibilities, a human life is open-ended. Authenticity is approached when we stand open to this open-endedness.

Before we investigate this, however, we must investigate in some detail that form of engulfment that most impedes authentic individuation—self-deception.

CHAPTER XII

Body-Self, Other Body-Selves, and Self-Deception

I have argued that the body becomes a self when it can contrast its productions and reproductions to the passing scene of the world. To be itself it must be spatial and temporal, and it must be able to contrast its ever-occurring experiencing to experienced things which come and go. Neither the already experienced nor the yet to be experienced are present, yet the experiencing of them which is the remembering and anticipating of them is the calling into presence of their absence. The calling into presence of the absent *constitutes* the calling as mine; it is my presencing, myself. But as we shall see, authentic individuation of self requires a vividness in the contrasting of experiencing to things experienced which is very difficult to achieve at certain moments.

We argued at some length that the body is involved in the very "citadel" of the self, in the "mental act" of its experiencing. We emphasize the shudder quotes around these terms, for we are criticizing dualism and mentalism. It is not that there is no truth in these positions. We would never deny that the body can be conscious, and that it can attempt—often successfully—both to conceal itself in certain ways from others and to project an appearance at odds with what it would project if it acted more spontaneously. The body is, in various ways and degrees, reflexive. But in regard to the conditions of identity of the self, mentalism grossly over-simplifies the situation. For it, experiencing is merely a mental act, and so it must render a far too easy and impoverished account of individual identity. Since, allegedly, a mental act is merely a private event within a personal chamber, all that will have to happen is that it somehow gain a sense of its own presence and of its place within a sequence of mental acts, and this distinguishes it from a sequence of putative events external to the chamber. If one assumes that mental acts are self-luminous atoms that form self-luminous molecules within an illuminated chamber, then one may think that all that is necessary for identity is available. The self *is* this chamber of mind and its contents and events.

The position does not grasp that the private, the mental, and the personal presuppose the contrast of the public and the bodily; a domain in which bodies are displayed to each other and in which the very meaning of self—and of the mental and the personal—is established for all involved. I must see others as self-ascribers and as other-ascribers and as those who see *me*—this body—as a self-ascriber and an other-ascriber. Hence the position cannot grasp how the body is involved in "mental acts" of experiencing, and it cannot see that the body's capacity to contrast the reality of its experiencing to the reality of things experienced involves an essential support from others *which at the same time impedes* the full realization of the contrast. That is, the body as *along-with* others and other things must be both mimetically *involved* with others and an integral element of the act of experiencing whereby the body can *distinguish* itself from others.

The great emphasis we have placed on the shadowy and peripheral status of the body lived primordially—its being *along-with* others and other things—should not blind us to its capacity on occasion to objectify itself for itself as "merely body." As part of its capacity to thematize the world scientifically, it can take toward itself the attitude of an observer, that of a physician, say. For example, it can regard itself as that which could lose a leg or a hand and still be itself. And, indeed, it could lose a leg or a hand and still be itself. This process of decimation has its limits, however, both physiologically and experientially or psychically. If we engage in an experiment of thought to determine at just what point the body-self *qua* physician for itself would regard itself as ceasing to be, we would encounter borderline areas in which we would not know what to say, but also fairly clear-cut cases. Can one imagine that he would really consider himself to be the same self if his head were to be severed from his body, and into the eye sockets were to be poured molten lead? It is highly doubtful.

Notice the wording of the thought experiment: imagine that he would *really* consider himself to be the same self.[1] If one imagines things in a completely fanciful way, then I suppose one can choose to call his head filled with lead himself, as he can in like manner fancy nearly anything to be the case. If, on the other hand, one imagines in the experimentally appropriate way that his decapitated body remains himself, then not only would one have to imagine it to be still living and functioning, but that

1. This carries over into our understanding of the de-facto bracketing of action in action which is theatre.

portions of it had taken over, to some minimal degree, the normal functions of the head—speaking, or thinking, or some remnant of seeing and hearing. James's sense that his self was located crucially in the movements of the throat and behind the eyes is most provocative. When I turn my head to look around, *I* look around. The body, particularly the head, is both I-myself and mine. It "houses" the distance receptors of seeing and hearing, which are essential to a self arising in the contrast between seeing and the seen, and between hearing and the heard.

The fact that the body can, to some degree, objectify itself has led Helmuth Plessner to speak of the "eccentric position" of the self—that it *is* its body *and* is "in" it.[2] Interestingly enough, he analyzes laughter as the body-self's sense that its loss of control as body in the spasm of laughing is appropriate given the total situation. So, one might think, it is his body that is momentarily out of control; he is not. But this loss of control is just what "one does" on such occasions. As the being who is this body, and who also is "in" it, I controlledly lose control of it.

Yet the fact remains that usually one's body is not objectified focally, and that one is for oneself simply identical with it. Thus the shock, often involving loss or diminishment of consciousness, in the instant of discovery that one's hand, say, has been severed by a savage fish, a wild animal, or a machine. What is sensed apparently is that it is not merely a hand that is lost, but a portion of the self. Sartre's analysis of consciousness in fainting is appropriate here: consciousness engages in a sympathetic magic in which its image of the event is felt to be identical with the event itself, so that to eliminate the image—through losing consciousness—becomes for it equivalent to eliminating the event. By fainting, the body-self denies that it has been reduced.

This, of course, is hardly an everyday occurrence, but strange things do follow in the everyday course of events from the fact that one's body is not typically objectified for itself. It has some presence for itself, and it is myself, but yet this presence is merely peripheral and it is already modeled mimetically on the behavior of others. It is oneself-as-peripheral-other-for-and-by-others. The "as" here is not thematic but is acknowledged only with difficulty, e.g., for me this time it was in writing this paragraph. The apparently solid and atomic center around which the perspectival panorama of the world always turns for me, turns out to be not solid and atomic after all. It is not in dyadic relationship to the world. The everyday sense of oneself as the central and utterly unique "chamber" in which "burns" consciousness of the world "out there" is delusive.

Thus, I need not try to see people as I *think* they see me, but only as

2. Helmuth Plessner, *Laughing and Crying* (Evanston: Northwestern University Press, 1970).

they really do. This is very difficult to accomplish, just because my sense of myself, whether I can acknowledge it or not, is my sense of myself-for-others, and yet I am in no position to see exactly how others do in fact see me at any moment. My habitual sense of myself-for-others is as pervasive and unnoticed as my lived body and my mood, and it must envelop the other person as I currently sense him there in space. I cannot leap out of my body to stand in his shoes and to see how I do look to him at that moment. Nor can I let his presence simply register itself within my "subject substance." I am already out there with him, automatically molding him and his perceptions (as perceived by me) to fit a body-self—my own—that must anticipate being seen by him in a certain way. At the most extreme point, and usually it is only momentary, my sense of myself is only what I take him to make of me, and my body is no longer a "housing" for myself on this side of him, but is lost within his animating gaze. This is the Dionysian merging of selves. One does what one thinks is expected of him. The inadequately individuated person sets up a scene projectively and is captured by the projection; he then plays the archaic "roles" demanded by the projection.

In and through my body I typically experience focally only others' aware bodies, and insofar as I accept their putative attitudes toward me as body-self (e.g., either "looking up" or "looking down" at me), I unwittingly build their bodily attitudes into myself, into my body: as the inevitable counterpart of their habitual looking up, I must habitually stand as looked-up-to; as the counterpart of their habitual looking down, I must slump habitually under their gaze. Or I carry around a head tilted up, although others are no longer taller and more powerful than I. Since there is this counterpart relationship, mimetic involvement is not always a simple one-for-one reproduction of others' bodily attitudes. The latter sort most often occurs in relationships of equality and reciprocity, or when aware of the other as not aware of oneself.

The most substantial and difficult-to-detect mimetic patterns are those incorporated in the self before the question could arise for it of whether or not to accept others' attitudes toward it. Since the pattern has become habitual, it has retreated into the margins of habitual attunement to the world where it is next to impossible that it should ever become sufficiently distinct to be objectified in the focus of consciousness. Since self-identity and self-awareness are a function of expression, and since expression is *already* of myself-as-other-for-others, I must constantly, to one degree or another, prejudge others as they relate to me, and thus must constantly prejudge myself. The upshot is a string of self-delusions into which the self can fall which is insidious and difficult to root out. The tightest snarl is self-deception, which we will discuss shortly.

Descartes had *some* point to make; there is *something* certain about one's own existence. Self-reference appears to be inevitable, for when I think, "I see a hat," I could not be mistaken in the way I can when I think, "He sees a hat." I could not identify something as a seeing which does not apply to a subject identified independently as "I"; there seems to be no identification of the seeing which is mine aside from an identification of it *as* my seeing.³ If the idea of the hat is false, it is either because there is no hat to be seen, or the seeing is not a seeing but an hallucinatory breakdown, and not because it is not I, but somebody else, who is seeing or remembering or only seeming to see and remember. Even if I only seem to see, then it is I and nobody else who only seems to do so.⁴

But from this it does not follow that I more easily know myself than I do other persons or other things. Sadly, it is just the reverse, usually. For ideas that are immune to error through misreference to the agent which is myself presuppose for their application a range of experience of my bodily self that is at certain points peculiarly susceptible to error. The certainty *that* self-reference is achieved is gained at the cost of predilection to error concerning *what* this self referred to is. Thinking "I see a hat" presupposes that one experiences the self or "I" as a being of the sort that is capable of seeing, and this involves intending a being which can take up a point of view of seeing and can have a perspective on an object in space; but this in turn involves the intending as mine of something in space that can see (in the ordinary sense of "see"). But—to use here just one gross example—I may be dreaming, curled up in bed and talking in my sleep, hence this presupposed identification of myself as seeing may be mistaken. *If* something is perceived, then I must be engaged bodily in the perceiving of it; but it may not be perceived. Even if one thinks, "I seem to see a hat," a hat is the kind of thing which presents itself perspectively in space to a space-viewer, and that viewer could only be intended as an embodied being with opened eyes taking a stance in space, an intention that may be mistaken. It is just because I *must* presuppose something definite about my body on the basis of a perception of the world that is so fallible, that the fallibility of what I presuppose about my body is so hidden from me. The necessary truth about the perceiving body is no better—and usually worse—than the putative contingent truths of the perceived world which it must presuppose.

Far from ensuring a realm of sure self-knowledge, the ubiquity and

3. Assuming the thematic mode in this short discussion of Descartes, assuming that we are identifying the seeing *as* a seeing. But the reasoning holds for the nonthematic mode: nonthematic experiencing of my seeing is nonthematic experience of me.

4. Cf. Adolph Reinach, "Concerning Phenomenology," trans. by D. Willard, *The Personalist* 50 (2) (Spring 1969):214.

necessity of self-reference make self-knowledge that much more difficult. The expressional configuration of the body is the most mistakable of all, and the dreams and encounters of the day are troubling and occluded in their own affective and expressive way. Ironically, the very necessity of self-reference involves an openness and indeterminacy of content of reference that leaves vast room for delusion. The "I" is like a naked magnetic pole which attracts layers of delusional junk and scrap.

Item: I am sitting in a diner. As the counterman goes about his business behind the counter in front of me, he looks at me, and he looks to me as if he needed me to look at him. For some reason I do not understand, I do not return his look when out of the corner of my eye I see that he again looks at me. The things he is doing, looking needy at one time, somehow sinister at another, would surprise him, I think. In a fundamental sense he sees his face through my face, and if I or others do not respond, or if we respond deceitfully, he cannot know himself. He turns and begins to gesture and to joke boisterously with a woman at the cash register. The woman laughs. This he construes, apparently, as her approval of him—he seems quite pleased— but she seems to me clearly to be laughing at him with contempt.

Absorbed in the world he thinks he acts upon favorably, his effects are intended, not his own expressive means. Hence his means are not focalizable and acknowledgeable to himself. Hence he cannot see that these means are noisome and contemptible to a woman of a different social class. Something works—she does laugh when he speaks—but just what he is doing he does not know, because what is working he does not know. That may just be grotesque, and someone else may have to tell him exactly what he is doing.

If she is pleased in response to his jokes, then he *must* have pleased her. Everything about his sense of his own life inclines him to believe that she is pleased, for, let us say, persons usually have been when he has joked with them, and he sees her as the person-who-reacts-to-his-funny-jokes. He sees her as a function of the sense he brings with him of himself-as-other-for-others. But she is not pleased.

The man has fallen into error about himself that is exceedingly difficult or impossible for him to root out unless he is helped by others to see what he is doing. But there are, unfortunately, even more difficult problems which beset those who would know themselves. We have assumed that the man is simply ignorant of what is happening when he jokes with her. There is, however, a kind of *intentional* ignorance about oneself into which one can maneuver oneself; this is self-deception. It is the kind of ignorance in which one has some sense of what one is doing, but so deploys oneself *vis-à-vis* the other that one cannot acknowledge to oneself the sense that one has of it. This sense is nonthematic intentionality: we cannot deceive ourselves about just anything, but only about that which it would be easy for us to be mistaken *if* we were simply mistaken. After all, how can we explain the way certain projects go through our minds—thoughts of strange sexual activity, say, or of mayhem—unless we suppose that the thoughts are ours but that we do not or cannot acknowledge them to be ours. In Jamesian terms, such an end of ours can crystalize a motor schema of behavior, but we need not be aware of the end *as* ours, nor need it *be* ours in the sense that it is the end of a thoroughly individualized self. We take dubious advantage of the real difficulties of self-knowledge.

To be intentionally ignorant of a project is to sense it nonthematically as something to be hidden. This can happen because one's experiencing life, which involves the body and its nascent and occurrent urges and tendencies, has a presence, but it is not presented to one; most of it is not reflected *as* what it is. But if one is to be *self*-deceived one must sense it nonthematically to be his own and to be hidden *and* must hide from himself his hiding of it. How is this feat accomplished?

In the sorts of self-deception I will discuss, it is possible because of the structure of the self which involves it on the deepest level with others. The rather high probability of self-deception, particularly in certain sorts of situations, is part of the price, I believe, for being individual bodies who are at the same time human selves. Deciphering, we trust, the ancient words of Anaximander that serve as epigraph for this volume, individual things must make reparation to one another—according to the order of time—for an injustice which, I believe, is simply the fact of their individual reality. This of course is not an ethical injustice, but a metaphysical one. What does this mean?

The self is a body experienced peripherally which is integral to its experiencing, but which is already formed mimetically by others, and which can so allow itself to slip into the influence of others that the person can believe he is only what he believes the other believes him to be. All that he can *acknowledge* is that feature of himself which is the object of the other's supposed construal; he cannot acknowledge his manipulation of self and other which has produced his construal of the other's construal. But he must have *some* sense of the to-be-hidden, and of his intention to hide it, otherwise he would not be self-*deceived*, but simply mistaken.

As organisms it is biologically necessary that we be separate, but as human organisms that are selves it is necessary that we share common linguistic, significatory, gestural, and physiognomic properties. Moreover, it is essential to fully human life that it be civilized, and essential to civilization that much biological activity be masked off and concealed, so that time-binding and person-binding signs, symbols, and communication can spring in all their interrelated structure from the bodies involved in the communication. Not only is the passing biological event concealed, but endeavor is made to conceal the concealing—for the very same general purpose of preventing distractions from communication (it needn't be communication of truth). Some of this is a concealing from self of the concealing of the to-be-concealed—self-deception. We are inclined, then, naturally toward a blurring of individual identities, toward concealment of various sorts, particularly in some circumstances.

Now, it is possible to accomplish the feat of sensing one's projects nonthematically as the to-be-hidden, and to hide from oneself the hiding of them, if one can allow oneself to so slip under the influence of the other (as one understands the other) that one can believe he is just what the other believes him to be—a person who is not hiding anything. The potentiality for self-deception as self-alienation through the other seems endemic to identity. The self as it is constituted through time involves a fusion of its more direct experience and view of itself (e.g., awareness of its bodily sensations) and its view of others' view of itself. Self-deception and con-fusion can occur in this fusion through the suppression from consciousness of a more direct experience of self by a contrived view of others' view of oneself—a view which is counter to the suppressed experience, and which, in its very contrivance, is itself suppressed as one's view. For example, for the purpose of not grasping one's own sensations thematically one con-strues others as incapable of sensing one's sensations, and this construal which hides the to-be-hidden (from thematic acknowledgment) is itself hidden as a hiding because it blurs and smears into the construal imputed to the other. One's nonthematic beliefs concerning the others' beliefs about one—being already beliefs modeled mimetically on others' believ-ings—collapse experientially into a single swarming pool of belief in which identities of selves are for the moment merged.

Evidence that this occurs frequently is great: the blurring of identity and forfeiture of free agency by seduced to seducer "as in a dream" (being manipulated by a salesman, for example); the similar forfeiture in mass movements of all sorts. Often the evidence takes the form of a disintegrated emotional denial when one is accused of self-deception about something, which suggests strongly that one is aware of it, but only nonthematically and nonfocally, and is stumbling in panic.

Let us cite examples. I appropriate one from Sartre, but turn it to my own purposes: A young woman is invited out by a man who, she knows, will try skillfully to seduce her. This troubles her. Nevertheless she accepts his invitation, for she finds him attractive, and, while engaged in an in-tellectual conversation, allows him to take her hand, a move which she knows—in a nonthematic and inexplicit way—sets the seduction in motion. She falls into self-deception. But, one might retort, the girl is hypocritical, not self-deceived, for surely she can see that that hand opened to his is *hers* and that *she* has accepted his advances. No, not so that she can acknowledge it, and later she will tell us sincerely that "it happened in a dream." She and the man conspire to make her aware of her flesh, but not *as* hers, not *as* herself.

What is going on here? The woman is troubled because she cannot accept her sexual desires for the man as her own, i.e., she is troubled because she is a body-subject. If her body were just another possession she might be annoyed by its perturbations, but not disgusted or frightened, for *it* could be blamed, not she. These frightened desires are the to-be-hidden, and they can be the first step in the process of self-deception (self-deception must begin and end with itself in self-deception) because they are nonthematic. That is, the man is skilled in seduction, and part of his skill consists in not directing the woman's attention directly to her body *as* her body, but to her body via her awareness of his body.

For the woman's nonthematic sexual project and desires to become nonthematizable for her, she allows herself to so slip under the influence of the other that she believes she is just what he believes her to be, and that he believes her to be incapable of sexual desires and projects. She allows him to stand in for her—to represent her—indeed, even to herself. *Here is one of her archaic "roles" into which she can slip nonthematically: "nice little girl for the big nice man."* At this moment she is an individual self in only a compromised sense. He stands in for her, and for key figures in her life who stood in for her earlier, and who interpreted her to herself.

This engulfment in the other is accompanied by a disintegration in the ordering of time. Her perception is mixed inextricably with her memory and fantasy. In both remembering and fantasizing the body is disengaged from the present and actual situation; thus even in situations which are more conducive to cognitive accuracy than is this one, there is a danger of confusing them. Likewise, remembering what is in fact a fantasy but remembering it *as* a perception must also easily occur. But in her present situation her current perception is easily lost in this whirl as well, since her body is now disengaged; not merely because she sits there passively, her hand in his, but because her awareness of her body is swallowed up in her awareness of his awareness of it. It is as if she perceives herself as remembered in his fantasies. She is a body-self dissociated from her body and the present moment and engulfed in a communal past. Rather than an articulated and ordered co-presencing of herself as prepubescent and herself in her current state as postpubescent, she collapses connivingly into her past and freely forfeits her autonomy and freedom. He stands in for her, but unlike the stage, this standing in is unacknowledgeable and in the deepest sense illicit.

Self-deception is like falling asleep. Not the least of the parallels is that one does certain things in order to fall asleep, e.g., one disrobes and goes to bed, but the effort is defeated as soon as one intends these things *as* in order to fall asleep. Indeed, whole verbal patterns are in service to self-deception and related activities. We commonly say, "I'm going to bed," not "going to sleep," or if we say the latter we had better not dwell on it if we wish to get to sleep. Likewise, all that the woman being seduced can and does acknowledge militates against the acknowledgment of what she does not acknowledge, and reinforces at every stage the nonthematizable process of self-deception. Imagine that her intellectual conversation has reached the apogee of such efforts—it is about Platonic love. Since the first step of the means to self-deception is, when acknowledged (and it can brim over into acknowledgment at any moment), the reverse of what she means to accomplish in the project of self-deception—i.e., the conversation is about the value of nonsexual relationships when what she means to accomplish through this is the hiding of sexual desires and the accomplishment of a sexual relationship—then the acknowledgment of the conversation as her goal will precisely subvert her awareness of it as her means (to the opposite), and indeed she will acknowledge it as her goal precisely in order not to be able to acknowledge it as the means which it is.[5] She is pathetically sincere.

It seems probable that there are basic similarities between many ordinary life situations and those which are structured by hypnotists: the passivity, the willfull forfeiture of explicit decision making by the subject to the hypnotist, the lack of sensory stimulation save what the hypnotist controls, etc. It seems that the facts of hypnosis, properly understood, might augment the conceptual working out of the transcendental investigation in which we are engaged: the disclosure of the conditions of identity of self.

In the next example the body-self deceives itself by an acknowledge-

---

5. It should be clear that I reject any approach which is exclusively that of "linguistic philosophy." Any attempt to pose the problem of self-deception in terms of how anyone could believe contradictory propositions seems to me to be out of touch with human existence. To assume that it is propositions that are the elements in self-deception is simply to assume the verbalizability and, probably, the acknowledgeability of the contents of mind, and this ignores the very stuff of self-deception, as I see it, which is the pre-predicative (or non-predicative), silent, acknowledgment-impeding *perceptual* content of mind. Nor will the rigamarole with "propositional attitudes," e.g., belief, help much, because the nonthematic is the half-believed, the nature of which must be discovered phenomenologically. The half-believed is often a matter of the decay of belief, and this involves the decay of the being of the believer.

ment-impeding construal of the witness, but this time it is through a discounting of him as a witness. (Of course, even in the first case the woman subtly discounts and degrades the man—in counterpoint to his obvious degrading of her—in the sense that she discounts whatever capacities he might have for engaging in a nonseductive relationship.) Item: there is a way in which I condemn another for being picky and squeamish—we are at dinner together, let us say—that discounts him as a witness to my behavior—he is "simply disgusting." The more picky I find him, the more my pickiness concerning his pickiness is obscured. The to-be-hidden is my pickiness; the hiding is an absorbing distraction in the other's pickiness, a repetition of archaic, nonthematic, communal, and habitual modes of rejection; the hiding is itself hidden because in seeing him to be a disgusting lump, I see him as being insensate, and I cannot see him seeing me to be anything at all, therefore cannot see that I do this in order not to see the pickiness in me. And so on, e.g., aggression against the other's aggressiveness undermines the capacity for reflective recognition of my aggressiveness. The dialogical, face-to-face situation gives way, and the experienced world is reduced to a simple mass of slime, as it were; my own pickiness and squeamishness dissolves and undermines any possible self-reflection and self-recognition. To another person looking on at us at the table, it may be clear from the posture of my body (e.g., arch, overbearing, putting down, or recoiled, cringing) that I am picky or squeamish, but I cannot see it, for I cannot see it through the person I am looking at—his seeing is discounted. I play the judge in order not to be judged. To "look down upon" and to "put down" is the way bodies behave in the inchoate, mimetically constituted community. Whether these stances remain turned upon others, or are turned upon myself—so that I become looked down upon or put down—depends upon the precarious slip and swing of events in a world in which human identities are not neatly individuated and set over against each other. I believe that I am only what the other believes about me, and that he can believe nothing.

Let us vary the example. Again, I look down upon the other for what I would condemn myself for if I had not undermined my ability to reflect—let us say the voraciousness and sloppiness of my eating. Self-rejection slips into other-rejection—a magical but in its way very real consumption of the other. The bodies merge experientially because they are isomorphic, as if two mirror images collapsed into each other. I condemn another with the very words which, if I could reflect, I would know apply to myself. Indeed I already know, in the sense that an incompletely individualized self has a pre-reflective consciousness. The self which refuses to let itself be penetrated by its own knowledge of itself is the self absorbed in a diffused, rejecting, mimetic community shared with the other. My expressivity is knowable for my own reflection only because initially it is known pre-reflectively through the expressive and responsive bodies of others. Reflection can be undermined and never occur if—on the pre-reflective level—the other can be either flatteringly masqueraded or discredited as a witness of my bodily being. For since my sense of individual self involves being other than the other and yet also for the other, and since, for example, he is pre-reflectively discounted as a witness of my behavior, I blur my individual self. Self-rejection which has remained at the pre-reflective level is dissipated through the atmosphere of one's mood and attitude. One's world is guilty. Self-rejection, picked up mimetically in an archaic and diffuse community of rejection, is fastened onto the other here and now. He becomes a picture of myself without my being able to acknowledge what I have done. With this we have developed Max Scheler's idea that in the tragic situation guilt cannot be localized. Neither can it be localized in the situation of tragic farce.

The body that one lives and that is inseparable from oneself enjoys a precarious identity. From "together with" the other in the field of experience as act and "sign," it can easily slip into "being together with" as an object, or even being coupled with or merged magically with the other. These are my archaic standings-in—the primitive "roles" I play in tragic freedom.

What is the shock which will connect the self within itself? Given our situation in which behaviors of the body are thrown out into the margins and tend to perpetuate themselves through the responses in others which the behaviors have always involved, it may be only that other person who will not bend in the usual circuit who can entice me into reflection by throwing back on me, mirror-like, but much more effectively than can a mirror, the disparities between my verbal protestations and the total background of my bodily behavior. Only I may be able to tell exactly what I am deceiving myself about, but only the other may be able to remind me to look for something.

Self-deception must be understood as a form of authorization. Both concepts are deepened thereby. We can understand, better than we did in the first section of the book, how authorization is a categorial and inescapable matter. Recall that we could say of the Old Man and Old Woman in *The Chairs* merely, as to Authorization, not authorized—apparently. This vagueness and tentativeness can now be removed. Through their hallucinatory conjuring of the approving authority they are authorized, but in a way which confirms them in their inauthenticity and self-deception.[6] Inauthenticity obtains whenever the person self-deceivingly manipulates the other's recognition so that his own individuation is subverted.

6. If it is thought that *authorization* connotes *authentication*, then substitute *confirmation* for *authorization*, e.g., confirmed in inauthenticity.

This will occur when either his particularity as a body in space or his mimetic sociality is subverted. In the case of *The Chairs*, it is more the former that occurs (insofar as the factors can be divided): the old people have lost touch with the actuality of persons in space and time. In a case we will mention below, where undue emphasis is placed on self-authorization through long-distance running, one's mimetic sociality is masked and undermined.

As one is authorized in his inauthenticity through manipulation of the other's recognition, so one is delivered from this state by allowing the other's recognition to manifest itself as it is. No manipulation is capable of freeing us entirely from the power of others; we can only further entangle ourselves by trying. We point out in passing that the role of the other in the theatrical exposure of self-deception is central. Here theatre understood as metaphor illuminates life both offstage and on. The actors as artists, together with the audience, catch the actors' characters in projects of self-deception. They locate the characters' undeliberate, pre-reflective and unthematizable purposes, some of which are self-deceptive. At times these purposes are quite clearly evident from the script, at other times their generation is a creative development which the script allows but does not clearly indicate. In the plays we have analyzed in detail, instances of self-deception are numerous. For example, *The Chairs* can be appreciated on many different levels, one of them being an exploration of self-deception: the conjuring of others before one in such a way that their views of one mask from one's sight the act of conjuring itself. The emperor would come to hear only a great message, not a conjuring trick, the old man thinks—but cannot say that he thinks, so lost is he in his conjuring. And so we think that he thinks as we watch him, and possibly learn to say that he thinks as we watch him.

Instances of self-deception in other plays are likewise numerous. For example, Ibsen's Nora and Helmar in *A Doll's House* exist in continual self-deception about themselves, each other, and their relationship, until others—Krogstad, Rank, and Helmar himself—so obtrude upon Nora's self-deceptive project that it is shattered. The artists and the audience see her project long before she can, and the drama and suspense of the play inhere largely in watching it develop and wondering if it can endure. We live her life along with her, but with a scope of vision and detachment which she lacks, and though we have seen the play many times we are filled with wonder at each new incarnation of our human predicament in its most dangerous form. Each time the disclosure of ourselves can be significantly new—we, the secret sharers, with our own projects of self-deception lit glimmering in the corners of our eyes. At its best, theatre can point the way to both authorization and authentication.[7]

7. Another classic example is Molière's Alceste, he who gives the title to *The Misanthrope*.

What we must underline at this point, however, is the emergence in our account of conditions of identity of self which are remarkably similar to the categorial potentialities of human being, the *existentialia*, of Heidegger's account. Independently of Heidegger we discovered that a condition of identity of self is that there be a body which can also be a subject, that it project possibilities, that it fall into step mimetically with others, and that it take over their attitudes toward itself. In germ here are all the *existentialia*.

In order to conceptualize this falling into pre-set and common ways of behaving and being, and into prescripted and prescribed attitudes toward others and oneself, we find that the most fitting and natural idea is the theatrical metaphor of "role." To begin to become a self one must play a "part" designed by others. To be at all one must be with others. And to do this one must learn a language of bodily "expression" that is only partially and occasionally verbal; fundamental structures are silent. Moreover, all of this occurs in nondeliberate global involvement in which one must constantly find oneself, but not focally and self-reflexively, necessarily; one must find oneself through one's moods. Finally, integral to all this is projection of possibility, or understanding, and it is usually unwitting projection. Take, for example, the woman in self-deception being seduced. From the breakdown in her projection of possibility we can learn what success would have been. She repeats her past in an autistic-like way. Projection of her life as temporal and transformative collapses into mere repetition of archaic "roles"—"nice little girl for the big nice man." As we said, rather than an articulated and ordered copresencing of herself as prepubescent and herself in her current state as postpubescent, she collapses connivingly into her past and freely forfeits her autonomy and freedom. She does not project the past *as* past from a present that is *new* and different, and she does not do this because she does not stand open to the future *as* future—and as incompletely predictable and as anxiety producing. An articulated unity in time, and the mood appropriate to that, has collapsed into a unity of engulfment, the loss of autonomy of self, the warm cacoon of escape from anxiety, and the mood appropriate to that. She "enacts" the sleepy child.

The key to this pattern of conditions of identity of self is the body as it exists with other bodies, that which Heidegger himself never adequately developed, I believe. We will now deepen our conception of the body as involved with others and as mimetic.

CHAPTER XIII

Self, Body-Image, and Mimetic Engulfment

The psychiatrist Paul Schilder writes of the body-image:

> We see parts of the body-surface. We have tactile, thermal, pain impressions. There are sensations which come from the muscles and their sheaths, indicating the deformation of the muscle; sensations coming from the innervation of the muscles . . . and sensations coming from the viscera. Beyond that there is the immediate experience that there is a unity of the body. This unity is perceived, yet it is more than a perception. We call it a schema of our body or bodily schema, or, following Head, who emphasizes the importance of the knowledge of the position of the body, postural model of the body. The body schema is the tridimensional image everybody has about himself. We may call it "body-image."[1]

But the location should not suggest something static. For no sensation can be located on or in the body unless it is registered as a change in what has gone on before. This can only be a change within the ongoing sense of the body—the body-image.

Schilder emphasizes that the "immediate experience" of "the unity of the body" is yet "not mere representation."[2] He seems to be agreeing that the body as lived cannot be regarded as just an object by the person whose body it is; it is far too enveloping and it is incompletely focalizable. He speaks of "the sphere" of processes in "the background of our minds," which obtain for us all in greater or lesser degree, whether we can con-

---

1. Paul Schilder, *The Image and Appearance of the Human Body* (New York: International Universities Press, 1950), p. 11.
2. Ibid., p. 11.

sciously acknowledge it or not. "The sphere" connects with the account we are developing of moods:

> The thinking of the child and of the primitive person is fuller of meaning than the thinking of the adult. They see more relations: everything is connected with everything else. Their thinking is full of symbolizations and condensations. An object means much more than the adult mind sees in it; it is not only animated but connected with all activities in the universe. Freud calls this type of thinking the action of the system of the unconscious; Lévy Bruhl and the French School call it primitive or pre-logic thinking. I prefer to speak of the sphere, and mean by this term the processes which go on in the background of our minds, bringing the single parts repeatedly into all types of varied relations and proceeding under the direction of the various instinctive tendencies from the general to the individual.[3]

Most significant is the way a person's body-image is connected with his direct experience of others' bodies as they are immediately lived by them. At this "immediate" level of experience the distinction between appearance and reality is washed out, and fusions and transformations between persons abound. Similarity tends to be experienced as identity. Schilder himself stresses that identifying relations between people are also object relations, and that a socialized and mimetic body-image is still *that* body's image, which he construes as that *person's*. But he lays little stress on those situations in which the other is not clearly and thematically objectified *as* other, and I believe he slips uncritically at times from a first-person phenomenological point of view, which is essentially integrable with a third-person point of view, into an exclusively third-person behavioristic one in which the conditions of identity of a body understood physiologically are simply conflated with conditions of identity of a self.

However, he concludes his book with the remarkable admission that what he regarded as our "immediate experience" of the unity of the body is "beyond our immediate reach":

> But the empirical method leads immediately to a deep insight that even our own body is beyond our immediate reach, that even our own body justifies Prospero's words: "We are such stuff as dreams are made on; and our little life is rounded with a sleep" (*The Tempest*). A discussion of a body-image as an isolated entity is necessarily incomplete. A body is always the expression of an ego and of a personality, and is in a world.[4]

Thus even the adult's body-image is beyond his immediate comprehension, for it loses itself in the encompassing sphere of relations. The adult's

3. Ibid., p. 249.
4. Ibid., p. 304.

body's immediate experience of itself is in terms of the world experienced by it. Schilder cites cases in which radical changes occur in the body through suggestions given it concerning changes in its world.[5]

We extrapolate: One's own body is "beyond his immediate reach," because the full field of what is experienced by him is not graspable, articulatable, and acknowledgeable by him. Things that an exclusively third-person point of view would automatically distinguish are blurred for the person as he actually lives them. Because from the third-person viewpoint persons are separate objects, we tend to infer mistakenly that in all moments of his experience the person himself must be decisively aware of the other *as* an object and *as* a separate one. This is an example of what James called the "psychologist's fallacy." It also violates "the principle of all principles" of phenomenology enunciated by Husserl: "[W]hatever presents itself in 'intuition' in primordial form (as it were in its bodily reality), is simply to be accepted as it gives itself out to be, though only in the limits in which it then presents itself."[6] Thus Schilder's potentially interesting dispute with Freud concerning the interplay of objectification and engulfment (or identification) soon becomes a pointless one. Since aggression against the father entails his objectification by the son, says Schilder, Freud "contradicts himself" when he asserts that the son can act out his aggression symbolically by consuming a common meal that symbolizes his engulfment with his father and their common substance.[7]

But the dispute cannot be fruitful as long as objectification and engulfment are regarded simply as mutually exclusive. The fundamental distinction between relationships that are thematic and those that are nonthematic is ignored. Likewise ignored is the possibility that a relationship can involve objectification on one level of experience—usually verbal—and engulfment on another. The psychologist's fallacy thrives because of a fixation both on verbal language and on the tacitly assumed primordiality of an atemporal third-person point of view. If someone relating to another is *asked* by a third person, Is this another person? then he must be thrown into the reflective or thematic state in which he must see focally and thematically (if he is sane) *that* the other is another. But I am also concerned about the many moments, particularly those of stress, but not exclusively those at all (say moments of drift, wash, and boredom) in which one is not in this state. There is always, presumably, in moments of waking consciousness a residual and implicit sense of ownness and self; without

5. Ibid., pp. 177–78.
6. Edmund Husserl, *Ideas: General Introduction to Pure Phenomenology* (New York: Collier Books, 1962), Section #24, p. 83.
7. Schilder, *Image and Appearance of the Human Body*, p. 254.

this there could be no sense at all of the other being other. And, indeed, without this one could not know that one of one's own intentions was to be hidden; one could not be—what one very clearly often is—self-deceived! Even the hypnotized person has some sense of ownness and self, one would think, for he balks if suggestions are made to him that he act in ways which are repugnant to him.

However, even if one is stating his otherness from the other and experiencing it thematically, one can still be behaving in ways that evidence profound mimetic involvement in the other—common stances, poses, attitudes, and attacks on things—and be doing this unwittingly. The fallacy overlooks the rapid or slow oscillation between the nonthematic, the relatively thematic, and the thematic—and between behavior which is congruent with what one says, and behavior which is not. Of course one person is relating to another, but it need not follow that he is relating to him either experientially or behaviorally at that moment *as* another and *only* as another. I can assert this last sentence confidently because the truth of its initial clause concerning separate persons presupposes a criterion of individuation of self which is quite crude; it is a criterion applicable from the third-person point of view exclusively. As persons, however, as conscious dialectically involved organisms, not as organisms *simpliciter*, they are not over against each other as objects would be, but very often indeed they are along-with each other mimetically, drifting together in a common tide of softened differentiation and entrancement.

I will continue to extrapolate upon, and to modify, Schilder's interesting findings. We quote now at greater length what we cited much earlier in the book:

> There is a community between my picture, my image in the mirror, and myself. But are not my fellow human beings outside myself also a picture of myself?
>
> A simple experiment may emphasize again that the community between the body-image outside and the body exists already in the sphere of perception. I sit about ten feet away from a mirror holding a pipe or a pencil in my hand and look into the mirror. I press my fingers tightly against the pipe and have a clear-cut feeling of pressure in my fingers. When I look intently at the picture of my hand in the mirror I now feel clearly that the sensation of pressure is not only in my fingers in my own hand, but also in the hand which is twenty feet distant in the mirror. . . . This feeling is therefore not only in my actual hand but also in the hand in the mirror. One could say that the postural model of the body is also present in my picture in the mirror. Not only is it the optic picture but it also carries with it tactile sensation. My postural model of the body is in a picture outside myself. But is not every other person like a picture of myself? . . . The sensations felt in the above

experiment cannot be attributed to projection. The experience of the sensation in the mirror is as immediate and original as the experience in the real hand. It is at least very probable that part of these experiences are given when we see the bodies of others, especially when one considers how little the optic experience concerning one's own body-image differs from the experiences we have concerning the optic image of the bodies of others.[8]

This is exceedingly valuable. But, as we said, we must expunge the suggestion that one's image in the mirror is one's primary image of oneself, and that one's optic image of oneself differs only a little from one's optic image of others. A crucial difference is that one has no primary experience of his own face. To cite again the example: I cut myself severely on the leg. Others rush over and I see them grimacing as they see the wound. Even if grimacing with pain should be a natural expression evident in a young child that is blind, yet for me the face of the other as he sees the wound reinforces my grimace through my sight of his face, and indeed his face fills out the body-image which is mine: *he* supplies a visually experienced face for *my* body-image. I do not say simply that he fills out my experience of my face, for in "the sphere" my image of my body and my image of his body are not perfectly distinct.[9] It is my body-image in the sense that it is experienced by my organism, and presumably would not exist if my organism died, but it is not my body-image if by that is meant that it is simply and directly *of* only my organism's face.

> [I]n the adult also body and world are continually interchanged. It may be that a great part of experiences will not be finally attributed either to body or world. I have mentioned the zone of indifference between body and world, and have stated that in a narcissistic stage the zone of indifference may play a more important part. After all, the image of the body has to be developed and built up.[10]

Perhaps then we can only say that in a face experienced nonthematically and probably unacknowledgeably as "our" face, I feel the distress of the experience, not just in the part of the body that has been cut.

8. Ibid., pp. 223–24.

9. Cf. Ronald Moss, "Distortions in Human Embodiment: A Study of Surgically Treated Obesity," *Selected Studies in Phenomenology and Existential Philosophy,* Vol. VIII, ed. R. Bruzina and B. Wilshire, (The Hague: M. Nijhoff, 1982). Moss shows how members of families, for example, tend to identify a fellow member's body as "our own," particularly obviously if that person's body is abnormal, e.g., greatly obese, and the family is protective of him or her.

10. Schilder, *Image and Appearance of the Human Body,* p. 123. Some evidence that body-images are the products of fusions and are communal is provided by E. H. Gombrich when he points out how some painters' portraits exhibit traits of both the painter's and the sitter's faces: see *Art, Perception and Reality,* ed. Mandelbaum (Baltimore: Johns Hopkins University Press, 1972), p. 40.

But not only does the other supply a visually experienced face, but also—and this a blind child would share with me—appropriate language, gasps, actions, gestures of contact, gestures of distance, all of which directly mobilize me mimetically, and become integral elements of the painful experience and of my life through time. Indeed, we are told by experimental psychologists that the intensity of a pain is in large part a function of the total context of behavior in regard to it learned from others (even if my movements in mimetic response to others are only incipent, these still make themselves felt).

Thus once we purge Schilder's text of physicalistic bias (body-images "melting together," etc.) we can make sense of his valuable insight that a boy "constructs" his own body and his father's of "similar material."[11] The boy must sense his body in some fundamental part through his immediate experience of his father's sensing both of his own body and the boy's; this is primary and nonthematic. As this boy becomes a young man, his father stands in for him as mimetic model. As experienced, as image for the boy, the father stands within the boy's body as the boy unthematically experiences it. In moments of engaged reflection or kinesthetic reflection, the boy may even be able to *recognize* it, particularly if, as a young man, he has some idea of what to look for. If the father suppresses response to physical discomfort, this will be the manner in which the boy, however unacknowledgeably, comes home to himself—unless there are powerful countervailing factors. If the father cowers before others, the boy will tend to do this also. If the father greets him happily, this will be the face that they both put on him, etc. He is engulfed in his father.

Of course, this is overly schematic. There are other adult models, e.g., the mother. Mimetically learned body-images may compete, or alternate to some degree, given various circumstances. Schilder also contends that persons sometimes take only parts of the experienced bodies of others and incorporate them into their body-images. They may also incorporate animals. And we would think that great physiological differences, or endocrinal or genetic differences, would predispose to a lesser degree of mimetic patterning, etc.

I give particular stress in this work to mimetic behavior learned undeliberately in the physical presence of others. But in an extended sense of mimetic it can mean all behavior that reproduces others' behavior, and the causal medium may be entirely genetic, e.g., behavioral traits may skip many generations. Or a son may inherit a father's traits entirely genetically, as we suggested was the case with Oedipus who was separated from

11. Schilder, *Image and Appearance of the Human Body*, p. 254.

his father at birth. Regardless of how mimetic behavior comes about, then, it tends to engulf us in other individuals, and our authentic individuation requires that we progressively distinguish ourselves as the distinctive beings that we actually are here and now.

It is true that a child's genetically inherited mimetic behavior may be quite different from the parental or otherwise authoritative behavior that he encounters in his immediate environment. If so, the mimetic influence of the present encounter will be considerably less than it otherwise would be; considerably less than if both elders and children inherited similar behavioral repertoires and the encounter in the immediate environment reinforced them. There are in fact many mitigating factors usually: the son has also incorporated, to some extent presumably, the mother's body-image, and the commodiousness of space and time and the separability of bodies allow the son "to be on his own" and to develop his individual identity through other relationships. He can unwittingly act out the body-image he shares with his father without competing with him for space, for objects, and for relationships.

But the bare bones of the tragic bind, and at its greatest possible intensity, are these: the son can constitute himself only out of his father's body as experiential material. Yet the corporate body-image is both his and his father's. Since each has a separate and distinct physiological body, they must be counted as two separate persons. But not yet being clearly distinct experientially, by way of body-image, the distinction within the identity fails to be fully articulated within the identity that each lives. Thus both will tend to claim a position that only one can hold. Hence, distinctness is achieved by the son only through supplanting or obliterating the father; or through the father anticipating the attack, and obliterating the son. But this is to attack the shared body-image which is the common ground and source of their being, and it is to suffer guilt and to make reparation needful. The guilt is rational, not necessarily neurotic at all, for it pertains to the conditions of individual identity itself. It is metaphysical or existential guilt.

This also pertains between daughters and mothers. But traditionally it has been less intense and focal. The key fact is that the female child is of the same sex as her mother; thus the earliest and most fundamental relationship has traditionally tended not to excite, but to blur and dampen the two women's experience of being distinct from one another, and to dampen their sense of further possibilities of distinctiveness.[12] With cur-

12. Another part of the picture, however, is the general feeling of their inferiority which women have picked up mimetically from the cultural environment and turned against themselves. It is probable, therefore, that women must band together as reciprocally confirming and valuing groups of women before their contrasting experiences *vis-à-vis* men will conduce to authentic individuation.

rent changes in child rearing, and in the self-consciousness of women, we can expect this to change. Women will probably be thrown earlier into closer contact with men, and their sense of their possibilities of distinguishing themselves from other persons will be heightened.

Because of powerful safeguards, this supplanting and obliterating of parents by children, children by parents, usually takes only psychological and symbolic forms; hence it is not surprising that the mode of reparation—reparation for the thought or impulse of aggression—is usually of a similar sort. In the symbolism of Christianity, persons are rebellious children of God who deserve to die. But God takes the form of a perfect and holy son, Jesus, who stands in for humans and dies in their place, thus redeeming them. (To be sure, Jesus is also God, so in a sense, the father also dies that through Him the children might live; the symbol of the cross is highly polyvalent and powerful.) The ritual of baptism reconstructs this experientially. In being immersed in the water one dies to his old, alienated self, and is "covered" by the one who has died to egoistic self and risen again as reconciled and faultlessly individuated self (perfect distinctness within the identity of the triune godhead). Having merged with this perfected individual in the ceremony, one is endowed with His power vicariously and is raised from the water in likewise perfected form.

The conditions of individuation of human identity are intrinsically dramatic, and the theatre-like ritual of baptism reenacts the evolution of the self. Indeed, the ontogeny of the evolution of the individual self can be viewed as recapitulating the phylogeny of the development of the race, with all its dramatic and semidramatic procedures. In the company of witnesses the self is stabilized as both individual and social—authorized— and on a level of history and continuity deeper experientially than the superficial one of linear dating. That this is a mystical solution will not disturb us as long as we recall that the problem to be solved is mystical. "We are such stuff as dreams are made on."

Thus the curse of Oedipus, that he should kill his father while trying to avoid doing so; the "cursed spite" that Hamlet must take his father's place and at the same time have to avenge his death and risk his own life; the bereft and feckless state of Vladimir and Estragon, who cannot contact Godot and who have given up their rights—all this can no longer seem to be mere theatrical diversion.

Finally, let us touch briefly on a speculation that opens up at this point. In the famous passage from his *Joyful Wisdom* entitled "The Madman," Nietzsche writes,

"Whither is God?" he cried. "I shall tell you. *We have killed him*—you and I. All of us are his murderers. But how have we done this? How were we able to drink up the sea? Who gave us the sponge to wipe away the entire horizon? What did we do when we unchained this earth from its sun? Whither is it moving now? Whither are we moving now? Away from all suns? Are we not plunging continually? Backward, sideward, forward, in all directions? Is there any up or down left? Are we not straying as through an infinite nothing? Do we not feel the breath of empty space? Has it not become colder?"[13]

And again, Nietzsche writes, "Ever since Copernicus man has been rolling down an incline, faster and faster, away from the center—whither? Into the void? Into the piercing sense of his emptiness?"[14] What does Nietzsche mean by the loss of center? It has to do with the loss of the conviction that the rest of the universe is turned toward us, registering us, valuing us, etc. But what does this amount to? If it is true that we are our bodies but are not simply centered in them—that experientially we are de-centered—then the person is for-and-by-others, mimetically involved in others, and yet as organism he is other-from-every-other. And since he is already mimed after an image that is not distinctly either here-and-me or there-and-him (for even if he is mainly indebted to a single other for his body-image, the image that they share is the fruit of their fusion and interaction), then the center of one's world is not an object at all, but is a betweenness, so to speak, which is a presence of meaningfulness. Now, if the sense of God is the sense of a shared, potent, and plentiful body-image which is sensed as a presence, but not simply localizable, and which need not be perceived as merely present and actual, as must be ordinary persons when they are present; and if this is a presence within which a person can live as he sunders his union with his biological parents and proceeds toward increased individuation; then in losing the sense of God one would lose the center and magnetizing goal for becoming an individual self. He would lose the center within which can reverberate his own autonomy. He would lose an engulfment that is at the same time liberating. He would lose his center and lose *charisma*.

Now perhaps this is only a stage in the individual's liberation. But in any case, "the imaginary playmate in the sky" ceases to be self-evidently ridiculous and puerile. Another horizon for the investigation of human identity is opened up. Beckett has written that "All poetry, as discriminated from the various paradigms of prosody, is prayer."[15] I take him to mean that it evokes a presence which sustains us independently of any attachment to anything which is simply localizable within any immediate environment.

13. *The Gay Science*, in *The Portable Nietzsche*, ed. Walter Kaufmann (New York: Viking Press, 1954), p. 95.
14. *Genealogy of Morals*, trans. F. Golffing (New York: Anchor Books, 1956), p. 291.
15. Deirdre Bair, *Samuel Beckett* (New York: Harcourt Brace Jovanovich, 1978), p. 181.

CHAPTER XIV

Identity and Theatre-Like Disengagement from Engulfment

No concept is more important to us, I suppose, than the concept of our own identity as selves, and yet no concept is more difficult to pin down in its application. We have extrapolated very freely on Kant's idea of the phenomenal self as that which arises because of the being's ability to contrast modes and changes of experiencing with modes and changes in things experienced by it. Because experiencing can change without any corresponding or similar change in the thing experienced, and because the thing experienced can change without any similar or corresponding change in the experiencing, the experiencing can gain a sense of itself as something in contrast to everything else, a sense of itself as its own—its self. Indeed, there can be experiencing of X when X not only is not present but when it no longer exists, and the self involves the ability to give presence in its experiencing to the absent.

We have involved the body essentially in the activity of experiencing, thus essentially in the self. Experiencing involves the experiencing body, and the self arises because the body distinguishes its experiencing of X from X itself. The body gains a sense of itself in its distinctiveness. As we see children gamboling in play and adults going about their business it seems unexceptionably true to us that the self arises because the experiencing body is separable and self-moving and is a constant agency of an indefinite variety of actions in regard to things that remain themselves, and so it can be experienced by itself and others as other from every other. No doubt this is fundamentally true and in outline correct, but it is prac-

196

tically impossible to assert it without doing so prematurely, without glossing over some of its conditions, difficulties, and presuppositions. For if to experience itself in its distinctiveness it must experience itself, and if to experience itself it must do so in terms of others' experience of it, then—one might think—it must somehow have experienced others' experience *as* the others,' hence different from and other than its own. It must have experienced itself in its distinctiveness before it can, by the hypothesis, begin to experience itself in its distinctiveness; the question of distinctiveness is begged, not answered. Any exclusively third-person approach will fall into this problem. To avoid it, such an approach will tend to underrate the importance of the being's experience of others' experience of him, and this lands it in an impossibly naive position.

To forestall the difficulty, we introduced the distinction between thematic and nonthematic experiencing. The body can experience itself in terms of others' experiencing of it but need not apprehend this at every moment *as* others' experiencing of it. Thus it can have an apprehension of itself as itself—and it can *be* a self which is for-and-by-others—and yet it need have no thematic apprehension of itself *as* a being which is for-and-by-others. We suppose that the body mimetically participates in the others, yet it is not necessarily aware of itself *as* itself-yet-mimetically-participating-in-the-other. With this we introduce a sliding scale of individual identity. We must speak of greater and lesser degrees of individuation of a human self. One becomes more and more individuated as one makes more and more of one's experience and activity experienceable by one *as* mimetically induced and yet *also* one's own. Certain essential social, legal, and political purposes require that cuts and distinctions be made rather arbitrarily in this continuum of psychical individuation; fine, but this should not deter us from exact thought.

It follows from this that we cannot tell exactly when the individual human self arises, nor even in many situations when it ceases to be. And situations in between, in which it is true to say of the person, "he was not himself," take on peculiar urgency and pathos. However, we will operate in that sector of the continuum of individual identity in which it is quite clear that we have a self before us. We then ask ourselves what processes must occur for this being to progress toward maximal realization of individual identity. In so doing we develop the connection most crucial for this section: the deduction of theatre and theatre-like activity as one condition for maximal realization.

The tendency to drift in with others and to fall into step with them must be regarded as fundamental and irreducible. We respond to things mimetically and undeliberately. As we have said, we reproduce their rhythm and magnitude through rhythm and volume of voice—speak for them—

or we trace in the air through gesture and posture their shape and movement and stand in for them "instinctively." With a small thing we kneel
down, contract the body, squint and narrow the focus of the eyes. With
a quiet thing we grow quiet in order to hear it, etc.

On this level of the person's experience there is no sharp distinction
between one's sense of oneself as subject and one's sense of things over
against one as objects. D. W. Winnicott records his interview with a young
poet:

> X. then went on to talk about the glorious irresponsibility of childhood.
> She said: "You see a cat and you are with it: it's a subject, not an object."
> I said.: It's as if you were living in a world of subjective objects."
> And she said: "That's a good way of putting it. That's why I write poetry.
> That's the sort of thing that's the foundation of poetry."[1]

Most obviously in the case of the human community, one participates
mimetically with the other through participating in his awareness of oneself. How is one to become aware of oneself *as* oneself-but-mimetically-
participating-in-the-other? Self-deception is a regression which is not "in
the service of the ego," to use the phrase alleged to be Freud's. The person
allows himself to become present to himself through another in such a
way that features of his own which distinguish him from others are obliterated, and obliterated so cunningly that his obliteration of them is
obliterated. The vehicle for this transaction is mimetically shared modes
of bodily being—shared body-images. For example, the woman being
seduced relapses into a mode of being which she shared with other little
girls, and which she allows to be evoked as a counterpart to the "protective" man who "of course" would attribute no sexual project to her.

The body merged mimetically with the other—either as a sympathetic
reproduction or as a counterpart reaction or as a compound of the two—
is neutral between, and basic and anterior to, the thematic distinction
between self and other. Yet a mode of mimetic behavior occurs in the
body which the body also audits; the body is both nascent "actor" and
nascent "audience." This contributes its sense to the body-subject's relationships to everything else. But it is not necessarily aware of the mimetic
behavior which it senses "in" itself *as* mimetic behavior induced in it by
others. We can suppose it spontaneously reproducing others' behavior,
but to be maximally its own individual self it must become aware of its
behavior *as* mimetic, general, and social and yet *as* its own as well. Since

1. D. W. Winnicott, "Communicating and Not Communicating Leading to a Study of
Certain Opposites," in *The Maturational Processes and the Facilitating Environment* (New
York: International Universities Press, 1965), p. 186.

one's body-image is made from "material" similar to that of others', the other will stand within one's body too closely to be discriminated as other. How is the power of the other to be broken without being lost completely? If we could somehow lose common, mimetically induced behaviors, we would cease to be socialized, cease to be human.

C. S. Peirce contended that the self's sense of itself arises as a supposition it learns in the face of the group's typically greater ability and knowledge; it must suppose itself to be an individual self in order to account for the ignorance and error that afflict it.[2] In being left out, and in stumbling to catch up, for example, the organism is singled out in its own eyes. Now this may very well be a necessary condition, and it is most suggestive. Yet it is implausible to suppose that this is necessary and sufficient for individual identity. If this were the only resource available, we could envisage the organism being individuated merely as an organism, but not necessarily one that is owned, acknowledged, and valued as "myself" by itself. The organism would be distinguished as a mote-like surd on the bright face of communal being. The body is not optimally ownable by itself as something merely limited and defective.

Since one is a being-in-the-world and a creature of space and time, one can grasp one's activity as one's own, thematize it, only if one can thematize space and time. But how do we do this as ordinary human beings and not just as reflecting philosophers or scientists? (They too must be human.) Space and time recede from us on every hand into the boundless. In order to go about most of our business, they must slip through our fingers as unnoticed as would a fog. One cannot be aware of the boundlessness of the boundless into which they slip. It is just here, on this page, pushed into a corner so to speak by our problem, that we can begin to see the seriousness of play. Play enables us to actively thematize space and time by setting up limits within space and time and playing within them. One models space and time within space and time and gains a grip on them, enabling them to be thematized, and along with this one can be thematized as a creature of—and a creator and agent in—space and time. The play of a child, say, is behavior that has set limits on itself, and has thus released itself to be known and developed. It is a bite, for example, that is self-referential, that signals itself as a bite, that limits and "frames" itself—a "play bite." It is only because it is a bite that it can signal itself to be a play bite. Yet it is only as a self-limiting bite that it can structure a setting of self-illumination, training, and discovery, rather than, say, panic, numbed hysteria, or insensate boredom. We begin to zero in on the problem.

2. C. S. Peirce, "Questions Concerning Certain Faculties Claimed for Man," *The Journal of Speculative Philosophy*, 1868, question no. 2.

Absorbed in others mimetically, engulfed in them, how can we begin to realize our behavior *as* induced by them and yet *as* our own as well? The body can get others off its chest—better, out of its chest—if it can enact them at its own impulse in play and as a fiction. One thinks first of the mimetic productions by children of parents, and of how the child listens entrancedly to himself. But he is not necessarily aware thematically and focally of his words and sounds *as* his enactments of others. *When we see what the actor does onstage we see that at which the child is aiming, however unwittingly.* If another can be enacted by a body—in the other's absence—then that body must realize both that it is a *person*, for it is the other person that it mimetically resembles and all recognize that only persons enact persons; and that it is *a* person because no one need be present to enact the other but he himself the actor! Moreover, he must realize that he is a free person, an agent, for the other is present merely as an enactment; no causal coercion plays from him to the actor. This behavior, then, must tend toward maximization of individual identity.

Let us put this major point a bit differently. The self is the body that has the other "in" it, but although this other is an element constitutive of it, in being enacted at will it is distinguished as merely an element of the enacting being. The other-in-me which is an element constitutive of me, but yet not the only one, can begin to be contrasted to the bodily self as it presently stands—I-myself here and now. To articulate the other in enactment is to articulate the enacting body as other from this other, and indeed other from every other, for every such is in principle enactable by this one. And to be thus other from every other person, one must be a person for others, and consequently a person for himself. It is the force of the fiction that breaks the power of the other without simply losing it. There must be sufficient distance between self and other so that the other is apprehended as other, and yet not so great that the self ceases to be recognizable by all as one of humanity's and society's sort, one of "our" sort.

In the light of the fugal structure of the self which we have appropriated from Kant, the self now exists at a point which approximates its maximal individuation, because the body can freely reproduce its others in a fiction, thus at a moment when the originals themselves need no longer be present, and hence when the body can be fully present to itself as its-body-and-itself in contrast to the absent others. To be a self is to *own* a body which also *is* one.

One is tempted to say that his voice, for example, is his own just because it emanates from his body. And, no doubt, the numerical distinctness of the body is a fundamental fact. But it is wrong simply to conflate conditions for individuating a body as a biological object with conditions for individuating a body-*self*. Given the "similar material" of the body-image, a body's voice may sound to it like "our" voice—or at least it may not be experienced as thematizably "its own." This engulfment is particularly likely if there is a shout, say, when one is along with others, and in response to an actual object of common concern in the environment.

The germ of art is present when a body shouts just to hear itself shout. This is play. And if it should enact another in the shout, in the absence of the other—not just "for the hell of it," but in the presence of guiding and authorizing witnesses—then this is the most decisive possible way for it to expel the other from engulfment in it. This is art proper. The enacting body as shouter and hearer of the shout becomes emphatically its own— it becomes an I-myself.

The same reasoning applies to soundless, gross movements of the body. Schilder speaks of "the fall of energy" and "the melody of movement." This is not illegitimate use of artistic metaphor. And yet, as experienced in everyday life, these movements quite commonly remain diffused through the others with whom one is in mimetic sympathy. For a body to gather itself as maximally individualized self, it must thematize its belonging to the world, its moody nonthematic attunements and involvements in the world. The most decisive possible way to do this is to enact such situations in the face of their absence. Both the body's belonging to the present and actual world and its transcending of it are spoken by it at once. This can only be the meaning which pure, freely initiated motions and sounds can have. And this can only be art and the art-like, this, the "inwardly" coordinated rhythms, motions, and materials which set up a "world" within a world in order to reveal the world and us in it ("inward," a mischievous spatial term, has the exact meaning here of the time of one's own—one's owned—life in space). The self is gathered when its freely initiated gathering of a "world" is gathered within the world.

We are not disembodied minds but body-selves, beings-in-the-world, and to find out where we are we cannot deduce our position from pure concepts as one instance of them. Concepts have instances, observed Kant, but space has parts. We must take that part of space to which we can have access and so isolate it and so set up reverberations within it that we can get some sense of the totality and of our place within it. We must try— and fail—to bound the boundless if we would reveal it. A place of geography is transformed to become a place for presencing.

These are presuppositions of theatre as art, as well as of behavior which is art-like, but they have tended to be obscured by modern realism. At its best this art created an illusion of space so convincing and cunning that it suppressed our consciousness of the conditions of its possibility. As early as 1300 Giotto painted scenes into which viewers felt they might walk.[3] This technique dominated painting, and increasingly the theatre as well, up until the current century. Stages came to resemble picture frames, housing a scene so seductive and mesmerizing that one was conducted into the represented world without realizing what made any such representation possible. There was pseudocontinuity in this one-perspective viewpoint. The proscenium formula for setting and scenery is "see-a-little-bit-of-it-and-imagine-the-rest-of-it-out-of-sight."[4] But that experience tended to slip into the boundless in practically the same unwitting and unthematized way as does everyday experience. The conditions of presencing, which are conditions of the bounding of space and time within space and time, were obscured. They are much more easily seen in the Greek theatre, in the Elizabethan thrust stage with spectators on its fringes, and in our experiments in this century with theatre in the round and with shifting playing area. When scenery and actors are used in these theatres they are quite evidently placed in real space and time, and around these pivots is generated—through compression, simplification, stylization, characterization—the space of presencing, the "world" of the play, its "space," "time," "persons," and "scenes." The inverted commas should restore to us the magnitude of the creative act, and the revelation of sense achieved thereby. James H. Miller writes:

> [A]n object in space is more abstract than a similar object that is framed, just as a statue is more abstract than a portrait. All we have to do is compare the figures in a wax museum to mannequins in a store window to realize that the wax figures are the curiosities and the mannequins seem more "natural."[5]

They are more "natural" because they *seem* to be what they *are*: art objects, works of interpretation.[6] Nothing could be more natural than that their actuality be unlike the actuality of the things they represent. That Greek actors at the birth of theatre wore masks should not surprise us. The transcendence of the artist calls out the transcendence of the auditor so that the auditor is put in touch with his own self. It is art which is most

3. James Hull Miller, "Staging in the Style of Store Window Display," Wisconsin Theatre Association, La Crosse Convention, April 1978, p. 2 (obtainable from 119 Ockley Drive, Shreveport, La. 71105).
4. Ibid., p. 8.
5. Ibid., p. 2.
6. A detailed "realistic" portrait seems natural because its two-dimensional surface and frame signifies that it is art. Actors on stage need not wear masks or heavy costuming to seem perfectly natural, because the inviolable zone of the playing area and the demarcation supplied by the stage lighting function something like the frame for the portrait.

obviously art that puts us in closest and most revealing contact with the heart of our reality: our ability to give presence to the absent or to the nonexistent. Thus the "melody of movement" referred to metaphorically by Schilder will most decisively come to be owned in the body-self's strictly artistic actions: literal melodies of movement in music, dance, theatre; and in those renderings which are most cognizant of the conditions of their realization—space, time, persons. Theatre illuminates the non-theatrical when it reveals it to be theatre-like.

Now let us discuss systematically the strength of the theatrical metaphor as it can be revealed at this point, the ways in which it can illuminate the individuation process outside the theatre in the world. After the chapters in which we discussed interpersonal engulfment in connection with self-deception and body-image, we began this pivotal segment with the demonstration of how enactment of another by way of a fiction is the most vividly obvious and effective way to become disengaged from engulfment and to maximize individuation in identity of self. We saw that what the actor does onstage is what children's play aims at or tends toward. We extrapolated from children's play to its theatrical limit onstage. We will now reverse our procedure and go back down the line step by step, seeing how the theatrical activity of the individual can illuminate through its metaphorical reach the more obviously theatre-like moments of individuation offstage, and then the less obviously theatre-like moments. The metaphor alerts us to possibilities, not all of which we would otherwise have seen. When these possibilities fall into a conceptual network which coheres with all that we have said so far, we will have attained our goal, at least the first sketchy statement of it: the connections between theatre, theatrical metaphor, and the conditions which make individual identity possible.

The power of the theatrical metaphor is so great that one could almost be forgiven for neglecting the question of its limits. There could be no stage actor unless he acted in and for a world—a world of other persons, an audience. Likewise, we find that the individual offstage must be a life-actor in and for the world; he must experience himself via the "audience's" experience of him; he does not have his reality in himself as presumably a match does within its sealed box. As the actor must make his mark on the responsive audience in order to read what he is doing—what he *is* as an actor—so must the person offstage. It is no accident that the essential life activities of conversation and dress can be developed to the point where they can be called "arts" in a true sense. They are deliberate, studied, and crafted displays for others. Even when one blurts something out more or less spontaneously it may be an astonishing *spectacle* even for the speaker.

One is returned to himself augmented, confirmed, and perhaps clarified by the other. One has left his mark on the other and through him upon oneself—*l'effet c'est moi!*—the effect, it is I!

In order to come home to himself as an individual, the life-actor like the stage actor must make his own to ever greater degrees what others have made of him. Although an inwardness that he does not share, or does not easily share, is also built up alongside this fund of mediated interpersonal experience, it must be alongside *it* if it is not to be lost in a smear of defensive projection and engulfment. As the actor cannot be an actor without the character enacted, so the life-actor cannot be a person without his various *personae*. But it does not follow that the actors are nothing but their characters or their *personae*.

It should be noted that in Carl Jung's lectures in London in 1935, which Beckett attended, the psychiatrist spoke of a little girl who died for no apparent reason other than that "she had never been completely born." Here emerges a key, perhaps the key, to all of Beckett's mature work: how does one—engulfed in the other—get born psychically as an individual self? One might almost say that in one form or another this is the theme, tacit or manifest, of all serious drama. The plot is this "movement of soul" toward differentiation and clarification of the selves involved.

As the actor must create a character, so the person must create a *persona*, or *personae*, if he is not to remain psychically unborn. Differentiation requires ultimately that he present that to the other. We cannot go from publicness and engulfment to privacy, pure individuality, and interiority. We can only go from being public and engulfed to being public and relatively more individuated; only when our publicness is owned and acknowledged by ourselves can we be genuinely individuated and inward by contrast. One of the few major differences between the actor's character and the person's *persona*—and we shall expand on this crucial theme later—is that the actor is more or less freed from his characters after each performance of them, while the person must die with his *personae* on his head. He remains forever responsible for them in a way in which the stage actor is not.

The Argentinian writer Jorge Luis Borges has written,

> It's to the other man, to Borges, that things happen. I walk along the streets of Buenos Aires, stopping now and then—perhaps out of habit—to look at the arch of an old entranceway or a grillwork gate; of Borges I get news through the mail and glimpse his name among a committee of professors or in a dictionary of biography. I have a taste for hourglasses, maps, eighteenth century typography, the roots of words, the smell of coffee, and Stevenson's prose; the other man shares these likes, but in a showy way that turns them into stagy mannerisms. It would be an exaggeration to say that we are on bad

terms; I live, I let myself live, so that Borges can weave his tales and poems, and those tales and poems are my justification. It is not hard for me to admit that he mas managed to write a few worthwhile pages, but these pages cannot save me, perhaps because what is good no longer belongs to anyone—not even the other man—but rather to speech or tradition. . . . Years ago, I tried ridding myself of him and I went from myths of the outlying slums of the city to games with time and infinity, but those games are now part of Borges and I will have to turn to other things. And so my life is a running away, and I lose everything and everything is left to oblivion or to the other man.

Which of us is writing this page I don't know.[7]

Of course, Borges is famous and an artist, and when others perceive him on the street they will perceive him to be famous and an artist, and he will probably perceive their perceiving him this way. The same is true, to an even greater degree, for the famous actor. The characters that the one writes and the other enacts will spill over into the *persona* or *personae* that they adopt willy-nilly when they walk in the streets. Hence we can expect that the difference they feel between their "public" *personae* and their "private" selves will be especially vivid and dramatic, and perhaps troubling.

But in its very vividness and exaggeration this calls our attention to a distinction applicable to us all which might otherwise be blurred and lost, and which can be troubling. Sometimes a person feels as if he were somebody else. The actor's character emerges from within the style and mood of the play as a whole, and the control he exerts as artist is in large part a responsiveness. In an importantly similar way the individual's dominant *persona* emerges from within the style and mood of the dominant group, and the control he exerts as private self must be in large part merely a responsiveness. Role onstage illuminates "role" off; style and mood onstage illuminate style and mood off.

In the essential offstage activities of conversation and dress we *are* by having our effects upon others mediated by them, and we are more fully individuated—not by giving up these activities—but by increasingly owning as one's own one's other's responses to one. The person cannot even defy the other through dressing and speaking unconventionally unless the other takes note of him and unless he takes note of his taking note. We suppose the hermit to suppose himself to be observed, or to be observable, by an ideal observer. To speak as a mature individual is to identify with the hearer's hearing of what one says, and yet not to submerge oneself in him. The more the "art" of conversation is developed, the more the speaker identifies mimetically—but not engulfedly—with what the hearer

7. Jorge Luis Borges, "Borges and Myself," *The Aleph and Other Stories, 1933–1969* (New York: E. P. Dutton, 1970).

hears. Likewise the "art" of dress requires that the wearer be able to take the viewpoint of the viewer and find this fulfilling of his own individual being. That this is analogous to what the actor does on stage cannot be doubted, and I take such "arts," at least minimally developed, to be essential to the structure of the maturely individuated self.[8]

Ideality is that attribute of the theatre that allows an incident that happened, say, three hundred years ago in a faraway place, to seem to be happening here and now. Giving such presence to absence is what chiefly characterizes theatre, but this ideality—if it is fine art—must possess two essential corollaries: (1) the repeatability of the performance, and (2) an inability on the part of the audience to alter the plot or the duration of time needed for it to unfold. As activities become less theatre-like, the distance between what is given presence in the conversation, for example, and what is, was, or could be present and actual becomes less. Let us say the conversation is giving presence to a person, it is about a person, and that this person is present. The more theatre-like and structured the conversation, the greater the distance between what we more or less immediately feel about him and what we express about him or make discernibly manifest to others. It is not just spatial or temporal distance that is relevant, but psychological distance generally. The less theatre-like it is, the less the distance, so that in certain situations with one's family, for example, the distance between what one immediately and privately feels and what one discernibly manifests is reduced almost to the vanishing point. After the sustained tension of "performance," these moments of relaxation and "freedom" may be a great relief.

But the notion of freedom here is equivocal. Although we are freer in the sense that there are fewer restraints against expression of the more or less immediately felt, the very absence of structures and restraints limits the extent and sometimes even the depth of feelings available to be expressed. That is, our ability to discern things about the others and about ourselves is limited by the collapse, or near collapse, of theatre-like ways of acting, being, and discerning. Hence in this respect we are less free; the scope of our ability to *be* is straitened. The effectiveness of action offstage may be dependent upon a very theatre-like "performance." But our success may leave us with the curious and troubling sense of being someone else. Borges' problem can afflict us all.

8. For example, we find in British English the interesting locution "bathing costume" for bathing suit. Note also this case: my infant daughter is playing with a large red feather. After picking her up and thinking that she may wish to play with the feather again, I stick it in my hair as the most convenient way of carrying it and preserving it. But I realize immediately that it must be seen by the others as worn-by-me-to-be-seen-by-others. So I remove it because it is not my intention in this instance to be so seen. My intentions must bow to a reality in which I am caught up unavoidably.

All arts and games, and all "arts" and "games," require that the present and actual situation be masked, suppressed, and controlled in various ways, in order that a certain facet of human life in its potentialities be focused and be allowed to develop unimpeded by extraneous events. All action involves judgment in the sense of selection.[9] Thus, an athlete slowly develops a particular bodily skill so that he can present himself at any appropriate time and place as its master. This will be a situation so structured that no other demands are made upon him. In general, a self can be affirmed and can exist only as that being which can hold more or less constant in its cognition and experience of itself through time; the athlete holds constant to certain abilities through time. Time can be transcended only through time; it cannot be escaped. Fine art magnifies this transcendence by preserving the uniqueness of a particular performance through great stretches of time.

Let us further articulate this first statement of our position that life is theatre-like. As we must distinguish stage actor as artist from himself as character, we find that we must similarly dintinguish life-actor as person from himself as "character," or *persona*. (These are distinctions of reason only; in neither case are there selves which are really separable from one another.) The key to understanding the stage actor's enactment of a character is the definiteness of the time span allotted deliberately by the artists to their activities as characters within the play's "world." No member of the audience is allowed to interfere with this unrolling of artistic events. If it is disrupted somehow the play can recommence some time later with no break in, and no time added to, its "world's" time. This is what makes possible the supreme ideality of theatrical presencing: its ability to call into presence things completely removed in fact from the immediate setting of the theatre house.

The more theatre-like is behavior offstage the more nearly the allotment of time to activity as "character" approximates—but never reaches—the definiteness and inviolability of time span allotted to activity as character onstage, and the more the offstage situation endorses and supports this inviolability. Thus this behavior approximates the ideality and distancing of the stage. A paradigm example of this is the urban cocktail party. Here the theatre-like arts of conversation, cosmetics, and dress are developed to their highest pitch. The party is conducted within a definite span of time, with invitations issued accordingly—"from five to seven in the evening, regrets only." In the paradigm case the persons are not acquainted with each other in a wide range of other settings, for example, in family settings. This approximates the anonymity of the theatre house and allows

9. See Justus Buchler's powerful work, *Toward a General Theory of Human Judgment* (New York: Columbia University Press, 1951).

the participants to hold back great quantities of knowledge of fact concerning themselves and others, as well as to inhibit a large range of immediate reactions to present fact, and to project an ideal image of themselves, of others, and of the world-viewed. If persons present are known to each other from other settings of very different sorts, then this knowledge may "leak" into the situation: as if light in the theatre house and disturbance there had distracted attention from the stage and weakened the cohesive force of the theatrical production.

The family situation is the paradigm case of social behavior at the other end of the spectrum: that which usually is least theatre-like. Though there are special family events, the person is more or less constantly with the others, and one's ability to limit his presence to a confined time is sharply reduced. Thus one's ability to achieve distancing and ideality is sharply reduced. One even gets to know the others in some of their private moments—when they did not think that any other person was aware of them. The more personally one knows someone is a function of the number of different settings in which one knows him.

Needless to say, perhaps, at this point, what the stage actor does in deliberate enactment of character in a highly protected setting and a sharply confined temporal span is to set traps for the disclosure of the tragic choices of "character" which people make undeliberately in situations which are not well protected, and in which they cannot typically acknowledge either that they made the choice or that they made it for any delimited period of time—if indeed there was any delimited time intended. Such offstage behavior, typically hidden from the person in the outer margins of his consciousness, has a strange quasi-eternal quality, as if it stood in an eternal "now"—that which does not change, so very much like death. Clearly, such behavior is often learned at an early age in the family. Theatre is a new source in time for the exhibition of the original sources—and the original rivalries, mimetic involvements, and self-characterizations—and for being disinterred from them.

There is, of course, a vast array of cases intermediate between the family and the cocktail party; they instantiate degrees of the theatre-like. Theatre itself can help illuminate them all, not only directly and explicitly in its various types of productions, but through our knowledge of the implicit structure of any theatre event. We will comment on rites as theatre-like later.

It is impossible to imagine what we would consider life to be like if we did not have theatre and the metaphor which springs from it. Take an ordinary sort of occurrence—a young child goes to live in the South of the United States for several years and returns with the speech pattern typical of the region. It is impossible to imagine how we would construe this in a world which somehow possessed no theatres and no behavior that is theatre-like. It is impossible to imagine what it would *be* in such a world. One *is* mimetically in the other's presence and is authorized in one's being by others. How would we experience our life as a human life without the concepts of role, presence, a part to play, the mimetic, scene, performance, audience, the tragical, the comical, *persona* and person, etc.—all of which involve more or less directly the concept of the theatrical? Even when the metaphor nears the end of its tether, as in a family encounter in which distance between what we more immediately and privately feel and what we discernibly manifest, between *persona* and person, nears the vanishing point, still there can be something very theatrical, for example, in how we berate or denounce each other; only the French notion of the *tirade* can do it justice.

Throughout the gamut of his "roles" a person is similar to a performer who is staging himself as a character, as Sartre has pointed out. For instance, even though one's emotions come and go, and even though one has experienced the fact time and time again that the merest smile from one who has hitherto been considered one's enemy is sufficient to melt one's emotion of hatred, still one "casts" oneself as "the one who hates X." It seems entirely appropriate to do so, for it seems that one is merely responding to the other's hatefulness. One parades oneself before oneself as an animated but changeless substance with essential attributes from which springs one's behavior, and deceives oneself as to his responsibility for doing so. One's model for himself is theatrical, either in a general and difficult to trace way, or perhaps in a way that is specifically theatrical or literary, e.g., "as angry as Achilles." This is a perversion of freedom. The person has "chosen" to curtail his freedom, to submerge himself in an engulfment of his own making, to turn himself into a mere thing, a bloody and avenging engine. Only a new theatre-like act, an act of imagination which reintegrates himself as free, as an individual, and as alive, can disinter and reanimate him.

We here encounter the domain of tragic freedom, self-deception, and engulfment in others and the world. It is the mission of art—particularly the theatre—to reveal this offstage reality. Not involuntarily, but not fully consciously or deliberately either, the person "casts" himself into "roles" available in the local environment. Others, in their own tragic freedom, encourage or entice him into these "roles" through being mimetic models for him; either this or the "role" he "chooses" is the only way out for him in an impossible situation. Perhaps a child is forced to choose between terrors: either to have an indefinite identity or one that is definite but shameful. Thus Sartre has written of the orphan Genet who is caught by his foster parents rifling through drawers and is called *thief*. To be a thief is less terrifying than to be nothing definite at all. He becomes what they call him. Practically speaking he is helpless. Nevertheless he "chooses" that identity and repeats the "choice" day after day as he grows to be an adult.

Occasionally we catch ourselves in these self-castings as *personae* or "characters"—and not infrequently at the urging of art: layer after layer, with "characters" standing in front of other "characters" as enacted responses to them, e.g., a person catches himself with chin up and teeth clenched at his desk heroically preparing a good lecture in the face of dwindling minutes on the clock.[10] But *why* do I do this, he asks? Behind this "character" he glimpses another, a child-like fugitive lurking in the dimmest reaches of voluntary life: himself as oppressed by time and powerless. The child-like character has "chosen" to be powerless in the face of time for all time; the "choice" stands changeless, as if it stood in an eternal now, so very much like death. He casts himself in the "role" of the heroic character in order to counteract and conceal the impotent character but he remains trapped in the confining and emasculating time of the character's life.[11]

But I am not powerless *now!* he says as he catches himself. I am a full professor, and I can be late *now* if I choose! etc., etc. We seek a new source in time from which to disinter ourselves and live anew. It is not only art which supplies this saving distance and detachment. It is also the art-like in our existence, those moments of imagination and of detachment within our involvement.

There is some value in referring to the face metaphorically as a mask. It is no accident that the word *person* derives from the word for mask, *persona*. Like a mask, a facial expression is for others to see. Usually it is modeled undeliberately on that of which we expect others to approve when they see us. It is integral to the "roles" which we expect others to expect us to play. In tragic freedom we cast ourselves in these available "roles," that is, we typically do not know that we have done so. Sometimes one does not know what expression he has on his face, and another must tell him what it is. But seldom in the ordinary course of events is the other motivated to tell us, for his interest is typically exhausted by the expression itself, and he cares not at all to arouse our potentiality to become aware

10. Concerning self-dramatization, note also Tolstoy's character Nekhlyudov in *Resurrection:* "All, all the best that a man can do, he felt capable of doing. His eyes filled with tears as he was saying all this to himself; good and bad tears: good because they were tears of joy at the awakening of the spiritual being within him, the being that had been asleep all these years, and bad tears because they were also tears of tenderness to himself at his own goodness" (Oxford University Press, 1916, p. 105).

11. See Maurice Natanson, "Man as an Actor." *Philosophy and Phenomenological Research*, Vol. XXVI, no. 3 (March 1966); especially "the watercooler" section.

of the expression and to transcend it in a creative act of our subjectivity. For example, vertical wrinkles between the eyebrows elongate the face and nose and must produce an expression of negative affect (other things being equal). The person who sees it is powerless to alter the visual impression that he has gotten, even if he should wish to shift his perceptual attitude. He simply confirms us in this expression of our being. Finally the face is pressed into this "mask" and is molded into permanent lines of expression.

However, even if one's face be permanently lined by the habitual expressions it has assumed, by the "mask" into which it has been pressed, a person is not a thing. If one recognizes a fact about his face he will no longer live stolidly within its grasp, but can seize other possibilities of existence, and can strive to counteract the fact of his own face. The open-endedness of one's subjectivity, creativity, and freedom is also a fact. To refer to one's face as a "mask" and to one's behavior patterns as "roles" is helpful only when we realize that metaphors are being used and that they have limits of applicability. The word *mask* used in the literal sense refers to a thing which becomes simply a different thing if its expression is changed, and *role* used in the literal sense refers to a prescribed pattern of conduct on-stage of which it makes no sense to say that it is good to counteract it.

The theatrical metaphor begins to break down just where we would expect it to do so: the dailiness of life, the dailiness of caring (or failure to care), the stickiness of our *personae*, their relentlessness, monotonousness, and momentousness—the mood of satiety with self—all this can find no direct parallel on the stage with its actors and characters shining there for a few hours. Moreover, there is something unspeakable in day by day living—unspeakably particular and private—and all art can do is to show in revealing ways that and how there is the unspeakable; it cannot live it in the way we must offstage. We reserve this discussion to the last section.

Now, what were we constantly presupposing as we worked out these parallels between onstage and off? Parallel in what common respects, in what common irreducible ways? First there is language, verbal and non-verbal; the parallels are unthinkable without that. Then there is role, on-stage literally, and offstage as those common ways of being together mimetically, those "roles" into which we must fall if we are to be. Then there is understanding as the projection of possibility. We cannot understand offstage as theatre-like unless we project the possibility that life both offstage and on can be projected in some manner theatrically, in those categories of possibility. Finally, and perhaps most dramatically, theatrical art's disclosure of the belongingness of mood to situation lets us see this pervasive, difficult to see belongingness offstage. But without that background mood in which we can have theatre, we could not have the belongingness of "world" to world, and world to "world." These are very similar to the ontological possibilities articulated by Heidegger which we have already seen to be presupposed by our analysis of convincing enactment in the theatre. Now they appear again toward the end of our analysis of the possibility of self-identity either onstage or off. We can say that we have been over this ground before, but that is only to say that we have come full circle and have made explicit what had to be implicit from the start if there was to be any circle of concepts at all. If we could not find any circle then we would succumb to vicious linearity—thought unable to ground itself. With the circle now first apparent, we can begin to fill in some of its more lightly sketched portions.

CHAPTER XV

Existence and Art: Self as Memorializing Structure of Possibilities

Aristotle observed that objects which in themselves we view with pain we delight to contemplate when they are reproduced with minute fidelity. We can, perhaps, appreciate this penetrating remark more than did Aristotle himself, for despite his belief that it is man's nature to gain a second nature through socialization, he thought that this socialization would best occur within a known set of forms of social life, and that man is a definite species of primary substance. Thinking within a post-Kantian framework, we do not regard a human self as being a substance. A condition for that would be that it be completely objectifiable. But we do not think that this is possible, either from the first- or the third-person points of view, nor do we think that there is some transcendent point of view in which both are synthesized—although art constantly struggles to achieve this. And the forms in which man could be adequately socialized do not seem to us to be all known, or even imaginable.

For us the delight of artistic reproduction is the delight of the production—the never-ending production—of the self. Reproduction in art is a special case of that contrasting of experiencing with objects experienced which is constitutive of the self. If a conscious body had never had the capacity to variously reproduce its life in art-like speech, gesture, dress, whatever—then we would have no reason to call it a self or a person.

"Of everything that happened to me to be able to say, 'Thus I willed it.' " This maxim of Nietzsche's, which celebrates freedom and autonomy, is most obviously exemplified in strictly artistic activity. To reproduce through artistic choice a tragic "choice" is to disengulf oneself from it, and from the indeterminate, death-like duration to which one committed oneself in that "choice." It is to establish oneself over against it as existing now, as free, and as real and alive—for after all, now in fact is not then, and one does not possess a nature that necessitates an autistic iteration of one's past. One seizes the possibility to appropriate one's past as one's own and as past. If this takes the form of a theatrical reenactment, then the reenactment is a memorialization for oneself and for others of our power over possibility.

It is not merely one's actual mimetic involvements with other persons that art makes thematically one's own. Already every actual or possible object in the universe to which one attends is his own in the minimal sense that it is his object of attention and his other. But the degree to which it can be made thematically one's own can be increased indefinitely. Here engulfment in the momentary and the narrow is replaced by equilibrating and vitalizing participation in the whole. Here world is mapped into "world." Here the objects that motivate, energize, and involve us one by one are compressed into simultaneous presence and into an intense if usually short-lived experience of total participation and total activity here and now. What is already one's own—the world at large—is acknowledged as one's own in one's "world" of art. The world is given back with the compounded interest of one's open-ended powers of involvement with it. Articulation replaces a moribund smearing and engulfment, at least for as long as one participates in the artistic activity.

We have spoken repeatedly of the difficulties inherent in the human source. To become human we must be mimetically engulfed in others, but to become an individual human we must sunder ourselves from these same others. Art is a centering into individual being that can bear the contradictions of source, because it takes the initiative from them and shares them memorially with others: those whose testimony is needed, and whose indifference has been destroyed by the artistic setting. Art is a new source in time for the reproduction, surmounting, and preserving of source. Art releases the power of time to distance us from source, and to wash out guilty attachment to it.[1] It catches up to source memorially and imaginatively and puts it where it belongs: behind it. Nietzsche spoke of artistic creation as the innocence of becoming.

Even in those cases in which the theatre artist grasps thematically actual mimetic tendencies of our everyday behavior, he must grasp them as instances of possible forms of behavior. This is to be no longer impacted in the actuality of this behavior. To grasp the actual through the fictional—

1. By "guilt" I follow Heidegger and mean a lagging behind one's possibilities as an individual (*eigentlich*) being.

or through any typification—is to be beyond the actual in the possible. The door is open for further progression into the purest invention. The self revels and swells with its ability to stamp as its own what had never before been incarnately imagined by anyone. It memorializes for itself and others—for itself through others—its power over possibility.

Ionesco has written,

> It has been said that what distinguishes man from the other animals is that he is the animal that laughs, he is above all the animal that creates. He introduces into the world things which were not there before: temples and rabbit hutches, wheelbarrows, locomotives, symphonies, poems, cathedrals and cigarettes. The usefulness of all these things is often only a pretext. What is the use of existing? To exist. What is the use of a flower? To be a flower.[2]

The purest inventions cannot help but reveal us, the inventors. Art can speak of us though not explicitly about us. Take a Mondrian color-pattern painting. Evident first is the brute fact of our freedom: we need not reproduce present and actual objects, or even nonpresent ones. The painting speaks of our power to abstract from objects altogether and to incarnate pure qualities: straightness, crossedness, blueness, redness. But the fact that it pleases us reveals more of who we are. It is just these varieties and these balancings of form and color and weight—and horizontality and verticality—that draw us into the painting and equilibrate us. To say that the painting "pleases the eye" is unhelpful ellipsis. For we must add that the eye pleased belongs to an upright, mobile, balancing being that is delighted by that which orients, balances, and draws it out in space and time. Or again, the cubist artist's display of perspectives that could never in fact be achieved simultaneously by a single viewer still speaks of that simultaneity through time which is of the self's deep structure. It speaks the syntax of self. Views achieved at different times are held together by anticipating and retaining mind. "Nonrepresentational" art represents us in the sense that it articulates and exercises our possibilities. It acts for us. Theatre is the art of vicarious experience, of standing in, *par excellence.* When it is taken as paradigmatic, the other arts fall into a comprehensible pattern.

Finally, "nonrepresentational" art often best "represents" our moods, because the impact of a situation in its wholeness is a matter of what is unfocused: marginally apprehended forms, backgrounds, tonalities, luminosities, and rhythms as these encompass us and block or facilitate our purposes. Success is achieved because individual objects which figure in

2. Rosette C. Lamont, ed., *Ionesco: A Collection of Critical Essays* (New York: Prentice-Hall, 1973), p. 1.

situations are *not* reproduced in identifiable form. Nor is abstract art limited to painting or music. Wilson and Ionesco, for example, utilize actual persons in their theatre, but the cumulative effect is similar to abstract art. Persons are not denoted as if they were objects viewable at a single abstracted instant of time; rather, the worldly structures of their moody experiencing through time are elucidated, and the structures of our experiencing are elucidated because of our identification with theirs. This can be enhanced through "nonrepresentational" sets, lighting, sounds, and costumes.

Beckett has said that he is not writing about something, but writing something. But the line between these must blur, for the writer cannot help but reveal himself as writer, and the great fantasies are those that reveal ourselves to ourselves from unexpected and otherwise inaccessible angles. In theatrical metaphor we use a man to give the appearance of another man—Burton or Olivier enacts Prince Hamlet. But we can go even further, and use a person to represent a rhinoceros or a horse. We have not removed ourselves from human actuality thereby.

In the play *Strider* the actor Gerald Hiken enacts a strangely colored horse, a piebald.[3] It is not merely that we learn what a horse in general, or this sort of horse in particular, means to *us*, thereby learning about ourselves indirectly. We learn about ourselves with a unique and unsettling directness. Take the crucial scene in which the horse as a young colt is being named by his owner. In perceiving fancifully and bodily how a horse might experience being given a name, and perceiving this through seeing a man enacting a horse being named, we re-present the event of *our* being named and explode the shell of stereotypical appearances that prevent this momentous englobing relationship from being experienced focally and in wonder. We are delivered into "the sphere" in such a way that its entanglements, engulfments, and moods can become thematic.[4]

Hiken, enacting the colt rolling on the ground and hearing the name he is being given, says softly, "Piebald" . . . "Piebald?" . . . "Piebald!" in a groping, fascinated voice. The revelation breaks upon him and upon us with dawning mystery and veiled alarm: How can *I* be the one who is named by the *other*? The physiognomic metaphors disclose the metaphorical nature of our own existence: ours is an actuality and particularity mediated by otherness, and we can come home to ourselves only by ap-

3. The original Russian version of the play was conceived by Mark Rozovsky, a writer and director who created the piece out of a set of improvisations between actors at a drama school.

4. It is impossible for a man to be a horse. But this is a "probable impossibility," as Aristotle put it in *The Poetics* (XXV-17). That is, the impossibility enacted as a fiction illuminates the essence or form, and this has instances in the actual world.

propriating this otherness as our own. We discover the key questions and ourselves as questioners and new possibilities of search open before us.

Pirandello objected that most art distorts the self through lending it a coherence which it does not really possess:

> For a humorist, causes in real life are never as logical and ordered as in our common works of art, in which all is, in effect, combined and organized to exist within the scope which the writer has in mind. Order? Coherence? What if we have within ourselves four souls fighting among themselves; the instinctive soul, the moral soul, the affective soul, and the social soul? Our consciousness adapts itself according to whichever dominates, and we hold as valid and sincere a false interpretation of our real interior being, which we ignore because it never makes itself manifest as a whole, but now in one way, now in another, according to the circumstances of life.[5]

But this is misleading. It is as if Pirandello thought that traditional "nonhumorous" art looks out at a distant disjointed self which it cannot accurately perceive. But the self is not just another denotable object about which art speaks. The artist cannot in any way express a disjointedness or dissonance in the self without to some important extent effecting an integration of the self. That is a basic reason why he composes his art. In so doing he composes himself. Elements are gathered together in the expression—although it is always a question of the extent to which this carries over into his everyday life. It is true that if we are to be informed about offstage life through art, we must try to subtract the unity which art cannot help but produce in the very act of revealing the complexity or disjointedness of existence. I say try to subtract because we can never know exactly what our life or the artist's life would be like if he had not produced the art at all.

We should note in addition, however, that identity of self does not require the identity of one personality. Nor need art, particularly theatre art which unfolds through time, render the self as requiring this. Theatre, whether humorous or not, can brilliantly articulate shifts in identity of personality, and it can grasp as a whole this array of shifts. We located identity of self in a body with the capacity for artistic or artistic-like reproductions of its life as its life. But it does not follow that each reproduction need emphasize the same elements, nor that it be done in the same style. It is even possible—though rarely found—that one system of reproducing that life be out of contact with another, in which case we have a multiple personality. We assume that it is a single self because of the

5. Luigi Pirandello, "On Humor," in *Dramatic Theory and Criticism*, ed. B. F. Gukore (New York: Holt, Rinehart & Winston, 1974), p. 752.

single body, and because we must assume this if we are to identify, as we do, this personality structure as multiple and as deviant. If we say that there are two *selves* in a single body then how are we to explain how one "self" feels violated by the other's presence (if it is aware of it)? There is nothing about the integrity of the body as a merely physiological entity which could explain this violation. Why shouldn't it be the happy site of a circus of selves? It must be because the body is a body-subject, a self, and *its* integrity is violated. We must say, then, that there are multiple personalities of a single body-self.

In human life the actual does not exist in isolation from the possible, the ideal, and the fictional. As Merleau-Ponty has said, we struggle with dream figures and our blows fall on living faces.[6] In pre-reflective experience, in the oscillations between daydream and perceptual awareness, the distinction between the veridical and the nonveridical blurs. As we have noted, Freud regarded the "primary process" as that in which reality cannot be adequately tested and the "subconscious knows not not." If, for example, my pre-reflective presence to myself is as a victim, then this constitutes my being whether I am in objective fact now victimized by others or not. It is only in yet-unachieved levels of reflection that the question of objective truthfulness can even be raised, and this requires a new engagement in time. Art can begin to comprehend through fantasy the role of fantasy in existence. Through the artistic "world" set up within the world the latter can begin to emerge through continuity and contrast. As creators know, art is controlled delirium: it is abandonment within bounds that have been artistically set, but the abandonment sets resonating bounds that were not deliberately set, and brings these to apprehension. To that extent we are no longer impacted in them, and we clear a room for the manifestation of those usually suppressed maverick tendencies that run under the wire, as Pirandello has put it. We encompass the present and past only in a new stance of commitment and openness toward the future.

When we attend to the theatre itself, and not just to the play in the theatre, we can see it to be continuous with dream, daydream and imagination. Just as the objects of these modes of consciousness do not present themselves within and against the stable background of world, but are wrapped about with characterlessness and indeterminacy, closing in upon themselves to form a created world, so in the theatre we have a focally attended stage wrapped about with an immobile and nonfocally attended audience—an effect heightened in modern times by a darkened area for

6. Quoted in Chaikin, *The Presence of the Actor* (New York: Atheneum, 1974), p. 11.

it.[7] The acting area is the place where the darkness and the dream of the encompassing world are thematized as such—a place filled with light where shadows spring forth as absences of light. There is reversal, or dilation, and the background springs into focal presence. We confirm ourselves in the light as beings who must endure much of our lives in supposition, darkness and ignorance.

Art moves ahead of us, exploring and experimenting. Because it thematizes our needs, longings, and fantasies it changes our lives; it begins to compose them. To what extent? We cannot at any moment tell exactly. We cannot tell when it will next illuminate and redirect our probing offstage and discover actualities—or when it will simply enlarge our sense of possibility and thus enlarge our lives.

The work of art might be called a substitute self, or perhaps a quasi self. It is deeply one's own and it speaks for one. Moreover, it is a concentrated and enduring expression; even the actor's artistry lives on in the memory of the auditor. Deliberately, skillfully, and frequently through trial and error, meaning is selected, concentrated, and funded in the stone, the canvas, or the performance. It is then unleashed for a relatively short time upon the viewer or the auditor. It calls more absence into presence than the artist present in his everyday mode of living ever could, and it does so even in the artist's absence (let us assume that the actor artist is concealed as a person, so absent in this sense). Since the essential function of the self is to call absence into articulated presence, the work of art is a consummation of self in the very moment that it breaks clear of self and becomes an independent existence.

But this "breaks clear of self" is figurative and somewhat misleading, because the concentration and connectedness achieved in the performance will open up new possibilities for integration and clarification offstage. To what extent? Again, we cannot tell until we begin to live with these insights offstage.

In Goya's drawings of war and ravagement what is gathered up seems to be the artist's compassion, his desire for justice, and his cruelty, all three. The actor does this also for his audience. Indeed, he does this for himself through doing it for his audience. In Elizabeth Swados's play *Runaways*, youthful actors, some of whom are actual runaways, enact on the stage their disruptive flights from family and social groups. As they enact this for us within the institution of the theatre, they recommit themselves to the culture and are more or less rewoven into it. In the case of *Oedipus Rex* the work of art holds together in solution elements which

7. Edward S. Casey, *Imagining: A Phenomenological Study* (Bloomington: Indiana University Press, 1976), p. 156 and *passim*.

the exclusively logical mind must find contradictory: engulfed dependency upon one's parents, one's source, and violent displacement and violation of them. Oedipus's act of social disruption and defilement is redeemed in part through the enactment of *Oedipus Rex* for the audience.

To realize in art the being of a conscious body is to realize combinations of elements posable by its consciousness which are strange or even repulsive to the logical mind. To use Freudian terms, art realizes both the primary and secondary processes of our bodily selves simultaneously. It seems clear that a person can experience contradictory states in a single moment, for example, desire and aversion with respect to the sexuality of a woman. Let us take one who is not one's mother. If it is said that the states are of her sexuality in different respects, such as desire for it as agency of confirmation and of pleasure, and aversion toward it as biologically reproductive, then it can be said either that this does not remove the co-presence of the contradictory states, since the aspects are not thus neatly separated in pre-thematic awareness; or that when made thematic and separate we still feel both emotions; or that contradictory states can exist at times relative to a single aspect.

The autonomy of the work of art begins to gather us as persons. As a body-self the artist is involved in that work which gathers and integrates the greatest number of his possibilities. To laugh at a glutton in a comedy who tears off pieces of food and forces them into his mouth is to glimpse what can perhaps be entertained only in laughter: desperate consumption as imaginary—yet certainly not unreal—antidote to separation and death anxieties, ontological ones. *This* void cannot be stuffed with matter, and yet the self is a body and the eating is not altogether unavailing. We experience the horror and the incongruity—we make the connection—and we laugh uproariously.

Art is like a vow which we make to each other. In artistic activity we are vowing to each other that it is valuable to do what we are doing— valuable to exercise our freedom and to bring ourselves to stand within the drag of the engulfment and fragmentation of our lives; valuable to assert now our individuality as a way of coming to grips with the communal, the mythical, and the timeless; valuable to select, articulate, and integrate what is otherwise smeared, inertial, dumb, and confused. Art memorializes our being-with others and other things at a level of recuperative and binding experience more fundamental than the practical social function of chronological dating which cuts our lives into an irreversible sequence of steps and stages.

For example, art overlaps—even if today only slightly and hesitantly— with the rhetorical vow made by the chief of the Nez Percé Indians, Joseph, when finally surrendering to the United States Army. Sweeping his arm toward the sky, he said, "From where the sun now stands, I will fight no more forever." Joseph invites Nature itself, its cycles and seasons, to stand in witness of his deed, and to stand in support of it. He stands in for Nature, and Nature for him. His deed memorializes itself and him: every subsequent moment will both reaffirm it and project it in commitment, as a monument of time is erected in time. Vaguely stirred by this manifestation of authenticity, we yet have difficulty recalling how such a vow was ever possible. We may feel that time atomizes us and reduces us to powder. Since the self does not develop in a simple linear manner from nonthematic apprehension of things to perpetual thematic apprehension, we require forms of memorializing life that will bind us in time prereflectively.

The plays of Beckett render the agony of time and choice. The tramps in *Waiting for Godot* simply wait; they are still tied to Godot. But note *Endgame*—it begins with the lines of the servant,

> CLOV: [*fixed gaze, tonelessly*]: Finished, it's finished, nearly finished, it must be nearly finished.
> [*Pause*]
> Grain upon grain, one by one, and one day, suddenly, there's a heap, a little heap, the impossible heap.

Clov breaks away from his master. Likewise the productions of Grotowski and Wilson seek to point the way toward the individuating engagement with time, the memorializing decision and vow.

The productions of Aeschylus and Sophocles stood with one foot outside of rite and one foot in. The contemporary productions we have studied extend a foot tentatively back toward rite. This theatre experiments with what has gone wrong with rite and how it might be corrected. By what witness can we swear today so that its constancy and power affirm and memorialize our right to be? Do we swear by the sun and the moon? Do we swear by science? By experience? Are these sufficiently Dionysian to gather us up in our many levels and to maintain us day by day? It is too facile to say that we swear by ourselves, or do not swear at all, for we have our identity through involvements, and we must swear by that with which we are involved if we are vitally to be. Although one did not ask for life, nor for those mimetic involvements through which one became human, in retaining one's life one remains indebted. One must swear by the value of one's involvements and one's being if one is to affirm one's right to be. This is no narrowly ethical or legal matter, but pertains to the price of individual identity itself.

The engrossing pursuit of authenticity lies in advancing and perfecting our individual reality, but this must exist in dialectical exchange with that in which we are engulfed. Theatre is only a sporadic experimentation, and realizing what it cannot supply may suggest what is needed: individuals in community gathered at regular intervals of world-time who affirm to each other—who reaffirm to each other and memorialize for each other— their right to be as individuals. We are left with questions.

Heidegger speaks of human existence as *Dasein:*

> Factical *Dasein* exists as born; and, as born, it is already dying, in the sense of Being-towards-death. As long as *Dasein* factically exists, both the "ends" and their "between" *are,* and they *are* in the only way which is possible on the basis of *Dasein's* Being as *care.* Thrownness and that Being towards death in which one either flees it or anticipates it, form a unity; and in this unity birth and death are "connected" in a manner characteristic of *Dasein.* As care, *Dasein is* the "between."[8]

But Heidegger places the words *connected* and *between* in quotes, and he would be the first to admit that we remain engulfed in the they-self, the mass, in order to evade the anxiety of death. We invest our care in distraction and idle talk. This is described well by Anthony Burgess when he declares that the essential function of language is to maintain social contact in the dark.

> Take speech as a flickering auditory candle, and the mere act of maintaining its light becomes enough. Tales, gossip, riddles, word-play pass the time . . . and out of these—not out of the need to recount facts or state a case— springs literature.[9]

But we must add that although great literature and theatre do not typically "recount facts or state a case," they thematize types and essences which can be exemplified in existence, and they thematize the darkness—the boundless. Even traditional comedy can thematize the darkness, although it tries to remain absorbed in the familiar social world, with its locations and dislocations. It is logomachy, an instance of the distraction of idle talk itself, to think that only verbal language in the simple assertive mood reveals human existence.

The ever-present potentiality to cease to be is a primary locus for self-deception. Let us say one is providing for his family by planning for his funeral and he envisions it. He must think of this as being experienceable if it is to make any sense to him, and he cannot neatly distinguish its being experienceable by him from its being experienceable by anyone. Thus he can pre-reflectively and self-deceivingly lose himself in that ongoing body of persons that he envisions looking on at his corpse. In this picturing of

8. Martin Heidegger, *Being and Time,* (Oxford: Blackwells, 1962), p. 426.
9. Anthony Burgess, *Shakespeare* (Baltimore: Penguin Books, 1972), p. 43.

his funeral his own eye looks on at his corpse, but it is an eye that is merged with others' eyes, and it is disowned by him. At an unthematized level of his experience, he thinks himself to be living on with the others; he thinks himself to be immortal; he flees from his death in self-deception. He cannot see that he is doing this just because in thematically seeing himself as dead he cannot see that he is seeing, thinking, or doing anything.

Theatre can help relieve this self-deception if through its "fictions" it can soften the impact of death and restore our contact with our own anxiety. If it can put us in touch with the mortality of our individuality, it can put us in touch with the potentiality of our individuality. It can thematize that anxiety which derives from unfinished business of individuation. For example, the youngster Johnny can say, "Johnny is a good boy!" just as his father would. But the danger is that development of self will be arrested at this stage, that the boy will never get beyond taking toward his organism the attitude of the social environment (as essential as this is). He verges on being just anyone, a statistic, a neuter. For, notice, presumably anyone who behaved this way in this setting would be accounted good. What is peculiar about Johnny's ability to behave this way—say, the particular difficulty or resentment that he experienced in meeting these standards—is ignored by himself. It is repressed, and to that extent he becomes amorphous and dissociated. One's countertendencies as a particular being are unacknowledged and become sources of unfinished business and anxiety. It is the goal of acting as fine art to articulate both one's particular potentialities as a conscious organism and one's communal-mimetic ones. I am both this body—these eyes, this nose, these teeth, these legs—and a body-for-and-by-others. This involves as its corollary the ability to sense the limits of the communal-mimetic—to sense that they are not all-inclusive. The ability to face what lies on this side of these limits—one's repressed particularity—is a function of one's ability to face and to ascertain these limits themselves.

Heidegger writes of anxiety,

> It brings one back to the pure "that-it-is" of one's ownmost individualized thrownness. This bringing back has neither the character of an evasive forgetting nor that of a remembering. But just as little does anxiety imply that one has already taken over one's existence into one's resolution and done so by a repeating. On the contrary, anxiety brings one back to one's thrownness as something *possible* which *can be repeated*.[10]

To appropriate one's death, says Heidegger, is to be individualized down to one's own self in uncanniness and thrown into "the nothing."[11] Because

---

10. Heidegger, *Being and Time*, p. 394.
11. Ibid., p. 322.

only the individual can die his death, and he can die no one else's, his death as lived-possibility-of-his-own is incomparable, so uncanny.

When we understand theatre we can see, however, that there is a theatre-like element even in dying (this point will be expanded and qualified in Part Three). The meaning of my isolation before my death is that my authentic interpersonal relationships are tested to the utmost. Heidegger writes, "*Dasein*'s Being is Being-with, its understanding of Being already implies the understanding of Others. . . . Knowing oneself is grounded in Being-with, which understands primordially."[12] If being-alone is priv- ative upon being-with, and if I can know myself only through the other, then my individual identity as a self-interpreting being will entail that I can be fully freed for my anxiety toward my death, and so understand it, only when I grasp that through me others are freed for their anxiety—not only toward their own deaths—but toward my death as well. If all my being is being-with, then I cannot be authentically toward-my-death un- less I am authentically being-with-others toward my death. If I do not think my death sufficiently important to grasp its importance for others, and the ever-present threat its potentiality is to *them*, then I do not grasp it as it is. For it is important, and the potentiality of my ceasing to be is a constant threat to those who are authentically related to me.

Solicitude for others involves, ultimately, solicitude for myself—a leap- ing in ahead of myself through the others that grasps my own potentialities as nothing else can. Not to be authentically toward myself through others is to be inauthentically toward myself through others. So given over to others am I that I am essential to them as an example of how a person can die authentically, and they are essential to me, both for this same reason and for others. In this sense a person's death is "relatable"—he can die for others and they for him. The dying person is the model who authorizes the witness, and the witness who takes this to heart authorizes the dying person, for assuredly he will "try this himself."

Art and the art-like can prime one and prepare one to be consciously and deliberately an example for others, and thus to understand—stand- under and bear—one's particularity and one's sociality even in the face of one's death. To be engulfed in others is to be engulfed in time. It is to be controlled by a past which drags one behind it. To catch up to one's past is to take a new initiative toward it; it is to claim a possibility as one's own, and this is to appropriate the future in a new way. Ever are we pulled beyond the art-like to art itself. To enact engulfment is to memorialize our capacity as persons in community to articulate our mortal individuality and independence within our mutuality and dependence. The memorial

12. Ibid., p. 161.

which is the artistic production stands within its own precinct, but it is visible beyond it. Its clarity and power can become a magnetizing ideal for life. Michaelangelo wrote,

> With so much servitude, with so much anguish,
> And with false concepts periling my soul,
> Sculpt I must, here on earth, bright things of heaven.[13]

Of course, theatrical enactment can also become the most pernicious self-deception if its ideality should be blurred, and instead of being a preparation for life and death, and an essential aspect of life, it becomes a putative substitute for living. Even at the requisite aesthetic distance, the actor artist is at closer quarters with his art work than is any other artist with his, and hence is most exposed to the danger of self-deception.

Still, the actor as artist is living even as he is performing, and he can seek to authentically answer death in his art even if he cannot cancel it. The void which is his possibilities and which he probes seeks an antidote in his art. For objects of art are those of the concretizing imagination: objects coming from we know not where, which are experienced as independent of present and actual existence, and as indefinitely variable. If such objects are set up on their special ground within existence itself, so that our fellows gravitate around them, and so that we focus on our work through them, then we have gained some control over the uncanny void from within, and through, this void itself. As artist I define my being through the medium of nothingness that might otherwise have paralyzed me. Actor and director Joseph Chaikin writes,

> The actor is able to approach in himself a cosmic dread as large as his life. He is able to go from this dread to a joy so sweet that it is without limit. What the actor must not do is to cling to any internal condition as being more or less human . . . more or less theatrical . . . more or less appealing. Only then will the actor have direct access to the life that moves in him, which is as free as his breathing. And like his breathing, he doesn't cause it to happen. He doesn't contain it, and it doesn't contain him. The "act" is one of balancing between control and surrender.[14]

Only the void which is possibility is equal to itself, and the ultimate possibility that beset me, death, has been answered—however inadequately—by a concretization of self within the void that, even as I live, outlives me. Through art and originality the self memorializes its life in time in the face of its death.

13. *The Complete Poems of Michaelangelo*, ed. J. Tusiani (New York: Noonday Press, 1960).

14. Chaikin, *The Presence of the Actor*, p. 10.

CHAPTER XVI

Summary and Prospects: Identity of Self

To be a self is to be a human body that is mimetically involved with other such bodies, but that nevertheless has a capacity to distinguish itself consciously from others and to regard its history and its prospects as its own. It can give presence to this absence as its own life, but it is never completely objectifiable either to itself or to others. The psychical birth of the individual is an open-ended process of theatre-like individuations emerging from theatre-like fusions. This psychical birth is never more than relatively consummated or relatively unconsummated. After a certain modicum of individuation has been achieved, the person attempts either to maintain his level of fusion unchanged—to repeat the voice of the group for the group—or to progressively distinguish himself from the group in ways that some at least of the group will confirm. Perhaps these others are merely anticipated or imagined. Subjectivity remains inherently open and ever incompletely objectifiable.

It is important to see how the incompletability of individuation of self and the incompletability of objectification of self are correlative features. As Beckett observed in *The Unnamable*, the self must objectify itself and must do so in terms established by others. Yet the self which is its own other and which is for-and-by-others must strive to become just its own self. But this is unconsummatable; the self as objectifiable and as that which bears marks of the communal can never implode and become identical with itself as a particular subjective substance. Authenticity of self is just this admission of futility made repeatedly by self-as-other to self as ever incompletely reflectable subject . . . to self as unnameable.

Our account augments Beckett in the following way. The self as body can enact—or "enact"—others freely in their absence, and can conclude that others mimetically "in" itself are constitutive of it, but not exhaustively so. Yet the body's consciousness cannot objectify itself as a particular consciousness. One reflects, and reflects upon one's reflections, but there must always be a reflecting, naming consciousness that can never be cornered and named by anyone. Consciousness is unencompassable and unsurpassable. Hence there is no possibility of taking others incorporated mimetically and adding them to one's own particular self "in itself" and achieving the sum which is oneself. One *is* one's "roles" but not *just* ones "roles," for one is also an unobjectifiable consciousness of "roles" actual and possible—even roles as yet unimagined. Each individual exists within the boundless void.

So the attempt to establish one's particularity for others and for oneself must be made, and yet it must be forever unfinishable. Similar to Beckett's view, authenticity of individual self consists in the admission to self by self of the unfinishability of the individuation of itself. We can say the word "I" easily enough—after a certain point—and we can know that it is spoken out of a particular history with a particular source. But we are never exactly sure of its content, for it is spoken toward a future that is indeterminate except for the fact that one will die at some moment, any moment. One's own potentialities, e.g., for fusion, and one's own yet-to-be-made choices exceed one's ability to objectify and catalogue them, and one's principles of conduct must be continually reaffirmed as one's own.

The identity of each self involves the identity over time of a problem of identity—however variously that problem manifests itself in each case. The person's ownmost, his "core," is an interrogative involvement with his involvements in which the question is asked: What is this history— who am I—in my sheer particularity? These are my others, and I am other from every other, but who precisely am I? It is a question that can never be answered definitively because one can be individuated from others through the experience of the uniqueness of one's body and still be unobjectifiable and unpredictable. One can slide unpredictably, even unimaginably, into engulfment in the encompassing others.

By "substance" is usually meant a being that is objectifiable. Usually it is also meant that if its circumstances and traits are known then its reactions to stimuli are in principle predictable. On both grounds I wish to deny that a self is a substance. Although a self requires an habituated body, and most of its reactions must therefore be predictable, still there are imaginative and psychically mobilized moments in which the self stands open to its life, and in which it can objectify and transcend some of its habitual reactions in ways that may surprise both others and itself. Even a self that appears hopelessly cowed or engulfed may effect a startling transcendence. Of course, it also may not.

One of the greatest joys and most powerful motivations to act is ontological and Apollonian: to *be,* to be most vitally one's own individual self. The body is individual and conscious and hungers after an eversharper sense of its particular significance. But perhaps the greatest fear is that one will be excluded from the company of other persons, because one has become so unusual that one has ceased to be comprehensible to them and confirmable by them. Hence the opposing motivation to act and the opposing ontological joy, the Dionysian: to lose this fear by losing one's individual identity in the corporate identity of the powerful mass of persons. Many are torn between these joys and many are brought to a psychical standstill between them. Only the artist, and only the person committed to the development of the art-like in his life, can synthesize the joys and tolerate the fears. In Part Three we will argue that the openness of the self's subjectivity involves the fact that the limits of the imagination cannot be definitively traced by the imagination itself, and that this has behavioral consequences. It incites to action, frightens, or induces a morass of indecision and defensive boredom.

The identity of self is the identity through time of a body in process which copes in one way or another with the problem of its identity. The problem of identity has itself an identity in the life of the person in question, and it contributes its share to the identity of that life; it is *his* or *her* problem of identity. To clarify this we must further develop the distinction between identity of self and identity of personality. What sorts and degrees of transformation of personality are compatible with identity of self? There is a vast spectrum, and its extent cannot be precisely delimited. Even in dramatic instances of change in identity of personality, usually nobody has any doubt that it is just that person who has undergone the transformation. Nor are we perfectly clear about what counts as transformation of personality. There is no definite line which, when crossed, signals this shift. We are stuck with definitely demarcated words to approximate an indefinitely demarcated reality. We must deal pragmatically.[1] We can only say that after a certain period of indecision it becomes easier to say that such a shift of identity of personality has occurred than to say that it has not—easier because it is more predictive of behavior and generally fruitful. Moreover, there may be shifts of personality which are but temporary or fleeting, and the more dazzling they are and the less they fit into a pattern, the more inclined we are to dismiss them with "he was not himself," and to rid ourselves of the problem of trying to understand them by eliminating them from our attention.

Now, can there be change of identity of personality—either permanent

1. The type of phenomenology I have developed in this book might be called transcendental pragmatism.

or temporary—so decisive that we would want to say that there has been change of identity of self, i.e., that there is a new self? First we should point out that certain sorts of very great change of personality would never prompt us to wonder about this. Someone whose personality remained childishly the same over the years would be the odd instance; developmental change is typical and expected. It is only very abrupt, great, and atypical change that would prompt us to think that even one personality of that self had been replaced by another. William James cites cases of religious and quasi-religious conversion in which a new system of personality traits are abruptly fused together around a new center of interest. "Subconscious allies" of conscious effort have been unwittingly released "behind the scenes," and at a word, a touch—often at the cessation of effort—they fall into a new pattern, a new habitual attunement to things.[2] A new funding and summing occurs, although it is wrong to say that there is total discontinuity. James speaks of the self as made of "variable material," and Justus Buchler argues that its boundaries cannot be precisely fixed.[3]

It is only when one personality of the bodily being suppresses or disowns the presence of the other that we are tempted to think even for a moment that the identity of the *self* is that of another self; that is, only when a personality can no longer acknowledge an earlier one as "myself at an earlier date," or when it speaks of this other personality as if it were another person. Only when the present personality can no longer appropriate the other one to itself is that continuity of career disrupted to the point that we are tempted momentarily to say that identity of a prior self no longer obtains.

But if this should happen the onlooking observer will probably detect distinctive continuities of behavior, and distinctive summings of past behavioral reality, which will prompt him in mature reflection to judge that he is seeing the same self. Even if the person himself claimed to be a different self, the observer would be dubious; he would tend to classify him as the same self become psychotic. And even if we should imagine the highly unlikely state of affairs in which no behavioral continuities are observable, the body with its distinctive physiognomy and continuity remains, and this is enough to deter us from judging decisively that a prior self has ceased to exist. We would suspend judgment perhaps. So strongly does the identity of the body figure in our judgments of identity of self!

2. William James, *The Varieties of Religious Experience: A Study in Human Nature* (New York: Longmans, Green & Co., 1902), Lectures VIII and IX.
3. See Justus Buchler's *Metaphysics of Natural Complexes* (New York: Columbia University Press, 1966), pp. 106–28, and *Toward a General Theory of Human Judgment* (New York: Columbia University Press, 1951), p. 8 and *passim*.

Only coma or insanity from birth which prevented that body from ever gathering a world in its experience, and from ever distinguishing its experiencing from things experienced, would seem to rule out emergence of a self. But if such gathering and distinguishing occurred later, this would probably count for the person and for others alike as identity of self over the *entire* stretch of the *body's* career, even though nothing from the period of the coma could be remembered by the person.

The point about identity of self is this: it can accommodate a great range of transformations of personality because we are hard put to discover *any* conditions which clearly disestablish a self while the body in question still lives and maintains a capacity for consciousness and for distinguishing its experiencing from the experienced (or at least has had or will have such a capacity). Theatre is an art which reaches out to encompass and thematize possibilities of personality change within the remarkably commodious matrix of identity of self.

There are cases in which body-images and "melodies of movement" that are incompatible and apparently discontinuous are incorporated mimetically. Thus two warring parents (or warring elements within a parent) can both be mimetically incorporated in roughly equivalent strength. Let us say they alternate unpredictably, and a schizoid person results. So why do we not affirm that a new self has appeared in the world because a new lived body has?

But at this point the conditions of identity of the physiological body and those of the lived or physiognomic body begin to overlap and to blur. Alternating physiognomic "possessions," alternating body images, will in time leave permanent physiognomic and expressive marks in the physiology; these marks others will recognize and the person will tend to recognize them through others' recognition of them and to be more or less confirmed in them as his own expressivity. More importantly, however, the continuity of the physiological entity supplies the locus without which even the discontinuity which occurs would be impossible. And unless we have a case of profound schizophrenia (and perhaps even if we do), there will be a continuous self because the body will probably, in some residual way, appropriate itself as the same through all its discontinuous physiognomic episodes. The person will be a confused and troubled self because of the discontinuity in physiognomy and personality; but there can be this discontinuity only because of the underlying continuity of the self.[4] Even

4. In the case of schizophrenia in which the body does not appropriate itself as the same through various episodes, and in which continuities of styles of behavior are not observable by a third party, one may be inclined to say that identity of self has not been achieved. Yet we do care for *that person*. Perhaps we should agree that we have an undecidable or borderline case and that our conceptual system breaks down. What is the justification for supposing that all cases must be decidable?

in more normal lives there are episodes in which the person endures as himself only because the physiological body supplies the abiding locus for the confusion. In those moments I am at least *this* abiding center of confusion, distraction, dismay, uncertainty.

The concept of identity of self includes in its scope a vast and open-ended domain of phenomena which we try to organize through it, and, indeed, this concept itself takes somewhat different shapes and emphases within the different contexts of its use. It is a tool that, like Proteus, changes as we use it. The danger with a metaconcept of identity, a tool of tools, is that formalistic prejudices will artificially restrict the concept of human identity worked on by it. Let us commit ourselves initially only to a very broad and flexible notion: all our mimetic involvements and individuations within the world, sequential or simultaneous, pertain to our identity as self. Even shifts of involvement so profound as to constitute shifts in personality—periodic or unique—fall within the continuity of a single self. A person is his professional "role" or "roles" and his certified competencies; he is what he expects others to expect him to be. He is also his familial involvements and "roles" and his informal competencies. He is—to stop at just these two orders of involvement—both of these even when they are sharply discontinuous, or when each is used to nullify or compensate for—or perhaps destroy—the other. The person also has his identity within the order of his memories, his daydreams, and his dreams. He is also himself when in the deepest dreamless sleep. Finally, we see that he is potentialities, both for mimetic involvement and for individuation, and that these elude anyone's ability to exactly demarcate them. He is—in principle—more than we can say about him.

If we say that he is this, then we must approach the specification of identity of self very generally, and say that it is the continuous relation between all this and any of the particular involvements or diremptions that momentarily or habitually take precedence and emerge for this body under the sun. Although we must suppose that the body undeliberately and pre-reflectively appropriates some of its past, present, and anticipated states and experiences and makes them its own (or has the capacity, or has had or will have the capacity), and that this is integral to what we mean by the self, still no set of central behavioral traits need persist, but only a continuity of transformations, some very fast, some very slow. Typically, of course, some habitual "melodies of transition" distinctive to that person do remain constant, or change very slowly. And typically, of course, standards of conduct are reappropriated as one's own. The point is that we cannot specify the degree of change sufficient to count as a new self. Because a person's identity as self is so flexible and commodious, his identity as personality is—or can be—his own most profound adventure.

It is to be hoped that this last statement is sufficiently controlled by the context of this book not to be misleading. The self is an occasionally conscious body that displays itself in a theatre-like way to others, and the first- and third-person points of view on it are deeply intertwined. We recall that mimetic fusion and interpersonal engulfment have been regarded by us as essential to becoming a human being. If individuation which is not mere fragmentation is to emerge, it must do so *out of* fascinated engulfment and fusion. The adventure of self is not an invention out of the blue. What *Hamlet* expresses prophetically, and *Waiting for Godot, The Chairs, Apocalypsis cum Figuris,* and *Letter for Queen Victoria* delineate, is that the problem of identity that crucially structures our identity today is a disruption in the mimetic "glue" that binds us with others. Time-tested mimetic attachments have weakened greatly, and new ones are being formed helter-skelter. Need we reappropriate world time so as to be confirmed by the stars and the seasons? What involvements can we find authoritative enough to authorize us as authentic individuals? How are we to authorize our questioning? We are questioning our questioning. In what does the seriousness of *this* questioning consist, so that we can endure in it beyond the mere curiosity of the moment?

Adapting an insight utilized by Nietzsche, T. S. Eliot writes, "In my end is my beginning." To fly off in ever-new directions is pointless. The significantly new must include an appropriation as one's own of one's sources in time. We *are* through appropriating activity; we declare what is ours and we make ourselves up as we go along. We do not make ourselves up out of nothing, however, for we are beings who are thrown into the world and into involvements.

Theatre is the art which is this tacit question—this experiment—in action: how much mimetic fusion with others, diremptions from them, and attendant transformations of personality will mark the course of selves through time? What will happen to them? Will they grow in vitality and in individuation or will they dissipate in a blur of self-deception and psychical middle age? This is the generic suspense that characterizes all good theatre, and we can say that the range of possible transformations of personality is very great. All this is compatible with saying that this range is usually curbed or masked from view in our everyday lives, for our potentialities for change, dimly apprehended, frighten us unless we can rise to the occasion through imagination and communal memorialization. To tolerate our potentialities for transformation we must experiment together.

The river presents itself as an image for identity of self over time. Although it is greatly different at its delta from what it is at its headwaters, still the river follows a single course from a single source and is just *that* process of transformations. Each transformation achieves continuity even as it achieves change. But this image for identity breaks down completely before the dialectic of the interpersonal. A river is individuated by its banks, and if these give way to the banks of another flow of water then one river or the other, or both, cease to be themselves. It is the nature of human beings that we cannot so easily tell when they cease to be themselves. Even when engulfed uncontrollably in others, one is still oneself— although not as an authentic individual. This person is the living body. But this is a body which typically has a capacity for consciousness, and consciousness is inescapably involved in communal and intersubjective structures.

The limits of transformation of self via mimetic response to others and diremptions from them cannot be set. If creatures from outer space should land on earth and should take toward us an attitude roughly comparable with that of adult teachers toward nursery pupils, the limits of our ability to follow them mimetically could not be determined by us in advance. Nor could the limits of our ability to then differentiate ourselves.

The actor is faintly analogous to the teacher from outer space who somehow understands us. He not only recaptures and exposes what lies between him and others, but in freely doing so begins to surmount it through individuation. Portions of many others' body images impacted in him may be reassembled in novel ways. Or he may project his mimetic skill and susceptibility into possible modes of being human conjured up through his kinesthetic imagination. When Aristotle said that poetry, for example dramatic poetry, is more philosophical than is history because it depicts things that might happen, we take "might" in a fuller sense than did he. We do not mean by it merely potentiality subservient to forms of actuality eternally set, nor do we mean by it merely chance. We mean the creative imagination active within a history which is linear, and which can be transformed by the unpredictable and the emergent. We include under the potentiality of mimetic reproduction the reproducing in concrete form of demands of mind. Instead of creatively and constructively transforming the tradition, these embodiments of mind may wrench us loose from it at certain points, and we so outrun our lines of communication that we become confused and wraith-like. Or these embodiments may become mere eccentric fancy and bizarre diversion, and the tradition solidify around us in moribund immobility. We require the imagination to be disciplined. It is in this light that I have analyzed theatre phenomenologically as incarnated thought experiments on the nature of human life.

Theatre is not a recounting of what has been, as is history. It keeps us open to the very moment of happening, and to the movement in the moment, and to possibility.[5] Theatre illuminates the theatre-like in our

5. Donna Wilshire, "Science and the Dramatic Imagination," *Performing Arts Review*, 4, nos. 3–4 (1973).

daily lives: A life is gathered up for itself only as it memorializes itself for potential others through its imagination and its lived future.[6] Identity involves risk—risk of engulfment and risk of fragmentation. There is no detached reproduction of a life as if by photography. Perversely enough, however, insofar as one thinks that there is, the thought tends to fulfill itself; a kind of detachment of the self within the self is produced. This is a metatransformation of the self which blights the possibility of all its other transformations. The person seeks to deposit existential possibility and anxiety in the vault of coolness and containment. The actor, on the other hand, keeps the unresolvable tension of universal and particular open and working.

The actor is an advance guard. He experiments with possibility in the form of dramatic ideality. He and the other creative ones stand on the edge of actuality and ventilate what would otherwise be a tomb. He sets before us visions of what is—or of what might be—the case. And he stands the risk of being deluded, distracted, or reduced to mush by that with which he experiments. For, to a degree that far exceeds all other artistic creators, he lends to possibility his own self as bodily being. Possessed by incarnated possibility he may be tempted to confuse this with quotidian actuality, or at least to prefer it to the detriment of the latter. If so, he goes out of touch with his own historical being as a particular body and he is reengulfed.

W. B. Yeats has written,

Heart-mysteries there, and yet when all is said
It was the dream itself enchanted me . . .
Players and painted stage took all my love,
And not those things that they were emblems of.

Those masterful images because complete
Grew in pure mind . . .[7]

Up to this point we have explored the powers of theatre and of theatrical metaphors. We have already glimpsed what some of the limits of these powers are. After a summarizing exposition of theatre itself as metaphor, we must now systematically delineate these limits. The self is open-ended and incompletely objectifiable, and finally exceeds the sure grasp both of theatre as metaphor and of the various theatrical metaphors embedded in everyday experience and in social science.

6. Even a diary must be intended by the writer as readable by others—even if "not to be read."
7. W. B. Yeats, "The Circus Animals' Desertion," quoted in Edward S. Casey, *Imagining* (Bloomington: Indiana University Press, 1976), p. 233.

PART THREE

The Limits of Appearance
and the Limits
of Theatrical Metaphor

CHAPTER XVII

Theatre as Metaphor

Paul Ricoeur comments on this line of Baudelaire's:

"Nature is a temple where living pillars . . ."

There is a triple correspondence between the body, houses, and the cosmos, which makes the pillars of a temple and our spinal columns symbolic of one another, just as there are correspondences between a roof and the skull, breath and wind, etc.[1]

Theatre is a primary site for the display of this triple correspondence. The display is achieved through the compression of elements afforded by the artistic medium: an enactment of events is occurring, not the events themselves. Displayed perspicuously together in their interconnections are elements which are usually isolated as they appear one by one in our focal attention. The physiognomy of human body-selves is shown to correspond to the physiognomy of the abodes that people construct in order to belong to the earth and to live under the sky. The cellar belongs to the earth and the attic to the sky. This is no mere metrical correspondence. It is the correspondence of things which evoke each other in human experience.

When we are up and about, the windows and doors of our abode allow us access to our world; at the same time, they contrast, interrelate, and extend our capacities for private and public involvements. The doors and windows are experienced as closeable as well as openable. The power of the public is latent within the private, and conversely. An abode with cellar and attic opens the world for its inhabitants differently than would a cave; it sums up more powerfully their being between-earth-and-heaven,

1. Paul Ricoeur, *Interpretation Theory: Discourse and the Surplus of Meaning* (Fort Worth: Texas Christian University Press, 1976), pp. 68, 62.

and their belonging to possibilities as well as actualities. It sums up more vividly the contrast between belonging to the opaque earth and to the open sky. In the detached involvement of the theatrical site this condensing and summing up of the abode can be made the explicit theme of discourse, whereas in ordinary life it is typically the implicit and hidden matrix of our behavior.

The power that bonds corresponding elements together is different from the power that can be exercised through them or upon them by calculative thought and manipulation. As Ricoeur has pointed out, the power pertains ultimately to the numinous and the sacred, evoked by religious and quasi-religious rites. The point of theatre is to show what happens when beings who belong to each other because they belong to the world encounter each other in their equiprimordial privacy and individuality. Theatre thematizes and memorializes events of encounter that otherwise might fly by in our experience and get lost. Item: it is one thing to smoke—a very strange thing really—and another thing for an actor to smoke in a Wilson play. In the midst of his chatting with other persons he lights the cigarette, and we *see* him summon with his miniature magic the power of light and fire in the lonely immensity of space that encompasses each of them. The smoke makes his breath visible, and in their abode on the earth the persons commune with each other, with the wind, and with powers of birth and mortality. If the cigarette should be passed from person to person, we would have an especially vivid—if heterodox—enactment of a sacrament of union.

In the abode made visible by the abode which is theatre, man the upright animal displays his potentialities as one of a family of beings caught between earth and heaven. He gestures, sits, lies down, rises, and gathers himself together communally and individually over time. Artistotle defined metaphor as the application to a thing of a name that belongs to something else by virtue of the similarity between them. Theatre involves physiognomic or symbolic metaphors: the displacement of appearances that belong literally to one thing so that they belong to something else that is made to resemble the first; for example, a *papier-mâché* structure onstage takes on the appearance of a tree in a forest; a living man becomes Hamlet, the long-dead prince of another place and day. Theatre is a metaphor for life, and into its "world" can be mapped the world, because elements of the world rooted ineluctably in lived situations are nevertheless also symbols of correspondence, and these symbols can themselves be symbolized and transposed in the theatre. They are lifted out of these lived situations in an act of concretizing abstraction and perceptual imagination. The result of this substitution is a compression in which a whole network of correspondences is displayable on the spot and within a limited duration of time. Instead of being engulfed in one symbol of correspondence and then in another, as we ordinarily are in offstage life, these symbols gather themselves together in a "world." Something that corresponds to something else substitutes for that thing in our comprehension and shares its power—breath, wind, potentiality; skull, roof, sky; pillars, backbone, supportive presence of erect human beings. Great theatre corresponds to these correspondences and shares and focuses their power.

We can also say that the world as it is experienced is protometaphorical in its structure. That is, a thing which corresponds to another—or symbolizes another—stands in for that other in our experience. As the popular song has it,

> I see your face in every flower,
> Your eyes in the stars above.

Theatre as explicit metaphor sums up, condenses, and thematizes these protometaphorical correspondences, so that the world is mapped into a "world."

The logic of correspondences bonds things together in numinous power, and they are gathered through discourse into the universe of the sacred. It is clear that this universe is now disrupted for many in the modern world, and it is important for us to see the role of theatre relative to this fact. As estranged as we typically are from primal symbolisms and energies—estranged through our calculative thought and our technology, which feed only on "data" and not on such symbols, and which pull us about as if we were leashed—still our primal mimetic affinities break through sometimes; at other times they form an undercurrent. These breakthroughs are all the more irruptive and uncontrollable because we have so largely lost the means to monitor and to leash them—artistic, religious, and artistico-religious rites. Still, our too-frequent mood of emptiness and strange sadness has its understanding—an understanding of lack of contact with our roots in correspondences. It is no surprise to see science fiction artists appropriate the perennial network of correspondences; for example, to present beings who are all head and breath, creatures of the wind, quasi-divinities from outer space who visit us and perhaps deliver us from our entanglements and problems—or from our lassitude.

Typically, though not always, there has been a tense and ambivalent relationship between religious rite and theatrical play. Both are concerned with symbolizing symbols of correspondence—with organizing and condensing such symbols—but theatre is a siren call to freedom, and it disturbs the rootedness of sacred symbols in natural periodicity and place. It tends not to wait for world-time to grant its permission for its enactments. No absence is immune to theatre's many-tentacled efforts to fetch it into presence. The full arsenal of language is at its disposal: from physiognomic metaphor rooted in the sensuous presence of the itinerant actor to the highly elaborated metaphors of verbal speech which spin out abstractions and distant references without apparent limit. Theatre becomes impious and willful, it can be said, and is so in regard to many of the same symbols as are venerated by religion. Family quarrels are the hottest of all.

Theatre, which has so often pulled away from religion, now pauses, as if it wondered how it might pull us back. This is inevitable, for it feeds off the same stock of symbols, and it suspects that this stock is being depleted. The point of our study has been to show that any attempt to understand theatre as an isolated craft is bootless. To study theatre is to find oneself in a vast sweep of human activities that circle back upon themselves. We cannot locate a core essence of human life that proceeds along a linear track of time and then adds activities like religion and art to itself as if they were baggage. We have labored to point out that we must understand ourselves in order to be, and that we must understand ourselves in theatre-like terms. This involves in turn an understanding of the theatrical. The key symbol upon which we have seized, and which binds up with its numinous power human life, religion, and history, is that of the exemplar individual. With him one so deeply identifies mimetically that his view of oneself becomes one's own view of oneself, and his view constitutes, authorizes, and empowers one. But though essential to one's human identity, this fusion must be disturbed, and the exemplar being must be displaced if one is to be humanly individual. A dialectic of indebtedness and guilt is set up that involves itself easily in the religious logic of guilt, vicarious atonement, and redemption, with all the principal parts played by the examplar being himself. It is no accident that the Christian plan of salvation has been called a drama. In the theatre, actors on stage symbolize through physiognomic-metaphorical means persons caught in the symbol-correspondences of mimetic engulfment and diremption offstage.

In the theatre, every correspondence between things of the earth and the sky, and between gods and men, is focused like a burning glass in the relations between individuals before us here and now on the stage. In the relationships between children and parents, for example, is compressed the symbolic power of relationships between servants and kings, or between persons and gods. Any disturbance in these relationships shakes the society at its foundations.

Through the proxy of theatre's drama we discover actual and possible "dramas" of everyday life in which we are tested and confirmed, both individually and collectively. The audience shares power symbolically with the "audience" of others in our everyday lives, and to construct our reality in the theatre within the gaze of the audience excites us. For the Greeks, both within and without the theatre, the audience included the ultimate witness-models—the gods. For us there are substitutes, "gods" everywhere of all shapes and sorts: nations, parties, companies, leaders, bosses. There is transfusion of energy from theatrical "world" to world, and from world to "world." We are caught in this whirl of authorization, and our roots are drilled down, toward greater authenticity and individuation, or toward greater inauthenticity. The power of theatre as metaphor is the power of meaning compressed: world compressed into "world," with energy flowing continuously back into world. No logic of statements committed to the primacy of linguistic atoms of meaning can grasp the primacy of the meaning we are discussing. Nor is there an other-worldly realm of meaning waiting to be applied to things or conveyed to others. Nor is meaning "minted" within the mind itself and then affixed to things when they register their presence before us through our senses. Meaning is the very presence—and the structure of the possible presence—of the sensuous, palpable, symbolically loaded world itself. The sense is in the sensuous, as Mikel Dufrenne frequently puts it.[2] No single thing in our physical neighborhood and present to the ensemble of our functioning organs is ever picked out in isolation from everything else. There is no reference to actual particulars unless the reference is "aimed" through some ideal sense or context. Nothing is presented without other things or other aspects of things being "appresented."[3] Thus things can be grasped only in terms of other things, things not themselves. And since perception is basic to that worldly presence of things-along-with-other-things which is meaning itself, then metaphor—that sensuous grasping of things in terms of what they are not—is endemic and fundamental to cognition itself.

The most fanciful and fantastic means—the purest metaphorical fictions—are the best suited to symbolize the symbol-things of life if by these means habitual engulfments of words in things, signs in things, and appearances in things are broken, and the ensemble of symbol-things is thus allowed to make new—or newly explicit—connections for us through their own powers. We have seen in *Hamlet* how the displacement of the appearance of a father to the appearance of a ghost destroys the habitual and stereotypical appearance of the father, and in that process re-presents the father so that the full extent of his mimetic powers over the son are

2. Dufrenne's major work is *The Phenomenology of Aesthetic Experience* (Evanston: Northwestern University Press, 1973).

3. I use the Husserlian term. It refers to that which is not presented directly to the senses (at least not at the moment), but which is related experientially to that which is, and which informs its meaning. For example, the front of a house cannot be presented without the back being appresented.

first perceivable. The stage metaphor of the ghost reveals the way in which a dead father's presence can haunt one. We have also seen in *Strider* how the displacement of the appearance of a person being named to that of a horse being named re-presents this fundamental relationship of being named so that its problems and powers are freshly evident. The fictional mediates the actual, explicates, and exposes it. The real is conducted to us through the irreal, or through the surreal, or through the supernatural.

Now if a specific metaphor is unavoidable and if endless variations upon it are endlessly revealing, then the metaphor is an essential one. Let us see how theatre is such a metaphor. Bruno Snell made the distinction between inessential and essential metaphors.[4] With the former there is some conceivable way to state in literal terms the comparison expressed by the metaphor: when a third term is found for the single aspect under which the relata are compared. For the latter there is no conceivable way to express it literally. This is the ur-metaphor which is "logically prior to and which always overflows any 'concept.' Insofar as the metaphorical verbalization of experience itself creates resemblances which could not be seen up to that time and, in that sense, were not there before, it would seem that there are 'necessary' metaphors."[5] Such metaphors are integral to the philosophical tradition (e.g., metaphors for cognition: "grasp," "illuminate," the "growth" of the mind, etc.), but are usually ignored by the tradition. They are pivots allowing us to turn knowingly toward the world.

We should note in passing, however, that the distinction between essential and inessential metaphors does not seem to be a hard and fast one. Take this relatively simple metaphorical line:

The road is a ribbon of moonlight.

There are literal terms to refer to the aspects under which the elements related—road, ribbon, moonlight—are compared. For example, a geometrical term for a curving line in space can refer literally and equally to roads, ribbons, and patterns of moonlight. But the assemblage of such terms would not only be cumbersome and after the fact, it would fail to express the totality of meaning that grasps us primordially in

The road is a ribbon of moonlight.

We should say that any good metaphor is essential, and that the only inessential metaphors are bad ones. Yet some essential metaphors lie

4. Bruno Snell, *The Discovery of the Mind* (New York: Harper & Row, 1960).
5. James Edie, *Speaking and Meaning: The Phenomenology of Language* (Bloomington: Indiana University Press, 1976), p. 193.

within the central grouping of our concepts. They ramify in every direction in the most complex and far-reaching ways. They are the coordinating tissue of our experience and allow us to turn knowingly toward the world and toward ourselves. But this is just to say that they allow us to be ourselves, for we are beings-in-the-world who must make sense of ourselves some way, and have at least the capacity to appropriate ourselves authentically as other from every other, as relatively consummated individuals.

The studies of meaning, of man, and, I believe, of being come into focus together at this point. Here are the essential links—irreducibly metaphorical ones—between self and world. If, as seems to be the case, the reality of the self is a function of its expression, if its expression is that gathering of itself over time as an embodied being-in-the-world which constitutes it (there being no distinctly human reality prior to expression), and if there is no knowing without expression of some kind, then expression is formative both of man and of the world as it is known by him.

The notion of essential and central metaphors works out, at a distance, the transcendental tradition as it moves from Kant through Hegel and up to Heidegger. Since language is metaphorical and appresentational, and is so in terms of the world as experienced by us, it is ineluctably anthropocentric. As Hegel put it, the Earth is the metaphysical center of the universe. We must understand the world in terms of ourselves. But, equally, since we do not exist to be understood prior to having expressed and known (to some degree) a world, and since the terms of all knowledge have a worldly sense, we can know ourselves only in terms of the world as we dwell in it and as it is known to us. Differently put, we must "go out of ourselves" to find ourselves; to find ourselves we must "come back" to ourselves from the world. As Bruno Snell stated, this ur-metaphorical level is that which cannot be grasped by the formal-logical principle of excluded middle.[6] Such talk falls by the way: "Either subject or non-subject, either subject or object." The metaphorically expressed reality is prior to the distinction between subject and object and overflows it.

Theatre is an essential and central metaphor for life. We can understand it only when we see how it is life-like. It is a mutual mirroring of actors and audience in which their common, mimetically induced behaviors are articulated relative to each person's equiprimordial individuality. It is an articulation and development of their identities as persons with personalities. On the other hand, when we begin our investigation of human identity in life offstage, we find that the full and natural expression of its conditions are in theatre-like terms. Theatre, we find, has already written

6. Quoted in Edie, p. 193.

large the process by which we become ourselves offstage. Life is theatre-like. We must display ourselves to others, and we must understand something of their response to this display if we would be ourselves. There is a metaphorical reality expressed in theatrical and theatre-like terms that is at least as basic as distinctions which we typically tend to speak of as the most basic of all: subject and object, self and others, offstage and onstage. These distinctions, we now see, are awash in the metaphorical and presuppose it.

It should not be surprising, then, that the notion of an actor's role is already extended metaphorically in the language of our everyday use for everyday situations: the "role" of the judge, physician, teacher. Or we can speak of a child's "performance" in class. These are essential and central metaphors because they contribute to the *creation* of the situations which they habitually describe and express. Integral to any situation is our comprehension of it. What is natural for us is to interact with the world in a way that is formative and transformative of it. The essential metaphor is like a magnetic emblem which is true of a situation because it has modified the situation to conform to itself.

Moreover, metaphors grow and change; for example, when we extend the metaphor in a deliberate "role theory." We both reveal and modify a situation: "Ah yes, the judge is performing and we are his audience—that explains it." We disclose aspects of these situations not disclosable otherwise, but we cannot do so without modifying the situation. To what extent? This is impossible to tell with any precision because we have unalterably changed the situation; we cannot reverse time and repeat cases that occurred before the use of the metaphor and compare them to the present cases. And when we try to remember earlier cases, or to refer to present cases in different cultural locales, our notion of such situations has been altered to some extent. Even a post-theatrical notion—if this could be imagined—would be post-*theatrical*. Only after the fact of metaphorical emergence—and always more or less under the sway of the fact—could we try to secure literal terms to refer to the respects in which onstage and offstage are similar, terms which are the *tertium quid comparationis*. Such terms must alter and diminish the initial metaphorical sense.

CHAPTER XVIII

The Truth of Art
and the Limits of
Theatre as Metaphor

Although theatre is an essential, central, and powerful metaphor, it is not an all-powerful one applicable without limit to the world. Its power over actuality derives from its fictionality, its imaginative reach. By means of its physiognomical and concrete imagination, encrusted binary oppositions of concepts are knocked apart—self and other, now and then, present and absent. As imagination is released between them and around them new room is left for the growth of mind. Yet imagination itself can sense something of its own limitations, its own inability to render in final thematic form the conditions of the experienceability of the world.

The theatrically and philosophically informed imagination can sense that its great strength was all along also its weakness: just because it is imagination it must come up short if there should prove to be—as I think there is—an indissoluble residuum of uncanniness and particularity in the factuality of human existence. Theatre can ground itself only when it uncovers its own limits—only when the artistic genre itself becomes tragic, beyond all the usual contrasts between tragedy and comedy. We shall follow a line of thought through theatre toward the ever-escaping final thematizability of the world and our deposit in uncanny factuality. Theatre itself we shall denominate primary metaphor; theatrical concepts embedded in ordinary experience and language and applicable to the offstage world we shall call secondary metaphor. But this should not suggest orders of importance; it is merely a stylistic device.

The difference between good art and bad art is that good art gives us the essence of actuality without the actuality, whereas bad art does not give us even the essence. In good art we get disclosure and development and at the same time a strange escape. We encounter actuality and transcend it. In bad art we get just escape and momentary distraction. And I do not mean to refer merely to good and bad representational art, for as I have said, it is just fantastic, semirepresentational, or nonrepresentational art that can best disclose certain structures of the totality of our situations.

But now we must fix more precisely the extent to which great art—particularly theatre art—does grasp the essence of things. Theatre reveals because it is imagination in concrete forms. It has both the limits endemic to imagination in general and to its concrete theatrical form. Let us discuss these limits in that order.

Nothing is more plausible—indeed nothing is more plausible to the imagination if it be critical—than that the imagination has some limits. This is brought home to us when we observe another age: to discern the shape of its civilization requires that we glimpse in outline the limits of its typical modes of imagination. Certain things it never calls into question, and this domain of the unquestioned forms the essential background without which the shape of what it does question, affirm, and imagine could not emerge in the bold and unblinking way that it does.

Each age sees something of its predecessors' limitations, but very little of its own. Moreoever, imagination is apt to attribute these limitations to factors extraneous to itself. As it experiences itself naively in its immediacy, it easily imagines itself to be limitless. For when it tries to imagine any definite limit to itself, it thereby imagines something that is not supposed to be includable within it; it imagines something about whatever it imagines to be unimaginable. Dimly aware of the contradiction in its own activity, it tends to erase the limit it has traced for itself.

But when imagination is reflectively critical of itself, it realizes that although it cannot tell just what its limits are, it can tell that it must have some limits. In these moments imagination realizes that all its variations on things pursuant to exposing their invariant features—the essence of each—must fall short of definitive conclusiveness, for it realizes either that its limits may have been reached without its knowing it, or that it could continue being productive for an unpredictably long period of time. Therefore it can conclude that the phenomenological reduction to essences can never be complete.[1]

Imagination carries limits and obstructions, as well as powers, within itself that it must assume are never totally canvassable and illuminable by itself. Imagination in the form of metaphor and symbol bubbles up end-

1. This conclusion has been affirmed by Merleau-Ponty in *The Phenomenology of Perception*, trans. Colin Smith (New York: Humanities Press, 1962).

lessly through our encrusted oppositions of concepts as set out by our reflective and analytical techniques. It disturbs these oppositions, sets them afloat, and leaves room for new conceptual and philosophical growth. Imagination is limited and yet its work is unfinishable. At its greatest extremity it realizes that though it must regard its fundamental concepts of reality as applying to the world and as characterizing it, each characterization is more or less provisional, and can be replaced by . . . it as yet knows not what.

To the endlessness of the imagination corresponds the boundlessness and indefiniteness of the imaginable. Things gain sense for us only within a context of imaginable relationships which mushrooms around us and spreads indefinitely into the universe. Every new answer leads to unpredictable new questions as the sense we can make of things changes. This must have been part of what Anaximander meant by the boundless, that which cannot be isolated before us and thematized as an object can be. There is no Archimedean point from which we can survey the boundless— each point is within it. If a point of view on things is to make sense it must lie within the domain of sense. Every reflective and scientific endeavor must spring from a pre-reflective matrix of experienceable things and a reservoir of sense that is inexhaustible by reflection. In philosophy we bound our concepts within other embracing concepts in an attempt to grasp the conditions of our grasping, but we must forever return to this boundless perceptual matrix if we would replenish our mental effort. In theatre we bound space, time, persons, and culture so that the boundless can begin to resonate within the enclosure. In each case we try to grasp the conditions both of knowing and the known—the intelligibility or being of beings, particularly the being of persons. Philosophy and theatre should complement each other within the boundless.

The critical imagination realizes that the conditions of the experience-ability of the world are not definitively stable, and thus that the world itself cannot be definitively thematized. Imagination frames the mystery of the world, the experienceability of which is never completely grasped. It restores us to perennial wonder, not merely to a wonder we will one day work our way beyond. It reminds us that only those things which are known are known, only those things which are illuminated are seen, and all the rest is darkness. But in being reminded we do, in a sense, see the darkness. It becomes—to use a phrase of the mystics—a luminous darkness, and this is the ever-retreating but ever-alluring goal of all philosophical thinking.

Now, we have not simply deduced the limits of imagination from out of itself, or from out of pure reason, nor will we now proceed in such a manner to deduce the limits of that specific form of imagination, theatrical art. For theatre art itself has seriously damaged philosophical arrogance of a rationalistic sort, and it has helped to guide our inquiry from the beginning. From the fate that we cannot fully understand in Oedipus, through Hamlet's final words, which speak not only for him, but for the play and for ourselves—"All the rest is silence"—to Lucky's word gasped out after he exhausts himself in his monologue and is thrown to the earth by the tramps—". . . unfinished . . ."—we recognize that theatre art has lived through the unfinishability of all description and all explanation. The endlessness of aesthetic interruption is vividly realized by Wilson as well. His art is a kind of hysteria which has been leashed and taught to speak. Such art is meta-artistic: in sounding its own limits it sounds also limits of existence and thought. In music the arresting silences of Bach's B-Minor Mass come to mind, as well as the three moments in the last movement of Mahler's Sixth Symphony in which the sound of a large wooden mallet on a wooden block is heard: musical tones reach their apotheosis in their limit—sheer sound.

What can theatre help teach us about its own specific limits as concrete imagination? From the beginning we have emphasized that it is the very fictionality of theatrical art that gives it its revealing leverage on actuality. It is almost impossible to emphasize this too much. But I do say almost. For one would emphasize this too much if one failed to point out that it is a concrete fiction which is possible only because of the actuality of the means necessary to produce it. These means are facts in the actual world, and if we do not understand them, we will not understand the limits of the facts that they can reveal. It is dimly analogous to saying that if we do not understand the specific actuality of a tool—say its weight, length, shape, and composition—we cannot understand the sorts of things it can and cannot do in the world.

Nor can we draw some simple distinction between the fictional content of the play and the actuality of the means necessary to produce it. From the beginning we have opposed the quasi-Platonic notion that the play itself is the ideal content of its prescripted and prescribing words, while the production is a mere passing and adventitious instantiation of it in the mundane world.[2] It is not Hamlet the ideality instantiated by Burton the actuality, but something like this: Hamlet-written-by-Shakespeare-and-played-by-Burton-and-others-before-us-and-along-with-us-here-and-now. We set up for ourselves concrete experimentations (on our essential possibilities) that arise from a tradition of such experimentations.

2. As perceptive as he often is, this Platonic or quasi-Platonic tradition has nevertheless been furthered by Aristotle, at least when he writes that the tragic effect can be achieved without the "Spectacle," its enactment by actors (*The Poetics*, VI-19, IX-10, XIV-2). The question is *to what extent* can the effect be achieved without the enactment?

If we do not understand the historical facts of the theatrical production we will have no adequate idea of its "content." There are, however, a few general things that one can say about any theatrical production. We will soon be more specific. Theatre is a fact that limits the facts that can be revealed by it. Theatre can reveal only because of its artistic control and restraint, which place limits on the actuality of its proceedings. But these limits can put us out of touch with the unrestrained horrors and joys and irruptions of everyday life. They can mask from our sight the darkest or most elusive or most terrifying senses and experiences in those momentarily unrestrained sluices, collisions, and imaginings offstage. Even when one grants that we may, in shock, faint away from, and obliterate, these senses, and that theatre may reveal something of them just because it defuses them and puts them in a limiting or fictionalized setting, still we pay a price for this transplanting revelation. It is plausible to suppose that there are some senses we cannot reveal at all, and others that we distort in the process of revealing. Likewise it is plausible to suppose that there is, in principle, no way of determining precisely where distortion stops and revelation begins. This is the artistic corollary of Heisenberg's principle of indeterminacy. We can stand outside the arts and establish, once and for all, their limits, only if we suppose that there is a god's-eye point of view accessible to us which need employ no artistic means of disclosure. We see no reason to suppose this.

Nevertheless we must be more specific about the limits of theatre's powers to reveal if we are to discharge the obligation we placed upon ourselves in the first section of this book to raise the question, So theatre's play must limit itself to be play and to be revealing—now what does this limitation conceal? Let us take the enactment of violence, the case in which distortion or concealment is perhaps most evident. The nature of the theatrical art requires that strict limits be placed upon the violence that can be done to the artists as they enact the violence between the characters, and also that the audience understand that these limits are in force. No doubt a great deal can be revealed about violence through the theatre's techniques of bracketing and aesthetic interruption. But what is concealed?

I suggest this: in the experience of violence in the world one realizes that his own and others' lives are in jeopardy. It is true that there is frequently a stupefying panic in which disbelief mixes incongruously with the conviction of actuality, as if bubbles were forming in molten lava. One finds it difficult to believe that the limits placed upon civil conduct have been breached. "This can't be happening!" But if one does not faint one does believe it, and despite the strange weightlessness of the pre-reflective perceptual field one's critical intelligence affirms the belief.

The confusion and sense of unreality in the theatrical experience of

violence, seemingly similar to the offstage experience, are really very different; hence, the theatrical experience is deceptive, and plays into the
hands of self-deception. While in the theatre, one is at least marginally
aware, on the critical level of consciousness, that the violence is not really
happening. But because one believes that artistic limits are being respected
one can, on the pre-reflective and pre-critical perceptual level of consciousness, give oneself so completely to the vividly evident enactments
that one does not on that level clearly distinguish artistic illusion and fact.
One is compelled by the bodily presences before him—his palms sweat.
The result is a kind of self-deception. Although one can say that one is
only in a theatre, one nevertheless tends to experience oneself pre-reflectively as on the scene of the violence, but passive, doing nothing to prevent
it or to protect those being injured.[3]

This is a confusion and corruption of the self that Plato could appreciate;
typically, the Greek artists did not enact violence directly upon the stage,
but instead made use of the spoken word, the narrative of messengers,
servants, or heralds, to convey information concerning violence. By this
means we learn, for example, of the violence done upon Laius, Oedipus,
and Jocasta in *Oedipus Rex*. It is as if the Greeks meant to tell us that in
regard to violence the communication is least deceptive and distortive
when entrusted to spoken words in narrative.

Now, there is no point in trying to diminish reflective and critical consciousness in theatre in order to eliminate the schizoid-like experience of
violence; for if we should succeed we would merely fall into different self-
deceptions and confusions. If the audience loses the detachment within its
involvement, it will become merely a mob, a "vacant building" possessed
by the actors. It will lose all sense and respect for the individuality and
otherness of the other, as well as for the fictionality of the play without
which actualities cannot be revealed. Instead of the play thematizing our
mimetic fusions, we auditors will be lost in them. The actors will absorb
the consciousness of the audience and be bereft of the relative detachment
and critical guidance which the audience might have supplied. Each actor
in every play will strive to be his own source, strive to be his father; each
actor will play Oedipus.

What if it were to be maintained, however, that all experience in the
theatre is deceptive in the way that the experience of violence is? I do not
believe that such a position could be defended. It is in the nature of violence
to disrupt the delicate balancings of the mind. Because we are animals

3. For more along this line of inquiry, which also includes an analysis of films (which I
believe to be more deceptive and confusing than is theatre), see my "Life, Death and Self-
Deception," in *Crosscurrents in Phenomenology*, ed. Bruzina and Wilshire (The Hague and
Boston: M. Nijhoff, 1978).

threatened by the environment our senses must fix on a theatrical scene of violence with compelling assent even though our reflective intelligence denies that it is actually happening. It is this that produces the schizoid-like split. A similar thing, of course, might be said about pornographic enactment, with the senses compelled in this case by the allure rather than by the threat of the environment. And the same reasons might be adduced for its failure to attain the status of fine art. In both cases the artists cannot achieve the level of control of the subject matter necessary for such art.

In regard to most other subject matters we do not generate a belief on the pre-reflective and pre-critical level so intense that it disrupts and confuses us in defiance of our critical faculties. With regard to these other subject matters we never fully believe on any level of consciousness in the actuality of the proceedings, and hence we are free to enjoy the essences detached by the encounters, and to try out the theatrical life experimentally to see if it accords with—i.e., organizes more revealingly—the life we bring with us from outside the theatre. In our very detachment we experiment with the structure of our involvement.

It must be conceded, of course, that weird things happen in theatre, and not just in pornographic or violent enactments; they are particularly arresting as they are discovered in rehearsal, and most particularly in improvisations in rehearsal. Often, however, one cannot tell whether they resonate and refer beyond the limits of the theatrical setting, or whether they are merely artifacts of these limits themselves. "We're only acting and we're getting away with things." Limits, then, would not reveal existence but simply structure a creation within the void; or they would allow embroidery to be piled upon life. There is only one test to discriminate here, but it is not decisive in all instances, especially in cases of contemporary art. It is the test of time. Does the finished artistic production gather up its artists and audiences in a way that deepens and renders more coherent the experience of all in their ongoing lives outside the theatre? Are questions answered which we hardly knew had been asked? Or, as Chaikin has written: "We ask wordless questions of our experience. . . . We ask questions and experience a dynamic silence. In effect we are joined to each other by what we don't understand." This itself is a discovery and a consolidation.

The actor performs within the animating gaze of others—the other actors and the members of the audience immobilized in their chairs. He presents himself to our sight as one who is seen, and as one who experiences himself to be seen; he experiences himself as experienced and authorized by the others. He absorbs their attention and swells with it; he is empowered in his transformation as the character. As we see him there, bathed in the light, licensed in his freedom, we may be tempted to think that his behavior is merely an artifact of the situation, and that his acting is just wish-fulfilling behavior—artificial life artificially induced—as an orchid can bloom in the arctic if placed within a glass enclosure and radiated with heat and light. But these wishes to be transformed in the animating gaze of others are not utterly dissimilar to wishes, means, and situations in the offstage world. For example, a person falls into a pose, say, of being brave; it is accepted by others as reality; it soon becomes the reality—that is, the person is enabled by others' belief in his bravery to do brave deeds. We live within the gaze of others, and can and do take leaps of transformation offstage. What blooms onstage under the intense, compounded gazes of those many others immobilized in their chairs may uncover similar behaviors in somewhat similar situations offstage. We cannot tell until we adopt this hypothesis and go look and see. And when we do we will not only look and see differently in the world, but we will exist somewhat differently, so there will be something different to be seen. Theatre reveals, but does not reveal at all clearly the limits of its ability to reveal. We can only say that some art makes our ongoing life more luminous and coherent than does some other art, or that it complements nonartistic modes of discovering the world. We can form no idea of total illumination.

Does theatre reveal what is the case or only what we would like to be the case? The distinction enshrined by the question is grossly misleading. For what could be more actual than the dreams and desires we do have? How can we know ourselves unless we know what these are? Theatre is peculiarly apt to reveal them.

Still, the question might be salvaged through refinement. Can theatre distinguish between what we want to be the case, and whatever *else* is the case, whether we want it or not? Theatre by itself (whatever that might mean exactly) cannot answer this question in a consistently reliable way. But this should not surprise or dismay us. For we have insisted that the event of theatre's "world" can occur only in intersection with the world. As is the case with any cultural institution, and with any human activity, the evidence from theatre becomes reliable only when it is fed into that network of experimentation and corroboration built up by all institutions and activities. Part Two of this book sketched this larger world of experience and discovered it to be theatre-like. There is no doubt that we identify mimetically with authority, rebel against authority in dramatic ways, take "roles," etc. But there are limits to the ways in which life is theatre-like. What these limits are cannot be precisely determined in every case. Particular questions concerning the reliability of particular theatre events can only be submitted to ongoing check and experimentation within the whole cultural matrix.

So our formula to the effect that good art reveals the essence of the actuality without the actuality is a bit too pat. For art itself is an actuality that influences and limits the actualities that can be bracketed by it and revealed in their essence. And try as it will, art cannot be sure of just what it has left out or of how much it has taken in. In the end, great art returns us to the plenum of actuality better prepared both to understand it and to experience awe in the face of its residuum of incomprehensibility. Great art attempts to strike against its own limits, and to set the boundless resonating within it. It both exalts and humbles.

What of the specific limits of a particular theatre piece? Let us take *Waiting for Godot*. It arises within the tradition in which the most theatrical of all themes is developed: identification with the authority, authorization by him, and alienation from him. We stand in for him and he for us, and then we endeavor to stand upon our own feet. The theme is practically obsessive in theatrical art, because it springs from our deepest ontological need, our need to *be* through interpersonal involvement. Theatre borders on ritual when it ties up the same threads so often that they are woven anew into the same pattern.

But *Godot's* point seems to be the breakdown in this pattern itself. The tramps' authorization by the authority has not been consummated, so they cannot begin to rebel meaningfully or to achieve a vital individuation. Yet when we dilate our inspection of the play we see that what was apparently a breakdown of the pattern is really but a distinctive new turn within it. The authority of the artistic spectacle set up for ourselves, through ourselves, and about ourselves moves to authorize us as the bearers of general human traits and potencies even as we experience together the narrower message of our failure to be authorized in the traditional ways. We feel, however, unfocally, that we are masters of our interlocked fates to the extent that we comprehend them through the play. In experiencing together our fragmentation, and our lack of empowerment-through-mimetic-involvement with traditional authority figures, we move to achieve mimetic involvement and authorization on another level; we move to authorize ourselves. Under the guise of the artistic other—he who is "in" us—we move to do so. The cries of individuation sound within the larger ensemble of the judging audience, and a new organism of mimetic community seeks to be born.

What justifies us in thinking that a disclosure of truth has occurred? In chapter 9, we deferred final judgment on the question of the truth of theatrical art. In general, we were prepared to say that theatre which is life-like and which appears to be true will have a very strong claim to being true if life turns out to be theatre-like. Life does turn out to be theatre-like, at least within the limits which we are trying to mark. The sorts of

254 / ROLE PLAYING AND IDENTITY

involvements which theatre expresses in its fictions are exemplified in the actual involvements of life. The mimetic enslavement of the tramps to the authority Godot, their insecurity over whether they have been authorized by him, and the flimsy things they do to distract themselves from their waiting for him strike a profound chord in us essentially mimetic and theatre-like beings. It may be that we hear the chord for the first time.

Authorization on a *categorial* level seems clearly to be established. We cannot reveal even a deficiency in authorization without employing a theatrical production that generates authorization on a different level; authorization is inescapable. The same can be said of all the *existentialia*. Any play that involves us at all will reveal that some role taking, some mood, some language, some projection of possibility are inescapable if we are to experience any enactment of anything. For example, there can be no disclosure of satiety or paucity of mood—or of mal-attunement—without a minimal mood of attunement between the participants in the theatre house; as a categorial matter, attunement is inescapable. Or, there can be no disclosure of a characteristic of projection of possibility offstage without a projection of possibility in the theatre house, etc.

But on the level of fact, the level at which we cannot help but exist in this one and only time of our individual lives—*are* we authorized or are we *not*? Most specifically, are we authorized as authentic individuals or are we not? Can our experience of *Waiting for Godot* answer this? Here is where the gravest difficulties begin for theory, for we cannot know ourselves without changing ourselves. We wrote in chapter 17 that second order theatrical metaphor embedded in ordinary talk and experience is like a magnetic emblem which is true of life because it bends life to conform to itself. Now, the event of a theatre piece's production occurs in the world, although not in the deeply habitual way in which a second order theatrical metaphor like the ordinary word "role" occurs. The question is whether in the very act of disclosing our lack of authorization the audience and the artists will *confirm* themselves in this lack and thus, paradoxically, authorize each other afresh. If the theatre event is true it is false. If it is false it is true.

I do not believe that we have a perfect paradox, however, because the theatre event is not a second order metaphor embedded in daily life, and because it is problematical whether the theatrical experience of lack of authorization will authorize us and authenticate us to any very significant degree. But it is important to mention it because it points to the open-endedness, uncertainty, and freedom of existence. This insight will also play a role in marking the limits of second order theatrical metaphor. A human existence is not a substance, and it holds an indefinitely large fund of unobjectifiability, creativity, and freedom. It is not that we can achieve no truth in art; but any truth we achieve disturbs that about which it is the truth and limits itself in more ways that it itself can comprehend; and so on through sequences of inquiry and levels of reflection indefinitely.

Let us be as clear as we can about this principle that each insight we achieve in the luminous focus of art casts a penumbra of uncertainty. It is indisputable, I believe, that our age experiences a breakdown in mimetic attachment and in authority at the deepest level, and that theatre, the mimetic art, reveals certain aspects of this better than any other investigation can. Take *Waiting for Godot* and *The Chairs*. Despite many important differences between the tramps on the one hand and the old couple on the other, their maladies fall into a single category: disturbance of mimetic attachment to authority. This truth is revealed clearly. And yet this very disclosure creates uncertainty. Is the disclosure of the breakdown of mimetic involvement with authority already the first step in its repair? Perhaps for some it will be. But just the opposite can happen, and I know of no way to predict which is most likely. In the very act of excavating the traditional foundation of authorization and bringing it to the light and to the air we further disturb whatever strength and solidity it possesses. That is, when our excavation thematizes this foundation, it is exposed for the first time as just one possibility among others of life and thought. It is lived as a possibility rather than as an unquestioned actuality. As Don Ihde has pointed out in his work on visual phenomena (but which can be extrapolated beyond such phenomena, I believe), to see a figure in a new way disturbs significantly the original way in which it was seen. The figure as it was first seen is now seen as only one of several possible ways of its being viewed, and it loses its strong conative grip on us.[4] Theatre can weaken constructive assumptions of life simply through thematizing them.

Moreover, as we have pointed out, any facet of mimetic involvement revealed by theatre must be revealed through mimetic involvement. In articulating in the theatre our lack of authorization we must be newly authorized to some extent, for actors and audiences authorize each other. But we cannot tell precisely to what extent. Is a piece like *Godot* living off the capital of a mimetic, authorizing tradition and not replenishing it sufficiently? Will such theatre ultimately undermine its own foundations? We cannot tell. The actuality of any mode of artistic production must limit its ability to reveal in ways that must escape its ability to reveal them. The involvements of our lives catch us up and carry us in ways that are only partially understood or controlled by human voluntary effort, for example, by art. W. H. Auden has pointed out that the thrust toward individuation in the West has reached a greater pitch than at any time in history. So

---

4. Don Ihde, *Experimental Phenomenology* (New York: G. P. Putnam's Sons, 1977).

great has it become that the traditional modes of mediating and equilibrating fusion and diremption, communal identity and individuation, Man
and man, often are incapable of performing their function, and we pitch
wildly from fusion and communalism to diremption and individualism.
Art has reached the stage of desperate creativity, and we cannot tell how
effective it can be.

But this uncertainty has its positive side. Every truth revealed by theatre
art—no matter how grim its disclosure of anxiety, insubstantialness, and
failure of authorization—can be revealed only through an immeasurable
upsurge of human transcendence, creativity, community, and freedom.
Even the articulation of death can be exhilarating. Also, the uncertainty
breaks us loose from what might otherwise be a paralyzing boredom. In
this light we can understand Nietzsche's cryptic observation,

> We have Art
> In order that we may not perish from Truth.

Yet a view of theatre as tragic cannot divorce itself from a view of life
as tragic. It is not as if it were merely in theatre that the truth we can attain
is limited. Any view of the world must limit itself to a set of assumptions
if it would project a network of possible ways for things to be, and there
is nothing in these assumptions themselves that guarantees that they can
canvass themselves and determine that they are all-sufficing to reveal the
world. Any view must limit itself in order to reveal, and it can provide no
assurance that it knows just what these limitations conceal. We cannot
focus on theatre through a super epistemological or scientific telescope in
order to ascertain just what its limitations are. There is no god's-eye point
of view accessible to us. Each mode of activity must stand open to correction and supplementation from every other. A disclosure must be from
a point of view, and each point of view involves more concealment than
it can disclose. And the same can be said of all points of view working in
concert, if that should be possible. There is no point of view that appre-
hends all possible points of view and the value of each.

Godot and *The Chairs* and much other contemporary art return us to
the darkness and unpredictability of our own individual-social natures,
and to our uncertain choices in the face of the natural shocks of everyday
life. Art at its best illuminates existence and finally creates a luminous
darkness of the inexhaustible residuum that we cannot understand. By
luminous darkness I mean that it is a darkness perceived *as* darkness. But—
except in death occurring while on stage—the artist outlives his performance. He is returned to the chaotic, strung-out, and non-luminous darkness of everyday life. We cannot hope to render without remainder this

non-luminous darkness so that it becomes luminous; ultimately we must simply respect its non-luminousness. We ought to know that after every artistic intimation of death we must die—out of the concert hall or theatre, or out of a lovely glade filled with light and the poet's song—and in a spasm in which we can appreciate neither the productions of art nor nature.

Let us now close this chapter. We said that great art sounds its own limits. There is, finally, a disturbing possibility: instead of the breakdown of art being rendered artistically within the art, it is perhaps necessary to experience the breakdown of art itself. Richard Foreman has declared:

> "Perfect" plays hypnotize us with an internalized formal image of a wholeness we ourselves do not possess and should not even dream of possessing. . . . [A] play . . . of undeniable excellence, "Waiting for Godot," nevertheless seems to me to paradoxically suffer from realizing its theme a bit too "perfectly" in terms of its formal strategies. As a result, while it was properly and productively disruptive of an audience's emotional habits at the time of its original "insertion" into theatrical history, I believe that its internal poetic strategies now seem a bit self-evident. . . . Moliere's "problematic" "Don Juan" and Strindberg's "defective" (especially in the second half) "Dance of Death" [are] plays that sort of "break down" formally in a way that suggests that something behind the text was almost too hot to handle![5]

I have only too recently attended a performance of Strindberg's *Dance of Death,* and it is difficult to admit that Foreman may have a point. But it should be considered. The paradoxical danger of the "perfect" play is that it seals us off from the life of the world that it should illuminate and open up to us anew. As Brecht feared, we will leave our pity and fear in the theatre, and not work it out in new probings and in new engagements offstage.

To adopt Max Scheler's insight, in no age before ours have human beings become so thoroughly problematical to themselves.

As we complete this chapter we close the first and most obvious stage of our account of theatre art and truth. For we turn from theatre art as metaphor to the theatrical metaphors at work in life outside the theatre. And yet these theatrical metaphors are not understandable in isolation from an understanding of theatre. So as we trace the limits of their ability to reveal existence we will be saying something more, however indirectly, about the truth of theatre art.

5. *New York Times,* January 14, 1979.

CHAPTER XIX

The Limits of
Theatrical Metaphors

Theatre is a fiction which is a metaphor of life; it is life-like. But only actual beings in the actual world can produce this fiction and participate in it; angels do not project it down from heaven. Theatre artists use their understanding of actual life to produce theatre, and what they use already bears the imprint of theatre and other cultural institutions. Life is already, in various ways, theatre-like. We live on the pivot connecting the fictional and the actual and can never leap off to land solidly on either "side." Indeed, in the case of human life, the idea of a purely fictional or a purely actual is a delusion—though no doubt we can and must dintinguish between living while onstage and living while off.

The reality of human life cannot be nicely distinguished from its appearances and the characteristic ways in which these come to be described. On a very general level the reality of a human being can be compared directly to the reality of a work of art.[1] Neither can be unless each comes to be through the appearances by which it is known and described. The reality of a piece of canvas exists independently of the appearances and the words through which it is identified, although some words and appearances are more revealing and more efficient in the way that they identify it. But if the canvas is the material substratum of a painting, then no identification of it *qua* canvas gets at the reality of it *qua* painting. At best we can locate extensions of pigment on the canvas, but we cannot reveal it as art. We cannot reveal what makes this bit of blue pigment the dress of the Virgin Mary, for example. Likewise we cannot use only spatial,

1. See Joseph Margolis, "Works of Art as Physically Embodied and Culturally Emergent Entities," *British Journal of Aesthetics*, XIV (1974), pp. 187–96.

temporal, and physiological terms to describe what makes a human body a human self. Human beings emerge in their reality through their appearances which fill the air of culture and which inform our common comprehension. Without being interpreted as humans we could not be human. "We are of such stuff as dreams are made on."

I wish now to spell out some specific aspects of theatrical art which apply metaphorically to offstage life, and which are already embedded in offstage appearances and descriptions. Just to distinguish them from theatre itself, we call them second order metaphors. While they are powerful and cannot be eliminated without unimaginable loss to life itself, yet they also are limited in what they form and reveal.

We first choose second order metaphors long present in ordinary English. Although we have dealt all along with the notion of "role," let us review synoptically its powers and properties. We cannot speak of the "role" of the physician without speaking of behaviors of his which are considered characteristic by those who characteristically receive and view his work. Thus "role" pulls in with it the companion notion of "audience," although it is not already deeply embedded in our ordinary language. We could still be said to "coin" this companion metaphor.

Now, the physician cannot be a physician unless he can "play" this "role" with some minimal success. Even if "what good physicians currently do" should appear to subsequent ages as injurious, a doctor cannot be a doctor unless he conforms to these expected pratices in some minimal way (unless, of course, he can prove to the relevant "audience" that they are injurious). He fights for his professional life to conform to these expectations, and if he should fail a part of his life is extinguished.

The same can be said of the "role" of auto mechanic. He "performs" successfully when the cars he works on "perform" likewise, and this is tied organically and inevitably to the expectations and evaluations of the relevant "audience" and clients. It is conceivable that a car "perform" too well, in the odd sense that its startling "performance" fails to fit into the community of expectations built up around automobiles' "performance."

The second order deployment of "role" is amplified by explicitly introducing the notion of "script," as certain sociologists and transactional therapists have done. So widely used is "script" that we witness it embedding itself perhaps in ordinary language. The interesting idea is that to learn a "role" is to learn a sequence of expected responses, a "story" or "plot." This is all the more binding on our behavior if the "script" is not explicitly spelled out; it is very difficult for us to acknowledge that such a "script" has been learned at all. The undeliberate and quasi-mechanical nature of the "role playing" is pressed home with the often used companion metaphor of a "tape." "Tapes from the past" play themselves out in our behavior without our knowing it.

Writers such as Eric Berne have attempted to render explicit some of these "scripts" and "tapes."[2] The most bizarre "plots" appear: for example, expectations and stratagems unthematizable by the participants which secure one or other of them short-term gains—"payoffs"—at the expense of long-term engulfments, immobilizations, and blockages of possibilities. The theatrical metaphor is linked to that of "games": There is a deep connection between theatrical, dramatical, and agonistic metaphors. The plausibility of these metaphorical interpretations is attested to by the degree to which a life falls into a recognizable pattern at their touch.

These double-edged ideas reveal the abyss beneath the facile notion that onstage life and offstage life are entirely separate. Neither "side" provides a firm footing for the literal description of it, while we then take such terms and extend them metaphorically to the other "side." In their metaphorical connection neither side is clearly *proton analogon*. Although there are theatrical metaphors, we cannot say simply that terms applicable literally and solely to theatre as a technical process isolated from ordinary life have then been extended to offstage life. For theatre derives its being from actual persons, artists, who are—among other things—attempting to spell out and elaborate "roles" encountered in their offstage existence. That we put offstage "roles" into quotes and do not do so with onstage roles is merely an arbitrary convention to distinguish them when we write. (Or merely an etymological convention, if we should agree that the word *role* was first applied to an actor by extension from the roll of his script.) To enact the role of Oedipus, say, with all the attendant prophesying and working of fate, is to illuminate through perspicuous integration "roles" and "tapes" of engulfments and dependencies offstage, and the stratagems employed—often tragically and blindly—to break away from them. There is an unplumbable and dateless history of give and take between the two "sides" of offstage and onstage. Over the abyss of our actual lives, which never surrender wholly to literal description, we cling to the logical principle of excluded middle—X is either A or not A—and to our neat oppositions of terms. We neither cling easily nor fall easily. Human actuality is the precarious intersection of fictionality and factuality and of presence and the present. That is, what is actual for us must be involved in various networks of idealization.

It does no good to dismiss role theorists with the curt, "There are no

2. Eric Berne, *Games People Play*, (New York: Grove Press, 1967).

scripts in life." For there are "scripts." True, role theorists seldom have any idea of what actually occurs when artists play roles onstage, and this is an important limitation of their theorizing. But this knowledge can lend more strength to the metaphor than they themselves have imagined, and we should trace this before we spell out the limits of the metaphor that this same knowledge helps us to discover.

First, even when a pre-written script exists the creativity of the actor is very great; the script can be unpredictably transformed.[3] This suggests that the individual's creativity is also possible with the "scripts" of life, *if* they can be brought to focal consciousness. Of course, theatre art can help us to thematize our impacted "scripts" and stratagems. And if we should consider the process in which theatre is created—particularly productions which arise exclusively from improvisations by actors—we may be able to grasp just how this thematization is achieved. For usually the merest sketch of a relationship is agreed upon by the actors, and they then open themselves to what reveals itself spontaneously as they interact. Perhaps a third party will confide privileged information as to motivation or situation to one of the actors, and out of this one-sided ignorance things emerge that surprise all. At this level theatre overlaps with psychodrama: the use of the stage to reveal and transform the pressing problems of the participants as persons.[4] And all this can suggest restraints and structures which can be imposed in ordinary life to deliberately explore in a theatre-like way the problems of the selves involved. Thus George Bach, a mar-

---

3. For example, Raul Julia in *Taming of the Shrew* drops to his knees and kisses the hand that Kate had placed beneath his foot as a symbol of her deference to him. She is "tamed," but now it is achieved through the love that has sprung up between them. I do not believe that this distorts Shakespeare's script. It is so good—so universal in its lineaments—that it can allow this interpretation.

4. I refer to the work of J. L. Moreno, e.g., the various volumes of *Psychodrama.* The title here refers to an activity that can be called a half-way house between theatre and offstage existence. The patient keeps his name and various others play significant persons in his life as they interact with him in situations crucial to his mental health. The aim is to disclose to him through these improvisations what the problems are and what possible ways there are for coping with them. He then tries out these ways in his everyday life. If they do not work he then returns to the psychodramatic "stage" for correction, reinforcement, or a new exploration. Clearly theatre in the strict sense creates characterizations that are often far removed from the artists' actual situations as persons. But, equally, there are times at which the connections are not so tenuous and indirect, and then theatre can be seen to overlap with psychodrama. Moreover, the stage actor taps his or her resources, problems, and experiences as a person, either studiedly or automatically, to a greater extent than the audience may realize. Very few actors weep, for example, with the mechanical facility with which persons whistle. The catharsis the actor experiences after finishing a great role—one of the "monsters" as Olivier calls them—has perhaps to be experienced to be understood. So depleted he may be by the "substitute self," the character, he has left on stage that he may have little energy or reason left with which to deal with the remaining problems of his life. If this should happen in psychodrama, of course, it will have been a failure.

riage counselor, aims to teach his clients to "fight fair," by which he means that only those problems that they can fight about with some control are to be brought up by them.[5] What he wants is an art-like fight.

Let us continue to ask how knowledge of the stage helps to mark the limits of second order theatrical metaphors. A world can be mapped into a strictly theatrical "world" only by such an extreme degree of control and of idealization that the consequences of many of the actions are prevented from occurring. Pestilence that "kills" does not kill the beings performing or auditing; "stabs to the heart" do not kill; "broken hearts" neither maim nor mend, but cease to be when the curtain falls and the mind turns from their contemplation. Theatre is a fiction which elucidates essences, some of which apply in existence.

One must admit that sometimes in a production the actor feels that it is all more real, in an important sense, than ordinary life: the coherence of the well-formed whole, the beginning, middle, and end; the vital sense it makes as it fits together and reveals even its own limits before the luminous darkness of the world; the intense involvement of the actor's faculties occurring within the limits which all involved have agreed not to breach, etc.

But the feeling of reality stems from the feeling of "reality" and from the intense activity that essences and ideas generate in human mind and experience. Within the margins of his consciousness the actor as artist is aware of that frame of aesthetic detachment and interruption which divides him decisively from the actual world and its strung-out events and non-luminous darkness. The actor as person does not cease to exist in the abyss of actuality as he performs; indeed, he feeds off this abyss as he performs. But the aesthetic frame he occupies also protects him from the abyss, and he knows this, marginally. Put briefly and apparently paradoxically, the world can be mapped into a theatrical "world" only if that "world" is localized in a certain way—shielded from the present and actual region of the world which the theatre house, with its seating for the audience, constitutes.

Only fine art achieves this high degree of localization and idealization. Thus every second order theatrical metaphor will mislead unless we repeatedly supply the qualification that the behavior to which it is applied cannot achieve this. Though essentially describable in ways that are extensions from fictions, the action so described is not fictional. We are not shielded from time, the world, and the full train of consequences of our acts; we are nakedly within time and the world. Second order theatrical metaphors are seriously limited because after their valid work of disclosure

5. George R. Bach and Peter Wyden, *The Intimate Enemy* (New York: William Morrow & Co., 1968).

through comparison is done, they must suggest that the behavior described by them is fictional.

The physician playing his "role" does not have an immobilized "audience" sitting in aesthetic distance from what he does. The full gamut of the consequences of what he does to the patient unrolls in time. True, the interpretation placed upon these consequences may be theatre-like, and tellingly so. Even if the patient should die, it may be thought not to be the doctor's fault, because in the "script" for that situation that each "plays" the doctor is king-like. But the patient dies nevertheless. Or if the "script" changes in the quasi-mythological cycles of actual historical time and the prescribed thing to do is to displace kings, then it is all the doctor's fault. But the patient dies nevertheless.

The aesthetic distance essential in strictly artistic acts requires both that the "world's" time be enactable within the world's time, *and* that it be impervious to world time and shielded from it in certain essential ways. Inevitably, either overtly or covertly, this shielding breaks down in off-stage life with its "roles." If we refuse to concede this we grow frenzied, I believe, and ultimately diabolical.

I have already pointed out that the self cannot be reduced to any set of "roles," not even to a set of imagined ones, because what it is cannot be divorced from what it makes its own. It can make its own the quest for a life as yet unimagined, even as it stands open to the possibility that ends all the others, death. It can stand open to world time and to the boundlessness of the sources of intelligibility. Finally, we experience, as simple facts accessible to all, the emergence of unpredictable and novel behaviors, as well as the frenzy, anguish, or stupefied dullness of persons who are expected to accept a description of themselves as "performers" falling within a limited set of "roles."[6]

The performer *qua* performer is no greater than his performances. But the "performer" is unimaginably more than his "performances"; possibility and expectation and tolerance form an ethical dimension of his being that is not possessed by the artist *qua* artist. Hence we must conclude that the second order theatrical metaphor can be pushed beyond its limits, *and there comes a point after which we should not speak even in shudder quotes of "performer" and "performances."*

Throughout our study we have found it to be an essential trait of actors' performances in the theatre that the time which they spend enacting the character is circumscribed and disconnected in certain ways from world time. As artists they know what their characters do not: that world time bounds and locates the time of the play, e.g., "three months of time

6. The classical statement here is found in Dostoevsky's *The Underground Man*. Its lesson is that we will be free at practically any cost.

centuries past in Denmark." Likewise it is an essential trait of actors' performances that what the audience members can know about them as persons, and what these members can do to intervene to deflect or block their enactment of characters in the play's "world," is typically very limited. If they should rush the stage, for instance, they cannot enter the play's "world," but at most can disrupt it, and they will soon be escorted out of the theatre by the police.

The parallels to the cocktail party situation are fairly close. As we have noted, the time in which one has to act is circumscribed, and the powers that others possess to pry into what one is doing and to disturb its course are limited. One's "act" need not last long, and rigorous conventional codes of conduct limit the extent to which others can test one, the extent to which they can look behind the "masks," shake the "stage setting," question the "scripts," peel away the "costumes" (although one's makeup may begin to run in the course of the party).

We should add a further parallel. Both onstage and at the party, the consequences of what the characters say and do are limited or lightened to some extent. All realize that the persons are only "performing," and that if one should encounter them unexpectedly in the street with their families after the party, one would probably confront quite different sorts of behavior.

But there is this crucial difference. While a text for a theatrical "world" can be suspended in mid-course, if necessary, and recommenced with no time added to this "world's" time, this cannot happen in our "performances" in the world. Even if one's makeup at a cocktail party begins to run, and one slips out to the powder room to repair it, still the time of one's "performance" has been interrupted and *extended*. This can have momentous consequences, e.g., the person one wished to meet may have left the party. Hence "performance" must be essentially different from performance.

Beyond this, however, there are many times offstage in which we are so completely unshielded before world time that we should not say even that we are "performing." It is inescapably evident that neither the conditions for performance onstage nor for "performance" at the cocktail party are met in the family. If one is a husband, say, there are no limits placed upon the time in which he acts in this capacity, or upon the ways in which the motives of his actions and quality of his actions are examined and tested. As the person acts in this capacity, time subjects him to merciless exposure. " 'Tis Time, Time, desireless, hath shown thee what thou art." To keep one's promise to remain faithful until death leaves no room for the demarcation of a time for a "performance" within the time of one's life. Hence it is more misleading than informative to use the second order theatrical metaphor and to speak of the "performance" of the husband.

This is not to deny, of course, that there are some similarities between the "role" of a husband and the role of an actor, but only to affirm that they are not sufficient to warrant the wholesale application of second order theatrical metaphor. Doubtless the social conventions relating to the behavior of husbands exhibit *some* similarity to the script of the actor which prescribes a portion of his behavior and which he must learn.

Likewise there are theatre-like aspects exhibited by many activities which should nevertheless not be described in exclusively theatre-like terms. Thus in most of his activities one habitually or deliberately stylizes his movements for himself and for actual or ideal observers. Yet we should be reluctant to apply only theatre-like terms to them. Take for example a situation in which one has driven into steep mountainous terrain and finds that the narrow dirt road has been washed out by floods. It is impossible to turn around or back up. The person begins to construct a road upon which the car can travel. Now, one may stylize one's movements for actual or imagined observers so as to appear "the resourceful explorer," "the courageous person," etc. Let us say that there are moments in which one is so absorbed in the task at hand and in the flood of consequences issuing from it that all deliberate stylization and all consciousness of stylization ceases. Yet stylization may occur habitually and automatically in one's bodily behavior, and this will probably show the effect of performances and "performances," both one's own and those typified and funded in the civilization as a whole. Moreover, there is something playful about what one is doing and this bears a striking resemblance to the theatrical and the theatre-like.

Whether stylization is deliberate and conscious or not, however, it is misleading to use exclusively theatrical metaphors to describe this activity. For they would conceal these distinctly non-theatrical aspects of it: The time of one's activities is not safely bound within the ongoing time of one's life, for these activities may be faulty and may even result in one's death. Nothing can be done to soften or confine the consequences of one's acts. Finally, there is no distinction made by the agent or by anybody else between oneself as person and oneself as "performer," hence the unqualified use of the concept of "performer" is misleading. The idea of the person as distinct both from the performer and the character, which is essential to our concept of what a theatre artist is, finds no application in this case. Activities like building the road over which one's car can travel are blessed moments of wholeness in which one says and does all in perfect freedom and perfect responsibility.

In such experiences we are not divided into a subject-self and an object-self, a performing self and a performed self. True, we are not at one with ourselves as a block of wood is at one with itself; but we are humanly unified because absorbed by the object of our concern. Our experience is a unitary one in which experiencing self and experienced self are lived through as indubitably one and the same actual person existing as actual. Even one's possibilities are actual as possibilities of one's very own. Thus one should not be referred to as "performer."

In regard to this point we should briefly note the situation of famous actors who are lured by the star system to perform their "own selves" in one transparent guise after another. Instead of acting being both an end in itself and a means to release them to their foreseeable and unforseeable possibilities as persons—and we to ours—it becomes a means of stifling these, and themselves, and us. Because to "play oneself" is to hedge oneself in through the time allotted to the playing of this "character," and because the actor acts without the full consequences of his acts occurring, the reality of his acts must wither as he performs them. Hence he must wither as a person. The self performs and "performs"—every human must do the latter and the actor must do both—but the self can be seized and contained in no finite set of performances or "performances." The self is that which escapes all final objectification—in part through the unpredictability of indefinitely many of its objectifications—and does so within a set of environments that cannot be contained and localized.

Only self-deception allows one to keep thinking that he is always only "performing," and that his "performances" generate effects which, if he chooses, can be limited almost entirely to a local environment, as consequences of performances can be. Even when he can be called a "performer," every "performance" is a reality which will characterize him in his individuality until the instant of his death, and, in a sense, beyond. It is forever true that he did it and not just a performer performed it. Thus not only is it the case that not all actions are "performances," but "performance" must differ essentially from performance.

Every act opens out directly onto a world that amplifies and records it unimaginably endlessly and that snatches it from one's grasp. We are left with consequences still incompletely known and still uncontrollable at the moment of our deaths. But we are morally responsible for actions done in our own person in a way that is different from those done as an artist. The self can deceive itself and believe that it is always "performing" and that its "performances" are more like performances than they really are. But it cannot escape itself, for the self *is* that being which deceives itself and suffers the effects for so doing. If he deceives himself about his own death and thinks he can confine himself to a nest of quasi-aesthetically framed local environments which he outlives, than he will live each moment in the stupefaction of that deception, and will die in the numbing—or perhaps frenzied—denial of what he is doing to himself. We must say that a person who "performs" his death so that he vaguely believes that he outlives it is the most wretched person imaginable, for he has failed to appropriate his own greatest power and pleasure as a self, which is just to come home to himself as he is.

Nothing we have said obliges us to deny that the role-playing metaphor is an essential one. The concept of "performing" may not apply *in toto* to all that we do offstage, but it is inescapable in most of everyday life, and to "perform" effectively as *persona* performed we must more or less mask from acknowledgment self-deceptively the larger context of time which encompasses the local context of the "performance." The press and shock of events are too great, and their outcome is too unpredictable, to adopt a stance of detachment strictly analogous to the actor's toward himself as character. Only thus can we explain why social blunders, bungled "roles" and "slippings of the mask," so much embarrass everyone in the situation: we can no longer lose ourselves in our mutual and unavoidable self-deception, and the forced acknowledgment that this is what we have been doing embarrasses us. "Performance" is unavoidably self-deceptive most of the time in a way that artistically disciplined performance need not be, and it seems to be an inescapable consequence of our being essentially social, essentially fantasizing, essentially private, and—if we may say so—essentially actual beings.

Unlike an actor who lays performance decisively behind him, the person offstage can go directly from one "performance" to another. That an actor can put performance neatly behind him only indicates the distance of ideality and control involved in it. He can voluntarily take up and leave the artistic stance of aesthetic detachment. But our "performances," as well as our activities that shouldn't be called "performances," involve us in the thick of things and in that gray area where voluntary and involuntary commingle. John Dewey asserted that great art can be more moral than morality, by which he meant that it can achieve through incarnated imagination new modes of integrating experience and winning satisfactions. But is is also true that we are responsible for our "performances" and our other acts in a relentless, twilight way that gives them a moral and existential seriousness distinct from that of actors' performances.

The actor onstage is engaged not only in a "conversation" with the audience but in a three-way dialogue between himself as person, himself as artist, and himself as character. Dilating through its differentiations, the self can open itself to itself. Kierkegaard describes an artist who is called upon at the age of thirty-four to undertake again the role which made her famous at fifteen—Juliet.[7] The problem is how she is to recapture the freshness and spontaneity appropriate to this character which was naturally hers as a person nearly twenty years earlier. But to be able to solve the problem is to achieve freshness and spontaneity on a level of self which is higher than what she was able to reach at fifteen. It is the level of ideality: her ability to summon into communicable presence that which in fact is no longer present. She comes home to herself as a life resurrectable through control and responsibility. She approaches the ethical stage of life in the mature fulfillment of the artistic.

But an equally important lesson is that this ideality has limits and the use of it at last must be abandoned. The actress who recaptures her youth through ideality must leave the theatre one day older. And she will be too closely enmeshed in the day as she lives it to idealize it; it will be too close and unpredictable to be given presence all at once and entire; moreover, it leads on to an indefinite number of other days which she cannot hem in and control. She will be abandoned to ethical responsibility in its relentless press, dailiness, and banality. She may possess an "art" of life, but it will not be art strictly speaking.

Kierkegaard refers to another actress who enacted as artist each of the stages of her life as she lived through them as person. Yet the actress who develops her ideality in order to grasp her evolving stages of life *as* her stages must also leave the theatre to reimmerse herself in a daily round that cannot be completely thematized and idealized as she lives it. If she should, in self-deception, enact her own death as she died we would be appalled. Even if she should know clearly that she is dying, we would think it greater homage to art to respect its requirements of control and its limits and to cease entirely from it. The point of great art is to reveal existence—including its uncanniness—and ultimately it does this through revealing the limits of art to reveal. Art should reveal that death is more than any artist can reveal through performing. Art reveals only through the distance of ideality, and this imposes definite limits on what can be revealed, and on when and how and by whom it can be revealed.

In sum: A performance requires that the performer bound what he enacts as character within his aesthetic control as artist, and within his ongoing life as person. But when he himself is dying he cannot as artist stand outside himself as dying character and aesthetically frame and bound himself. If he should poison himself, for example, there will come a time when he cannot control the movements of his body. In his dying he is thrown into the boundless. He cannot artistically perform his own death. And since the application of the concept of "performance" requires that

7. Søren Kierkegaard, *Crisis in the Life of an Actress* (New York: Harper Torchbooks, 1967).

the person's behavior as *persona* be bounded and controlled within his ongoing life as person, and since this is impossible in this case, the person can "perform" his own death only in the most abysmal self-deception.

To refuse to acknowledge the limits of art and artistic metaphors is both to undermine art and to reduce one's life to compulsive narrowness and frenzy. One mode of refusal is so obvious as almost to escape attention for that reason. It is the attempt to fill up one's life with artistic involvement so that no room for anything else remains. When one isn't performing he is auditing someone else's performance, and when he is doing neither of these he is remembering when he did do so, or anticipating when he will do so again. But when artistic activity is used to escape from the twilight struggle of ordinary life with its moral and prudential problems, the activity loses its dialectical dependence upon this struggle, and art shrivels in significance.[8] William James, himself an artist, advised us never to allow great excitement to be built up by art unless it is to be released later through engagement in the everyday world; for example, the "heroic" should lead to the heroic, on however small a scale, if we are not to become flaccid and self-indulgent. There is something crudely moralistic in his injunction, and it bears a trace of contempt for essences and the vitality of mind, but he has a point.

Other attempts to impress artistic forms directly and deliberately into offstage life aim to transform it rather than to supplant it. William Saroyan explains why he cultivates passing relationships: "Brief friendships have such definite starting and stopping points that they take on the quality of art, of a *whole* thing, which cannot be broken or spoiled."[9] Now, no doubt, human life is art-like over a great extent of its range. To be at all we must create a self for ourselves which is displayable to others, and we must do so in a way that is analogous to an actor creating a character. The fact that more and more of our relationships in our mobile society are perforce passing ones—only emphasizes the parallel to an actor and his passing relationships to people in the audience whom he does not know individually and probably will never see again. Saroyan goes on, "In a chance meeting you have been thrown together accidentally, total strangers, in order to pass along . . . the essence of your own story and reality. You are not there to acquire more story, to have more material to carry with the rest of the material that still hasn't been really understood, or certainly hasn't been used, and you are there anonymously." The word

---

8. No doubt it is true that artists often express contempt for conventional morality. But in nearly every case, I believe, great artists are sensitive to some or all of the basic virtues of justice, love, wisdom, courage, temperance, and they have participated in one way or another in the struggle to achieve them.

9. William Saroyan, *Chance Meetings* (New York: W. W. Norton & Co., 1978).

anonymous again reminds us of the actor presenting himself to an audience.

But we must wonder: how far can the theatrical metaphor be pressed? How far ought it to be pressed? We mold ourselves in trying to know ourselves. If all interpersonal relationships were of this brief sort then one would acquire no new "material" to be reduced to its "essence." One would become empty, a mere shell, a *poseur*. Moreover, one's relationship to himself cannot be brief, and if he is to respect himself it must be for being abidingly true, abidingly open, and abidingly reliable not only toward himself but toward others whom he respects for the same reasons. Ultimately, I think, the relationship must be toward himself alone: in an experience which no one else can live through as he does, and in a life for which only he is directly responsible ethically day by day.

Let us note, however, that Saroyan is *writing* about these brief art-like relationships. It is not just that this renders them doubly aesthetic. He is calling these passing relationships back into presence. He does not let them wholly die. He memorializes them for himself and others through exercising his power over time and possibility. His life with others is woven up, at least in his present aloneness.

Still, the present aloneness of the writer is an important fact. He writes of people who are not present and who perhaps do not remember him at all, and he writes for people who likewise are not present and who have met neither him nor them. Such modes of lonely presencing have grown typical of our culture. There is a stark contrast between them and events of theatre in which all are present as they memorialize their life in time together. Of course, in contemporary theatre the persons present are usually strangers; there is lacking a definite community that can grow together through art. The greatest of all contrasts to Saroyan's lonely communications would be those theatre-like and regular rites of church and state that weave our lives together over their daily strung-out expanse. During these rites we say to each other and to ourselves: This is what members of our group have done before; we do it again, and in so doing memorialize it for others who will follow us.

The realities of rite wane, at least in the West. Hence, we increasingly find attempts to force life directly into artistic form. One thinks first of apocalyptic stage visions meant to excite the audience to new modes of behavior beyond the theatre walls. Or one thinks of productions which involve audience participation. The latter in particular defeat the realities without which theatre cannot exist: the distance of ideality and artistic engagement which must surround all that art can do. Theatre can be a new way of constituting the meaningfulness of the world. It can probe, excite, and suggest. But the question always remains to be asked: Can the purposes initiated and insights won there be realized and corroborated off-stage? Can we live with them?

Very significant as well are attempts to force life directly into artistic form through adoption of radically art-like and theatre-like styles of life. In its most exaggerated form this life is exemplified by the pop artist Andy Warhol. It is said that he has attempted at times to live his life as if it were literally an art work or a series of art works. He attempts to fashion a course of events with strictly artistic style, and although some improvisations are perforce allowed, beginnings and endings of the fashioned series of events are to be controlled as an artist-director controls a production.

But only a God who created the world with the very conceptual tools with which he designed and measured it could achieve this.[10] We cannot bound the universe within which we stand as if it were a framed work of art, because our modes of reflection and projection of meaning are never fully reflectable to us; thus our rational reconstruction of the sense of the world must always be incomplete. The universe for us must be boundless, whether we acknowledge it or not, and attempts to usurp the place of God can only be ridiculously or wretchedly diabolical. Such attempts miss the actuality of human life—the "material" out of which essence is to be distilled. They must be empty and more or less crazed and delusional, no matter how intense be the momentary excitement that they succeed in generating.

Finally, the limits of second order theatrical metaphor suggest limits of first order metaphor, or theatre itself. We come full circle again. The corollary of this "performance" mania is a performance mania onstage. This occurs so easily that we might call it the occupational hazard of the actor as person. It occurs when the actor does not allow the audience to be co-creator, but so dazzles and mesmerizes them that each member loses that detachment within his mimetic involvement that is his foothold in individuality and critical reason. Artistic balance is upset, and the audience almost literally becomes a single mass, a mob, a corporate body without a face indwelt by a presence in a mask—as Claudel's actor put it. For the performer the ultimate impiety and artistic mistake is to think that he can create the other by a sheer act of his own will. It's as if he would create his own source, and so become his own father. Like Oedipus he is the seed, the sower and the sown. He forgets that he cannot ground himself or bound himself, and that only by God can he be set upon before and behind, to use the Psalmist's phrase. So dangerous is acting, I believe, that

10. See Sidney Hook, *The Metaphysics of Pragmatism* (Chicago: Open Court Publishing Co., 1927). Hook's frontispiece is a print of Blake's "Ancient of Days" laying out the universe with dividers.

there is some reason to call it the diabolical art. Not the least of the danger is that the actor's fear of his inadequacy as a person will prevent that inadequacy from being remedied. His success as an actor—his being loved as a character—will prevent him from acknowledging that he is afraid to be desired, loved, and judged as an actual individual with a life unrolling indefinitely in time. His success traps him in exhibitionism.

An environment for us can be neither absolutely local and insulated, nor total and all-inclusive. Every situation must present itself as one of an indefinite number of others, simultaneous or sequential, and as in a world that overflows our ability to thematize it. It is this that gives depth and solidity to the experienced world and to the things in it. Everything experienced as actual is presented as more than can ever be said about it, as more indeed than can ever be experienced of it, and as causally interactive and consequential in more ways than can ever be predicted. Not even the stage environment is absolutely local, thus how much less so can be an offstage environment. For example: Is a man faking? Yes, let us say—he is so in the short view and in the immediate situation; he is acting so as to mislead those present. But it may be the beginning of a new kind of life for him and for us. His deceits generate actual consequences in the world which may finally change his pretentions to realities. They become self-fulfilling prophecies. As James put it, the truth is what one can "come out with," those courses of events that prove most coercive over belief in the long run; and the report on the long run is never wholly in. We die not knowing just what we have done or what we have become.

1. The "Art of Life"

What, finally, are we to do with the most venerable instance of second order theatrical metaphor, the art of life—*ars viva*? We cannot begin to itemize all the ways of living that have been described, or that might be described, under this rubric. It seems, however, that they all have this in common: the artist of life has learned that *now* is the only time in which to really live and make a difference in the course of events, and yet also that this now is included in the encompassing time span of the ongoing world. That is, the life-artist has learned an involvement which is at the same time a detachment; he stands toward himself in a manner analogous to the way in which the actor as artist stands toward himself as character. He is involved, present, spontaneous, and yet also self-controlled.

However, salient differences emerge. First, the quality of a performer *qua* performer is nothing but the quality of his performances. Yet we are reluctant to assert this equivalence between a "performer" and his "performances," for we sense that a distinctive ethical and ontological measure is in order, and that a self is more than can ever be itemized as a set of actual or possible "performances" or "roles." Recall Aristotle's insight that the quality of an aesthetic activity is determined exclusively by the quality of its artistic product, while the quality of an ethical activity is determined in essential part by the state of mind and state of being of the person whose activity it is.[11]

Moreover, we remember that one of the most famous treatises on *ars viva* is *The Art of Holy Living and Holy Dying*. But as we have seen, the "performance" of dying must be fundamentally different from a perform-ance of dying (which is possible when the actor enacts someone else's death), because the "performance" cannot be bounded within a larger time of the "performer's" life—hence if we must speak of "performer" at all we must speak of a self-deceived one. Only if the "performer" believes that his life is contained within a higher, divine life—or continued as a presence for God—can he "perform" his death in a manner that is not a wretched imposture. But, then, this "audience" is so different from a mundane one that the "performer's" behavior is on a different level from that of any performer or any "performer" who displays himself for the mortals grouped about him. If one thought he were truly named only by God then the as-if of that "performance" *is* one with which he could die. God would be the supportive "audience" in the "performance" of dying. It would be a "part" no one else could play, and the "role" of an invoked presence of divinity in the maturation of individual identity should not be underestimated, as I have pointed out before. But now the inverted com-mas weigh so heavily on the words that they settle into a domain different from that of theatre. Second order theatrical metaphor has not led us astray, perhaps, but it is at the end of its tether. Of course, some will believe that it has led us into self-deception on a massive scale.

One can think of Kant's moral philosophy as a distant extension of theatrical metaphor, which is nevertheless too distant to warrant the un-restrained application of theatrical terms metaphorically. He thought that pure practical reason required that if the ethics of duty were to make sense one had to suppose both an afterlife in which the good person can be happy and a god who grounds this domain. But these are postulates and cannot be strictly proved. One is morally obliged to live *as-if* they were true; it is an act of faith and a kind of enactment. One is launched toward that horizon also intimated by great art: that sense of purposiveness in the universe which we cannot precisely describe, and to which we can ascribe no specific purpose. This domain beyond all our science nevertheless in-

11. Aristotle writes, "(1) The [ethical] agent must act in full consciousness of what he is doing. (2) He must will his action, and will it for its own sake. (3) The act must proceed from a fixed and unchangeable disposition." (*Nichomachean Ethics*, Book 2, Chapter 4).

spires that science to seek ever further for explanations. It is piety that buffers us from diabolism and frenzy. Any attempt to achieve an art of life that is artistic in anything like a literal sense must be an attempt to bound the boundless.

2. Erving Goffman's "Role Theory"

Erving Goffman has developed one of the most vivid and suggestive adaptations of theatrical metaphor for social theory. In his aptly titled *The Presentation of Self in Everyday Life*,[12] he links the human person to his appearances to others, and to himself via others. Ostensibly, then, we are not to seek the self as an "in itself" hidden away which emits, perhaps, signs of itself, but as a dialectical "construction" of appearances. The apparent relevance of this approach to our own is unmistakable, and it becomes insistent when Goffman compares the presentation of self with the presentation of a character by an actor.

Goffman has a keen eye for discovering similarities between onstage and offstage life, and his work is well worth studying. But planted at the bottom of his theory of the self is an idea of appearance that stunts and distorts the theory. It is evident in a questionable quotation from Santayana which he uses as an epigraph for his book:

> Masks are arrested expressions and admirable echoes of feeling, at once faithful, discreet, and superlative. Living things in contact with the air must acquire a cuticle, and it is not urged against cuticles that they are not hearts; yet some philosophers seem to be angry with images for not being things, and with words for not being feelings. Words and images are like shells, not less integral parts of nature than the substances they cover, but better addressed to the eye and more open to observation. . . .[13]

Appearances of self are linked to masks which in turn are linked to cuticles and shells. The material aspect of appearance as sign is increasingly stressed at the expense of the ideal, revelatory, and semantic aspects (to use C. S. Peirce's distinction). Appearances are things, so particular things, so particular things behind which the particular self can be hidden. The crucial thesis central to any phenomenology worthy of the name (and also to any sociology, I would think), that appearances are structured as essentially shareable and mutually intelligible senses or essences, so that to see the particular self as a structure of appearances is to see it as essentially social and predeliberately as well as deliberately revelatory—this cardinal point is increasingly obscured. His notion of appearances harbors nominalism

12. New York: Doubleday Anchor Books, 1959.
13. Ibid.

that assumes general senses are mere general names—mental shortcuts for blurring real differences among real things, which are always particulars. Since an appearance is one particular thing, that of which it is the appearance must be another, and it is eminently that which can be concealed by the appearance. Persons must seem to be alienated from their "roles," and to be essentially asocial or antisocial.

The notion of appearance which Goffman brings to all his analyses, so to his analysis of theatre, must distort theatre, and so further distort off-stage life when he applies his theatrical metaphor to it. His nominalism can gather up only fragments of the actor's project, not its wholeness. He construes as manifest appearance, as one real thing, the character played by the actor, whereas the actor himself must be another particular thing, just momentarily hidden by the character he plays. This is an oversimplified reading of appearances. We are never aware merely of the character, as if it were an animated Platonic archetype viewed by the "eye" of the mind. We are always aware of Hamlet-played-by-this-actor, and often focally aware of this. Nor is the actor aware only of the character (in the sense of his awareness being only the character's awareness), but he is aware of both this and what the character cannot know, and of the audience as aware of him-as-playing-Hamlet-in-this-manner, and so on.

Above all, the actor is aware at moments that he is expressing via the character some of his own deepest feelings and insights as person and artist, and that this, given the hush of the audience, also expresses others' feelings and insights. The audience in turn knows that something of very general, yet also of very personal, import is afoot, and they accept this not as a deceit practiced on them by the actor, but rather as the successful realization of the socially sanctioned contract into which they and the artists and managers of the theatre have entered.

Goffman, however, must see the actor's artistry as a kind of deceit. Inevitably, then, he must construe role-like activity offstage as a kind of deceit. Given his reading of role playing onstage, his version of the role-playing metaphor leads him to think that we persons offstage are distinct beings in isolation from our "roles." Then either it is claimed that the real self is unknowable (because we are always "role-playing"), or that it is glimpsed when the role, like a mask, slips. Goffman asserts that what we glimpse is the "look of one who is privately engaged in a difficult, treacherous task."[14] The task is that of "impression management," the manipulation of other "presented" selves through the impressions of oneself which one gives them. So the naked face we glimpse must be a nonsocial or antisocial one. Now, I believe that this is not only an alienating and demoralizing idea of the self, but that it is false.

14. Ibid., p. 235.

It is not that persons are incapable of the most wretched and laughable or the most brutal antisocial acts. These occur with a frequency that numbs the mind attempting to attend to them. Our situation, I believe, is a bit more tragical and a bit less farcical than Goffman thinks it is. Since we are not essentially nonsocial, antisocial, personal, and particular merely, but also essentially social—our antisocial acts, generated with relish, must also damage ourselves, however subtly.

Despite many surface changes of approach, Goffman's more recent *Frame Analysis* is still burdened with the same nominalistic assumptions concerning appearance and reference, so it cannot move far from his earlier book.[15] He has reoriented his approach from a theatrical model to a cinematographic one. He advances the interesting idea that events are humanly and socially significant for us because they are "keyed" or "framed" in a certain way, e.g., the "same" event which can be framed as serious— say the impending entry by one's employer through the door—can be reframed as comical: while the door is still shut one mimes holding a club over the spot at which the employer is expected soon to stand. We step outside the situation and comment upon it. Frames can frame other frames without limit, but presumably always within the strange outermost frame "without a rim," which is not imposed by us, he says, but is ultimate reality.

Consonant with what he takes ultimate reality to be, Goffman wants to say that there are "primary perspectives" which are not framings or keyings; for example, descriptions of events in their (allegedly) purely physical aspects, e.g., mass, shape, velocity. "When no keying is involved, when, that is, only primary perspectives apply, response in frame terms is not likely unless doubt needs combating, as in reply: 'No, they're not merely playing; it's a real fight.' Indeed, when activity that is untransformed is occurring, definitions in terms of frame suggest alienation, irony and distance."[16] But it is not clear how a fight or anything else could be apprehended without any transformation whatsoever, without any conceptualization, or—using the terms in the broad sense that they seem to allow—without any keying or framing. Goffman halfway suspects that serious activity has meaning only relative to the nonserious, and since the latter is keyed, the former must also be to some extent. Hence he writes, in the sentence immediately following the above quotation, "When the key in question is that of play, we tend to refer to the less transformed counterpart as 'serious' activity. . . ." Instead of the "untransformed" we find the "less transformed."

Goffman's nominalism, like that of Hobbes, Hume, and Locke, wishes

15. Goffman, *Frame Analysis* (Cambridge: Harvard University Press, 1974).
16. Ibid., p. 46.

to assert that "behind" socially and subjectively mediated and framed appearances there stands the physically real particular "in itself" (in the case of Locke it is a "something we know not what"). He is disturbed, however, by his own notion of primary or untransformed perspectives, and soon, wishing to cover his bet, refers to primary perspectives as those which are "no more transformed than is felt to be usual and typical for such things."[17] But this introduces a line of thought that immediately cuts beneath his own dichotomy of physical and social perspectives, with the physical supposed to be primary. For both physical and social perspectives would be generated out of a common historical and social matrix of transformation and interpretation. It is that level on which he himself operates, but uncritically; he does not thematize it in reflection.

He is disturbed in turn by this incipient line of thought. He senses, evidently, that if it were developed it would require him to revise the notion of the "outermost unimposed frame" so that this could not be a matter of uninterpreted physical particulars merely. His analysis of sociality would have to penetrate to a level of interpretational analysis with which he is unprepared to deal. So he merely makes the statement and does not develop it.

The results for his "role-playing" theory are predictable. "Play" is merely derivative *vis-à-vis* "reality" and "earnest."[18] And art, specifically cinema and theatre, is merely a copy of what already stands perfectly intelligible "in itself."[19] So, in interpreting offstage life according to either the cinematographic or theatrical model it must seem to be merely the copy of a copy, the shadow of a shadow.

As we have seen, however, Goffman is not clear on what role-playing and "role-playing" are supposed to be derivative from. This presumably is the "really real," what we would see *if* we could attain a pure (untransformed?) primary perspective on the physical particulars themselves. Consequently we are made to feel that there might be an alternative to the radical superficiality and silliness of social life as he understands it.[20] If we could see, however, that there is no alternative to this "superficiality," then it would no longer appear to be such.

It is important to see how Goffman's underlying notions of appearance and reference must excite the niggling, ever-frustrated suspicion that there must be an alternative. Appearance may be essential to reality in Goffman's view, yet it is also its antipode, and if—particularly in *Frame Analysis*—

17. Ibid., p. 47.
18. Ibid., pp. 41, 130, 138, and 145. But on 155 he expresses some misgivings, as if he were again trying to cover his bet without really working out the alternative position.
19. Ibid., pp. 79 and 130.
20. Ibid., p. 563.

there is found to be nothing behind it in the way of self—then human life itself can only be taken to be a deficient mode of reality. A person is composed *merely* of appearances.

For example, Goffman writes of what he takes to be the common way of construing self: "Behind current role, the person himself will peek out. Indeed, this is a common way of framing our perception of another. So three cheers for the self. Now let us try to reduce the clatter."[21] His method of reducing the clatter is to compare the offstage situation to the onstage situation, in this case a radio show in which a few performers enact many characters:

> Now it happens that knowing followers of the show come to appreciate that the personality sustained by each player across his several parts may itself be somewhat put on, at least tailored to increase its power as typification of a possible way of being. . . . Once again we are reminded that a sense of the humanity of a performer is somehow generated by discrepancy between role and character, which discrepancy itself can be manufactured for the effect it produces. If such is true of role-character contrasts, what about person-role contrasts?

The conclusion is clear: Life offstage is a multileveled performance, essentially comparable to the actors in the show who enact various characters: the self that appears behind the various social roles it performs is itself another performance. There is no substantial or atomic self behind the appearances. Now, I agree with Goffman about this, but since I construe appearances differently, I develop a theory of identity of self different from his. As he leaves the matter, we cannot account for our deepest intuition: that the "performance," the "dramatic effect," of life offstage is fundamentally more serious than any performance onstage. Though it bore us or disgust us, it matters more.

Goffman maintains that as the novelist or poet corrects his proofs and tinkers with his style so as to appear spontaneous and real, the enactor offstage enacts himself as life-actor and his self is exhausted by these various enactments.

> A sense of the person can be generated locally. And this discrepancy between person and role, this interstice through which a self peers, this human effect, need no more depend upon the world beyond the current situation than does the role itself. Whatever a participant "really is," is not really the issue. His fellow participants are not likely to discover this if indeed it is discoverable.

21. Ibid., p. 294.

What is important is the sense he provides them through his dealings with them of what sort of person he is behind the role he is in.[22]

The distinction which Goffman draws between what "really is" ("if indeed it is discoverable"), and "the sense he provides them . . . of what sort of person he is behind the role he is in" is symptomatic of the trouble in his thought. He cannot see that the distinction is artificial and misleading; that what a self *really* is involves integrally how it *appears* to be to others. He does not see that the experiencing body must bind its presence to itself through others and other things in a way that vastly exceeds and encompasses the time of the immediately present local situation. Similarly to Beckett's characters—but more benightedly, for the tramps can call into presence an abiding absence—persons under Goffman's model must work frenziedly to shore up a moment-by-moment reality within the local environment. They cannot really succeed.

We cannot accept the distinction which Goffman introduces between who the self really is and the sense it gives others of who it is behind the "roles" it is playing. Because the self *is* that bodily being that synthesizes its experiences beyond local environments and current "roles," and that *must* give an impression to others that it is doing so. Some of the impressions given voluntarily may be misleading, manipulative, or fatuous, but that does not set aside the chief point to be made.

It is possible to validly extrapolate from the activity of the performer onstage to the offstage situation: the time of his life as artist encompasses and supports the time of his life as character. Likewise the time of the person's life must encompass and support the time of any local "performance" by any of his *personae*. The theatrical metaphor begins to attenuate, however, when we sense that the quality of deliberateness in the artist's binding of time is significantly different from that of a person's binding of time offstage.

Goffman has left out the most important member of my "audience"— myself, myself as present to myself in all my "roles." He ignores the self-conscious structure of the self, the I-me polarity, one's accumulating and changing sense of one's passing life in all its episodes, the time-spanning consciousnesses of self that are integral to the self itself. They weave and reweave *one* bodily history as *one's own* . He treats only of what William James called the social self, or "selves." As Kurt Reizler put it aphoristically, the I responds to an indefinite number of me's.

Of course, if one does not approve of what he is doing in his "roles" offstage or does not see their importance, then, indeed, he will feel alienated. But desperately so, just because it is himself from whom he is alien-

22. Ibid., p. 298.

ated. He is at odds with himself. He may try to assuage his guilt by taking an attitude of aesthetic distance from his "roles," like an actor toward his roles. But, assuming a vestige of rationality, this will only increase his guilt, because he is then responsible for taking toward himself a manifestly inappropriate and escapist attitude.

The theatrical metaphor, as employed by Goffman, blurs fundamental distinctions between off and onstage. Onstage all roles are perceived as fittingly and properly: (1) composed or made up, and (2) causally inefficacious in their thematic import *vis-à-vis* the immediately surrounding offstage world (e.g., the actor whose character is killed appears immediately afterwards in a bar). But offstage such composition for the moment is not condoned if exposed (it is phony, a confidence trick), nor are all "roles" so composed. The analogy blurs the distinction between the morally sanctioned and nonsanctioned, and between those behaviors fabricated for the moment and those that are integral, habitual, appropriate, sanctioned, and perceived by all to be so—those constitutive of who I am. It is a reductionism that sees all "roles" as more or less phony, and that cannot explain how we can be concerned not only to appear good, but also—however feebly—to be so. Nor can it explain how we may not merely fear exposure of our failings, but fear that we will *not* be exposed— and corrected. Guilt is not just fear.

But at long last, the secondary metaphor of "role" can be stretched only so far. Sociologists attempt to anchor it by relating it to social position, e.g., the "role" of the physician. But if it is connected to social position it must follow some general rules or patterns, be repeatable, and be "enactable" by an indefinite number of individuals. But any creative or spontaneous act falls outside this matrix, as does any repetition of the presocial limb coordinations and self-mimeses "built into" the body perhaps before any social-mimetic acts were. Goffman's role theory misses both the presocial and the supersocial (the moral, i.e., as understood by Kant), neither of which is necessarily nonsocial or antisocial.

I am responsible for my behavior offstage in fundamentally different ways from my behavior onstage. Ethical responsibility is a condition of the identity of the self; I *am* the being and *no* other, who is responsible for behavior, the consequences and parameters of which cannot be confined to the frame of a work of art. In aestheticizing behavior through his role theory, Goffman contributes to the devitalization of the self. His position, verging on nihilism, is expressed hyperbolically in one of Nathaniel West's novels, which depicts an old actor alone in a house in the Hollywood Hills: in the process of actually dying, the actor enacts the role of a character who is dying. This strikes us as being depraved and wretched because the man has confused aesthetical and ethical standards.

He self-deceivingly thinks that his activity will be judged by standards of performance that will leave untouched his status as a being who performs (or that touch him only professionally), whereas his very being is expiring in odium and confusion. Encompassing every role, either off or onstage, is the capacity for a transcending consciousness of role which can judge the goodness of the activity, a judgment which in turn is judgeable on the basis of the appropriateness of its standards of judgment. This open-ended subjectivity is tied to the incomparable particularity of the body.

What if it is maintained, however, that this transcending consciousness of "role" is just another "role"—a "role" that evaluates "roles," a "meta-role"— and one that is just as culturally conditioned as any other, thus for which I am not responsible? The reply to this is direct: given the indefinitely prolongable reflexivity of consciousness, hence the ever-retreating, unobjectifiable subject-self, I can become aware of this "meta-role" as an intentional *object*, an activity for which I am responsible, hence *I* cannot be reduced to it. Subjectivity is something like a mirror, which can reflect everything except its own present act of reflecting.

The crucial lapse in Goffman's thought is that he does not develop his observation that "primary perspectives" are "no more transformed than are felt to be usual and typical for such doings." If he had he might not have concluded that the ultimate "frame without a rim" is the total assembly of physical particulars. Human selves, however complex, are then nothing but particular objects *within* this world (although they "exude" expressions). But as I have used the term *world*, it includes the evolving *sense* of it as the all-pervasive ground of intelligibility which confers meaning on any particular being.[23] The self, then, is both a particular body and that which is a presence to itself within this overarching presence. The sense of the world is perpetually enriched through the cultural activity of artistically and quasi-artistically created "worlds." Still, its presence is the boundless horizon of all our experiences—the primordial constancy in which the constancy of everything else is sustained.

---

23. Since the world as we know it is a concatenation of things and processes *meant*, it can be argued that we should always write *world* as "world." But all else would have to be put in quotes also. The lack of contrast would militate against the sense. And to distinguish the *world* of the play we would have to write it as " 'world.' " The cumbersomeness of this argues against its adoption.

CHAPTER XX

The Limits of Appearance

The Lord whose oracle is that at Delphi neither speaks nor conceals, but indicates.

—Heraclitus

Our age prides itself on its objectivity. We like to think we speak not merely of what things mean to us but of what they are in themselves. This is a delusion. If we refer to things only in terms of mathematical measurement, say, then we interpret their existence within a framework of meaning imposed by ourselves. It is only because we grow forgetful of our own framework that we forget ourselves and the indefinite number of ways in which we might interpret things. We then forget that before any allegedly objective rendering of them we must belong to the world in a primordial mimetic attunement or diremption from attunement; the world must be ours and we must be its before we can set ourselves off from any of the things in it. If I am to rebel meaningfully from someone he must be *my* opponent; I must be attuned to him in some residual way.

What is left of this mimetic attunement when it is forgotten? If we forget about the moon no change is suffered by it, but if we forget about our own potentialities then they do suffer. A vivid example of this impairment is the employment by a reputedly objective social science of a theatrical metaphor for behavior—a "role theory"—which has lost touch with its sources in the theatre and in our artistic and artistic-like life which maps the world perpetually into indefinitely many "worlds" and reinterprets the world accordingly. It forgets that we cannot be reduced to a set of "roles" because it has forgotten that the two-pronged conceptual projection of roles and "roles" is a necessary and yet limited manifestation of an indefinitely extendable array of our potentialities. It forgets that we exist over an abyss of possibility and freedom—which is to say that there is available no definitive description in literal terms of either the strictly artistic onstage life or the quasi-artistic offstage life, and that we teeter perpetually between the two over the abyss of possible interpretation and freedom.

Thus "role theory," of the sort we have examined, leaves us finally without guidance concerning what we are to make of ourselves and how we are to move within a world which we must make our own in one way or another.[1] The function of religion was to assure us behaviorally that though the world escapes any final description by us, and is mysterious, still it is ours—our own abode—because we were created to belong to it by divinity. What the world means to God or to the gods is also—to an extent conformable to our limitations—what it must mean to us, and in our rites we make this meaning our own. To feel alienated from the world is a more or less schizophrenic condition, since we are beings-in-the-world and must belong to it in some way. Contemporary antidotes to this are several: e.g., rigidly authoritarian and conformist styles of life, which mask from sight the abyss of possible interpretation and possible action in which we move perpetually, or the use of psychedelic drugs, which impart to us a transitory feeling of participating in the cosmos, of being empowered and authorized by it, and at the same time of being securely ensconced within ourselves. But since the effects of the drugs are transitory, and since the drugs themselves can be taken from us, they cannot characterize us as we are. For a person *is* the activity of synthesizing experience beyond local environments, and this includes his powers of initiative and responsibility. Modes of cumulatively mediating and articulating primordial mimetic engulfment and achieving authentic individual identity are generally lacking.

The desacralization of theatre parallels in illuminating ways the desacralization of society. What a Greek audience at *Oedipus Rex* saw was seen as witnessed-also-by-the-gods. We can only suppose that things, events, and personages had the vividness and solidity of meaning that only symbols can have —and ones that are not apprehended *as* symbols. They had sacred significance because everything was experienced as for-and-by-the-gods. The theatre was an excellent locale for suggesting the witnessing and authorizing gods in each of their quarters: earth, under the earth, and in the sky. Thus theatre could exist in a continuum with those strictly religious rites in which man's covenant with the gods was explicitly confirmed. *Hamlet* was—and perhaps for many still is—the turbulent site for the transition from a sacral to a desacralized experience. Theatre today produces its works in an era that has been desacralized for most of us, and only intermittently—and by somewhat desperate means in physiognomic

---

1. I do not wish to leave the impression that Goffman's thinking is representative in every respect of "role theories." Limitations of space have prevented me from examining others' thought, e.g., the very valuable but rambling work of Kenneth Burke.

symbol—can it call up that numinous power which comes from contact with our undeliberate mimetic participation in the world: our ability to feel that the world is ours—our community's and our individual own—in love, fear, covenant, recreation, and invention. It points toward a religion that may never be born, or reborn.

In one important respect, rites are more like theatre than is a cocktail party. All three hold for demarcated segments of world time, yet both theatrical performances and (most) rites can be interrupted, if necessary, and can resume with no time or material added to the performance or to the rite. Although they occur in a segment of world time, they also transcend this segment in a way that a cocktail party cannot. Rite, however, *unlike* theatre, transcends this segment in such a way that it ties its participants deeply into world time. For the rite occurs on days of the calendar designated holy, and in commemorating the authority of the founder (or inspirer) of the rite as one who lived in world time, it authorizes the participants as persons, not just as performers. There is some value in regarding the rite as a chain of "enactments" down through the generations in which the authority of the founder is transferred through his or her proxies and authorizes the participants. But the embeddedness of the rite in world time renders these "enactments" fundamentally different from enactments; even with shudder quotes the word *enactment* is misleading. In rites of passage, for example, one is confirmed as a being who transforms one's biological identity through involvements with others—rites of puberty, marriage, death. In marriage one is more than a performer, and in death the community confirms one even in that departure from community which cannot be performed. In our lonely, nearly riteless modes of dying—drugged, say, in an old persons' home—death has grown wild, as Philippe Ariès has said; it is less than human.[2] Our marriages are frequently little more than "shows," for with the decay of the rite we cease to be bound within the whole time of our lives. Adolescents, finally, resort to desperate measures to prove that they are adults. We may feel as if we stood on the edge of a precipice, with the wind sublimating us, blowing away our substance into the void.

As Chaikin well put it, in our art we ask wordless questions of each other and are united by what we do not understand. Theatre displays before us fragments of premonitory symbols, indications of transcendence: new sorts of engulfments, dissolutions, and as-yet unpredictable achievements of individuation. We struggle and hope that the abyss of our lives and the possibilities that it holds will resound in authorization and empowerment. We strive for an art, and for an art of life, that will break

2. *L'Homme devant la Mort,* translated as *The Hour of Our Death* by Helen Weaver (New York: Alfred A. Knopf, 1981).

through to new and difficult identifications. Perhaps the most difficult and needful identification is with ourselves as aesthetically and "aesthetically" distanced from ourselves. The power in which we would participate is the power to monitor and moderate our own impulses rather than being engulfed in them. But the self that reflects upon itself is the same self that participates in the world, and it can wither from lack of sympathetic involvement. Any form of viable Stoicism requires some sense of participation in the powers of nature, whether it proclaims the formula of Marcus Aurelius or not: Oh Nature, let thy will be my will.

Perhaps we can strive for no goal beyond our playing and striving itself, for only in this is creation of meaning. When any metaphor—for example, the theatrical metaphor—reveals its limits, we are not delivered thereby to that which transcends metaphor, to that which is utterly definitive and literal. We are delivered to the indeterminate, the boundless, the unglimpsed, the Open. Heidegger quotes Rilke:

. . ."[L]ike the moon, so life surely has a side that is constantly turned away from us, and that is not its opposite but its completion to perfection, to plenitude, to the real, whole, and full sphere and globe of being."

The globe of Being of which he speaks here [Heidegger continues], that is, the globe of all beings as a whole, is the Open, as the pure forces serried, boundlessly flowing into one another and thus acting toward one another. The widest orbit is the wholeness of the whole draft of attraction. To this widest circle there corresponds as the strongest center, the "unheard-of center" of pure gravity . . . When we are touched from out of the widest orbit, the touch goes to our very nature. To touch means to touch off, to set in motion. Our nature is set in motion.[3]

We think of Nietzsche's *Unschuld des Werdens*—innocence of becoming—in which play within the totality of beings has become its own necessity, and in which "nothing happens for the sake of anything—which is the same as to say perhaps that everything happens for the sake of everything."[4] A "world" of play would embrace the world and map it, but it does so ever incompletely. In this play, life becomes precious because it is risked in the boundless. We find ourselves only by losing ourselves in a world which we cannot encompass; we return to ourselves through a finite expression of the boundless, a "world." We think that never before

3. Martin Heidegger, "What are Poets For?" in *Poetry, Language, and Thought*, Albert Hofstadter (New York, Harper Colophon Books, 1975), p. 124.

4. Albert Hofstadter, "Validity versus Value," *Journal of Philosophy*, 59 (Oct. 11, 1962): 608ff. Quoted in Rose Pfeffer, *Nietzsche: Disciple of Dionysus* (Lewisburg, Pa.: Bucknell University Press, 1972), p. 209.

has so much been risked, and standing in the periphery of play lie possibilities of desperation and discouragement.

We cannot confine the world before us as if it were just another object in the world. We map the world within the world. Around all our projects and their focal objects lies the openness of the boundless. We are unshielded before it, as Heidegger says. It is that within which any objectification must occur, so it cannot itself be definitively objectified. Nor can we step out of it, for any point to which we could step must be within it. Any concept is good for so much and no more. In great art we affirm this unshieldedness more or less explicitly so that, it is hoped, we will be able to live it implicitly day by day.

Around and beneath and through the network of distinctions we raise—in the circumpressure of the world—flow mimetic fusions and affinities which we cannot adequately describe or predict. The distinction between self and not-self is not the clear and decisive matter that the words themselves suggest. The self comes to birth already permeated with not-self, and without the behavioral flow of the mimetic and the communal there would be nothing against which the conscious body could push in its irruptive moments of individuation. Nor is the individuation ever complete, nor is it ever completely grasped. We are essentially particular and private and essentially communal and involved, and the paradox is worth no more and no less than any attempt at harmonized utterance: all attempts are incomplete within the boundless.

The physiognomic expression of the body expresses possibilities of fusion and diremption that lie ahead of writable language which is discursive. It concerns what this language has had to forget to become that system of oppositions that is essential to what it is as prose narrative. What is observable onstage has a corollary in the plastic and graphic arts. In a manner sharply reminiscent of Schilder's idea of "the sphere," Kenneth Clark writes of the work of Leonardo da Vinci:

> The pointing finger and the smile—the one indicating a power outside our field of vision, the other reflecting an inner process which is equally beyond our comprehension—had a symbolic importance to him even in his early work. And as his sense of mystery was intensified and confirmed by his researches, the use of these symbols became more conscious. The Mona Lisa has been irreverently described as "the cat that's eaten the canary": which expresses well enough the smile of one who has attained complete possession of what she loved, and is enjoying the process of absorption. And Leonardo has discovered that this mysterious, continuous process has the same rhythm as that in which rain pours from the clouds, wears away the earth, flows to the sea, and is sucked up into the clouds again. In the Louvre St. John these two symbols of mystery are united and concentrated, and this gives the image

its obsessive power. Attributes of grace, the smile and the turning movement, become extremely sinister, because they are now indistinguishable from attributes of continuous energy; and these, being beyond human reason, are felt as hostile to human security.[5]

This idea of continuous energy and absorption is fundamental to our study. Nothing could better convey the powers and dangers of mimetic engulfment than Leonardo's pointing, smiling, and somehow sinister figures. They suggest the precarious identity of human individuals: we slip into aggressive or submissive fusion at the merest breath.

But it must be pointed out that, more often than not, attempts to describe the "inner process" of experience—that which is signified, says Clark, by the smile—are self-defeating. From Democritus on, the temptation has been to say that we directly perceive only unsharable alterations and states in our own minds. The reason given is that a single thing affects different perceivers differently, and we never know exactly how the other perceives it. But this is a self-defeating theory. For how do we know—except by direct perception—that there *is* a single thing that affects different people differently? We must know what we can experience in common before we can even surmise that we also experience it differently. Nearly all doctrines of inwardness and of ineffable and unsharable sensations presuppose naive notions of objectivity, intersubjectivity, and individuation, and they can be no better than these notions. Lying at the base of a theory of knowledge and a theory of man, as they usually do, the theoretical superstructure must be stunted by them.

It is only *eventually* that we can speak meaningfully of privacy and ineffability—but eventually, of course, we must. Everything we see is saturated with the interpersonal, the mimetic, and the historical. To be alone in a high mountain meadow, for example, lying so close to a small flower that it appears blurry, is to be in the presence of something identifiable with a Latin name, something whose sort is regarded, valued, and identified by others. Yet in the very moment that I withdraw my head, focus on the flower, and utter its name I grasp that I have not said all that can be said about it, and indeed that all that I or anyone could say about it would leave it incompletely known. And I apprehend simultaneously both the boundlessness of the thing itself as it is knowable by the community and the incredibly full particularity and privacy of my own experiencing of it here and now. No one else could live through what I have just lived through, just as I have lived through it, nor can I ever be sure

5. Kenneth Clark, *Leonardo da Vinci: An Account of His Development as an Artist* (Baltimore: Penguin Books, 1959), p. 16. The same upraised finger and smile are to be found in the depiction of St. Anne in Leonardo's "Madonna, Child, St. Anne and St. John."

that when I tell the other what this is like I am telling him that it is like his experiencing it. For the other's experiencing in its living flow is not directly accessible to me, nor is mine to him. His thinking and feeling is untransferably his, and mine is mine.

Correlative to each person's being and having a particular body is sensory variability from person to person, and sensory anomalies. Since some are detectable, e.g., color blindness, it is plausible to suppose that others exist in this and in other sense modalities, and that some of these escape our ability to imagine to test for them.[6] Nevertheless, in artistic activity we grope into this area and seek that it be confirmed by others. It would seem that even my sensory uniqueness can slip into dissociation unless the attempt is made to make it my own through others. So even in this most private sphere there is a movement toward interpersonal exchange. There is no denying my particularity and privacy, but we must avoid understanding it simplistically. Thus if we would be authentically individual persons we must strive perpetually to disengage ourselves from self-deceiving engulfment in others, but it is equally self-deceiving to think that we can ever arrive at a stage of pure and permanent particularity. As a named being who strives to appropriate his particular history as his very own, I cannot be reduced to an intersection of universal attributes, no matter how densely it is drawn. Nevertheless a human cannot be given a particular name unless he exemplifies the universal traits of humanity, otherwise a dog might be given that name, or a plant or a stone. To appropriate my life I must stand in for others who can name and describe me. The particular self can never stand denuded of all actual and possible fusions and identifications with others.

The "power outside our field of vision" and the "inner process which is equally beyond our comprehension"—those traits which Clark attributes to Leonardo's paintings—are coordinate and interdependent. I sense that nobody else could live through my experience as I have just lived through it, *and* that the boundless as the unspeakable and communal permeates every dimension of experience, whether "inner" or "outer." Sensory anomalies and variations from person to person are very significant, but allusion to them is not necessary to establish the aspect of uniqueness and uncanniness in each person's experience. As a unique history of lived-through experiencing there is no way of directly comparing my experiencing to others' experiencing. But this inability typically remains unthematic and unacknowledged because ordinarily we feel no need to compare our experiencings, so we do not try. We feel no need because there could be no unique experien*cing* at all without common objects experien*ced*, and the traits which we similarly and variously experience these *objects* to

6. After all, it is vision that is the distance and theoretical sense par excellence, the most easily objectifiable and discussable sense.

possess, and which we can communicate, are sufficient for most purposes to express to others, and to ourselves through others, how we individually feel about the things. Nevertheless our directly lived and incomparable experiencing persists uninterrupted, as if it were a shadow in the center of our field of vision which is so constant that it is no longer noticed. It is incomparable hence uncanny.

Leonardo's characters with their smiles and upraised fingers indicate the swirl of mimetic interfusion and continuous energy linking persons within the boundless, and they have a sinister quality. They are disturbing because they disclose that there is no secure attachment in either the private and particular or in the public and the communal, but only a perpetual teetering between them that can lose its balance. The product of the interaction of the public and private aspects of the self is not consistently predictable or controllable. A corollary is that there are no sets of literal terms shorn of all artistic metaphor which can be used to refer adequately to the public domain on the one hand, and the private on the other. Indeed, art and the art-like are the inevitable attempt to mediate domains that cannot exist apart from one another, but which cannot exist together peaceably and securely either. We are as essentially speakable, communal, and periodically engulfed as we are unspeakable, private, and uncanny, and we cannot predict what will happen to us, or exactly what we will choose to do. We are unshielded. There is no refuge in either the public or the private, but only unending dialectical exchange and teetering between them. We exist as a complex of tensions which is unresolvable within any local environment and over any confinable time. At best we have the vow and the memorializing moment of our commitment of will. At worst we have the suppression and attempted destruction of an aspect of the self.

D. W. Winnicott has written,

> I suggest that in health there is a core to the personality that corresponds to the true self. . . . I suggest that this core never communicates with the world of perceived objects, and that the individual person knows that it must never be communicated with or influenced by external reality. . . . Although healthy persons communicate and enjoy communicating, the other fact is equally true, that *each individual is an isolate, permanently noncommunicating, permanently unknown*, in fact unfound. . . . Rape, and being eaten by cannibals, these are mere bagatelles as compared with the violation of the self's core. . . . For me this would be the sin against the self. . . . The question is: how to be isolated without having to be insulated?[7]

There seems to be some truth in this. If I could conceive it happening at all, I could only dread that another be able to live through my experi-

7. D. W. Winnicott, "Communicating and Not Communicating Leading to a Study of Certain Opposites," in *The Maturational Processes and the Facilitating Environment* (New York: International Universities Press, 1965), p. 187.

encing just as I do, for that would be to empty my identity into him and to be obliterated. As the feeling and thinking body that I am moment by moment, my privacy and unfoundness and unspeakability are integral to my continuity and density through time, integral to my identity. In some moments, in my essential privacy and essential publicity, I am merely a site for swirling confusion. But I am just this site, this locus, and it belongs with the inertia of the conserved and habituated lived-body. This sees me through as the being that is myself.

Yet I distrust Winnicott's notion of a core of the self. It suggests that there is a refuge, and that the "inner" and private is somehow more real than is the "outer" and public. But neither is more real than the other, and one's identity must involve an ever incompletable mediation of each through the other. No doubt one's particularity and privacy are inexhaustible, and yet artistic and quasi-artistic activity is precisely the attempt to share it in such a way that the person can comprehend it in the terms which make it comprehensible to others. I am named by others, and yet if my individuality is to develop I must guide myself and others in ever further ways of naming myself. I speak of myself and make myself ever more nameable . . . but I speak *to* whom? Not only to others, but to my own self through others, and this subject self, this auditing, feeling, viewing, naming self is never completely objectifiable and nameable. The ever-ongoing naming self cannot be strictly isomorphic with the named self. There is one self, but as naming and ongoing and pulled toward particularity it cannot be exhausted as it is named through others. There is a particularity of experienc*ing*, but the self cannot thematize itself as a nakedly particular object experienc*ed*. I must approach myself through others asymptotically, ever unreachably. The perpetual finding can be endured and enjoyed only because I sense that there must always be an unfound. I can exist as a self identical to itself through time only if I exist simultaneously as the named and the unnameable.

Heidegger describes our age as the time of need. We approach the time of greatest need, he says, for we have grown oblivious to the need itself. Perhaps, though, the self-closing darkness will become so profound that it will set itself off from a background and become aware of itself as a need. It might happen if our enduring and playing and our living and dying had that vividness and solidity of sense which comes when we experience ourselves as witnessed-by-a-god. If this were to occur we would experience our lives as summed up perpetually through time because summed up in the experience of the witnessing god. We could be coherent in our depths because our simultaneity through time would be coherent and summed. Symbols shared with the god would not refer to mere facts or actualities which come and go, but would pertain to the time transcending reality of myth, that which is most concrete for us just because it is not merely a factual account of a given segment of time. "We are of such stuff as dreams are made on." But how could we possibly experience ourselves as witnessed-by-a-god?[8]

Now, it might seem that contemporary theatre of the most compelling sort is in agreement with Heidegger that the gods have fled. We think of *Waiting for Godot, The Chairs,* and *Apocalypsis cum Figuris.* And yet the absence of divinity is so keenly felt that its presence hangs over these productions. It is as if we were compelled to ask *ourselves,* "What would a *god* see and sanction in these mimetic experimentations and gestures toward the unknown?" Nietzsche wrote: "We have killed God. Mustn't we become like gods ourselves to seem worthy of the deed?" We may wonder whether divinity can be escaped. We revert to Emerson's "Brahma" in which the poet speaks these words for the god:

> They reckon ill who leave me out;
> When me they fly, I am the wings;
> I am the doubter and the doubt.

Perhaps the ever-unobjectifiable source of creativity is all that we can mean by divinity—cruel and joyous both, and in unexpected ways. We do not know quite what to say. But modern art does suggest new metaphors for divinity. As Robert Wilson participates as an improvising actor in his own productions, and as an action painter like Jackson Pollock does not calculate and objectify the painting and establish himself as something clear and distinct over against it, so creator and creating issue into creation in a rush of union and spontaneity. The actor as artist and creator exists only a hair's breadth removed from himself as character and created; the abyss of communal and creative life pours through the locus of his particularity.

We are not sure how far these metaphors apply, however. Even a production of *Oedipus Rex,* occurring at a specially appointed place and at a periodic time, supervised by Sophocles and presented to an audience many of whom knew each other, for they lived and worked together in the larger community—even here the production occurred at some little remove, apparently, from the mythical time of rite *per se.* How much less for us can art knit up our lives day by day through its time binding symbols, we who live rootlessly in a post-industrial age, our everyday minds dominated

8. See two penetrating articles by Claude Lévi-Strauss, "The Sorcerer and His Magic" and "The Power of Symbols" (in *Structural Anthropology* [New York: Basic Books, 1963]). He compares the psychoanalyst and the sorcerer. The latter acts out the relevant social myth while the patient is the entranced audience. The former is the authorizing audience—as well as a surrogate authority figure—while the patient acts out and constructs his own myth, only individual myth being possible in an industrial society, says Lévi-Strauss. When the cure is successful it is so because the myth organizes and mobilizes the patient's life; the stranglehold of complexes is broken by their being thus "objectified." These points can be brought to bear upon problems and opportunities of contemporary theatre.

by data, by signs which refer to external or causal relationships in the passing scene, and our nonscientific consciousness a mere grabbag of mythical fragments? In our consternation we may try to break away completely from the past and to reject all religiosity as prideful, pretentious, and disturbing. Shouldn't each self be content to silently monitor and authorize itself?[9] But isn't that a delusion? Can we live vitally at all without tapping in some way powers of mimetic fusion and vicarious justification?

Recent theatre is an attempt to map the world in a new way: a metatheatrical attempt by theatre to delve more deeply into its own resources as creative art so that it can project a new image of the world as creative. We would like to participate in the flowering of the world. We question at a new depth our own nature as questioning beings-in-the-world. The experimentation in questioning let loose upon the stage, or in whatever art, is the only answer that is forthcoming. We find merely an enigmatic smile—so disturbing to our security as to be sinister—and a finger pointing beyond anything to which we could yet give presence. With all our science, the powers of nature become ever stranger to us.

Can we be authorized through ourselves and through one another as a community of experimenters and searchers? Or will we always demand beings who are gods in the old mold, and in whom we lose ourselves in child-like abandon—empowered in a way that seems at least to block authentic individuation at some point? Federico Fellini, commenting on the abduction and killing of the statesman Aldo Moro, has said: "The Catholic myth of sacrifice is protective, so we don't know how to confront reality without myths. The Moro incident was accepted almost as liberation: Society has made a mistake, and Moro has paid for it. But the time has come to make ourselves responsible, to become adults."[10] But it is not perfectly clear that such engulfment with its transfer of power and virtue vicariously can be outgrown. It might even be argued that we shouldn't try to do so unless we have found our way toward some viable substitute in self-authorization.

Those who dismiss religious practice as regressive and self-deceptive typically have no idea that the sense of the presence of the divine can allow a person to disengage himself from engulfment in those authorities who just happen to be present in his local environment. Thus it can abet the process of individuation. True, this sense of the divine may be one which has not transcended the religious biases of its local institutional origin, so that its liberating effect is limited radically. And of course we encounter problems of meaning and truth in the notion of the divine that tax our intelligence, creativity, and perseverance to the utmost.

9. I am indebted to discussions with Albert Ellis on this point.
10. *The New York Times*, February 18, 1979.

But for the person to think that he has taken a giant step in eliminating regressive fusion and self-deception simply because he has eliminated the "patent" self-deception of belief in deity is just to be more vulnerable to less obvious dangers of engulfment and self-deception. These are inherent in the cloud of secular authorization through which we must try to steer our more or less individuated existence. We seem to be as primitively engulfed in our everyday companions and in their opinions of us, and in modish thinkers, party chiefs, rock stars, models of taste, consumption, or aggression—and in the masses that follow them—as ever the human race was engulfed in anything. Professors and scholars are no exception. Paid to think for ourselves, and usually tenured and given the greatest security, we are frequently engulfed in the latest styles of research and stylization of self, and oblivious or contemptuous of those who adopt different styles and who belong to different groups. This may prompt us to conjecture that since all of us will be engulfed in some way, the best we can do is to attempt to be engulfed benignly. Christians' belief that "we are one in the body of Christ" swims before the mind with the luminous glow of a creature from the deep seas. It is a belief that is not as easily outgrown as some had thought.

We will be authorized in some way, and the open-ended process of individuation of self can easily founder in self-deception and engulfment. Perhaps the risk is greater now, given our modernist conceits concerning progress. Human institutions have grown uncertain and this uncertainty undermines the rites that mediate individuation within communal structure. The problem is compounded by a peculiarly modern experience of loneliness which defends itself through engulfment. If we do not understand the risk of being human, and the price of individual identity, then our leap into the void of our possibilities will be dangerous self-indulgence merely.

Sophocles had the chorus in *Antigone* chant, "There are many weird things, but nothing weirder than man." This has not changed. Perhaps our proclivity to make war and to murder is part of the puzzle on which we have been working in this book. Is murder an anxious attempt by us beings of weak and precarious identity to authorize ourselves? If persons die by our agency, doesn't this confirm our efficacy as agents? Moreover, mightn't this be equivalent experientially to the murdered person's dying for us, standing in for us in death? If we were to be freed from death by this miserable magic, wouldn't this authorize us? I suppose we would finally feel important enough; but this authorization would subvert our authenticity. For that requires that we value authentic life for itself, and value it in whomever it is exemplified, either as actuality or potentiality. Moreover, we can be authorized in authenticity only by those who are trustworthy and just in their judgments; only by those who are themselves authentic.

We can now state definitively—in our own terms—the problem of human existence to which Christians believe their faith provides the solution. Human individuals are beings of weak and precarious identity. Each is a vulnerable and absolutely particular body, yet each must define itself according to general ideas and communal patterns. Each of us draws the line between "myself" and "not myself," but each draws it in a different place. Each person is absolutely individuated through his body, and the perspectival panorama of the world turns constantly around it. Indeed, one must take great care of one's body; one must be somewhat egoistic just to survive. One will tend to believe pre-reflectively and irrationally, "I'm at least half of all there is—and at least as important as everything else!" The others who obstruct and coerce one destroy this belief on occasion, but one is not thereby attuned to the whole and its creative ground. For one's identity is not confined to the envelope of one's skin, but is mediated by others. The person slips into a corporate egoism and irrationalism: "My group is weightier and better than all other groups."

Our nature is sinful; we either fall naturally into destructive engulfments with egoistic impulses deriving from our separate bodies—and this sets individuals against individuals—or we fall the other way and are engulfed with our local group—which sets group against group. The problem of the precariousness of our identity is solved only when we are reconnected to the divine creative ground out of which all beings spring. But, weak, unstable, and confined to our perspectives, we will be annihilated by this contact unless God becomes a human individual, allows himself to be annihilated, conquers the annihilation, and we participate in this destruction of egoism vicariously and are redeemed. Sinful engulfment is destroyed only through divine engulfment.

But what of those who do not believe? How are they to cope with an identity which does not cease to be weak, precarious, and problematical just because the religious solution is unavailable? Theatre provides some minimal guidance. It is the art of standing in that illuminates standing in and the realities of identifying and authorizing relationships. As it gropes for new ways of being individually human, its groping is humans' groping, and it breaks out unpredictably and fragmentarily in trepidation, exhilaration, discouragement, elation, and dread. It is easier to speak of self-authorization and self-authentication than it is to understand it or accomplish it. Thus George Sheehan, for example, speaks of our hero-less age, and advocates that each person become his own hero through feats of running.[11] This idea should not be dismissed out of hand. Whatever en-

11. George Sheehan, M.D., *Dr. Sheehan on Running* (New York: Bantam Books, 1975), pp. 204–205.

hances the powers of the individual body will tend—other things being equal—to enhance the individuation of the self. But the danger is that the person will conclude that running is sufficient to produce maximum individuation of self, and that he will define his individual identity as existing in isolation from others. A "me against the world" attitude emerges. If this happens his mimetic involvement with others is masked, he remains engulfed, and the process of authentic individuation is blocked at this point. Thus running as a form of self-authorization would confirm one in inauthenticity.

Long ago Pythagoras advised us not to call the gods to witness, a person's duty being rather to strive to make his own word carry conviction. And no doubt it is essential in order to be maturely individuated to be able to believe, "With no possible witness to this deed I do it." But this means only that there can be no actual human witness of the deed other than the agent. It does not follow that this person will not *imagine* witnesses. The ever-unobjectifiable subject self, the I, is not a different self from the objectifiable self, the me, and it cannot be sane and become a pure and absolute particular insulated from others and the world. There is no way to purge the self and its imagination of all exemplar individuals incorporated mimetically as witness-models of its life. Nor should we wish to do so if we could. These include authorizing, stabilizing, and empowering others—although, to be sure, some are malevolent, rejecting, and destructive of self. Never to take toward oneself in any way the attitude of a respected and confirming other, and never to live within his or her gaze, is to exist without support and without stability. The I is not an object in the world, but is rather the limit of the world as experienceable: the moment-by-moment limit of what is projectable and imaginable as worldly by this particular body as it lives in the world. What is projectable is a function of one's gaze upon things, others, and self, but one's gaze includes the gazes of others mimetically incorporated into one's sensing body, and not all of them can be objectified and excluded from the self. Such gazes are more inward than one's inmost and are indistinguishable from one's own.

When art encounters its limits it points beyond itself. As we draw our study of theatre and the self to a close, we glimpse the rite of authorization and authentication that theatre suggests but does not provide: *a ceremony in which persons gather together at regular intervals in world-time and confirm each other as beings who are to be born as individuals through progressively articulating their mimetic fusion with others.*

Sinister and precarious aspects of mimetic involvement could be acknowledged in the ceremony. Yet this would not be just another intellectual exercise in which we attempt to objectify mimetically incorporated exemplar figures and witness-models in order to separate the benign from the malign. If all vestiges of the confirming and authorizing other could somehow be objectified, then mimetic involvement with the other would appear to be just one of many possible arrangements, and the person would lose the incorporated other's unquestioned, supportive grip in his pre-reflective life. To change the metaphor, it would be as if a creature from the deep seas were to be brought up to the surface: it would burst before our eyes. The numinous power of mimetically incorporated authoritative persons, derived through correspondence with gods and supernatural beings, and all unwittingly—these potent physiognomic symbols—would be perceived *as* symbols, that is, *merely* as symbols.[12]

Let us sketch a bit further. In this rite of authorization and authentication suggested but not provided by theatre we could strive, both hesitantly and trustingly somehow, to feel our way to mimetic involvements which are not exclusionary, and which do not project in a paranoid way sinister and destructive aspects of the involvements onto other groups and persons. In order to become who we are each of us has had to be defined by membership in groups which are local. The groups in turn have defined themselves as other than—and, typically, better than—other groups. We are drawn into the "drama" of competition and aggression. How, then, can we identify effectively with humans wherever they are found? The rite could cultivate whatever tendencies for such identification there might be. Perhaps a natural piety could be revived in which individuals are disengulfed not through defiance of their particular sources but through respect for them, and, equally, through respect for the interdependence of all persons. A silence could occur in the face of whatever possibilities for guidance and for authentication as individuals might appear before us. With this openness to potentiality within the boundless "sphere," guilty attachment to source might be washed out—that archaic attachment which stifles capacities both for increasing individuation and for more extensive mimetic involvement, because it keeps us engulfed in merely local groups.

In our time of need, however, it is not clear whether vital and authentic individual identity is still possible for us. It is not clear whether we know how to desire it. Abandoned to our possibilities and to the circumpressure of the world, we who seek proper relatedness to our particularity, to our sources, and to others can only strive to create such an identity. We must aim for a community of compassion in which each recognizes the tragic aspects of the other. We must cope with the problem of recreating our history in such a way that it becomes indistinguishable from an invention.

12. Cf. Sean Healy, *The Roots of Boredom* (Teaneck, N.J.: Fairleigh Dickinson University Press, forthcoming).

INDEX